The Bosnian Muslims

THE BOSNIAN MUSLIMS

Denial of a Nation

Francine Friedman

WestviewPress

A Division of HarperCollins*Publishers*

Copyright © 1996 by Westview Press, Inc., A Division of HarperCollins Publishers, Inc.

Published in 1996 in the United States of America by Westview Press, Inc., 5500 Central Avenue, Boulder, Colorado 80301-2877, and in the United Kingdom by Westview Press, 12 Hid's Copse Road, Cumnor Hill, Oxford OX2 9JJ

Library of Congress Cataloging-in-Publication Data
Friedman, Francine, 1948–
  The Bosnian Muslims : denial of a nation / Francine Friedman
    p.   cm.
  Includes bibliographical references and index.
  ISBN 0-8133-2097-6 (hc.)—ISBN 0-8133-2096-8 (pbk.)
  1. Muslims—Bosnia and Hercegovina—Ethnic identity.   2. Bosnia and Hercegovina—Ethnic relations.   3. Nationalism—Bosnia and Hercegovina.   I. Title
DR1674.M87F75   1996
305.6'971049742—dc20   95-43377
                                                                CIP

The paper used in this publication meets the requirements of the American National Standard for Permanence of Paper for Printed Library Materials Z39.48-1984.

10   9   8   7   6   5   4   3   2   1

Contents

Illustrations

Preface

The entity we once knew as Yugoslavia has exploded into a number of as yet territorially undefined landscapes. Yugoslavia's fascinating mixture of domestic unity for foreign policy purposes paired with internal instability because of the centrifugal forces engendered by national particularism have kept academicians and international decisionmakers alike interested in that country's fate. Undoubtedly, its new visage in the post–Cold War era will rivet international attention for a long time to come.

The unique Yugoslav domestic and international relations before its breakup were frequently described by a characterization attributed to Sir Fitzroy McClean, who came to know Yugoslavia well during his World War II sojourn there. The quip went that Yugoslavia possessed seven neighbors, six republics, five nations, four languages, three religions, two alphabets, and only one Yugoslav—Tito. Later the remark no longer applied, not only because the "only real Yugoslav" died in 1980 but also because a new nation was recognized—the Bosnian Muslims.

This book traces the origins of the Bosnian Muslims, following their maturation from relative international obscurity to important political actor in Yugoslavia to contemporary victim of ethnic cleansing. The introduction presents the problem of the Bosnian Muslims and provides a broad overview of conceptual concerns in the study of ethnicity while introducing the definitions and conceptual tools this volume employs. Chapters 1 through 8 examine the political and social development of this group from the Middle Ages to the present, chronicling both domestic and international influences that may have produced their precarious contemporary position. The final chapter reflects on the odyssey of the Bosnian Muslims as an illustration of the fact that we would be wise to view international affairs not merely from the conventional perspective whereby events are interpreted and decisions are made solely in the context of clashing governmental interests. Instead, we should also view certain international events as consequences of the search for ethnic identity.

I first undertook the research for this book many years ago, believing scholars of the Balkans had for the most part overlooked an interesting and increasingly significant group within Yugoslavia. Resources on this subject were surprisingly few and, with some notable exceptions, not overly scholarly or analytical. I had hoped that my research would fill a small gap in the literature on the Yugoslav peoples.

Much to my dismay, my research agenda was overtaken by international events. The Bosnian Muslims have not only become a household word internationally but are in danger of becoming a homeless people. The sudden collapse of the second Yugoslavia and its implications for the Bosnian Muslims entailed massive rewriting of this book. A change in focus was necessary to deal with the issue of the continued existence of the Bosnian Muslims as a discrete national unit—an issue the war in Bosnia and Herzegovina has only recently raised. Of necessity, therefore, this book has become a kind of interim report, rather than a definitive characterization of the Bosnian Muslims.

None of the actors involved in this horrid conflict is entirely blameless. Nevertheless, it is difficult to ignore the fact that Bosnia and Herzegovina unwillingly became a pawn in a game of chauvinism played out in the lands of the former Yugoslavia and that the Bosnian Muslims, again not entirely blameless for the fate now befalling them, may have had fewer pieces to play than the other actors involved. How did the Bosnian Muslims come to be in this situation?

After more than two years of mind-numbing atrocities, this is still an open question. The research presented here is intended to contribute to the scholarly inquiry into this question by delving into the historical and sociopolitical position of the Bosnian Muslims to discover how their domestic situation, as well as externalities, influenced their options within Yugoslavia and the way post–Cold War changes in the international environment had a strong impact on the Bosnian Muslim situation. I have sought in these pages to discern what behaviors, activities, and events may have influenced the trajectory of Bosnian Muslim history onto the current ominous path and to apply these findings within the context of social science theory on ethnicity to try to understand their tragedy.

Bosnia and Herzegovina had a long history as a unique, discrete area—often with a distinct legal status—in and of itself. Its history is also replete with toleration of its many religious and, later, national communities. Perhaps a greater understanding of the danger and virulence of unrestrained national chauvinism will demonstrate how such chauvinism can ruin a multinational area. Conceivably, in the future that understanding will undermine the attraction of chauvinist nationalism so that all the actors in the Bosnian tragedy will seek alternative, peaceful methods to express their uniqueness and to realize their national aspirations. Dare we hope for a continuation of the tradition of tolerance begun in that land during the Middle Ages? I write these words in early 1995, when this is but a faint hope.

Francine Friedman

Acknowledgments

One of the most gratifying parts of writing this book was the opportunity to confer with some of the brightest and most generous scholars in the field. I am particularly grateful for the comments on earlier versions of this manuscript by Robert J. Donia, Alex N. Dragnich, John V.A. Fine Jr., Zachary Irwin, John Lampe, Fred Warner Neal, Robin Alison Remington, Dennison Rusinow, and Paul Shoup. Whereas I would not burden them with responsibility for any errors of fact or interpretation in this work, their thoughtful and incisive comments pressed me to dig ever deeper and look even further for clues to the Bosnian Muslim catastrophe. Those issues they suggested I deal with in this work but that space and time limitations have precluded will be the subjects of further research efforts.

Interlibrary loan facilities at Ball State University and Vanderbilt University were invaluable in helping me locate the sources for researching this subject. However, I was also most fortunate to be able to utilize the resources of the following universities: the Hebrew University of Jerusalem, the University of Pittsburgh, Stanford University and the Hoover Institution, Case Western Reserve, Indiana University at Bloomington, the University of California at Los Angeles, Vanderbilt University, Temple University, St. Mary's University (San Antonio), Trinity University, the Ohio State University, the University of Pennsylvania, Claremont Graduate School, Ball State University, the Library of Congress, and the University of Illinois at Urbana-Champaign (through its Summer Associateship program). Connie McOmber, staff cartographer for Ball State University's Department of Geography, produced the maps.

My good fortune in regard to this project continued with the devotion to the publication of this book exhibited by Susan McEachern, senior editor at Westview Press. Her encouragement was a significant factor in my finishing this book in a timely manner when events seemed continually to overtake the writing. Associate Project Editor Scott Horst ably guided me through the last stages of preparation when the technical points might otherwise have been overwhelming.

Finally, the support of my family was vital to the completion of this volume. Their understanding of the time I needed to spend away from them, their devotion to its completion, and their undertaking of some of the more mundane tasks involved in putting the manuscript together evoke my gratitude. I dedicate this work to them.

F. F.

Note on Usage and Pronunciation

The various South Slav peoples have been known by different names during different parts of their history. The term *Bosnian Muslim* is of recent origin. The terms *Bosnian Serb* and *Bosnian Croat*, which are less than one hundred years old, referred respectively to Orthodox and Catholic populations in the geographical area of Bosnia. The peoples inhabiting this area did not begin to differentiate themselves from their neighbors in anything other than religious terms until the nineteenth century, when nationalistic terms such as *Slovene*, *Serb*, and *Croat* became fashionable. Therefore, whereas in this book I use the terms Serb and Croat to refer to inhabitants of the South Slav lands throughout their history, as has been the scholarly custom, I do so with the understanding that it was not until the mid-nineteenth century—when Croat and Serb nationalism enveloped Bosnian Catholics and Orthodox, respectively—that these people thought of themselves in those terms. Furthermore, whereas Bosnia and Herzegovina were at one time separate entities, I use Bosnia and Herzegovina or simply Bosnia to denote the territory of post–World War II Bosnia and Herzegovina, since the period of their separation is not an integral part of the story told here.

I utilize indigenous spelling of certain terms and proper names, as Serbo-Croatian writers do. For the reader unfamiliar with the complexities of the Croatian form (Latin alphabet) of the Serbo-Croatian language,

c is pronounced as **ts** as in fi**ts**
ć is pronounced as **ch** (soft) as in mu**ch**
č is pronounced as **ch** (hard) as in **ch**est
dj is pronounced as **j** as in **j**est
j is pronounced as **y** as in **y**ell
š is pronounced as **sh** as in **sh**out
ž is pronounced as **zh** as in seizure

Finally, I am aware that on the present subject political overtones are imputed even to choices of spelling. Thus, I have arbitrarily chosen to use Herzegovina, not Hercegovina, in the text simply because most U.S. commentators use that spelling and not because I wish to imply a certain bias.

The Former Yugoslavia
and Its Neighbors

Cartographic Services, Department of Geography, Ball State University

Introduction: Ethnicity, the Concept of a Nation, and the Bosnian Muslims

"Nation: a group of people united by a common error about their ancestry and a common dislike of their neighbors."[1]

"Communism is dead! Long live nationalism!" could easily be the cry of the 1990s. The twentieth century will leave in its wake vicious ethnic-based dramas being played out not only in less-developed parts of the world but also in more industrially advanced countries. The contemporary Balkan conflicts—with their tangle of ethnic, territorial, demographic, historical, and other problems—have darkened what for many people should have been the joyous post-Communist era. Instead, the region is enduring a series of ethnic-based confrontations, including, in the former Yugoslavia, the largest and bloodiest military conflict in Europe since World War II.

Many commentators have lamented the fact that we have entered an era of rampant ethnonationalism. For example, in 1975 Harold R. Isaacs, in his classic pioneering study *Idols of the Tribe,* prophetically characterized the condition in which the planet finds itself during the 1990s. He portrayed the international arena in 1918 and 1945 as "experiencing on a massively universal scale a convulsive ingathering of people in their numberless groupings of kinds—tribal, racial, linguistic, religious, national."[2] He further depicted that epoch (and, coincidentally, portions of the present global situation) as "the world breaking into bits and pieces, bursting like big and little stars from exploding galaxies ... each one straining to hold its own small separate pieces from spinning off in their turn."[3]

A moving example of Isaacs's characterization is the fate of the Bosnian Muslims, a constituent nation of the former Yugoslavia. Since the late 1960s, Europe's westernmost Islamic community has been considered politically and juridically equal in stature within Yugoslavia with the Serb and Croat nations, with which the Muslims share common Slavic origins. For a Communist country that in principle is atheistic to legitimate the status of an avowedly religious group was no casual action. I argue, however, that official recognition of the Bosnian Muslims made them vulnerable to Serb and Croat pressures, because neither group would accept the Bosnian Muslims as anything more than a religious entity—certainly not as a national entity. International television audiences are currently witnessing the fruits of this denial of Bosnian Muslim nationhood. Furthermore, that nation is in danger of being fragmented and even

1

destroyed, as portrayed most movingly in the siege of Sarajevo and the attempted destruction of the Muslim presence and culture in various other areas of
Bosnia and Herzegovina. I attempt to document in this book how the Muslims
have arrived at this sorry condition.

Although the Bosnian Muslims are the main focus of this work, a constant
undercurrent is the centrality ethnicity has come to occupy in international
affairs and its actualization, often in the form of virulent chauvinistic nationalism. The remainder of this introduction discusses certain concepts—such as
nation, state, nationalism, and ethnic group—that infuse this book. An understanding of these conceptions—particularly of nation and ethnic group, the
nature of their demands on the loyalties of individuals, and their relation to various social and political constructs—may illuminate certain aspects of the
Bosnian Muslim tragedy that have been ignored to date.

The Study of Ethnicity and Nationalism

It is an interesting commentary on the times that starting in the mid-1970s, academicians and policymakers expressed renewed interest in ethnicity, a subject
they had virtually ignored since the turn of the twentieth century.[4] However, an
explicit definition of the concept of ethnicity continues to elude many analysts.[5]
Even Senator Daniel Patrick Moynihan, who early recognized the importance of
ethnicity in international politics, was reluctant to "tidy up the taxonomy,"[6] to
define more closely what attributes delineate an ethnic group from a nation or a
state and what the terms *nationalism* and *ethnonationalism* signify.

If we search the literature, these terms are rather difficult to quantify or differentiate precisely because analysts tend to use them in different ways. Whereas in
the West (Western Europe and the United States) the term *state* is often used syn-
onymously with *nation* to describe the political organization of a society, in
Central and Eastern Europe, including the former Yugoslavia, these two terms
have been differentiated. For our purposes in discussing the situation of the
Bosnian Muslims, the term *state* is used as a juridical concept signifying the
political organization of a sovereign, territory-based group of people. *Nation*,
however, specifies a psychological construct or state of mind of a group of people who share a sense of solidarity that has little or nothing to do with citizenship. In this sense and in this area of the world, then, a nation exists because a
group of people believes it exists.[7]

Historically, the concept of *ethnic group* has been widely understood to have
a slightly different connotation from that of a nation. Members of an ethnic
group share a common interest or characteristic and, by extension, certain common developmental experiences.[8] However, analysts do not widely agree on the
precise difference between the terms *ethnic group* and *nation* or on their manifestations in the forms of ethnicity and nationalism. Thus, whereas Michael G.
Roskin characterized the ethnic group according to a linguistic (or other) criterion for membership rather than by a genetic connection among people,[9] Paul R.

Brass described ethnicity as "subjective self-consciousness" with an element of standing or prestige with regard to other groups.[10] Brass's characterization of an ethnic group as reflecting psychological affinity, and his definition of the concept of *nationalism*, emphasizing a nation's consciousness of its uniqueness and interests, as well as its sense of opposition to other nations in the promotion of its own aims and interests, were most compelling and influenced the conceptualizations in this book. Nevertheless, the lack of a distinctive analytical divide between ethnicity and nationalism leads me to concur with Anthony D. Smith that a reassessment of this field of study must conclude that both the study and the empirical realities of ethnicity and nationhood are "intimately related."[11] The terms thus become somewhat interchangeable, as reflected in the ensuing pages.

The logical extension of the recognized affinity between ethnicity and nationalism is found in the term *ethnonationalism*. This term forges the concepts of ethnic group and nation, emphasizing "the political dimension of solidarity."[12] Ethnonationalism differs from nationalism in intensity, membership, or the degree of mobilization of its adherents.

The problem of definitions becomes thornier when we discuss group dynamics in the former Yugoslavia. Yugoslavs wielded these terms, which Western political scientists seem to employ equivocally, much more precisely and from a different perspective. Thus, the term *nation* (*narod*) was used to signify those South Slavs who lived mostly within Yugoslavia and who were distinguished by their own titular republics. Included within this group immediately after World War II were the Serbs, Croats, Slovenes, Montenegrins, and Macedonians. The Yugoslav term *nationality* (*narodnost*) denoted those Yugoslav populations living in large clusters within Yugoslavia, such as the Hungarians and Albanians, the majority of which lived in states bordering Yugoslavia. Nationality status gave them special rights of national self-identification but not possession of their own republic, like the aforenamed nations. Finally, the term *ethnic minority* (*etnički manjine*) stood for those people, scattered throughout Yugoslavia, who did not fit into the other two groups. Note that the Bosnian Muslims were not specifically included in any of these categories until the late 1960s. As is discussed throughout, the ambiguity of their position within the lands of the South Slavs was thus reflected in the Yugoslav conceptualization of nationhood. When discussing Yugoslavia's peoples, I employ the terms *nation* and *nationality* to reflect the Yugoslav usage and use the term *ethnonationalism* to portray the political repercussions of the actualization of national identity.[13]

Ethnicity and the Modern State

The contemplation of the importance of ethnicity in the international arena was virtually subsumed after World War II by considerations of the viability of the state and international organizations, as well as a yearning for the creation of a world state or other ideal types of political organization and social order.[14]

International politics at the time consisted of problem solving by coherent dominant groups that controlled clusters of other, weaker groups through force and by the mystique of overwhelming power displayed in various cultural, geographical, economic, and psychological ways.

Suddenly in the 1970s, however, these concerns were undermined by the realization that other forces had become equally or even more important for the analysis and comprehension of current events.[15] As Isaacs put it,

> The "soft" facts of life we are dealing with here have to do with such matters as physical characteristics, name and language, history and origin, religion, nationality. These are the stuff of which group identities are made and group identities have become, more than ever before, the stuff of which politics is made, world politics and politics everywhere in the world.[16]

There may be nearly nine hundred extant ethnic groups today.[17] They are able to exert tremendous influence in many parts of the world, often as a destabilizing force. It was reported in 1974 that almost half of the independent countries of the world had recently experienced "ethnically inspired dissonance."[18] This is not surprising when we note that in 1972 only 9.1 percent of the existing states were considered ethnically homogeneous.[19] The recent nationalistic turmoil in the countries of the former Communist bloc may have reversed the trend somewhat. Nevertheless, the rest of the world's inhabitants remain ethnically divided in various proportions, with some states sporting as many as five numerically significant ethnic groups.[20] The implications of this ethnic crazy quilt are startling. For example, all but 15 of the 164 significantly violent disturbances involving states between 1958 and May 1966 were the result of ethnic, tribal, or racial disputes.[21] We do not have to await the compilation of more current data to conclude that many of the contemporary conflicts throughout the world originated from ethnic strife.

Social theorists had previously argued that the economic conflicts that accompanied the development of industrial society would be more enduring than conflicts based on ethnic or cultural divisions. They did not credit the strength of attachment to an abstract sentiment such as ethnicity, since it did not seem to have the same immediate or direct impact on day-to-day life as economic matters. The "new ethnicists," however, foresaw an era of nationalist challenges to the authority of those states that contain ethnic minorities within their borders. They viewed ethnonationalism not as a result of a particular grievance but as a natural situation in a world in which one's security no longer depends on belonging to a powerful state. The desire for self-determination would not be easily satisfied by the same sporadic and halfhearted concessions with which government had met economically inspired challenges.

The current tragedy of the Bosnian Muslims can be seen as only one more example of the trials and tribulations of seeking self-determination. Throughout the rest of this book I explore the origins of the Bosnian Muslims and their national development. I focus on whether their evolution from tribe to nation, which in many ways is little different from the development of the Serbs and Croats, made them a target for the other South Slav people. Although the area has periodically been unstable and violent, the murder and mayhem we now witness are unusual. Perhaps an appreciation of the historical, political, cultural, economic, and social factors surrounding the Bosnian Muslims will facilitate an understanding of the motivations of the current outbreak of violence and will help observers comprehend the difficulties that will ensue if the South Slavs seek reconciliation.

NOTES

1. J. F. Brown, "The Resurgence of Nationalism," *Report on Eastern Europe* (14 June 1991), p. 37.

2. Harold R. Isaacs, *Idols of the Tribe: Group Identity and Political Change* (New York: Harper & Row, 1975), p. 1.

3. Ibid., p. 11.

4. In fact, the word *ethnicity* only began to appear regularly in dictionaries during the 1970s. Nathan Glazer and Daniel P. Moynihan, "Introduction," in Nathan Glazer and Daniel P. Moynihan, eds., *Ethnicity: Theory and Experience* (Cambridge: Harvard University Press, 1975), p. 1.

5. See, for example, Walker Connor's demarcation between "ethnic group" ("a basic human category [i.e., not a subgroup], characterized by unity of race and culture") and "nation" (an ethnic group that has acquired a sense of group identity). "The Politics of Ethnonationalism," *Journal of International Affairs* 27 (1973), pp. 2–3 (note). Connor bemoaned the U.S. academicians' tendency to lump the concepts of ethnic group and minority together, when "ethnic group" is defined as "a group with a common cultural tradition and a sense of identity which exists as a subgroup of a larger society," as did George A. Theodorson and Achilles G. Theodorson in *A Modern Dictionary of Sociology* (New York: Crowell, 1969), p. 135. See also Talcott Parsons, "Some Theoretical Considerations on the Nature and Trends of Change of Ethnicity," in Glazer and Moynihan, *Ethnicity*, pp. 53–83; and Wendell Bell and Walter E. Freeman, eds., *Ethnicity and Nation-Building: Comparative, International, and Historical Perspectives* (Beverly Hills: Sage Publications, 1974) for additional explorations of ethnicity. For a discussion of how various writers have attempted to define ethnicity, consult Konstantin Symmons-Symonolewicz, "Ethnicity and Nationalism: Recent Literature and Its Theoretical Implications," *Canadian Review of Studies in Nationalism* 6 (Spring 1979), pp. 98–102.

6. Daniel Patrick Moynihan, *Pandaemonium: Ethnicity in International Politics* (New York: Oxford University Press, 1993), p. 4.

7. See, for example, Anthony D. Smith, ed., *Ethnicity and Nationalism* (Leiden: Brill, 1992), and Hugh Seton-Watson, *Nations and States: An Enquiry into the Origins of Nations and the Politics of Nationalism* (Boulder: Westview Press, 1977), which wrestled with the definition of the nation, as well as its origins. Joseph Stalin was far more secure in his characterization of a nation: A nation had a common language, territory, economic life, and psychological makeup, or "community of culture." *Marxism and the National and Colonial Question* (New York: International Publishers, 1934), pp. 6–8.

8. See Michael G. Roskin's discussion of the ethnic group in Eastern Europe in *The Rebirth of East Europe* (Englewood Cliffs, N.J.: Prentice-Hall, 1994), p. 9.

9. Ibid.

10. Paul R. Brass, *Ethnicity and Nationalism: Theory and Comparison* (London: Sage, 1991), p. 19.

11. Anthony D. Smith, "Introduction: Ethnicity and Nationalism," in Smith, ed., *Ethnicity and Nationalism,* p. 1.

12. Robin Alison Remington, "Ethnonationalism and the Integrity of the Sovereign State: The Disintegration of Yugoslavia," paper presented to the Conference on Race, Ethnicity and Nationalism at the End of the Twentieth Century, University of Wisconsin–Milwaukee, 30 September–2 October 1993, p. 2.

13. See Anthony D. Smith, "Ethnocentrism, Nationalism, and Social Change," *International Journal of Comparative Sociology* 13 (1972), pp. 1–20, for a discussion of the difference between ethnic consciousness, or ethnocentrism, and nationalism.

14. Thus, for example, according to Edward Allworth, U.S. policymakers were painfully unaware of the potential for violence within the Soviet Union because of its nationality question. "Restating the Soviet Nationality Question," in Edward Allworth, ed., *Soviet Nationality Problems* (New York: Columbia University Press, 1971), p. 2. Allworth further suggested that many writers approached the nationality question in the Soviet Union from a negative and adversarial point of view that may be part of the reason for the "lack of substantial conceptual or theoretical progress needed for studying Soviet nationality problems effectively as a whole in America or the USSR" (p. 10). The cataclysmic events that shook the Soviet Union at the beginning of the 1990s might not have been so surprising, nor might the West have been so unprepared for "winning the peace," had Soviet ethnic studies been pursued with more refined theories and conceptual tools.

15. The academic community's response to the strong correlation between international instability and ethnic conflict was an avalanche of monographs and journal articles examining ethnicity, nationalism, ethnic consciousness, and the role of ethnic groups as transnational actors. In 1978 alone, at least two new journals were launched that specifically treated such issues: *Ethnic and Racial Studies* and *Nationalities Papers.*

16. Harold R. Isaacs, "Power and Identity: Tribalism and World Politics," *Headline Series* (Foreign Policy Association) 136 (October 1979), p. 9.

17. Abdul A. Said and Luiz R. Simmons, "The Ethnic Factor in World Politics," in Abdul A. Said and Luiz R. Simmons, eds., *Ethnicity in an International Context* (New Brunswick, N.J.: Transaction Books, 1976), p. 17.

18. Nathan Glazer and Daniel P. Moynihan, "Why Ethnicity?" *Commentary* 58 (October 1974), pp. 38–39. Observing an apparent widespread change in attitude in the West from the tumultuous 1960s, Theodore Hershberg was led to observe that "the Age of Aquarius is being replaced by the Age of Ethnicity." "Toward the Historical Study of Ethnicity," *Journal of Ethnic Studies* 1 (Spring 1973), p. 1.

19. Walker Connor, "Nation-Building or Nation-Destroying?" *World Politics* 24 (April 1972), p. 320.

20. Ibid.

21. Said and Simmons, "The Ethnic Factor in World Politics," p. 16.

1

Origin of the Bosnian Muslims

*"On the road, when I met people, I asked them always about the past.
Only in this way could the present become comprehensible."*

—Robert D. Kaplan[1]

"The Balkans produce more history than they can consume."[2]

Boundary changes have been infrequent since World War II. However, contemporary clashes over frontiers in Central Europe, encouraged by irredentism, reinforce the fact that national groups rarely dwell within clearly demarcated borders. Settlement patterns harken to deeper imperatives than fair boundaries. Central Europe, once the scene of large multinational empires, is a striking example of how national groups, previously subjugated by imperial designs, can rise as states in their own right with perceived injustices to be corrected, stolen lands to be reclaimed, and enemies to be vanquished.

Perhaps the most poignant example of the nastiness of national-boundary problems and the deadly attempts to redress perceived injustice is found in the territories of the former Yugoslavia. This land has been traversed and conquered so many times by so many peoples that it is not surprising that most of twentieth-century Yugoslavia's internal frontiers, as well as some external borders, are contested.

Yugoslav intellectuals, as well as politicians, continue to view the origins of the South Slavs, their settlement patterns, and their political conditions as central to a consideration of the legitimacy of contemporary territorial and political demands. Serb and Croat claimants are currently attempting to carve out their own realms at the expense of the Bosnian Muslims, a national group once relatively unknown except within Yugoslavia. The anguished odyssey of the Bosnian Muslims may be a foretaste of what other nascent national entities will have to endure to achieve self-determination in the post-Communist world order.

Who are the Bosnian Muslims, and how did they come to this sorry pass? Was there something about the history of the various Yugoslav peoples or about their twentieth-century unification or the institutions and regimes they created that encouraged the depredations of ethnic cleansing in the name of ethnic homogeneity? In attempting to confront the issue of the viability of the Bosnian Muslims as a nation and to understand why they have suffered at the hands of their compatriots, we must, of course, consider contemporary conditions. However, first we must search for clues in their singular history to discredit the dubious claim that today's murder and mayhem are merely a renewal of racial hatreds rather than a contemporary land grab.

Early Balkan Settlement

Although the earliest immigrants into the Balkan Peninsula may have arrived around three thousand years ago,[3] the ancestors of today's South Slavs likely first crossed the Danube and then the Drava Rivers in the middle to late sixth century.[4] The names Serb and Croat,[5] not used meaningfully by Balkan inhabitants until the nineteenth century,[6] were probably taken from later-arriving, possibly Iranian groups who were assimilated by the Slavs already in the Balkans during the seventh century. There is every reason to believe that the antecedents of today's Serbs and Croats, who were part of the larger Slav movement westward, were originally of the same Slavic stock, becoming differentiated only because of settlement patterns rather than by racial and cultural differences.[7]

Encouraged, ironically, by the invasion of the Turkic Avars, the Slavs created a substantial number of settlements in the area. Until the arrival of the Avars, Slavic settlement of the Balkans had been fitful at best. The Slavs were living a wild and primitive life unhampered by leaders or other authority, but when the Avars appeared, they either conscripted the Slavs or forced them to flee south of the Danube. Together, the Avars and some of their Slav subjects wreaked havoc on the borders of the Byzantine Empire. The Byzantine army was occupied with a war against Persia and could not spare troops to control the Balkans. The Slavs and Avars gained and retained control of the Pannonian area of the Balkan Peninsula for three centuries, during which time many South Slavs fell into a sedentary existence, settling and cultivating the land. Ancestors of the Croats inhabited what is now Croatia, Dalmatia, and western Bosnia. Forebears of the Serbs settled in what is now southern Serbia, Zahumlje, Trebinje, Pagania, and Konavli.

Avar military aspirations effected the first cooperative, albeit sporadic, Slavic merger to wage war against Byzantium.[8] However, the Avar-encouraged merger of South Slavs was not a lasting or a profound union, for the Slav colonists were not subject to strong unifying political leadership during this era.

The Byzantine counterattacks against the Avars and their Slavic cohorts were generally unsuccessful, partially because of Byzantine Emperor Maurice's capricious leadership and later because of the ineptitude of his successor, Phocas. But even when the Avars and Slavs were defeated in a battle, it was the military contingents rather than the Slavic settlers who were adversely affected. The settlers merely continued to diffuse throughout the area. They gradually mingled with and assimilated the indigenous Illyrian populations, who had settled perhaps as early as 1800 B.C.[9] in the northwest—including present-day Serbia,

Croatia, Bosnia, Dalmatia, and northern Italy, as well as Transylvania and Romania.[10]

Avar strength began to decline during the second decade of the seventh century, culminating in the Avar defeat by the Frankish King Charlemagne in 796. The Slavs accepted his rule, and control of the Balkan interior from the head of the Adriatic across to the Black Sea devolved to the Slavic tribes.

The Slavs had settled widely throughout the Balkans, breaking the land tie between Constantinople and the few remaining Romanized cities in Dalmatia. Thus, the eastern and western sections of the empire, already estranged, were now cut off from communication with each other. In contrast to the eventually revitalized western part of the empire, the east became a dreary place. The flavor of the Slav-settled Byzantine lands was captured in the following passage:

> In the lost areas urban life disappeared or declined; many of the towns became little more than villages. Commerce as well as communication across the Balkans virtually ceased owing to both urban decline and the insecurity of the roads. Christianity as a religion of the Balkan population almost disappeared in the interior. Literate culture more or less died out.[11]

The Slavic tribes continued to maintain their primitive tribe-centered organization. The early Slavic patriarchal clans were organized in a series of small, independent districts, each of which was called a *župa,* meaning "bond" or "confederation," led by a *župan.* Often, some clans affiliated and chose a *grand župan.*

The religion of the Slavs, too, remained primitive for some time. The early Slavs appear to have followed an animistic type of religion, believing they were surrounded by invisible spirits that could be either benevolent or hostile. They also worshiped a supreme being and supported priests and medicine men. When the South Slavs were finally brought to Christianity, the ancestors of the Serbs accepted the gospel and rites of the Eastern Church as preached by Cyril and Methodius in the ninth century. Although the forebears of the Croats appear to have been introduced to Christianity by missionaries from Rome as early as the late seventh century during Pope Agathon's reign (678–681), they do not seem to have accepted it wholeheartedly until the ninth century.[12] Reflecting the eastern versus western split in the empire, the acceptance of different religious rituals exacerbated the differentiation of the Serbs from the Croats that geographical and historical factors had already initiated.

The Balkans in the Middle Ages

As the tenth century drew to a close, the outlines of the political and demographic landscape of the Middle Ages emerged. The Bulgars had long been dominant actors in the Balkans, but other Slavic states also arose, only to be merged with stronger neighboring empires. Ancestors of today's Slovenes and Croats were Frankish vassals, although at times the Croat lands also fell within the Byzantine sphere of influence. However, the Croats, allied with their Dalmatian cousins, were finally able to throw off Byzantine and Frankish domination in the late ninth century and build an independent Croat state that lasted for two hundred years. Some contemporary Croats insisted that the foundation of the Croat kingdom was laid as early as the end of the eighth century to the middle of the ninth century.[13] However, the independent Croat state was only finally realized under Branimir (879–892) and the Kingdom of Croatia under Tomislav (910–928). In fact, the strength of Croatia during this period may have compared favorably with that of the Serbs, who were unable to resist Bulgar incursions.[14]

The Serbs became politically and militarily active in the region at about the same time Croat fortunes were ebbing, in the wake of Tomislav's death in 928. Croatia was forced to seek Byzantine assistance against the Serbs, as well as against the Venetians and others who were attacking Croat-inhabited lands. Hungarian power, however, overwhelmed the Croatian kingdom, which lost its independence to the Hungarian monarch Ladislav and then to Ladislav's successor, Koloman, through the Treaty of Zagreb in 1102.[15]

In the latter part of the twelfth century, Stjepan Nemanja united Serbia, founding a powerful dynastic state. Serbia and Byzantium were at loggerheads throughout the rest of the Middle Ages. The Serb kingdom grew stronger and more aggressive, particularly in the fourteenth century, whereas Byzantium was racked by civil war. The upshot of all the alliance manipulations among the Serbs, Byzantines, and Bulgars was that the newly created Serbian patriarch crowned the Serbian King Stjepan Dušan emperor of the Serbs (and the Romans, as he called himself[16]) in 1346. Dušan's territory then extended "from the Danube to the Gulf of Corinth and from the Adriatic to the Aegean,"[17] making Serbia one of the most powerful forces in the area.

The existence of the medieval Croat and Serb kingdoms is fairly well documented, but what of Bosnia? Historians have found relatively little written evidence about Bosnia and Herzegovina's early history, in part because its mountainous terrain discouraged casual travelers and other observers. We do know that many peoples—including the Serbs, Croats, Hungarians, and Byzantines—controlled parts of the region at various times from the tenth through the twelfth centuries. In fact, lacking historical sources to the contrary, some Croats claimed absolute suzerainty over Bosnia and Herzegovina based on certain periods of domination,[18] just as the Serbs put forward their claim based on possession of Bosnian lands during Časlav's reign in the middle of the tenth century and control of Hum (modern Herzegovina) from the mid-twelfth century to the early fourteenth century.

The polemical fray was joined, however, by Bosnian Muslim historians who sought to demonstrate the validity of the contemporary Bosnian Muslim nation as the legitimate successor of an independent medieval Bosnian state. These scholars complained that some Serbs and Croats cavalierly dismissed uniquely

Bosnian manifestations of state authority as mere tribal unions.[19] They rejected Serb and Croat claims on Bosnia based on possession of the land during the Middle Ages, pointing out that sovereignty over Bosnia was passed around so frequently for a time that the inhabitants felt no allegiance to any of their erstwhile suzerains. Finally, the fact that the inhabitants of the area all spoke a similar language merely obfuscated the fact that they formed a distinct national unit, albeit Slavic, like the Serbs and the Croats.[20]

Hard facts to clarify early Bosnian history are decidedly lacking, and such evidence is sometimes difficult to find for Serb and Croat history in regard to Bosnia as well. Nevertheless, we can discern some outlines of Bosnian medieval history beginning in the twelfth century with the ever increasing independence of Bosnia from its often nominal Hungarian overlords. Under Ban (Governor) Kulin's stewardship (1180–1204), Bosnia became an important regional actor. Kulin's peaceful reign and concentration on economic development permitted Bosnia to become increasingly independent of Hungary, although during the late twelfth century Bosnia sought and received Hungarian protection from the territorial designs of Serbia. Hungarian interference in Bosnian affairs may have been minimal,[21] but Hungary increasingly resented Bosnia's growing independence and sought to increase its influence. In one notable intercession, Hungarian leaders were able to convince the pope that religious heresy was rife in Bosnia, causing him to support a crusade there between 1235 and 1241. Hungary marched into Bosnia to eradicate a heretical religion from Bosnia and neighboring areas. But was there religious heresy in Bosnia, or did Hungary initiate these claims simply to exert influence over Bosnia?

Medieval Religious Practice in the Balkans

Nationalist inclination infuses the scholarly discussion of religion in medieval Bosnia. The issue of medieval religious practices and membership may seem arcane, yet it is central to the identity claims made by various Yugoslav nationalists and thus to the problem of the political and national status of today's Bosnian Muslims.

At the geographical, political, religious, and cultural crossroads between Occident and Orient and on the line of bifurcation between Rome and Byzantium, the lands of the South Slavs received missionaries from both the Catholic and Orthodox centers, who attempted to win converts throughout the Balkans. Rome's emissaries succeeded in instilling Roman Catholicism in Croatia and neighboring Dalmatia, whereas missionaries from Byzantium converted much of Serbia. Lying between Serbia and Croatia, Bosnia was subjected to conversion attempts by both sides. Again, however, mountainous terrain became an important factor, as Bosnia was protected from intensive attention by either side. It would not be surprising, therefore, if the conversions that took place in Bosnia produced localistic interpretations of the mainstream religious practices interspersed with rituals from the pre-Christian ages rather than zealous and doctrinally precise adherents.

Thus, controversy surrounds the existence and character of medieval religious practices in Bosnia. Most of the controversy surrounds the nature and existence of the *Crkva Bosanska* (Bosnian Church), members of which some claim are ancestors of today's Bosnian Muslims.

Two major lines of argument have been pursued regarding the Bosnian Church. The first was advanced by many Yugoslav scholars,[22] supported by some British scholarship, who utilized documents originating under Pope Pius II (1458–1464). They asserted the existence in Bosnia of the Bogomils, a heretical dualist sect—that is, a sect positing that life is reducible to the clash between good and evil. Bogomilism arose first in Bulgaria and then spread throughout the Mediterranean, including Dalmatia; to the extent it penetrated eastward, it eventually reached Bosnia.

The Bogomils reviled the concept of the church as the mystical body and representative of Jesus on earth and echoed a Manichean belief in a perpetual struggle between the principles of good and evil. The Bogomils denied God's rule over all facets of life, stating that at first God ruled only over a spiritual realm. Eventually the elder son, Satanel (the prefix "el" indicating divinity) revolted against God out of pride and was joined by angels who believed that under Satanel they would have to labor less.[23] When Satanel's revolt failed, he was exiled from heaven and created earth as his own realm. This is the origin of the Bogomil belief that matter and the visible world were part of the evil spirit's realm. The Bogomils had only contempt for the Hebrew Bible's writings, which they considered to be inspired by Satanel. Exceptions were the Psalms and the sixteen prophets. From the New Testament they especially revered the Acts of the Apostles, the Epistles, and the Apocalypse.[24]

From these beliefs arose the practices attributed to the Bogomils, who believed the path to salvation lay in the renunciation of material things through asceticism. The souls of those Bogomils who successfully avoided sin were assured of returning to the spiritual heaven. The uninitiated, who did not bind themselves to the ascetic life, were doomed to endure another exploited existence in the unjust material world. The initiated—who, by the way, did no manual labor— were revered by laypeople, for they carried the Holy Spirit within them.

The Bogomils also rejected all official Orthodox and Roman Catholic Church ceremonies, the liturgy, and the sacraments. They particularly repudiated water baptism, since water came from the material world. Initiation was performed "by the laying on of St. John's Gospel."[25] Their services, held in private homes, consisted of recitation of the Lord's Prayer, "the ceremonial breaking of bread, and the exchange of benedictions with the believers."[26]

The attractiveness of the Bogomils as forebears of today's Bosnian Muslims lies in the desire of Bosnian Muslim nationalists to demonstrate a separate and distinct origin through the unique character of religion in that area. This would indicate that their direct ancestors were originally separate from either the

Orthodox or the Catholic inhabitants and would obviate equally vehement Croat and Serb claims on Bosnian lands based on the supposition that Bosnia was originally an integral part of their respective cultural legacies.

The other side of the controversy is championed by John V.A. Fine Jr., and others,[27] who are convinced that the Bosnian Church was a local institution that broke from the Catholic Church on ritualistic grounds. This view persuasively disputed the contention that the Bogomil heresy had much, if any, influence in Bosnia. Scholars contradicted the heretofore widely accepted hypothesis that the discovery of unique *stećci* (medieval tombstones) proved the existence of the Bogomils. Instead, Fine and others argued that decoration on the *stećci* was often reminiscent of Christian tombstones that would have been abhorrent to Manichaeans. Ivo Sivrić, of the Order of Franciscans, cited inscriptions of a variety of tombstones on which he observed appeals to the Trinity and signs of the cross. These marks seem to demonstrate that the "heretics" at least nominally held some mainstream Christian beliefs, revering both the Trinity and the cross,[28] and did not eschew the concept of an omnipotent God, a veneration of saints, and the use of church buildings decorated with religious art—all of which the Bogomils would have repudiated.

Thus, these scholars have advanced the thesis that the Bogomil heresy has been incorrectly confused with the Bosnian Church, which constituted an indigenous separatist and schismatic—but not Manichaean—sect. The Bosnian Church originated as a result of the Bosnian refusal of Hungarian attempts to control Bosnian Catholicism by appointing a Hungarian bishop. Rejecting Hungarian meddling, the Bosnians expelled the bishop to Croatia and set up their own independent church, known as the Bosnian Church. According to Fine, Bosnian Church adherents (*kr'stiani*) and not Bogomils were among the ancestors of today's Bosnian Muslims, along with members of other medieval religions who later converted to Islam. Bosnians followed the doctrines of the Bosnian Church because the influence and doctrinal purity of mainstream Christianity in Bosnia had simply dissipated, as have some other theologies historically, without adequate supervision by "educated keepers of doctrine."[29] Thus, the Bosnians drifted into the schismatic religion when adequate religious instruction became unavailable and not because they had particular doctrinal arguments with the mainstream churches.

This view of Bosnian religious practices is more compelling than the Bogomil version, which would have invested Bogomilism with greater strength in Bosnia than the evidence indicates. Indeed, to inveigle its crusade, Hungary played upon the fact that the Catholic Church considered many people to be heretics merely for continuing to practice such "pagan" or indigenous (not mainstream) rites and customs as they had heretofore followed. The Bosnian peasant, on the other hand, did not consider it heretical to synthesize his or her traditional usages with the new ones imposed by Christianity.

Bosnia was not firmly integrated into the organization of either Roman Catholic or Orthodox ecclesiastical institutions. In fact, the jurisdictional line between Rome and Constantinople ran through Bosnia, which permitted a certain vagueness about which church should control the lands.[30] This ambiguity was exacerbated by Bosnia's remoteness from the centers of either religion, which left it open to any aggressive ideology or religion that swept through it.

To add to the confusion, Bosnia had long been an area of political dispute. It remained torn between its leaders' attempts to increase Bosnia's independence and Hungary's desire to control Bosnia. This jurisdictional confusion permitted some of the bans of Bosnia to realize increasing independence for their lands.

The bans and succeeding rulers practiced toleration of, even indifference to, the variety of religions extant in the land. Even when the rulers became Catholic from the mid-fourteenth century on, this toleration extended to the independent Bosnian Church.

For some, adherence to the schismatic Bosnian Church may have been synonymous with the type of feeling that passed for patriotism in Bosnia in the Middle Ages. Threatened nobles may have organized defense of their territory from incursions by armies from Hungary, thus transforming a local religion into an ideology of opposition to the acquisitiveness and meddling of neighboring areas.[31] Hungary's accusations against Bosnian heresy may have reflected the ulterior motive of jurisdictional jealousy.[32] Although ecclesiastical complaints were directed to Split, the home of the Catholic bishop, he was nevertheless denied his appointed influence in Bosnia. Thus, religious problems based on nontolerance were brought from outside Bosnia, a situation reminiscent of the contemporary conflict in Bosnia and Herzegovina.

Whatever the origin of the claims against Bosnia, the crusade turned into a Hungarian war of conquest of Bosnia.[33] Ban Kulin's previous "abjuration" of heresy or his ability to demonstrate that heresy was not rife in his land could hold off the crusades only so long.

The 1235–1241 crusade against Bosnia, led by the Hungarian king's brother Koloman, governor of Croatia and Dalmatia, began after Kulin's death and the banishment of his Catholic son, Ban Stjepan, in favor of an alleged follower of the schismatic religion, Matej Ninoslav (1232–1250). Fine has suggested that the Bosnian Church, which was strongest and most effective during this time of chaos, became an autonomous church between 1234 and 1252, developing out of the existing Catholic monastic orders of the region rather than as an offshoot of any dualist heresy.[34] However, at this juncture it appears that adherents of each of the two explanations of heresy in Bosnia met at a crossroads of sorts. Apart from the Bosnian Church, stated Fine, there did exist a growing heretical movement (called by some historians Manichees, Cathars, Patarenes, or simply Bogomils). The Bosnian Church had long been able to remain free of these heretical influences, but "the wars threw all Bosnians together to repel the invader, and also, by making the populace anti-Catholic, attracted many toward the heretical movement."[35]

Any deviations from Catholicism by the Bosnian Church that resembled heretical practices may have been continued by the monks "as a reaction against domination from a foreign culture by means of an organized attempt to revive or perpetuate certain aspects of the native culture in the face of pressure to change."[36] Anthropologists call this a "nativistic movement" and seek such a reaction particularly among the more privileged inhabitants who felt their position was somehow threatened.[37]

Mid-thirteenth-century Bosnia apparently fit this characterization rather well: Hungary threatened the political leadership with loss of authority. The local religious leadership would have been exterminated had the established Catholic Church organization been reintroduced into the region by Hungarian force of arms. It is not inconceivable, therefore, that many Bosnians may have participated in a dynamic resistance against Hungary regardless of whether they shared the same religious rituals.

Koloman captured some territory from Ninoslav in 1237,[38] but the Bosnians later regained it when Hungarian troops were mauled by the Tatars. Ninoslav reincorporated the lost land and avoided further crusades against Bosnia by appealing to Pope Innocent IV. Ninoslav stressed his conversion to Catholicism and successfully pleaded that he had supported and protected religious practices inimical to the church in his realm only because he relied on the schismatics to help fight for Bosnian independence from foreign incursion.[39]

The pope, having investigated Ninoslav's protestations, agreed that there should be no more Hungarian-led campaigns. He also permitted Catholic services in Bosnia to be conducted in the Slavic language and writings to be rendered into the Glagolithic form so Catholicism could be more easily propagated in the region.[40]

Ninoslav's agreement with the pope brought some tranquil years to Bosnia, particularly since Hungarian ecclesiastical control was successfully deflected, but in the years following the death of Ninoslav rebellion against the established Catholic Church spread throughout Bosnia. Catholicism disappeared from Bosnia,[41] and as soon as the Hungarian armies left, the Bosnian Church reemerged.

The competing claims over the genesis of the Bosnian Muslims may never be resolved because of the dearth of original source materials and documents from either Bogomils or members of the Bosnian Church. Yet scholars have marshaled what little evidence remains to pursue these two lines of inquiry.

Some notable scholars have questioned the strength of heresy in Bosnia. Sima Ćirković believed Christianity was only weakly rooted in Bosnia because of its relative geographic isolation and difficult terrain. Since Bosnia was less accessible than other areas, dualist ideas that filtered through might have found fertile soil, since there were few Christian centers in the area that could have stanched such ideas before they became widespread.[42] Fine also cautioned that "in a country of Bosnia's intellectual level and geographical conditions, ideas just do not spread as easily" as proponents of the Manichaean hypothesis claim. He thus discounted papal alarmism about rampant heresy, claiming that Bogomilism, as well as other religions, would have "circulated slowly," if at all.[43]

Church Attacks on Heresy in Bosnia

Whether Fine's sophisticated analysis of the existence of a separate Bosnian Church will induce a generally accepted reinterpretation of previously held theories or analysts will continue to credit the Bogomil version, the fact remains that it was widely believed in Rome and the West that heresy was rampant in Bosnia. The possibility that the alleged heresy may have been a successful propaganda campaign by Hungary to regain control over an increasingly independent Bosnia was not widely credited. Evidence points to some activity by the Bosnian Church in the mid-fourteenth century, although it was probably not a state church as some scholars have claimed.[44] More likely, the Bosnian Church gained adherents because Bosnia had no official ties with Catholicism for seventy years during the struggles against the Hungarian crusades. It would, therefore, not be surprising if church buildings had been abandoned or, in the absence of clerics, if the ignorant population had reverted to non-Catholic rituals.

In the mid-1300s, a Franciscan mission entered Bosnia to win that region back to the Catholic Church. The mission seems to have succeeded over the next several decades to the extent that most of Bosnia's rulers from Stjepan Kotromanić (1318–1353) on were Catholic[45] (except possibly for King Ostoja [1398–1404, 1409–1418][46]). However, they seemed to remain tolerant of the Bosnian Church.[47] On the other hand, we do not know how successfully the Catholic Church reached the general population.

Bosnia's independence, and consequently its status in the area, continued to grow. Inheriting from his uncle Ban Stjepan Kotromanić a vastly increased Bosnian land (which included Catholic-inhabited areas formerly controlled by Croatia, as well as for the first time Orthodox Hum [Herzegovina]), King Tvrtko I (1353–1391) annexed considerable neighboring territories from both Serb and Croat lands. With his vastly expanded landholdings and increasing economic and commercial strength, spurred by Kotromanić's development of lead and silver mines, Tvrtko styled himself king of Serbia, Bosnia, and Primorje in 1377, as well as of Dalmatia and Croatia by the last decade of the fourteenth century.[48] At this point, then, Bosnian leaders clearly considered Bosnia an independent entity until its conquest by the Ottoman Turks in 1463.

The Bosnian Church was finally extirpated under King Stjepan Tomašević (1443–1461), the price demanded by the pope for the king's request for aid against the Turks. Most Bosnian Church members converted to Orthodoxy, Catholicism, or Islam, whereas a small number sought protection in Herzegovina, following the head of the Bosnian Church, who emigrated there.

The Ottoman Invasion and Conquest of Bosnia

The battle of Kosovo Polje in 1389 proved to be a momentous event for the Balkans. Although the battle was a draw, large Serb losses helped to open the

Balkan Peninsula to the Ottoman Empire, ending Serbia's pretensions of building a Balkan empire during the Middle Ages.

The Ottomans approached Bosnia and nibbled away pieces of its eastern
reaches. In 1451, Vrhbosna (contemporary Sarajevo) fell. Then in 1463, the ultimate push for Bosnia began.

The Ottomans' conquest of Bosnia followed their usual invasion scenario:

> First, they sought to establish partial or total suzerainty over the country. Then they
> made an effort to take over direct control by eliminating the native dynasty. Finally
> they employed a policy of progressive incorporation of the land into their organiza-
> tion by temporarily including non-Moslem leaders and their warriors in the Osmanli
> *timar*-system and by converting the people to Islam.[49]

However, Bosnia, domestically fragmented (into Bosnia—the king's lands—and
Herzegovina—the duke's lands[50]) and exhausted by Hungarian interventions,
became the Ottomans' most successful and one of their easiest conquests in the
Balkans.

Post-Tvrtko medieval Bosnia had been unable to attain a uniform sociopolitical structure to counter the Turkish onslaught.[51] Ottoman raiding parties
increased the tension already gripping the land as rivalries among the leading
Bosnian nobles further weakened domestic cohesion. Accelerating Turkish
interventions coupled with civil war made Bosnian territory an easy target for
Ottoman absorption.

Some historians have posited that the members of the Bosnian Church or the
Bogomils—whichever view of the schism one accepts—aided the Ottoman
advance into Bosnia to deflect further Hungarian attacks[52] or that they did so
out of rage over the conversion of King Stjepan Tomašević from Bogomilism to
Catholicism.[53] There is more evidence, however, that aid from Bosnian inhabitants may have come because they believed they could continue to possess their
lands under Turkish aegis or that the indigenous schismatic Christians saw in
the Islamic Turks a lesser evil than the intolerant Roman Catholics. Early Islam
appeared to be more tolerant with more equitable laws than Christianity.[54]
There may also have been a feeling of kinship—that is, the Muslims allowed rev-
erence of Jesus, even as they acknowledged him in their religion, whereas the
pope considered both the schismatics and the Muslims to be enemies.[55]

Fine, however, disputed that the Bosnian Church was significantly aiding the
Muslim conquerors by citing the absence of such concerns in various letters
written at the time by high personages deeply involved in the defense of Bosnia.
He observed that

> the lack of notice given to them as a factor both before and after the [Turkish] con-
> quest suggests that such Patarin cooperation with the Turks had not been on a large
> scale and had not been significant enough to have had any real effect on the out-
> come of the struggle.... A few years earlier the king had told the Bosnian Church
> clergy to accept Catholicism or leave; a majority accepted the new faith and a hand-
> ful went to Hercegovina. Apparently the populace, indifferent about the issue, went

on living as they had previously, with no great indignation against the king or
Catholics for exiling a handful of monks.[56]

Fine emphasized, however, that Catholic persecution of the Bosnian Church
began only four years before the fall of Bosnia (1459–1463). For the entire previous period, the Bosnian Church had been tolerated or possibly simply ignored.[57]

When the Turks finally conquered Bosnia, many Bosnians converted to Islam,
but this was a slow process throughout the late fifteenth and the sixteenth centuries.[58] There is little evidence of forced conversions (except for an occasional
overly enthusiastic pasha).[59] Census data, for example, demonstrated that in
1489 there were 25,000 Christian hearths and 4,500 Muslim hearths in Bosnia;
however, the census covering the period 1520–1530 showed that the number of
Muslims did not begin to approach the number of Christians until thirty years
after the Ottoman invasion.[60] This suggests that large-scale Islamization of peasants and town dwellers may not have begun in earnest until the end of the fifteenth century.[61] It further suggests that not all religious conversion was to
Islam. In fact, the Orthodox Church gained a number of converts from the
Bosnian Church and even from Catholicism because the Orthodox Church was
favored over the Roman Catholic Church under Ottoman rule.[62]

Reports that Turkish feudal landlords sometimes directed reprisals against
non-Muslims after domestic riots, sparing only those who were or who became
Muslims, did not mention how frequently this practice occurred.[63] Most scholars agree, however, that the Islamization of the Balkans was "for the most part
peaceful and voluntary"[64] and that the Ottomans allowed the non-Muslim
indigenous people autonomy in local and religious affairs in return for their loyalty to the sultan. In fact, the Ottoman administration may have been torn
between the benefits of increasing the number of Muslim faithful and the economic ramifications of encouraging Islamization: The conversion of a Christian
to Islam entailed financial loss to the Ottoman Empire, since the "infidel tax"
could no longer be collected.[65]

If the Ottoman Turks were so tolerant of their Christian subjects, why did so
many Bosnians, who finally had such uncritical sovereigns, turn to Islam? The
immediate answer as implied by the earlier discussion of medieval Bosnian religious conditions is that there was no strong Christian religious organization in
Bosnia to capture the allegiance of the Bosnian peasants. Therefore, when Islam
entered the area with its dynamic and well-ordered organization, the Bosnian
peasants, most of whom were religiously unengaged because of weak Christian
proselytizing, responded enthusiastically.

Furthermore, opportunism may have played a role in the individual choice of
religion. The ability of Bosnians to identify with the higher civilization represented by the Muslim religion and to acquire the political, monetary, and social
advantages accruing to followers of the state religion in the Ottoman-held
regions was an important factor in accepting Islam. Only Muslims could hope to
rise to the highest positions within the Ottoman Empire.[66]

Much of the conversion to Islam occurred among townspeople because Ottoman administration was centered there. Merchants gained greater freedom of movement and more secure transport of goods if they were Muslim. Professional soldiers also converted to Islam to ensure rapid advancement, particularly because the Ottoman armies were so successful during the fifteenth and sixteenth centuries.[67]

Although conversion was less rapid and widespread than that in the towns, Islamization also made inroads in the villages. Many peasants likely found seductive the fact that tax and rent benefits, as well as equal civil status with all other Muslims—no matter how highborn—accrued only to Muslims. A final motive for the conversion of Bosnians to Islam may have been the appeal of the "warlike and conquest-oriented ideology" of Islam as a way to wreak revenge on the previous aggressors, the papacy and Hungary.[68]

Nevertheless, conversion to Islam did not banish from the peasants' daily lives elements of Christian, pagan, and even what might have been deemed "heretical" practices, which differentiated them from the local Muslim aristocratic and religious intelligentsia.[69] The "universal" religions of Islam and Christianity share the concept that the "present is devalued" in favor of later "salvation," or status reversal in a different system.[70] The Bosnian peasants would thus have had to make minimal changes in their outlook on life and its rewards. They would have experienced little frustration if they had not immediately acquired wealth and status, which they would also have been denied under Orthodox or Catholic rule. Furthermore, "the social role that was assigned to an individual by society was justified and accorded significance as a manifestation of religious duty."[71] Thus, Fine described what may have been the attitude of most Bosnians when they converted to Islam:

> Probably few Bosnians in accepting Islam underwent any deep changes in patterns of thought or way of life. Most of those who became Moslems probably lived as they always had, retaining most of their domestic customs as well as many Christian practices. They adopted now a few Islamic practices, which quickly would acquire great symbolic value and which would soon come to be viewed as the essentials of Islam.[72]

To summarize, some scholars have contended that medieval Bosnians easily converted to Islam in reaction to previous excesses and persecutions by Catholic leaders.[73] The egalitarian concept that granted persons of any nationality who embraced Islam access to the best positions in Ottoman society was also attractive. Superficial similarities existed in the simplicity of the rituals of the heretics and those of Islam. Even more powerful a lure may have been that Islam and Christianity shared concurrent religious and political dimensions. The level of commitment of indigenous Christians on either dimension, therefore, would not have been compromised by entering Islam.

Finally, the number of new adherents to Islam could have been influenced by the lack of strong and committed leadership of the schismatic church, as well as of the Roman Catholic and Orthodox Churches in Bosnia. Common people must have felt spiritually adrift without an effective alternative church organization to guide them, thus increasing their vulnerability to the blandishments of Islam.

Despite the increasing popularity of Islam throughout Bosnia, the Catholic Church staged a modest comeback in the mid-fifteenth century by converting some Bosnian Church believers to Catholicism.[74] Those who refused to convert to Catholicism, Orthodoxy, or Islam went to Herzegovina in exile.[75] Thus, the schismatics disappeared very rapidly after the fall of the medieval state of Bosnia, although isolated reports of their existence persisted.[76]

The picture that emerges after the Ottoman destruction of the Bosnian state in 1463 is one of a gradual conversion of many Bosnians to Islam but at a differential and usually slow rate in various areas.[77] Unquestionably, the general ignorance about religion and ritual contributed to the ease with which Bosnians accepted Islam. Furthermore, Islam was well supported by institutions and clerics who guaranteed familiarity with Islamic tenets, unlike the medieval Christian churches in Bosnia, whose haphazard local institutions exhibited a remarkable inability to excite religious or even communal loyalty to the church. Furthermore, backsliding from Islam was deterred by making it punishable by death.

Much has been made of the heretical Bosnians possessing an effective indigenous church that influenced the history of Bosnia and thus that of the Bosnian Muslims to the present day. For the contrary view, I again cite Fine:

> The Bosnian Church exerted relatively little influence on political developments or upon society. And as an inefficient religious organization existing in the middle of a peasant society quite indifferent to religious matters, its religious and moral influence was also small. Thus the legacy of the Bosnian Church is nil. And though frequently historians have used the Bosnian Church to explain the Islamization of Bosnia, it is more accurate to explain that phenomenon by the absence of strong Catholic, Orthodox, or even Bosnian Church organizations.[78]

Apparently, some historians have given greater importance to the role of the Bosnian Church in medieval Bosnia than did its contemporaries. Henrik Birnbaum, in fact, emphasized the period of Ottoman rule of Bosnia and Herzegovina, not the medieval era dominated by heresy, as "the very key for our understanding of the present ethnic situation" in that region.[79]

Nevertheless, some contemporary Croat nationalists have claimed that the Bogomils were a group of ethnic Roman Catholics who embraced Manichaeism and then, under persecution from the Roman Catholics and the Orthodox, converted to Islam. As ethnic Croats, then, the Bosnian Muslims would have been the direct successors of the old Croatian kingdom,[80] and throughout time, they provided the continuity that allowed modern Croat nationalists to claim them and their territory as Croatian patrimony.[81] One of the earliest proponents of this claim was Ivo Pilar in *Die Sudslawische Frage und der Weltkrieg*.[82] Pilar, like other Croat nationalists, considered the Muslims to be "Islamicized Croats who, through conversion, acquired a new locus of cultural identification that entailed the loss of Croat national consciousness."[83] Other, more contemporary writers also subscribed to this view.[84]

This view denigrated the Serbophile claim that the Muslims were actually Orthodox settlers in Bosnia who converted from Orthodoxy to Islam when the Turks invaded that area.[85] Instead, contemporary Orthodox inhabitants of Bosnia were considered "descendants of migrants who came to Bosnia under Turkish rule, or of Catholics who embraced Orthodoxy under the influence of the well-organized Orthodox Church."[86] Serbophiles rejoined by claiming Bosnia's Catholics for their own, stating that in the sixteenth and seventeenth centuries some Orthodox immigrants converted to Catholicism[87] and claiming that Bosnian rulers were at one time vassals of the Serbian kings.[88]

To counter these Serbophile and Croatophile hypotheses, Muslim nationalists have advanced a third option. They have contended that today's Bosnian Muslims were descendants of the Bogomils. This unique ancestry made the Bosnian Muslims a product of a distinctive Bosnian Slav culture wedded to the ensuing Islamic culture to create an original and exclusive Bosnian Muslim group. Bosnian Muslim nationalists believe their unique historical and social development has differentiated them from the other inhabitants of Bosnia and Herzegovina and made them legitimate claimants to control of that land, on a par with today's Serbs and Croats. During the early twentieth century, as we shall see later, some Bosnian Muslims also touted Gothic heritage for the ancestors of today's Bosnian Muslims to differentiate them from the Slavic roots of the Serbs and Croats and to base Bosnian Muslim history on national rather than any other basis, such as class distinction.

With the strategic importance of Bosnia and Herzegovina—both geographically and politically—in post–World War II Yugoslavia and the current contention among Serbs, Croats, and Muslims over its land, it is no wonder that a plethora of arguments and counterarguments surrounds the circumstances of medieval religious practices in Bosnia. None of the concerned groups, however, has been able to advance conclusive geographic or ethnographic claims on today's Bosnian Muslims to the exclusion of all other counterclaims. The abundance of conversions and migrations that occurred during the Middle Ages has produced a welter of mixed backgrounds—too mixed to be deciphered—which makes claims of original descent too confusing to be of much use. Claims based on historical events are equally impossible to credit. On the other hand, throughout much of its history, Bosnia and Herzegovina has been a discrete geographical area populated by adherents of assorted Christian rituals living together more or less harmoniously. The Ottoman conquest, however, inserted a new religion and social structure into the mix. The result was that many Bosnians who converted to Islam began to develop a strong sense of identity with their Islamic coreligionists that created tensions between them and their non-Muslim Slavic relatives, the Orthodox and Catholics.[89] The importance of the mobilization of a population by appeals to religion is the focus of Chapter 2.

NOTES

1. Robert D. Kaplan, *Balkan Ghosts: A Journey Through History* (New York: St. Martin's Press, 1993), p. xxi.

2. *Yugofax* (12 October 1991).

3. Karl H. Menges traced the origins and movements of the earliest Slavs in *An Outline of the Early History and Migrations of the Slavs* (New York: Department of Slavic Languages, Columbia University, 1953). For an overview of the Balkans during the Neolithic Age, see Marija Gimbutas, "The Neolithic Cultures of the Balkan Peninsula," in Henrik Birnbaum and Speros Vryonis Jr., eds., *Aspects of the Balkans: Continuity and Change* (The Hague: Mouton, 1972), pp. 9–49.

4. For a discussion of the problem dating Slav colonization of the Balkans, see Peter Charanis, "The Slavs, Byzantium, and the Historical Significance of the First Bulgarian Kingdom," *Balkan Studies* 17 (1976), pp. 8–12.

5. According to Salim Ćerić, the name *Serb* first appeared as part of the name of a city in Asia Minor, Gordoservom, in 680–681. Ćerić thus concluded that the Serbs had entered the Balkans at least several decades earlier. *Muslimani srpskohrvatskog jezika* (Sarajevo: Svjetlost, 1968), p. 18. Constantine Porphyrogenitus wrote that the Croats entered the lands bordering ancient Dalmatia at the invitation of Heraclius, who was hard-pressed by the Avars in the seventh century. In R.J.H. Jenkins, ed., *De Administrando Imperio*, Vol. 2: *Commentary* (London: Atholone Press, 1962), pp. 115–116. The Serbs were directed to the land that later became Serbia at around the same time. Jenkins, *De Administrando Imperio*, p. 133. Roy E.H. Mellor placed the ancestors of the Serbs and Croats in the Balkans almost half a century earlier. *Eastern Europe: A Geography of the Comecon Countries* (New York: Columbia University Press, 1975), p. 41.

6. For more on the significance of group names and self-identification in the Balkans, see Robert J. Donia and John V.A. Fine Jr., *Bosnia and Hercegovina: A Tradition Betrayed* (New York: Columbia University Press, 1994), pp. 71–74; and Jenkins, ed., *De Administrando Imperio*, pp. 116–117, 132.

7. The Slovenes, a third group of South Slavs, were probably not an offshoot of the Serb-Croat migratory group but may have been a completely separate tribe. See Mellor, *Eastern Europe*, p. 44.

8. Oton Knežević, "Bosna i Hercegovina od seobe naroda do XII. st.," in Krunoslav Draganović, et al., *Poviest hrvatskih zemalja Bosne i Hercegovine od najstarijeh vremena do godine 1463* (Sarajevo: Napredak, 1942), p. 166. See also Francis Dvornik, "The Slavs Between East and West," (Milwaukee: Marquette University, Slavic Institute 19, 1964), p. 2.

9. Mellor, *Eastern Europe*, p. 42. See Harry Hodgkinson, *The Adriatic Sea* (London: Cape, 1955), pp. 40–41, for a brief description of the ancient Illyrians.

10. William M. Sloane, *The Balkans: A Laboratory of History* (New York: Abingdon Press, 1914), pp. 56–57. Vladimir I. Georgiev placed the various peoples in this region according to linguistic criteria in "The Earliest Ethnological Situation of the Balkan Peninsula as Evidenced by Linguistic and Onomastic Data," in Birnbaum and Vryonis, eds., *Aspects of the Balkans*, pp. 50–65. John V.A. Fine Jr. also located some Illyrians in northwestern Greece and in Albania. *The Early Medieval Balkans: A Critical Survey from the Sixth to the Late Twelfth Century* (Ann Arbor: University of Michigan Press, 1983), p. 9.

11. Fine, *The Early Medieval Balkans*, p. 36.

12. Anthony Knežević, *A Short History of the Croatian Nation* (Philadelphia: Croatian Catholic Union, 1989), p. 12.

13. See, for example, ibid.

14. Contemporary Croatian nationalists further claimed that by harboring Zacharia—the Serbian pretender—and other imperiled Serbs from the Bulgars, Croatia, "the leader of civilization among the southern Slavs…prevented the destruction of the Serbian people." Ibid., p. 17.

15. Some Croats insisted that Croatia remained independent of Hungary even though the Hungarian king was also recognized as the king of Croatia. Knežević, for example, cited an 1107 treaty according to which Croatia was not incorporated into Hungary nor required to pay taxes to Hungary as merely a reacknowledgment of the rights conferred on Croatia and its Dalmatian allies by Byzantium four hundred years earlier. Ibid., p. 22.

16. John V.A. Fine Jr., *The Late Medieval Balkans: A Critical Survey from the Late Twelfth Century to the Ottoman Conquest* (Ann Arbor: University of Michigan Press, 1987), p. 307.

17. Enno Franzius, *History of the Byzantine Empire: Mother of Nations* (New York: Funk and Wagnalls, 1967), p. 390.

18. For a succinct presentation of the Croatian case for control of Bosnia and Herzegovina based on historical and geographical factors, see Stanko Guldescu, "Bosnia and Herzegovina in Medieval and Modern Times," *Balkania* 6 (October 1972), pp. 11–15. Knežević also implied historical Croatian domination of Bosnia and Herzegovina when he wrote that from the time of Prince Branimir the Croats always "allied with the Western Church and culture—with the exception of the population of Bosnia and Herzegovina, which, with the coming of the Ottomans, largely accepted Islam." *A Short History of the Croatian Nation,* p. 14. Mellor stated that Hungarian historians "look on Bosnia as the original core of the Croat kingdom." *Eastern Europe,* p. 48. On the other hand, Sima Ćirković's *Istorija srednjovekovne bosanske države* (Belgrade: Srpska književna zadruga, 1964) forcefully argued that Bosnian lands belong to the Serbs.

19. See, for example, Nada Klaić, *Srednjovjekovna Bosna: Politički položaj bosanskih vladara do tvrtkove krunidbe (1377 g.)* (Zagreb: Grafički zavod hrvatske, 1989), p. 8.

20. Enver Redžić, "O posebnosti bosanskih muslimana," *Pregled* 60 (April 1970), p. 459. In that source Redžić also mentioned the diffusion of Islam throughout the area as a factor that led some to confuse Bosnian Muslims with other Yugoslav Muslims—a fallacy, in his opinion.

21. John V.A. Fine Jr., "Was the Bosnian Banate Subjected to Hungary in the Second Half of the Thirteenth Century?" *East European Quarterly* 3 (June 1969), p. 167.

22. The more well-known twentieth-century Yugoslav historians who supported the Bogomil explanation were V. Ćorović, *Historija Bosne* (Belgrade: Srpska akademija nauka i umetnosti, 1940); A. Babić, *Bosanski heretici* (Sarajevo: 1963); and Ćirković, *Istorija-srednjovekovne bosanske države.*

23. Steven Runciman, *The Medieval Manichee: A Study of the Christian Dualist Heresy* (Cambridge: Cambridge University Press, 1947), p. 75.

24. Fine, however, cited the edicts of a synod in 1211 that maintained that the Bogomils rejected the entire Hebrew Bible as containing only the sayings of Satan. *The Early Medieval Balkans,* p. 175.

25. Arthur J. Evans, *Through Bosnia and the Herzegovina on Foot During the Insurrection, August and September 1875, with an Historical Review of Bosnia* (London: Longmans, Green, 1877), p. xxxvii.

26. John V.A. Fine Jr., *The Bosnian Church, A New Interpretation: A Study of the Bosnian Church and Its Place in State and Society from the 13th to the 15th Centuries* (Boulder: East European Quarterly, 1975), p. 116.

27. See, for example, Vatro Murvar, *Nation and Religion in Central Europe and the Western Balkans—The Muslims in Bosna, Hercegovina and Sandžak: A Sociological Analysis* (Brookfield: FSSSN Colloquia and Symposia, University of Wisconsin, 1989), pp. 4–5; and Colin Heywood, "Bosnia Under Ottoman Rule, 1463–1800," in Mark Pinson, ed., *The Muslims of Bosnia-Herzegovina: Their Historic Development from the Middle Ages to the Dissolution of Yugoslavia* (Cambridge: Harvard University Press, 1994), p. 33.

28. Ivo Sivrić, *The Peasant Culture of Bosnia and Herzegovina* (Chicago: Franciscan Herald Press, 1982), p. 177.

29. Fine, *The Bosnian Church*, p. 16.

30. Zoran Batusić argued, however, that Bosnia was influenced more by Roman Catholicism than by Orthodox Christianity. "E Pluribus Unum?" *East European Reporter* 5 (March–April 1992), p. 22.

31. Ćerić, *Muslimani srpskohrvatskog jezika*, p. 62; and Nedim Filipović, "Forming of Moslem Ethnicon in Bosnia and Herzegovina," in Ranko Petković, ed., *Moslems in Yugoslavia* (Belgrade: Review of International Affairs, 1985), p. 1.

32. Fine detailed the jurisdictional wrangling over Bosnia and accusations of heresy in *The Late Medieval Balkans*, pp. 44–45.

33. Fine, *The Bosnian Church*, p. 142. Janos de Asboth suggested a Hungarian ulterior motive for denouncing Bosnia to the church—namely, that it was around this time that the Bosnian mines began to be worked successfully. *An Official Tour Through Bosnia and Herzegovina with an Account of the History, Antiquities, Agrarian Conditions, Religion, Ethnology, Folk Lore, and Social Life of the People* (London: Swan Sonnenschein, 1890), p. 45. Whether the mines were indeed operative at this early date is questionable. See Ćerić, *Muslimani srpskohrvatskog jezika*, p. 59, for a brief description of economic conditions in Bosnia in the Middle Ages.

34. See Fine, *The Bosnian Church*, p. 150. In *The Late Medieval Balkans*, pp. 481–482, Fine described the organization of the Bosnian Church.

35. Fine, *The Bosnian Church*, p. 150.

36. Ibid., p. 151.

37. Ibid.

38. Henry Charles Lea, *A History of the Inquisition of the Middle Ages*, Vol. 2 (New York: Harper, 1887), p. 294. Fine considered the commercial charter Ninoslav issued to Dubrovnik in 1240 as evidence that the Hungarians did not capture all of Bosnia's territory. *The Late Medieval Balkans*, p. 145.

39. Lea, *A History of the Inquisition*, p. 297; and Fine, *The Late Medieval Balkans*, p. 145.

40. Lea, *A History of the Inquisition*, p. 297.

41. Ibid., p. 302.

42. John V.A. Fine Jr., "Review of Sima Ćirković, *Istorija srednjovekovne bosanske države*, Belgrade, 1964," *Speculum* 41 (July 1966), p. 527.

43. Fine, *The Bosnian Church*, p. 31.

44. Ćerić, for example, stated that Bogomilism may have been the state religion, even followed by some of the bans, for nearly half the time of the existence of the independent Bosnian state between the second half of the eleventh century and the mid-fifteenth century. *Muslimani srpskohrvatskog jezika*, p. 58. See also Janko Lavrin, "The Bogomils and Bogomilism," *Slavonic Review* 8 (December 1929), p. 279.

45. Fine, *The Late Medieval Balkans*, p. 281.

46. John V.A. Fine Jr., "The Medieval and Ottoman Roots of Modern Bosnian Society," in Mark Pinson, ed., *The Muslims of Bosnia-Herzegovina: Their Historic Development from*

the Middle Ages to the Destruction of Yugoslavia (Cambridge: Harvard University Press, 1994), p. 6.

47. Fine, *The Late Medieval Balkans*, p. 482.

48. Ibid., pp. 393, 398.

49. Milos Mladenović "The Osmanli Conquest and the Islamization of Bosnia," *Slavic and East European Studies* 3 (Winter 1958–1959), p. 219.

50. Heywood, "Bosnia Under Ottoman Rule, 1463–1800," p. 29.

51. Henrik Birnbaum, "The Ethno-Linguistic Mosaic of Bosnia and Hercegovina," *Die Welt der Slaven* 32 (1987), p. 10.

52. Ćerić, *Muslimani srpskohrvatskog jezika*, p. 66.

53. Lavrin, "The Bogomils and Bogomilism," p. 281.

54. Franzius, *History of the Byzantine Empire*, p. 131.

55. Brian W. Aldiss, *Cities and Stones: A Traveller's Jugoslavia* (London: Faber and Faber, 1966), p. 108.

56. Fine, *The Bosnian Church*, p. 341.

57. Fine, *The Late Medieval Balkans*, p. 582.

58. Heywood projected that among the urban population in the western Morava Valley, for example, Islamization peaked around 1540, after a very slow start in ca. 1475, and then declined sharply. "Bosnia Under Ottoman Rule, 1463–1800," p. 32. Milos Mladenović estimated that "by the middle of the sixteenth century two-thirds of the population was Muslim," including aristocrats as well as commoners. "Family Names of Osmanli Origin in Bosnia and Herzegovina," in Donald P. Little, ed., *Essays on Islamic Civilization Presented to Niyazi Berkes* (Leiden: Brill, 1976), p. 245. In 1624, the apostolic visitor Masarechi described a massive conversion of forcibly Catholicized Bogomils to Islam after Bosnia was conquered. Muhamed Hadžijahić, Mahmud Traljić, and Nijaz Šukrić, *Islam i muslimani u Bosni i Hercegovini* (Sarajevo: 1977), p. 39. Turkish tax rolls, reports by English diplomat Paul Ricaut (1628–1700), and a narrative of the janissary law also point to a large Islamization of non-Catholic Bosnians. Hadžijahić, Traljić and Šukrić, *Islam i muslimani*, pp. 46–52.

59. Fine, *The Bosnian Church*, p. 382.

60. Speros Vryonis Jr., "Religious Changes and Patterns in the Balkans, 14th–16th Centuries," in Birnbaum and Vryonis, eds., *Aspects of the Balkans*, p. 169.

61. Filipović, "Forming of Moslem Ethnicon," p. 2. The rich towns the Ottomans created to house their administration, to serve as centers for communication and commerce, and to propagate the Islamic way of life lured many—particularly peasants—to Islam. Alexander Lopašić, "Islamisation of the Balkans: Some General Considerations," in Jennifer M. Scarce, ed., *Islam in the Balkans; Persian Art and Culture of the 18th and 19th Centuries* (Edinburgh: Royal Scottish Museum, 1979), p. 58. Filipović termed the Ottoman towns "the vital core of the material and spiritual culture of that [Ottoman] civilization." "Forming of Moslem Ethnicon," p. 11. This accords with Ćerić's statement that the villages distant from urban areas were spared the pressures of Islamization because a Turkish administrative presence was absent in the rural areas. *Muslimani srpskohrvatskog jezika*, p. 51.

62. Fine, "Medieval and Ottoman Roots," pp. 14–15.

63. Ćerić, *Muslimani srpskohrvatskog jezika*, pp. 48–49.

64. Steven L. Burg, "The Political Integration of Yugoslavia's Muslims: Determinants of Success and Failure" (Pittsburgh: Carl Beck Papers in Russian and East European Studies, University of Pittsburgh, 1983), p. 3.

65. Fine, *The Bosnian Church*, p. 382; and Lopašić, "Islamisation of the Balkans," p. 50.

66. Miloš Mladenović, "Family Names of Osmanli Origin in Bosnia and Herzegovina," in Little, ed., *Essays on Islamic Civilization*, p. 245; and Lopašić, "Islamisation of the Balkans," p. 50. This point supports the contention of Ralph C. Beals that "in practice, the universal religions [predominantly Buddhism, Christianity, and Islam] become closely wedded to the power structure and stratification systems of the major pre-industrial civilizations of Europe and Asia." "The Rise and Decline of National Identity," *Canadian Review of Studies in Nationalism* 4 (Spring 1977), p. 153.

67. Lopašić, "Islamisation of the Balkans," pp. 49–50.

68. Filipović, "Forming of Moslem Ethnicon," p. 13.

69. William Lockwood, *European Moslems: Economy and Ethnicity in Western Bosnia* (New York: Academic Press, 1975), pp. 25–26. Hadžijahić, Traljić, and Šukrić concurred that Islam as found in Yugoslavia contained many Slavic-Bogomil-Islamic and Catholic-Orthodox-Islamic syncretistic characteristics. *Islam i muslimani*, pp. 81–89. See *Islam i muslimani*, pp. 53–57, for a discussion of the Islamic influences on Christian ways of life in the Balkans after the Ottoman conquest.

70. Beals, "The Rise and Decline of National Identity," p. 153.

71. Ibid., p. 154.

72. Fine, *The Bosnian Church*, pp. 386–387. As a result of this strange amalgam, certain rituals were still followed within post–World War II Bosnia in spite of religious differences, certain holidays were still celebrated by all community members, and many superstitions were held by all citizens that had no basis in the twentieth-century religious makeup of the population. Spiro Kulišić, "Razmatranja o porijeklu muslimana u Bosni i Hercegovini," *Glasnik zemaljskog muzeja u Sarajevu* 8 (1953), p. 156. For example, Milenko S. Filipović mentioned "godfatherhood," a "Christian ecclesiastical institution" that has been retained even by the Bosnian Muslims. "Forms and Functions of Ritual Kinship Among South Slavs," *International Congress of Anthropological and Ethnological Sciences* (6th) (Paris: Musee de l'homme, 1962), pp. 77–79. The Islamicized population, like the Christians in the area, still clung to some pre-Christian practices and beliefs, such as the existence of fairies and vampires. Ćerić, *Muslimani srpskohrvatskog jezika*, p. 47. See also Hadžijahić, Traljić, and Sukrić, *Islam i muslimani*, pp. 82–91.

73. See, for example, *Evans, Through Bosnia and the Herzegovina on Foot*, pp. lxxxvii–lxxxviii, citing the eyewitness account of a doctor at the University of Bologna, J. Bapt. Montalbano, *Rerum Turcicarum Commentarius*, written before 1630. See also William G. Lockwood, "Bosnian," in Richard V. Weekes, ed., *Muslim Peoples: A World Ethnographic Survey* (Westport, Conn.: Greenwood Press, 1978), pp. 111–112; A. P. Vlasto, *The Entry of the Slavs into Christendom: An Introduction to the Medieval History of the Slavs* (Cambridge: University Press, 1970), p. 234; Lopašić, "Islamisation of the Balkans," pp. 49–51; Lea, *A History of the Inquisition*, p. 314; and Ćerić, *Muslimani srpskohrvatskog jezika*, p. 51.

74. Fine, *The Late Medieval Balkans*, p. 486. Aleksandar Solovjev wrote that the majority of the people only insincerely crossed to the "Greek faith." "Nestanak bogumilstva i islamizacija bosne," *Godišnjak Istorijskog društva BiH*, Vol. 1, cited in Ćerić, *Muslimani srpskohrvatskog jezika*, p. 63.

75. Lockwood, *European Moslems*, p. 25; Birnbaum, "The Ethno-Linguistic Mosaic of Bosnia and Hercegovina," p. 14; and Hadžijahić, Traljić, and Šukrić, *Islam i muslimani*, p. 40.

76. Thus, Aleksandar Solovjev observed that Bogomilism did not die easily: "We see that in a year (or two) after the destruction of the Catholic king and kingdom [of Bosnia] warring heretics were found who returned to the old faith, killed the monks and demolished the Catholic church, the same as once during the time of Ban Ninoslav. This was the last isolated spasm of irreconcilable Bogomilism." "Nestanak bogumilstva i islamizacija Bosne," *Godišnjak Istorijskog društva BiH,*" cited in Ćerić, *Muslimani srpskohrvatskog jezika,* p. 69. And Bogomils, Patarines, and Manichees "in the neighborhood of Bosnia" were mentioned in documents of the sixteenth century, whereas "Patarine books" were discovered in Dubrovnik. Hadžijahić, Traljić, and Šukrić, *Islam i muslimani,* p. 41. Nevertheless, Fine stated that "references to Patarins ... after 1463 in Bosnia and after 1481 in Hercegovina are amazingly few." *The Bosnian Church,* p. 375. Filipović cited the last mention of a "krstjanin" (Bogomil) in 1533. "Forming of Moslem Ethnicon," p. 3. And finally, Lovett F. Edwards claimed that "the last-known Bogumil family—that of Helež—is supposed to have died out in the village of Dubrovčani as late as 1867." *Introducing Yugoslavia* (London: Methuen, 1967), p. 194. See also Lavrin, "The Bogomils and Bogomilism," p. 282.

77. Fine, *The Bosnian Church,* p. 384. Fine also pointed out in this regard that "changes of religion were a general and common occurrence at this time, and that the widely discussed 'Islamization' was only one aspect of this broader phenomenon." Nevertheless, it was less common to pass from Islam to Christianity because of the terrible penalty exacted for openly abandoning Islam. Fine, *The Bosnian Church,* p. 385.

78. Ibid., p. 387.

79. Birnbaum, "The Ethno-Linguistic Mosaic of Bosnia and Hercegovina," p. 10.

80. According to Murvar, the borders of Ottoman Bosnia included most of the old Croatian kingdom. *Nation and Religion in Central Europe,* p. 22.

81. See, for example, *Massacre of Croatians in Bosnia-Hercegovina and Sandžak* (Toronto: Croatian Islamic Centre, 1978), pp. 9–17.

82. Vienna: Manzche K.U.K. Hof-, Verlags- U. Universitäts-Buchhandlung, 1918. See also Mahmud Kemal Muftić, "Hundred Years of Mistakes in Croatian National Politics," *Balkania* 5 (January 1970), p. 26, which emphasized conflict between "Croats and Croat Muslims," and Andrew Ilić, "The Truth About the Croatian Catholics and Croatian Moslems," *Balkania* 5 (October 1971), p. 21, for an impassioned rejoinder; also Stanko Guldescu, "Bosnia and Herzegovina in Medieval and Modern Times," *Balkania* 6 (October 1972), pp. 15, 20.

83. Cited in Pedro Ramet, "Religion and Nationalism in Yugoslavia," in Pedro Ramet, ed., *Religion and Nationalism in Soviet and East European Politics* (Durham: Duke University Press, 1989), p. 302.

84. See, for example, *Economist* staffer K. F. Cviic, "Yugoslavia's Moslem Problem," *World Today* 36 (March 1980), p. 108.

85. Pedro Ramet, *Nationalism and Federalism in Yugoslavia, 1963–1983* (Bloomington: Indiana University Press, 1984), p. 146.

86. Cviic, "Yugoslavia's Moslem Problem," p. 108.

87. Ramet, *Nationalism and Federalism in Yugoslavia, 1963–1983,* p. 146.

88. Murvar, *Nation and Religion in Central Europe,* p. 132.

89. See, for example, V. Ćorović's entry "Muslimani u bosni i hercegovini," in *Narodna enciklopedija srpsko-hrvatsko-slovenacka* 2 (Zagreb: Bibliografski zavod, 1925).

2

Bosnian Muslims in the Ottoman Empire

"Where the Turk trod, no grass grows."

—Yugoslav proverb

The arrival of the Ottoman Turks in southeastern Europe opened the first chapter in the history of the Bosnian Muslims. Previously Bosnians had only more or less perfunctorily followed various Christian rituals; institutionalized religion was not that important to most medieval Bosnians in the absence of many clergy of mainstream faiths. The adherents of these various religions lived throughout the country in geographically consolidated groups, with the Orthodox dwelling primarily in the south and east, Catholics in the north and west, and schismatics (members of the Bosnian Church or Bogomils) in between.

When Islam arrived in Bosnia in the mid-fifteenth century, it brought a profoundly institutionalized religion and a sociopolitical structure that relied on religious differentiation. Islam offered social and economic advantages to many, particularly the persecuted "heretical" or schismatic Christians, as well as Orthodox and Catholic inhabitants who converted. Nevertheless, the process of Islamization only slowly produced an indigenous native Muslim community in Bosnia. The interactions between this Muslim community and its non-Muslim neighbors became a key element in the two groups' ability (or lack thereof) to cohabit peacefully. The initial Bosnian Muslim impulse for exclusionary self-determination and reactions to that impulse were forged during the Ottoman period.

Social Structure

Ottoman society,[1] with its strong urbanized characteristics, was imposed on the largely rural Balkan region. Two main elements characterized this society. First, in the Ottoman social structure, everyone had a fixed place, rights, and duties. In principle, even the lowest inhabitants were safeguarded from capricious actions. In this respect, the Balkan peasants may have preferred Ottoman rule to the arbitrariness of their former rulers. Nevertheless, the advent of that rule introduced a more rigid feudalism than medieval Bosnia had heretofore experienced, making the Christian peasants nothing more than serfs on the lands of the foreign invader. Second, the Ottoman social and political structure exhibited Turkish and Byzantine elements superimposed on traditional Muslim practices.[2]

The Bosnian Muslim elites undoubtedly experienced many prosperous years under the Ottoman regime in return for their staunch support of the empire.[3] Whereas the conquered non-Muslim peoples labored to support the ruling Turkish nation, those who had converted to Islam controlled the lands and property. They became a hereditary nobility, persons of substance in the Ottoman lands who retained political rights non-Muslims were denied. Thus, the old medieval ruling class in Bosnia was destroyed, was converted to Islam and transferred to Anatolia, or was co-opted into the military with the attendant privileges.

The Ottoman social system that was imported to the Balkans was long a suitable one for stimulating military and political successes. And success naturally breeds loyalty, particularly from those who benefit the most. The Porte (the imperial government) was in a position of supreme control that was shared with no other numerically, monetarily, or hereditarily superior economic or social group. The sultan maintained loyalty by recruiting the professional Ottoman class from a variety of groups in society; he could thus withdraw favor and bestow it on another element when the previously favored group became unmanageable. The Turks made the development of a middle class impossible (outside of perhaps "a primitive class of merchants and craftsmen mostly of oriental origin" in the towns).[4] Therefore, below the titled nobles in the countryside was the free peasantry, composed mainly of converts to Islam, who by law could own and work their own lands. The majority of inhabitants, the *kmets* (serfs), gave a portion of their harvests to their landlords. The *kmets* were predominantly Christian (Catholics and Orthodox) and very rarely Muslim, especially from the nineteenth century on.[5]

Traian Stoianovich described six or more estates into which Ottoman society was divided.[6] For our purposes, however, within the Ottoman social structure individuals could be distinguished, in broad terms, by two characteristics. The first dichotomy was between state employees, defined broadly as "men of the sword" (*'asker*) and "men of the pen" (*ulema*, or clergy), and others. State employees enjoyed greater privileges and power and a markedly higher standard of living. Ottoman state functionaries[7] were differentiated from the majority of the population, called *raya* (members of the flock—that is, non-Ottoman-subject inhabitants). The term *raya* originally included Muslims and non-Muslims, urban and rural dwellers who were feudal dependents as opposed to those belonging to the ruling strata of Ottoman society. Later, however, particularly from the eighteenth century on, *raya* began to be used to refer only to the dependent (largely Orthodox, with some Catholic) Christian population.[8]

Those who worked for the state generally professed Islam. However, the leaders of the various *millets* (the organization of non-Islamic religious denominations into separate self-governing communities for both religious and legal purposes) were considered to be agents of the Ottoman state and thus often shared some of the privileges of Muslim state functionaries.[9]

Thus, the second dichotomy—which, in fact, overlay the first—was between Muslims and non-Muslims. For the Ottoman rulers, this was the important division of society. Because the Turks had destroyed the indigenous political institutions denoting national identity, only a person's religion, not ethnicity or geography, categorized him or her in Ottoman society. The Ottoman conception of community was thus religious rather than ethnic, which left the non-Muslim peasantry free to give their loyalty to their own leaders, who represented the continuity of their own ethnic group. Loyalty to the Ottoman state was not strongly encouraged by the Turkish bureaucracy. The lack of a middle class in the Ottoman Empire to provide cross-cutting cleavages in the population further inspired the ethnic particularism that has been the hallmark of this region from the end of the Turkish occupation to the present day. The difference in status, opportunity, and standard of living between Muslim and non-Muslim Slavs was clearly evident.

The Christians, of course, resented their lower social and political status. The distance between the positions became so profound—as expressed in different social, cultural, and political preferences—that even the later Yugoslav experience could not totally erase the mutual dislike caused by the disparity. The resentment between the groups was also not easily erased—a resentment born at least in part from the different experiences of the medieval and premodern eras. Robin Remington characterized the development of the Croat and Serb national identities "as nations without a state in the womb of competing empires" that relied on ethnonationalism for survival.[10] The ruling Bosnian Muslims, on the other hand, survived handily as a unique group in Bosnia and protected their class privileges.

The Turks did not particularly want to assimilate their subjects, so they did not assault the communal identity. For example, they encouraged the sociopolitical distinction between the free (Muslim) peasantry and the *kmets*, who were largely Christian. Herein lay one of the seeds of the empire's destruction. The emphasis on the administrative integration of each religious group and the exclusivity of Islamic religious affiliation prohibited any basis for a common Ottoman citizenship. In the end, stronger communal ties developed among the indigenous populace, since non-Muslim individuals did not identify with the government elites. Whatever political allegiance did exist was directed to the sultan and his representatives as the governmental authority. The growing religious loyalty and communal identity of the non-Muslim subjects were focused on their own groups and elites.[11]

During the early centuries of the Ottoman Empire, tolerance for the practice of all religions "of the Book" (the Hebrew Bible) was widespread. Christians and Jews were considered "protected" peoples,[12] although by definition being a Muslim was clearly more rewarding. Conversion of the non-Muslim subjects to Islam was in principle the goal sought by Muslims. Nevertheless, since mass conversion would have produced economic and social chaos in the Ottoman system, tolerance of the Ottoman state—particularly during its early years in the Balkans—toward its non-Muslim subjects is not surprising.

This toleration weakened during the early sixteenth century when Sultan Selim I conquered new lands. Muslim religious leaders began to emphasize the Islamic nature of their state and induced succeeding sultans to take a more conventional position in religious matters. This conservatism translated into decreased tolerance of non-Muslims and a stricter differentiation between the free Muslim peasants and the Christian *kmets*. There were even reports of attempted forced conversion in the seventeenth century.[13] The Orthodox community responded to this treatment with periodic rebellions against Ottoman rule.

The *millet* system also eventually encouraged the tendency of the South Slavs to combine the religious with the national. This system held the various religious leaders responsible not only for their religious duties but also for governing their flock. If taxes were paid in a timely manner and there was no disorder, the leaders of the *millet* were free to organize their communities without Ottoman interference. Eventually, the religious leaders also became the representatives of their constituents in secular matters and took responsibility for their education. Primitive ideas of nationalism, which began in nineteenth-century Croatia, thus filtered into Bosnia through the largely Croatian Franciscans, who proselytized and organized their flock in Croatian lands. Inevitably, their teaching of Catholicism became infused with a national ethic, which Catholic Bosnians imbibed.[14]

Meanwhile, the Orthodox *kmets,* too, were receiving nationalist messages, influenced by the Serbian fight for independence from the Ottomans. The Orthodox won ever more autonomy from the Porte through a series of successful rebellions, culminating in 1878 in an independent Serbian state to the east of Bosnia. As a result, their sense of self-identification as Serbs spread to their coreligionists still in Bosnia and on the Military Frontier established by Austria-Hungary as a buffer against the Ottoman Empire from the sixteenth through the eighteenth centuries. Increasingly, pride in Serbian accomplishments was internalized by the Orthodox people living in Bosnia and Austria-Hungary, so that the concept of being Orthodox began to merge with a sense of being Serb. Of course, Muslims could not be sanguine living next to the new Serbian state peopled with their former dissatisfied Orthodox serfs, because the geographic proximity of a restless population threatened to cause further unrest among the already disgruntled serfs, who seemed to want territorial union with Serbia.

In time, then, the religious leaders began to express their constituents' national aspirations, and the religious and the national became intertwined. When nationalism arose, the religious element also came to the forefront as one of its ingredients.

Decay of the Ottoman Empire

The weaknesses of the Ottoman feudal system—which was based on the social, economic, legal, and political separation of various groups—took their toll on Ottoman society beginning in the mid-sixteenth century, although this fact did not become apparent until the nineteenth century. Continued military success was crucial to the health of the Ottoman Empire. The resultant territorial expansion supported the Porte and secured the prosperity of those who participated in battles and won property. Ultimately, however, the imperial feudalism of the Ottoman Empire was doomed by progress and by the vitality of Western civilization. The slow but inexorable growth of democratic forms and the transformation of absolute to constitutional monarchies created the conditions for more stable social relations in the West. The result was an economic prosperity that feudalism could not match.[15]

The success of European capitalism in the late seventeenth century and Europe's alluring markets undermined Ottoman attempts to industrialize or to increase their share of global commerce.[16] Although the Ottomans still supported a huge empire, Europe (mainly Austria-Hungary and Venice) had succeeded—through military as well as diplomatic means—in whittling away some of the Ottoman holdings. Austria-Hungary's Military Frontier (*Vojna Krajina*), populated largely by Orthodox settlers who had migrated from Serbia when the Ottomans invaded there,[17] held the line against further Turkish assaults on Europe. War plunder—on which local loyalty to the Porte was based—stopped and, in fact, was reversed, with a concomitant strain on fealty to Ottoman interests. Thus, a mixture of internal and external circumstances substantially weakened the empire and unsettled many of its inhabitants.[18] However, the three major problems that threatened the viability of the Ottoman Empire in the Balkans were (1) the ever stronger defiance of many Muslim landowners and tax farmers against the state apparatus; (2) the collaboration of nationalistic Christian *kmets* with other, non-Christian *kmets* and other, non-Turkish nations; and (3) the increasing interest of Russia, France, and Great Britain in Ottoman affairs and their attempts to interfere in the foreign and domestic policies of the Porte.[19]

Bosnian Muslim Elites Against the Porte

The end of the eighteenth century ushered in an era of economic and social decline for the Muslim population in the Ottoman Empire. Agrarian relations were regulated by the September 1859 Safer Decree, which assigned to landowners and *kmets* alike obligations to each other and to the state, as well as granting them privileges.[20] Even so, the Christian communities bore a heavier tax burden than their Muslim neighbors. For example, the Christians paid church taxes,[21] taxes to support the military forces—although they were not allowed to enlist (as well as a head tax on each male in place of the military service he was not permitted to perform)—and taxes on the produce from land and personal possessions. They even had to support service to the state that was occasionally required, such as road and public-works labor (corvée), and the provision of livestock and carts when requested.[22] The tax burden became even more onerous during times of war. Muslim peasants also had to pay some of these taxes, but they had access to redress from the courts, which was usually denied Christians.

However, despite their oppressive tax burden, the Christian communities may have been healthier in certain respects than the Muslim population, which was subject to many demands not required of non-Muslims. The Christians did not have to provide soldiers for the empire; doing so weakened the Muslim population at home when the young men were away fighting. Furthermore, rural life may have protected the *kmets* from plague and other diseases, a fact that was demonstrated in the eighteenth century by the large growth in the Christian population relative to that of the Muslim.[23] Although the *raya* were subject to many obligations, their social organization and religion were largely untouched by the Ottomans. The relative independence of the Orthodox Church under Ottoman rule contributed to the rise of Serb nationalism among the Orthodox people who were subject to Turkish dominance.[24]

The restiveness felt in other parts of the Ottoman Empire did not radically manifest itself in Bosnia and Herzegovina until the nineteenth century. Bosnian Muslim elites then found themselves often directly opposed to the Ottoman administration.

Distinct conservative opposition to the Porte crystallized during the reigns of Selim III (1789–1807) and his nephew Mahmud II (1808–1839). These sultans resolved to stem the empire's decline in the European lands by reforming the Ottoman agricultural, military, and socioeconomic systems. They wanted to restore legitimacy to the entire system by modernizing the bureaucracy and the relation of workers and owners to factors of production and, in doing so, to fend off the threat of great-power intervention on behalf of the beleaguered Christian peasants.

The resultant reform, or *Tanzimat,* had four major aims: (1) to establish an efficient bureaucracy that would treat Muslims and non-Muslims as equals under law, (2) to tighten central control over the more independence-minded provinces of the empire, (3) to replace tax farming with a modern system whereby taxes would be collected by paid tax collectors rather than local nobles and would be levied according to census information, and (4) to substitute European legal foundations for Islamic law.[25] The reforms failed to produce the desired results in Bosnia. The local Bosnian authorities only reluctantly implemented the attempts by European-influenced Ottoman officials to improve the lot of the *kmets,* if they did so at all. They particularly resisted modernization of the Ottoman socioeconomic, military, and administrative systems. They opposed introduction of both the European model of public education and a legal system separate from Muslim law, fearing the result would be a secular state with a reduced role for religious institutions.

The Porte decided to abolish the janissary (Bosnian military elite) order as part of the reform effort. Since the janissary constituted a large part of the local gentry, it is not surprising that this policy was met with resistance. The janissaries' support for Ottoman policy had been declining ever since the implementation of European military techniques in the mid-1700s. Aligned with the *ulema,* who resented the penetration of European customs and ideas into Muslim society, some military leaders and landowners became more influential within society, which commensurately decreased stability in the empire. By the mid-nineteenth century, when nineteen of the twenty-three Turkish battalions stationed in Bosnia were composed almost entirely of Bosnian Muslims, the loyalty of many of these army units to the Porte was questionable.[26] Most of the janissary corps were eliminated by the late 1820s, and the local feudal landlords became increasingly alienated from the Porte. The Bosnian Muslims were particularly incensed that some of the reforms would have increased the religious liberty of the Christians and augmented their legal rights including equitable taxation.

Agricultural problems also explain the failure of the *Tanzimat.* Owners of *chiftluks,*[27] lands controlled by feudal landlords, were as predatory as tax farmers. The position of the Balkan Christian peasants under the Ottoman Empire began to deteriorate by the end of the sixteenth century. Not only did Muslim peasants seize communal and reserve lands, but feudal landowners gained hereditary ownership of the *chiftluks.*[28] This change in land relations created a class of hereditary nobles, which made the system ripe for abuse. Local Muslim nobles bitterly fought reformers' attempts to curb their demands for ever more income from the peasantry.

The owners of *chiftluks* began to protect their property with private armies, which served numerous functions. They were used against rivals and the central government when it became too predatory. But private armies were also mobilized against any peasant actions seen as contrary to the interests of the *chiftluk* owners, including the peasants' tendency to escape to the freer mountain villages and thus to abandon the landlords' *chiftluks.*

Furthermore, increasingly the *chiftluk* owners were not answerable to higher authorities for the treatment of their *kmets.* The widespread growth of *hassachiftluks,* private farms of *chiftluk* owners, enabled more effective resistance of the feudal landlords to the central government, since under this system they no longer administered the land on behalf of the sultan. Their loyalty was increasingly directed to the region they considered home rather than to far-off Constantinople.

The agrarian practices traditionally followed by the Ottomans in the Balkans produced large levels of rural underemployment and underproduction. Taxation practices were draining an unconscionable proportion of the peasants' income. Nevertheless, the local Muslim landlords rejected any attempts at reform. Adhering to the *Tanzimat* would have cost the landlords revenues because of greater taxation and increased protection of the peasants by the state. Additionally, the feudal landlords were unused to a capitalist system. They could not perceive how they could benefit from such a system and were frustrated as they anticipated their loss of dominance.

The Muslim feudal landlords feared a decline of privilege and fiercely opposed the possibility of an improved situation for the Christian *kmets* and merchants.[29] Furthermore, the authorities lacked the requisite force to impel resistant landlords to follow principles clearly foreign to their civilization. Rebellions against the Porte were led by the Bosnian *beys* (aristocrats) in 1821, 1828, 1831, and 1837.[30] After 1859 the Porte was partially successful in instituting land reform,[31] whereas the Bosnian *kmets* and the landlords were still divided by their different economic and political interests. With the expansion of the reforms, however, and attempts by the Porte to restructure and centralize the administration of the area, the uprisings began to take on a distinctive antigovernmental (and often anti-Christian) tone, and the Bosnian Muslims successfully challenged the central government.

The landlords considered the Porte's reform efforts a direct attack on their privileges, favoring peasants' over landlords' interests. They particularly resented what they considered to be foreign intervention as the great powers forced more reforms on the Ottoman Empire. The gap between the indigenous Muslims and the Ottoman Turks widened. Further, the Christian *kmets* did not find their lot eased despite the battlefield victories of the central government. On the contrary, the landlords who had suffered during the disturbances imposed heavier burdens on the peasants in an attempt to recoup some of their economic losses.[32]

The difficulty of reforming the Ottoman Empire was increased by the fact that the empire was a Muslim rather than a Turkish entity. Alterations or reform of the empire could be accomplished only with great difficulty because of the religious basis of the society under Islam.[33] In reality, therefore, the "westernizing" reforms were progressive only to the extent that they were meant to update some of the outdated practices within the empire. The *Tanzimat,* a socially conservative movement, depended on a landed class to counter the Muslim traditionalists and thus still ran counter to the interests of the mainly Christian peasants, even though one of the reformist aims was ostensibly to better their lot. The so-called reforms, then, did introduce some new norms into the traditional Ottoman system. However, on the whole the *Tanzimat* failed because the local nobles who wanted to perpetuate the feudal system were stronger than the reformers who believed the empire had to develop alternative production relations similar to those that were appearing in other areas of Europe.[34]

The Bosnian Muslims had some rather peculiar allies in their resistance to the *Tanzimat*. Many of the conservative leaders of the Christian communities were themselves resistant to change. Before the reform, they had been permitted to maintain foreign connections and to possess some feudal properties with the same obligation to help in times of war as that of other landowners.[35] The Christian Church establishments had come to terms with the Ottoman system and, in turn, had developed a privileged position in managing their own communal affairs. Therefore, these churches discouraged the new movements to westernize and secularize Balkan society.

The anomaly of a Christian Church supporting the establishment to the detriment of its own constituency is perhaps more explicable when we note that the Orthodox Church, which spoke for the majority of Christian inhabitants of this part of the Ottoman Empire, was controlled (from the mid-eighteenth century on) by Greek officials from Constantinople, who received legitimation and favor from the sultan.[36] Their desire to protect their position explains the resistance of church officials to modernizing tendencies that might have undermined their privileges. However, Leonard Bushkoff made the telling point that "while collaboration with the Turk enabled the Church to preserve the Byzantine heritage, the attendant loss of morale and intellectual vigor left it defenseless against the Western ideas which ultimately undermined this very heritage."[37]

The Ottoman system and state were under relentless attack from both internal and external forces. The reform period had not attenuated the chronic problems faced by the Ottoman Empire. The indigenous nobility resented the loss of land to foreign conquerors and reform attempts. They also opposed any improvement in the status of their Christian subjects. The *raya*, on the other hand, felt little loyalty to the Porte and, despite the halfhearted reforms designed to better their lot within the empire, began to react more positively to Croat and Serb nationalist agitators from Austria-Hungary who spoke of national independence.[38]

Rise of South Slav Nationalism in the Balkans

Deeply resentful of the perpetual discrimination under which they lived, the Orthodox peasants longed to improve their economic and social lot, which had only worsened as a result of the reforms. Thus, following the Muslim versus Porte rebellions in the first half of the nineteenth century, the area became inflamed by large-scale revolts mounted by the Christian peasants against both the Muslim landowners and the Porte. Beginning in the eighteenth century, with the expanding market economy and new educational opportunities, a new type of leader had arisen from among the non-Muslim peasantry to lead these revolts. Designated by the Ottomans as officials in various localities, these peasant leaders, whom the Ottomans hoped would ensure the continued proper functioning of the various socioeconomic units, became community leaders. Eventually, these leaders were able to parlay their increased prestige and status within officialdom to encourage greater communal identification among the non-Muslim masses.[39]

Uniting a new sense of political identification with an already well-developed religious identification, these new Christian elites fostered the gradual development of incipient forms of national divisions within the Ottoman Balkan areas. The new elites took advantage of the Balkan Christian tendency to give their first allegiance to the family, the village, and the church.

The political structure with which the Ottomans had ruled the Balkans was losing control under the impact of two forces: modernization and nationalism. The introduction of a gradual internal modernization into the Ottoman Empire only accelerated both the weakening of traditional feudalism and the growth of embryonic nationalist feelings within the Balkans. The Ottoman elites used the screen of Islam in the early nineteenth century to counter developing unity among local inhabitants, but a few members of the Ottoman elite were also beginning to nurture a greater sense of Turkish national identity. Their attempt to base the Ottoman Empire on the principles of a modern European state was thus met with an equally determined anti-Ottoman force composed of incipient Balkan nations.

One conflict pitted local janissaries in Bosnia against Christians, who tried to protect reforms granted to them by the Porte but rejected by the janissaries. When the Porte eventually supported the janissaries after initially underwriting the Orthodox defenders of the reforms, the Christians intensified their revolt, led by Karageorge Petrović in 1804 and his successor, Miloš Obrenović, in 1815.

The peasant revolts in the early nineteenth century ended with the Porte's grant of autonomy to the Christian inhabitants of north-central Serbia. Further peasant revolts were successful in Herzegovina and then in Bosnia in 1857–1858 and 1861–1862, respectively. The Orthodox peasant masses experienced a newly awakened sense of communal unity—perhaps the first stirrings of primitive nationalism in various parts of the Balkans. They were often aided by local Orthodox priests' resentment of the distant Phanariote (Greek-speaking administrators from Constantinople) hierarchy that had been imposed on their community. This growing unity of purpose exploded in 1875 in a large Christian uprising against the local Muslim elite. The great powers intervened, and the Ottomans were forced to forfeit control over Bosnia and Herzegovina to Austria-Hungary.

External Influences on the Ottoman Balkans

Austrian and Russian military successes against the Ottoman Empire further encouraged South Slav unification. Austria fought a number of wars against the Ottoman Empire, as a result of which it expanded into the Balkans; the Habsburgs then transplanted thousands of Serb settlers in western Bosnia and eastern Croatia to the borders of their newly acquired territory to serve as a bulwark (*Vojna Krajina,* or Military Frontier) against Ottoman counterinsurgency. But the French Revolution had awakened a desire for national self-determination and political and cultural liberty among the South Slav inhabitants of Austria-Hungary, a desire that eventually spread to the South Slavs of the Ottoman Empire.[40]

Meanwhile, Russia was pursuing its own imperialist aims. In 1768, Catherine the Great had forced the Turkish sultan to acknowledge that Russia was the protector of all Orthodox Christians in the Ottoman Empire. Thus, Russia assumed what became an ongoing anti-Muslim role of natural ally and protector of the oppressed (that is, Orthodox Christian) peoples in the Balkans in their search for the right to self-determination.

Russian soldiers eagerly fell in with the need to "fight for Christendom." The Balkan problem also fulfilled Russia's need for foreign adventures whenever it was necessary to divert potentially revolutionary attention away from internal problems. Increased influence in the Balkans would aid in the fulfillment of Russia's historical desire for sovereignty over Constantinople and the Straits and for an outlet to the Mediterranean's warm waters through the Balkans.[41] To achieve this expansion for Russia, the Ottoman Empire had to be carved up. Russia sought Serbian cooperation during the Russo-Turkish War (1806–1812) in return for grandiose promises to negotiate Serb independence from the Turks. These promises did not materialize, however, when the Porte and Russia finalized the Treaty of Bucharest in May 1812, which effectively ended the Serbian Karageorge rebellion against the Ottoman Empire. In effect, Serbia became a special case within the empire, a political entity whose citizens obtained certain heretofore nonexistent rights. Miloš Obrenović led a second Serb revolt in 1815 against the Ottoman Empire's reimposition of dominance in 1813. With Russian pressure against the Porte implicit, he received a formal grant of limited autonomy under Ottoman rule, guaranteed by the 1826 Treaty of Akkerman between Russia and Turkey.[42]

Later in the nineteenth century, other major powers became more active in Balkan matters. England, for example, was interested in perpetuating the status quo in the Balkans. Benjamin Disraeli was determined that the Ottoman Empire should remain intact to protect Britain's Mediterranean interests and its direct access to India from the threat of Russian expansion. The British Empire was also interested in the agricultural potential of the area and in pursuing commercial ties. Thus, Britain's military representative to the Porte, Colonel Rose, declared that the fall of the Ottoman Empire "would be the signal for the ruin of British trade and commercial interests,"[43] since Russia's claim to be the sole protector of Turkey's Orthodox Christian subjects and its proposal to annex the Danubian principalities threatened Great Britain's carefully crafted balance of power in the region.

The paradox of these imperial political and commercial interests is obvious: "Autocratic" Russia pursued self-determination for the Balkan nations, whereas the "liberal, progressive" powers cherished the status quo in the Balkans by prolonging the life of the Ottoman Empire.[44] The insidious as well as overt attacks by external imperial powers hastened the decay of the empire, which was already reeling from corruption and dissolution. When Russia defeated the Ottoman Empire in 1878, the Ottoman presence in Europe receded.

The weakness of the Ottoman Empire encouraged the South Slavs of Austria-Hungary to dream of some kind of union with their fellow Slavs who were subjects of the Turks. Unlike the case in the Ottoman lands, capitalism appeared in Habsburg lands and caused the rise of a bourgeoisie among the South Slavs. As was the situation among Western Europeans, the South Slav middle class in Austria-Hungary was influenced by the spread of the ideologies of liberalism and nationalism, upon which it began to base its political program. Nevertheless, the political development of Western Europe differed in a fundamental way from that of the Balkans (as well as from most of the rest of Eastern and Central Europe). Western European states were created by dynasties, which developed the core political unit first and then, in partnership with a strong middle class bound in allegiance to the king or the state, the different ethnic groups led by feudal nobles. A similar evolution in the Balkans, stated Boris Furlan, might have occurred if the Ottoman Empire, with its focus on religion rather than ethnicity, had not conquered the Balkans and allowed the creation of nations to precede that of states.[45] In the West, the formation of a state encouraged attempts to develop a national basis, whereas in the Balkans the rise of nationalism led to attempts to form a state by those who were not yet independent from the Ottoman or Austro-Hungarian Empires.[46]

The Habsburg Serbs and Croats, seeking greater autonomy within Austria-Hungary, were not necessarily of one mind about how to achieve such autonomy. Within both the Serb and the Croat movements, some sought to form new independent states on the basis of the reestablishment of the former glory of the Serb or the Croat medieval kingdoms.

The alternative was to deemphasize their individuality and attempt to forge a common state based on their shared South Slav origins. This approach, which ran counter to the centrifugal tendencies of the pan-Serb and pan-Croat movements, constituted the Illyrian movement. Launched by Ljudevit Gaj in the mid-nineteenth century, it became popular among Croat intellectuals as the first movement to emphasize the common foundations binding the South Slavs in the Austro-Hungarian Empire. The movement was aimed at focusing South Slav energies against the Hungarians rather than on historical or religious differences that separated the various South Slav peoples. Illyrianism even promoted tolerance of the domestic Muslims in the Ottoman Empire when Bosnia and Herzegovina was able to be liberated from Ottoman rule. Illyrians thus approached local Islamic leaders to neutralize domestic Muslim support for Ottoman rule in the Balkans.

The Illyrian movement developed into Yugoslavism in the mid-nineteenth century under the tutelage of Josip Juraj Strossmayer and Franjo Rački.[47] These leaders attempted to bolster support for a Yugoslav state among the Serbs and Croats in Austria-Hungary so that the South Slavs could attain political unity based on the conception of their common ethnic roots and shared culture. Most Serbs in Austria-Hungary, however, rejected Illyrianism and dreamed of a greater Serbia bolstered by the inclusion of Bosnia and Herzegovina;[48] they supported the Christian anti-Ottoman revolts. Nonintellectual Croats also retained their narrowly nationalistic dreams. The idea of Yugoslavism thus almost disappeared between 1878 and 1903, as relations between the Serbs and the Croats became increasingly marred by contradictory nationalist and territorial aspirations. The large Serbian minority in Croatian lands, which yearned for Serbian rule, inhibited the creation of an autonomous Croatia within the Austro-Hungarian monarchy. Similarly, Belgrade's pan-Slavic greater Serbian vision hindered the creation of a decentralized Yugoslav state in which autonomy-minded Croats could feel comfortable.[49]

The peasants of Bosnia and Herzegovina were also restless. In the end, they too rebelled against the Ottoman Empire, taking advantage of the weakening legitimacy of the Ottoman government as it lost control both internally and externally. Rebellious Muslim notables enlarged their authority, and bold foreign armies damaged the integrity of the empire. Under this situation of widespread rebellion and conflict, the Balkan Christians forged their own revolt against social conditions. When capitalism entered the Balkans, the smoldering social conflicts brought about by persistent inflation and oppression increased to the flash point in 1875, when social rebellion became a quest for independence from Ottoman rule and ultimately removed Bosnia and Herzegovina from Ottoman control.[50]

Bosnian Versus Ottoman Identification

Bosnia and Herzegovina was governed by a centralized military regime. Control over the area was vital for continued Ottoman control of the rest of the Balkans.[51] Yet in the Bosnian *eyalet* (province), relatively few residents of Turkish descent had not become acclimated to and part of the local Bosnian culture.[52] The Turks no longer encouraged settlement in Bosnia from other regions of the empire as they had upon first conquering Bosnia. Most population transfers to Bosnia during the latter years of Ottoman rule were those of previous inhabitants returning to their former homes.[53]

In addition to containing scattered administrative, military, and legal officials and the garrison troops, the indigenous nobility represented the Porte on the local level. Data collected in 1879 indicated that this group may have amounted to slightly over 1.5 percent of the Muslim population and a little over 0.5 percent of the total population.[54] (By 1910, their numbers were no more than 2.0 percent of the Muslim population and only 0.7 percent of the total population in Bosnia.[55] See Table 2.1 for population figures.) Despite their small numbers, however, the indigenous elites dominated the province. In fact, although the

TABLE 2.1   Population of Bosnia and Herzegovina, 1890–1991

Year	Population (in thousands)
1890	1,402
1900	1,678
1910	1,898
1921	1,890
1931	2,323
1948	2,563
1953	2,847
1961	3,277
1971	3,746
1981	4,124
1991	4,354

SOURCES: 1890–1910: John R. Lampe and Marvin R. Jackson, *Balkan Economic History, 1550–1950: From Imperial Borderlands to Developing Nations* (Bloomington: Indiana University Press, 1982), p. 281; 1921–1991: Robert J. Donia and John V. A. Fine Jr., *Bosnia and Hercegovina: A Tradition Betrayed* (New York: Columbia University Press, 1994), p. 86; and *Statistički Godišnjak.*

central government was able to retain tight control over the district chiefs representing it, the chiefs, in turn, had little control over the local feudal landlords, who made their own agrarian and other policies.[56]

The Bosnian Muslim community found itself in an increasingly anomalous position under Ottoman rule. Some felt a sense of unity with their Turkish conquerors based on their shared religion. The Bosnian Muslims, however, generally exhibited a kind of local, perhaps geographic patriotism that set them apart from the Ottoman Turks, possibly even categorizing them as an incipient—albeit not initially overt—segment of the rise of South Slav nationalism.[57] Perhaps the best expression of the ambivalent position of the Bosnian Muslims in the Ottoman Empire came from Frenchman Henri Massiau de Clerval, who reported for the French on Bosnia and Herzegovina during the Crimean War. De Clerval observed that the position of the Bosnian Muslims was unenviable. They were divided from their Bosnian compatriots by faith, custom, and lifestyle. The local Bosnian Muslim aristocracy supplied the Ottoman central government with many high-level dignitaries[58] and identified with the ruling group as the defender of Islam, despite disagreements with certain of its policies.[59] Furthermore, the Ottoman Empire served as the guarantor of the Muslims' feudal holdings. It is no wonder, then, that the Muslim nobility was often helpful in putting down rebellions by anti-Turkish forces in the Balkans.[60]

The Bosnian Muslims were separate from the Ottoman Turks, however, on the basis of their native language, although Serbo-Croatian was a court language of the Porte. Furthermore, despite the numerous Bosnian Muslims who were elevated to high positions by the Porte, many Bosnian Muslim elites considered their base of power and their prime loyalty to be at the local level rather than at the central government level.[61] In fact, the local nobles resented their vassal obligations to their feudal suzerains, who in return gave them only rarely utilized military protection. Thus, in response to reform pressures from the central government and increasing restiveness by the *kmets* locally, the local aristocracy often increased the pressure on the *kmets* to expand production—thereby risking their nonsupport—while allying themselves with other local landowners who were in the same position to resist the increasingly onerous demands of the central government. The Bosnian Muslims were thus mistrusted and misunderstood by both the Ottomans and the local non-Muslim Bosnians.

The confusing welter of names for different persons in different situations further illustrates the complexity of the Muslim, as opposed to the Bosnian, identification of the Bosnian Muslims. The Serbo-Croatian-speaking Muslims of Bosnia called themselves *Bošnjaci* (Bošnjaks) to emphasize their regional origins. Even the Turks in Istanbul called the Bosnian Muslims *Bošnjaci*,[62] although in Constantinople the word *potur* appeared in certain documents to signify the Islamized Bosnian population, as opposed to those with Turkish origins.[63] Bosnian Christians and even the Bosnian Muslims themselves often called the Serbo-Croatian-speaking Muslims *Turci* to distinguish them from Bosnian Christians.[64] Bosnian Muslims, however, often applied the pejorative term *Turkuš* to Ottoman Turks to differentiate themselves from the Turks in the ethnic sense.[65] The word *Turčin* was generally applied to Slavic Muslims in all regions of the Ottoman Empire.[66]

The term *bosanski narod* (Bosnian people or nation) appeared in the nineteenth century in a letter by a Muslim functionary to Knez Miloš using the Cyrillic alphabet.[67] Of course, this could have merely been an easy way of referring to the population as a whole and may have been devoid of ethno-political overtones. However, in the nineteenth century, the Porte habitually began to refer to the Bosnian inhabitants—of all religions—as Bošnjaks.[68] On the basis of this evidence, Birnbaum argued that "the awareness of being Slavs never ceased also among the Muslims [of Bosnia and Herzegovina] right up to the decline and fall of the Ottoman Empire."[69] Presumably, then, Islamization did not significantly separate the Bosnian Muslim community from its Christian cohabitants communally (that is, as Bosnians) or, in certain ways, even socially.[70]

The fact that both the Christians and the Muslims in Bosnia spoke the same language did not necessarily create a strong bond of identification between the two groups, since "language was not yet considered a significant criteria of group affiliation."[71] Despite the fact, then, that the Bosnian Muslims seemed to have the potential for two mutually exclusive identities—Bošnjak and as part of the ruling Muslim elite—no evidence indicates that they exhibited any significant, recognized, and formal Bosnian Muslim ethnic identification during this period.[72]

Bosnian Muslim internal group unity on a social, cultural, and conceptual basis does not seem to have always been strong. Instead, significant divisions within the Bosnian Muslim community occasionally appeared that essentially corresponded to the divisions that occurred within other groups in the Ottoman Empire.[73] In this vein, Salim Ćerić compiled a nonexhaustive list of the opposing economic and social forces within the Ottoman Empire during the seventeenth and eighteenth centuries that could also apply on occasion to the Bosnian Muslim community: feudal landlord versus *kmet,* state versus *kmet,* state versus feudal landlord, Muslim feudal landlord versus Muslim nonfeudal landlord, rich Christian versus poor Christian, and so on.[74]

There is evidence that differences between urban and rural Bosnian Muslims that were overlaid with class distinctions were also significant. William Lockwood chronicled occasional friction between landed interests and urban administrators. These indications of a rural-urban distinction that existed and that has continued into the twentieth century are not accepted by all observers. However, one cannot dismiss the fact that an important element of the current Bosnian conflict is the fact that in Bosnia and Herzegovina a disproportionate share of Bosnian Muslims are urban dwellers compared with the more rural Serbs and Croats. This situation became obvious during the time of the Ottoman Empire when "Moslem peasants as much as Christian peasants perceived the predominantly Moslem townsmen as 'a clique which exploited them economically and ruled them politically ... an opportunistic group of people who had a common response to daily issues and behaved as a class conscious of its own interests.' "[75] The ruling class was described by one analyst as made up of parasites, "landowners who throughout their lives never saw their estates, officials, army officers and soldiers."[76]

Rural inhabitants considered tax demands to be urban exactions on rural dwellers. Thus, class differences among the Bosnian Muslims exacerbated urban-rural cleavages. During the earlier years of Ottoman rule, the various classes in Bosnia and Herzegovina had apparently coexisted more or less peacefully. However, the aristocracy gradually became more demanding of the lower classes, and class conflict sharpened commensurately.[77] During the seventeenth and eighteenth centuries, particularly around Sarajevo, Muslim peasants and similarly aggrieved small landowners and poor urbanites, often supported by individual members of the *ulema,* frequently expressed their frustration violently.[78]

Lockwood thus concluded that "it is difficult if not impossible to conceive of aristocracy and peasantry as constituting a single, meaningful, social category during the feudal period, regardless of specific context. Social boundaries between aristocrat and peasant were as sharp as between any two ethnic groups."[79] Muslim peasants, like Christian peasants, could not hope to become wealthy landowners despite belonging to the ruling religion; the difference in lifestyle and social networks was too great to bridge. They could, however, possibly attain personal freedom, perhaps through military service, an option not open to their Christian counterparts.[80]

Bosnian Muslim writers on this issue, in attempting to strengthen their national pedigree, have presented an alternative interpretation of Bosnian Muslim unity and self-identification. Salim Ćerić, for example, contended that "on the basis of the described historical development, among the Islamicized Slavic population in the central parts of today's Yugoslavia grew a feeling of distinctiveness, a special culture and a special mentality, that made it a special nation."[81] Avdo Sućeska agreed with Ćerić that the Bosnian Muslim community, by form and content, was a "united and complete Muslim society, [a] distinct ethnic community ... with distinct interests and aspirations."[82] Nevertheless, Sućeska also stressed that the Bosnian Muslims were strongly connected with the Ottoman state, especially—although not exclusively—through Islam. Thus, "through the united faith of Islam which represented the ideological lever of the Ottoman Empire, Muslim society in Bosnia adopted a united political ideology and represented a united cultural circle."[83] Henrik Birnbaum concurred with these Yugoslav scholars that "the role played by religion, affecting all facets of life, as well as the privileged political status and favorable economic conditions enjoyed by the Bosnians-turned-Muslims contributed to set the Islamized portion of the population apart from its Croat [that is, Catholic] and Serbian [that is, Orthodox] compatriots."[84]

What Ivo Banac termed the "continuity of Bosnian regional consciousness"[85] was advanced by the privileged circumstances under which the Bosnian Muslims lived during Ottoman rule. They had greater political autonomy and a lower tax burden than other Ottoman subjects. Furthermore, from the seventeenth century on, they were permitted to inherit fiefs, as ownership of private-property estates increased and military-feudal land ownership (*timars*) decreased. Conscious of their distinctiveness, many Bosnian Muslims spoke the "Bosnian" language. In this view, all Bosnian Muslims, despite differences in class and social status, were interested in maintaining the privileged position membership in the Islamic religion provided. This unity called forth an equal and opposite determination by the Christian *raya* to "enter into every combination of Christian forces that would have destroyed the Turkish reign, which the Muslim population protected. So occurred the ideological separations based not only on class but similarly on religious differences."[86]

Others have argued in favor of a Bosnian geographical-historical identity, stating that during the Ottoman occupation a unique "oriental-Islamic cultural heritage" developed that pervaded even Christian life. This heritage was reflected in the clothing, literature, art, and architecture, and in the adoption of Turkish and Arabic expressions into the Serbo-Croatian language, which came to be reflected in certain rituals of the Christian churches.[87] Proponents of this opinion imply that such a cultural effect occurred because there was, in fact, a common pre-Ottoman culture and history shared by all Bosnian inhabitants.[88]

As this discussion illustrates, scholars differ over whether class or other elements prevented the formation of a national self-identification by the Bosnian Muslims during the Ottoman conquest. One argument holds that the Bosnian

Muslims had separate interests, and thus goals, based on a class division or on rural-urban factors. The Muslim nobility, which identified strongly with the Ottoman Turkish conquerors, was occasionally pitted against the Muslim peasantry, who were discriminated against just like the non-Muslim peasants. The second view is that Muslims of all classes were able to override their differing class interests and form a unified group on the basis of their shared religion or emerging common linguistic or shared territorial foundations during the Ottoman era.

Perhaps the reality lies in a synthesis of elements of both positions. It is conceivable that the Bosnian Muslim nobles and peasantry during Ottoman times did indeed have some divergent interests and loyalties. Day-to-day life for the common person—even Muslims—cannot have been easy at that time, particularly because of having to suffer the depredations of a luxury-seeking ruling class. However, the shared belief in Islam and the concomitant feeling of privileged status that comes with belonging to the dominant religion or worldview could somewhat ameliorate antagonisms. There is indeed evidence indicating that some Muslim landowners eventually saw that in the face of increasing assaults on the Ottoman Empire by non-Muslims, intra-Muslim class conflict was counterproductive.

Thus, in the end the obvious decay of the Ottoman Empire would have provided strong impetus for the conscious decision of Bosnian Muslim landowners to stake their fortunes on unity with their fellow citizens, forgoing the class exigencies of uniting with the broadly Ottoman class of aristocrats. Some Muslim nobles did not easily make the transition from Ottoman administrator or feudal landlord to representative of general Bosnian Muslim interests when Ottoman rule over Bosnia ended. Those who felt they could not exist except as representatives of the Ottoman Empire, who could not live under the regime of the Habsburg infidels, or who feared retribution for their treatment of Christian subjects emigrated to other Muslim lands, especially Turkey. Some of those who remained in Bosnia during the decline of the Ottoman Empire in the Balkans and its replacement by Austria-Hungary, however, soon found it beneficial to represent themselves as leaders of the interests of the Bosnian Muslim community as a whole.

Overall, however, the evidence does not strongly favor a deep-seated *national* identification by Bosnian Muslims during the Ottoman period. Whereas one could easily observe the development of some common cultural traits that distinguished them from the non-Muslim population in Bosnia, there is no indication of Bosnian Muslim ethnic consciousness as that which was merging Croatianism with Catholicism and Serbianism with Orthodoxy. Thus, whereas the Ottoman period may have encouraged a consolidation of Bosnian Muslim interests and the decline of the Ottoman Empire may have fostered an understanding by Bosnian Muslim landowners that their best interests lay with local patriotism rather than with continued loyalty to the Porte, nevertheless there are few convincing data to indicate that the Bosnian Muslims under the Ottoman Empire can correctly be identified as a distinct national entity or that their self-identification had become politicized—that is, ethnonationalistic. This was so even under the duress of the 1875 rebellion by the Orthodox peasants in Bosnia and Herzegovina against their Muslim landlords, which became a bid by Bosnia's Serbian Orthodox population for freedom from Ottoman rule and union with the independent state of Serbia.

NOTES

1. For a detailed discussion of the Ottoman social structure, see Salim Ćerić, *Muslimani srpskohrvatskog jezika* (Sarajevo: Svjetlost, 1968), pp. 78–115; and Wayne S. Vucinich, "The Nature of Balkan Society Under Ottoman Rule," *Slavic Review* 21 (December 1962), pp. 597–616.

2. Peter F. Sugar, *Southeastern Europe Under Ottoman Rule, 1354–1804* (Seattle: University of Washington Press, 1977), p. 31.

3. See Ćerić, *Muslimani srpskohrvatskog jezika,* pp. 100–104, for a catalog of incidents in which Bosnian Muslims played significant roles in furthering Ottoman imperialism.

4. Boris Furlan, "The Nationality Problem in the Balkans," lecture delivered at the Hoover Institution, Stanford, California, 20 February 1943, p. 3.

5. Citing the findings of the Turkish historian Ömer Lutfi Barkan in "Essai sur les données statistiques des registres de recensement dans l'Empire Ottoman aux XVe et XVI siècles," *Journal of the Economic and Social History of the Orient* 1 (1958), pp. 9–36, Sugar estimated that 18.8 percent of the hearths in the Ottoman Empire during the 1520–1530 census period were Muslim, 80.7 percent were Christian, and 0.5 percent were Jewish. *Southeastern Europe Under Ottoman Rule,* pp. 50–51. This amounted in the Balkans to 194,958 Muslim hearths, 832,707 taxable Christian hearths, and 4,134 taxable Jewish hearths. The non-Muslim population thus equaled 4.29 times that of the Muslims. Nedim Filipović, "Postankarska obzorja," cited in Ćerić, *Muslimani srpskohrvatskog jezika,* p. 76. Most of the Muslims were located in ten of the twenty-eight Balkan districts of the Ottoman Empire, including Bosnia and Herzegovina. Speros Vryonis Jr., "Religious Changes and Patterns in the Balkans, 14th–16th Centuries," in Henrik Birnbaum and Speros Vryonis Jr., eds., *Aspects of the Balkans: Continuity and Change* (The Hague: Mouton, 1972), pp. 162–163.

6. Traian Stoianovich, "Factors in the Decline of Ottoman Society in the Balkans," *Slavic Review* 21 (December 1962), pp. 623–625.

7. Sugar estimated that the privileged encompassed only about 10 percent of the population. *Southeastern Europe Under Ottoman Rule,* p. 33. Avdo Sućeska described members of the upper echelons in "Istorijske osnove nacionalne posebnosti bosansko-hercegovačkih Muslimana," *Jugoslovenski istorijski časopis* 4 (1969), p. 51.

8. Atif Purivatra, *Jugoslavenska muslimanska organizacija u političkom životu Kraljevine Srba, Hrvata i Slovenaca* (Sarajevo: Svjetlost, 1974), p. 14 (note).

9. Henrik Birnbaum argued that the term *millet,* originally signifying a non-Islamic religious group, gradually took on the meaning of national group or minority within the Ottoman Empire. "The Ethno-Linguistic Mosaic of Bosnia and Hercegovina," *Die Welt der Slaven* 32 (1987), p. 13. The patriarch of Constantinople was the head of the Orthodox *mil-*

let, by far the largest of the *millets*. He was considered the spokesperson for the Orthodox *millet* in all its dealings with Muslim authorities and held jurisdiction over all legal and moral matters on the local level pertaining to its members. Charles Jelavich and Barbara Jelavich, *The Establishment of the Balkan National States, 1804–1920* (Seattle: University of Washington Press, 1977), p. 4.

10. Robin Alison Remington, "Bosnia: The Tangled Web," *Current History* 92 (November 1993), p. 365.

11. Kemal Karpat, *An Inquiry into the Social Foundations of Nationalism in the Ottoman State: From Social Estates to Classes, From Millets to Nations* (Princeton: Princeton University, Center of International Studies, Research Monograph no. 39, 1973), p. 8. See also Jelavich and Jelavich, *The Establishment of the Balkan National States*, p. 5.

12. The term *dhimmi* was applied to those who were "protected" or "tolerated" peoples. The term signified indigenous "people of the book [the Hebrew Bible]" (mainly Jews and Christians) who were to be protected from pillage, slavery, exile, and massacre according to the *Covenant of 'Umar* between the Ottoman state and its subjects. *Dhimmis* could become Muslims through voluntary conversion or through the system of *devshirme*, the forced conversion of Christian youths who were taken from their villages as a special type of tax levy and forced to serve as slaves of the sultan in various capacities. Although the children were originally meant to form a special military cadre, the janissaries, in practice any other profession could also be attained. For that reason, a family that had ambitions for a son might have sought rather than avoided the collectors for *devshirme*. For a discussion of the genesis and treatment of *dhimmis*, focusing particularly on the Arab treatment of *dhimmi* peoples, see Bat Ye'Or, *Dhimmi Peoples: Oppressed Nations* (Switzerland: Editions de l'Avenir, 1978).

13. Sugar, *Southeastern Europe Under Ottoman Rule*, p. 65.

14. Robert J. Donia and John V.A. Fine Jr. pointed out the more contemporary manifestations of the excesses of this strong sense of Croatian nationalism by the Franciscans (and many of their congregants) during the World War II Croatian atrocities against Serbs. *Bosnia and Hercegovina: A Tradition Betrayed* (New York: Columbia University Press, 1994), p. 65.

15. Ćerić, *Muslimani srpskohrvatskog jezika*, pp. 33-35.

16. Robert W. Olson, "The Ottoman Empire in the Middle of the Eighteenth Century and the Fragmentation of Tradition: Relations of the Nationalities (Millets), Guilds (Esnaf) and the Sultan, 1740–1768," *Die Welt des Islams* 17 (1976–1977), p. 73; and John R. Lampe and Marvin R. Jackson, *Balkan Economic History, 1550–1950: From Imperial Borderlands to Developing Nations* (Bloomington: Indiana University Press, 1982), pp. 47–49. See also Stoianovich, "Factors in the Decline of Ottoman Society," pp. 625–628, for an analysis of the effect of the disparity between wages and prices on the Ottoman social order.

17. It was the descendants of these colonists who declared independence from Croatia and later unsuccessfully attempted to create an independent state of Herzeg-Bosnia.

18. Sugar suggested that these circumstances included "a drastic change in the training, personality, and activities of the rulers; the growing influence of the *enderun* [members of the inner service, including women and eunuchs, who served in the inner section of the Ottoman imperial palace that contained the ruler's residence] on state affairs coupled with factionalism in the *birun* [members of the outer service who served in the Ottoman imperial palace outside of the residence of the imperial family] and the establishment of close ties between members of the inner and outer services; the growing corruption that

resulted, in part, from the emergence of these factions; the sudden inflation at the turn of the sixteenth and seventeenth centuries, supposedly caused by the shift of world trade from the Mediterranean to the Atlantic and by the influx of silver from the Americas into the Ottoman Empire; a conflict between the old Turkish element (*beys, gazis,* and *sipahis*) and the descendants of slaves, which conflict split the rank of the 'professional Ottomans'; changes in the organization and composition of the military establishment; and, finally, the inability of the Ottoman Empire to expand further." Sugar, *Southeastern Europe Under Ottoman Rule,* p. 187. The second half of Sugar's volume evaluated and described the significance and ramifications of each of these factors in the decline of the Ottoman Empire. Ćerić credited the following factors that allowed the West to become so much stronger militarily than the Ottoman Empire: the increasing specialization of the military establishment and its more systematic training, the introduction of weapons of greater accuracy and killing capability, and the greater ability to mobilize the masses for military duty. Better communications networks and domestic relations ensued because of more efficient organization of governmental power. *Muslimani srpskohrvatskog jezika,* p. 35. Wayne S. Vucinich contended that "the Ottoman Empire was weakened by its policy aimed at preserving each of several distinct cultures, whether out of religious sincerity or political expediency. The administrative and legal diversities, socio-economic disparities, the Muslim religious exclusiveness, the isolation of ethno-confessional entities, and a state and social system based on war—all of these created a ramshackle empire which was bound to fall to pieces once the overwhelming police power crumbled." "Reply," *Slavic Review* 21 (December 1962), p. 638. Furthermore, according to Ćerić, the Turkish feudal landlords became so delirious about their military success that they ignored their relations with the "producing" population, the *kmets.* Although landlords could lose their property for failure to satisfy military obligations, they would not lose their land because of mismanagement. *Muslimani srpskohrvatskog jezika,* pp. 36–37. The economic problems of the Ottoman Empire were of crisis proportions. Agriculture was not developing effectively, and agrarian relations were a major cause. By the time the Porte was able or willing to take steps to increase production by improving the conditions of the *kmets,* "the society was so weakened and impoverished that it could not be preserved." Ćerić, *Muslimani srpskohrvatskog jezika,* p. 41. Halil Inalcik added two other factors that aided the decay of the Ottoman Empire: "population increase accompanied by economic stagnation, and the destructive financial and political consequences of long years of war with Iran and in Hungary." "The Ottoman Decline and Its Effects upon the *Reaya*," in Birnbaum and Vryonis, eds., *Aspects of the Balkans,* p. 347.

19. Jelavich and Jelavich, *The Establishment of the Balkan National States,* p. 99.

20. For more on the provisions of the Safer Decree, see William Miller, "Bosnia Under the Ottomans," *Gentleman's Magazine* 61 (October 1898), p. 347.

21. Donia and Fine pointed out that the Ottomans, who favored the institutionalized Orthodox religion over Catholicism, permitted the Orthodox to exact church taxes on Catholics, who also tithed to the Catholic Church. *Bosnia and Hercegovina,* p. 39.

22. Dame Millicent Garrett Fawcett described the brutality of the system under which the Christians lived in *The Martyrs of Misrule,* in Eastern Question Association, *Papers on the Eastern Question,* no. 11 (London: Cassell Petter & Galpin, 1877), especially pp. 7–11.

23. Jelavich and Jelavich, *The Establishment of the Balkan National States,* p. 7.

24. Indeed, Fred Warner Neal considered that "the merger of religion and nationalism probably was as complete in the case of Serbia as it has ever been before or since." "From

Particularism to Unity: The Kaleidoscope of Nationalism(s) in Yugoslavia," *American Universities Field Staff* (Southeast Europe Series) 2 (1954), p. 3. See Vucinich, "The Nature of Balkan Society Under Ottoman Rule," pp. 606–610, for a discussion of some of the forms of social organization used in this area. Current and historical manifestations of the *zadruga* are highlighted in Robert F. Byrnes, ed., *Communal Families in the Balkans: The Zadruga* (Notre Dame: University of Notre Dame Press, 1976).

25. Robin Okey, *Eastern Europe 1740–1980: Feudalism to Communism* (Minneapolis: University of Minnesota Press, 1982), p. 100. See also Ćerić, *Muslimani srpskohrvatskog jezika*, pp. 94–99, for a description of some elements of the reform and their effects.

26. Robert Donia, "Imperial Occupation and Its Consequences: The Army and Politics in Bosnia and Hercegovina, 1878–1914," unpublished paper, Ohio State University, Lima (1979), p. 3.

27. The term *chiftluk* originally referred to the amount of land a pair of oxen could plow in one day. Only at the beginning of the sixteenth century and certainly by the mid-seventeenth century did the term come to signify a social institution or a large agricultural estate later transformed into quasi-private property. Stoianovich deemed the *chiftluk* a "transition from a social and economic structure founded upon a system of moderate land rent and few labor services to one of excessive land rent and exaggerated service." Traian Stoianovich, "Land Tenure and Related Sectors of the Balkan Economy, 1600–1800," *Journal of Economic History* 13 (Fall 1953), pp. 401–402. There were two types of *chiftluk*—the *raya-chiftluk*, the land over which a *kmet* could exercise usufructuary rights in return for taxes and labor, and the *hassa-chiftluk*, the private farm of the owner of the *chiftluk*. Stoianovich, "Land Tenure and Related Sectors of the Balkan Economy," p. 398.

28. Nedim Filipović, "Forming of Moslem Ethnicon in Bosnia and Hercegovina," in Ranko Petković, ed., *Moslems in Yugoslavia* (Belgrade: Review of International Affairs, 1985), p. 6. Filipović suggested that this creation of hereditary fiefs resulted from the fact that the decay of the Ottoman Empire beginning in the late sixteenth century made the defense of Bosnia dependent upon the "material power of Bosnian spahis." "Forming of Moslem Ethnicon, " p. 14.

29. Jelavich and Jelavich believed that had the local Muslim landlords permitted the land reforms to be carried out, the Serbian revolt might have been postponed. *The Establishment of the Balkan National States*, p. 28.

30. Paul Hehn, "Capitalism and the Revolutionary Factor in the Balkans and Crimean War Diplomacy," *East European Quarterly* 18 (June 1984), p. 166. The 1831 revolt of the Muslim landlords occurred after the end of the Russo-Turkish War (1828–1829), when Sultan Mahmud II attempted to push through his reforms. He met with strong resistance, however, from the Muslim landlords in Bosnia and Herzegovina. Led by Husein Gradaščević, the landlords raised an army and with their Albanian allies defeated the sultan's forces in 1831, capturing the city of Travnik, formerly the capital city of the Bosnian *eyalet* (the administrative district of the Ottoman governor-general). They demanded autonomy for Bosnia and an end to the government's reform program; in return, they would continue to give allegiance to the sultan. But in 1832 the sultan defeated the increasingly fractionalized rebel forces.

31. Lampe and Jackson, *Balkan Economic History*, p. 284.

32. George G. Arnakis, *The Near East in Modern Times*, Vol. 1: *The Ottoman Empire and the Balkan States to 1900* (Austin: Pemberton Press, 1969), p. 256; and Ćerić, *Muslimani srpskohrvatskog jezika*, p. 111.

33. Jelavich and Jelavich, *The Establishment of the Balkan National States*, p. 100.

34. Ibid., p. 17.

35. Ćerić, *Muslimani srpskohrvatskog jezika,* p. 30.

36. Donia and Fine described the Ottoman's obvious signs of favoritism of the Orthodox over the Catholic Church within the Balkans in *Bosnia and Hercegovina,* pp. 39–40.

37. Leonard Bushkoff, in a critical review of *The Balkans in Transition* by Charles and Barbara Jelavich, *Balkan Studies* 5 (1964), p. 129.

38. Serbian agents scattered throughout the Ottoman and Austro-Hungarian Empires to stimulate support for the concept of the unification of all Serbs with Serbia. See David MacKenzie, "Serbian Nationalist and Military Organizations and the Piedmont Idea, 1844–1914," *East European Quarterly* 16 (September 1982), pp. 323–344.

39. Karpat, *An Inquiry into the Social Foundations of Nationalism,* p. 8.

40. For a discussion of the forces that influenced the South Slavs and the role of language and literature in their national awakening within the nineteenth-century Austro-Hungarian Empire, see Stanley B. Kimball, "The Austro-Slav Revival: A Study of Nineteenth-Century Literary Foundations," *Transactions of the American Philosophical Society* 63 (November 1973).

41. Russians were by no means of one mind diplomatically on whether to aid their fellow Slavs against the Ottoman Turks. In the end, Russia did declare war on the Porte, but this occurred two years after the opening salvos by the Balkan Christians and after assuring itself in 1877 of Austrian neutrality toward the adventure. Jelavich and Jelavich, *The Establishment of the Balkan National States,* pp. 146–148. See also Arthur J. May, *The Hapsburg Monarchy, 1867–1914* (Cambridge: Harvard University Press, 1951), p. 124. Leonard Bushkoff blamed the change in the Russian attitude toward the Balkans on "the social and political changes signified by German unification and the weakening of the Habsburg Empire," as well as on "the relative decline of Russian military capacity vis-à-vis the industrialized European powers" between 1856 and 1917. Review of Jelavich and Jelavich, *Balkans in Transition,* p. 130.

42. Michael Gavrilović, "The Early Diplomatic Relations of Great Britain and Serbia," *Slavonic Review* 1 (June 1922), p. 91. Lawrence P. Meriage pointed out that although the revolt did not have nationalistic aims, the resulting establishment of the *pashalik* (jurisdiction of a Turkish governor, or pasha) of Belgrade as a discrete unit within the Ottoman Empire provided the first step for the maturation of Serbian nationalism. "The First Serbian Uprising (1804–1813): National Revival or a Search for Regional Security," *Canadian Review of Studies in Nationalism* 4 (Spring 1977), pp. 198–199. The fact that Serbia was now a defined political entity was emphasized by the provision that the Porte had to negotiate with its Serbian subjects through their deputies. Gavrilović, "The Early Diplomatic Relations of Great Britain and Serbia," p. 91.

43. Hehn, "Capitalism and the Revolutionary Factor," p. 158. For more on the deterioration of the Ottoman Empire's foreign trade position during the last quarter of the nineteenth century, see Şevket Pamuk, "The Ottoman Empire in the 'Great Depression' of 1873-1896," *Journal of Economic History* 44 (March 1984), pp. 107–118.

44. Furlan, "The Nationality Problem in the Balkans," p. 5.

45. Ibid., pp. 1–2.

46. Ibid., p. 3.

47. For a description of the brief nineteenth-century flirtation with union based on Yugoslavism, see James Bukowski, "Yugoslavism and the Croatian National Party in 1867," *Canadian Review of Studies in Nationalism* 3 (Fall 1975), pp. 70–88.

48. Paul Shoup, *Communism and the Yugoslav National Question* (New York: Columbia

University Press, 1968), p. 8; David MacKenzie, *Ilija Garašanin, Balkan Bismarck* (Boulder: East European Monographs, 1985), p. 51; Robin Okey, "State, Church and Nation in the Serbo-Croat Speaking Lands of the Habsburg Monarchy, 1850–1914," in Donal A. Kerr, ed., *Religion, State and Ethnic Groups* (New York: New York University Press, 1992), p. 55; and MacKenzie, "Serbian Nationalist and Military Organizations and the Piedmont Idea," p. 323. Illyrianists expected a Croatian cultural reawakening to become the impetus for eventual South Slav union. Influential Serb intellectuals, however, considered Croats to be Serbs according to linguistic criteria, thus foreshadowing the Serb-Croat distinctions in self-identification that would become a major problem in twentieth-century Yugoslavia.

49. Jelavich and Jelavich, *The Establishment of the Balkan National States*, p. 248.

50. Because the rebellion ended with Austria-Hungary occupying and eventually annexing Bosnia and Herzegovina, some scholars have accused the Habsburg monarchy of involvement in sparking the anti-Ottoman revolt. The extremely large Austrian interest in the area suggested that "Austrian officials in Dalmatia, many of whom were Serbs and Croats, incited the Bosniacs to rebellion in 1875." May, *The Hapsburg Monarchy*, p. 120. However, this view begs the question of Austria-Hungary's interest in maintaining a status quo in the Balkans to forestall Russian incursions, exhibited, for example, in the monarchy's aid to the Turks during the Herzegovinian rebellion of 1858–1862. Austria's later failure to assist the Ottoman Empire during the insurrections of 1875–1878 was a product of its altered situation as a result of its defeat by Prussia and the consequent formation of the Dual Monarchy in 1866–1867.

51. Ćerić, *Muslimani srpskohrvatskog jezika*, p. 108.

52. On the basis of the census for the period 1520–1530, Vryonis asserted that 96,500 hearths in Bosnia and Herzegovina belonged to Muslims who had converted to Islam, leaving about 30 percent of the additional Muslim hearths listed attributable to Turkish immigrants. Vryonis, "Religious Changes and Patterns in the Balkans, 14th–16th Centuries," p. 164.

53. Birnbaum, "The Ethno-Linguistic Mosaic of Bosnia and Hercegovina," p. 12.

54. Peter F. Sugar, *Industrialization of Bosnia-Hercegovina 1878–1918* (Seattle: University of Washington Press, 1963), p. 13. William Miller broke down the population figures of the 1895 census, reflecting 1,568,092 inhabitants in Bosnia, into 42.94 percent Orthodox, 21.31 percent Catholic, and 34.90 percent Muslim. "Bosnia Under the Austrians," p. 341.

55. Donia and Fine, *Bosnia and Hercegovina*, p. 76.

56. Ćerić, *Muslimani srpskohrvatskog jezika*, p. 104.

57. Birnbaum contended that despite all of the obvious differences between the Bosnian Muslims and the Bosnian Croats and Serbs, "the Slavic Muslims of Bosnia in many respects remained very much similar to their Christian—Catholic and Orthodox—fellow countrymen even though, precisely because of their different conditions, they no longer fully identified with them." "The Ethno-Linguistic Mosaic of Bosnia and Hercegovina," p. 18.

58. Carl Max Kortepeter counted at least seven Bosnian grand viziers to Ottoman sultans, perhaps the most famous of which was Sokollu Mehemmed (1565–1579), who attempted to modernize the communications networks throughout the Ottoman Empire. *Ottoman Imperialism During the Reformation: Europe and the Caucasus* (New York: New York University Press, 1972), pp. 248–251. Vladimir Dedijer counted nine grand viziers from Bosnia and Herzegovina and pointed out the importance of Bosnia to the Ottoman

Empire by the fact that Serbo-Croatian became the diplomatic language used by the Porte. *The Road to Sarajevo* (New York: Simon and Schuster, 1966), p. 29. Muslim historian Safvet Beg Bashagitch identified about seven hundred Muslim notables hailing from Bosnia. Cited in G. H. Neville-Bagot, "The Muslims of Bosnia and the Other Autonomous States of Yugoslavia," *Islamic Review* 48 (June 1960), p. 33. Vatro Murvar detailed the contributions of twenty-five viziers of "Croat" nationality. Since he included those mentioned by the other authors, it is obvious that what is "Croat" for Murvar means "Bosnian" for other authors. *Nation and Religion in Central Europe and the Western Balkans—The Muslims in Bosna, Hercegovina and Sandžak: A Sociological Analysis* (Brookfield: FSSSN Colloquia and Symposia, University of Wisconsin, 1989), pp. 24–43.

59. Henri Massiau de Clerval's previously unpublished report on conditions in Bosnia and Herzegovina at the time of the Crimean War, addressed to the Minister of Public Instruction, Archives des missions scientifiques et littéraires Tom V. (Paris: 1856), cited by Ibrahim Kemura, "Bosna i muslimani u očima jednog posmatrača iz sredine XIX stoljeća," *Glasnik Vrhovnog islamskog starješinstva u socijalističkoj federativnoj republici jugoslaviji* [hereafter *Glasnik VISa*] 32 (September–October 1969), p. 420.

60. Steven L. Burg, "The Political Integration of Yugoslavia's Muslims: Determinants of Success and Failure" (Pittsburgh: Carl Beck Papers in Russian and East European Studies, University of Pittsburgh, 1983), p. 6. Birnbaum suggested that the call to arms was the only time the Porte addressed an appeal to a common religion to the Bosnian Muslims. "The Ethno-Linguistic Mosaic of Bosnia and Hercegovina," p. 13.

61. Sugar, *Southeastern Europe Under Ottoman Rule*, p. 236.

62. Sućeska, "Istorijske osnove nacionalne posebnosti," p. 52.

63. Muhamed Hadžijahić, *Porijeklo bosanskih muslimana* (Sarajevo: 1990), p. 87.

64. William G. Lockwood, "Living Legacy of the Ottoman Empire: The Serbo-Croatian Speaking Moslems of Bosnia-Hercegovina," in Abraham Ascher, Tibor Halasi-Kun, and Béla K. Király, eds., *The Mutual Effects of the Islamic and Judeo-Christian Worlds: The East European Pattern* (Brooklyn: Brooklyn College Press, 1978), pp. 212–213. Even today, stated Bernard Lewis, "in the secular republic of Turkey, the word Turk is by common convention restricted to Muslims … [On the other hand] while the non-Muslim resident of the country is not a Turk, the non-Turkish Muslim immigrant, whether from the former provinces of the Ottoman Empire or from elsewhere, very rapidly acquires a Turkish identity." "The Return of Islam," *Commentary* 61 (January 1976), p. 43. Furthermore, according to Lewis, the practice of calling Muslims "Turks" was followed throughout most of Europe at the time because of a widespread "unwillingness to recognize the nature of Islam or even the fact of Islam as an independent, different, and autonomous religious phenomenon." "The Return of Islam," p. 39. C.N.O. Bartlett noted that "Muslim" and "Turk" lost their synonymity in Yugoslavia only in the 1950s when Turk, as with Muslim, took on national rather than religious affiliational overtones. *The Turkish Minority in Yugoslavia*, Bradford Studies on Yugoslavia, no. 3 (Bradford, West Yorkshire: Postgraduate School of Yugoslav Studies, University of Bradford, 1980), p. 1.

65. Ćerić, *Muslimani srpskohrvatskog jezika*, p. 120; and Burg, "The Political Integration of Yugoslavia's Muslims," p. 6.

66. Atif Purivatra, *Nacionalni i politički razvitak muslimana* (Sarajevo: Svjetlost, 1970), p. 6; and Burg, "The Political Integration of Yugoslavia's Muslims," p. 6.

67. Sućeska, "Istorijske osnove nacionalne posebnosti," p. 53.

54 _Ottoman Empire_

68. Birnbaum, "The Ethno-Linguistic Mosaic of Bosnia and Hercegovina," p. 13. Thus, the terminology for the Bošnjaks became identical to that used for other minorities within the empire in reference to "language, territory, and national specificity" (p. 13).

69. Ibid.

70. William G. Lockwood noted in his anthropological study of the Muslims in western Bosnia that "differences between groups in a single locale tend to be closely related variants rather than totally different traits." _European Moslems: Economy and Ethnicity in Western Bosnia_ (New York: Academic Press, 1975), p. 49.

71. Lockwood, "Living Legacy of the Ottoman Empire," p. 213. The 1910 Austrian census of Bosnia and Herzegovina showed that 2,289 people knew the Turkish language and 448 were familiar with the Arabic language. Ćerić, _Muslimani srpskohrvatskog jezika_, p. 45. Aleksandar Solovjev differed, however, citing Paul Ricaut's observations of a sect of "Muslims in Bosnia, Herzegovina and Sandzak' (the Potur) who felt half-Christians, who spoke the same language as their Christian neighbors, and felt a solidarity with them." "Engleski izveštaj XVII vijeka o bosanskim Poturima," _Glasnik Zemalskog muzeja u Bosni i Hercegovini_ 7 (1952), p. 106.

72. Lockwood thus persuasively concluded that the Bosnian Muslims "were no different ... than other Moslem subjects of the Empire.... They were considered by both Christians and other Moslems, and thought of themselves, as the establishment, and an integral part of the Empire." Lockwood, "Living Legacy of the Ottoman Empire," p. 213. See also Bogdan Denitch, "Religion and Social Change in Yugoslavia," in Bohdan R. Bociurkiw and John W. Strong, eds., _Religion and Atheism in the U.S.S.R. and Eastern Europe_ (London: Macmillan, 1975), pp. 370–371. Karpat pointed out that in the early nineteenth century, Turkey "accepted as 'Turks' the former Ottoman subjects who were Muslims, allowing them to migrate freely and to settle in Turkey. Among these there were Bosnians, Herzegovinians and Pomaks who were Slavs by language and race, did not speak Turkish, but were Muslims by religion." _An Inquiry into the Social Foundations of Nationalism in the Ottoman State_, p. 2. See also Ćerić, _Muslimani srpskohrvatskog jezika_, pp. 161–162, concerning conditions in Austria-Hungary that impelled the emigration of some Bosnian Muslims to Turkey.

73. Lockwood, "Living Legacy of the Ottoman Empire," p. 213.

74. Ćerić, _Muslimani srpskohrvatskog jezika_, p. 41.

75. Lockwood, "Living Legacy of the Ottoman Empire," p. 213. See also Sućeska, "Istorijske osnove nacionalne posebnosti," p. 51.

76. Furlan, "The Nationality Problem in the Balkans," p. 3. See Sugar, _Industrialization of Bosnia-Hercegovina_, pp. 8–12, for a description of types of land-ownership in the Ottoman Empire and a discussion of the significance of those different types for the Bosnian Muslim inhabitants.

77. Ćerić, _Muslimani srpskohrvatskog jezika_, p. 94.

78. Sućeska, "Istorijske osnove nacionalne posebnosti," p. 51.

79. Lockwood, "Living Legacy of the Ottoman Empire," p. 214.

80. Sućeska, "Istorijske osnove nacionalne posebnosti," p. 50.

81. Ćerić, _Muslimani srpskohrvatskog jezika_, p. 116.

82. Sućeska, "Istorijske osnove nacionalne posebnosti," p. 50.

83. Ibid.

84. Birnbaum, "The Ethno-Linguistic Mosaic of Bosnia and Hercegovina," p. 18.

85. Ivo Banac, _The National Question in Yugoslavia: Origins, History, Politics_ (Ithaca: Cornell University Press, 1984), p. 41.

86. Purivatra, *Jugoslavenska muslimanska organizacija*, p. 14.

87. See Muhamed Hadžijahič, Mahmud Traljić, and Nijaz Sukrić, *Islam i muslimani u Bosni and Hercegovini* (Sarajevo: Svjetlost, 1977), pp. 53–80.

88. Burg, "The Political Integration of Yugoslavia's Muslims," p. 5. Muhamed Hadžijahić cautioned that at that time this feeling of a common homeland could not be confused with a feeling of a common Bosnian nation. *Od tradicije do identita: Geneza nacionalnog pitanja bosanskih muslimana* (Sarajevo: Svjetlost, 1974), p. 88.

3

Bosnian Muslims Under Austro-Hungarian Rule

"I hate the corpses of empires, they stink as nothing else."

—Rebecca West

The Bosnian Muslims had always lived under Muslim rule. More important, since the Ottoman Empire was a nonnational entity, the Bosnian Muslims—like all other inhabitants of the empire—had identified themselves by their religion.

Occupation by Austria-Hungary in 1878 changed their circumstances dramatically. Not only were the Bosnian Muslims forcibly separated from the non-Slav Muslims of other South Slav lands, who remained under Ottoman tutelage, but they were also separated from other Slavic Muslims in the South Slav lands of Macedonia, Montenegro, and Novi Pazar. This alone might have encouraged the differentiation of Bosnian Muslims from surrounding communities, but the fact that national orientation in the Habsburg Empire was considered more significant than religious orientation ensured their isolation from other Muslim influences.[1] Now the Bosnian Muslims were administered by non-Muslims (religiously aligned in Bosnia and Herzegovina with the minority Catholic Croats). For the first time, then, the Bosnian Muslims were faced with the challenge of political rather than religious self-identification as forces on all sides attempted to forestall their development of a narrower communal loyalty in favor of a larger, politically motivated fealty. The relatively short period of Austro-Hungarian control over Bosnia and Herzegovina (1878–1918) is thus the story of the political awakening of the Bosnian Muslims.

Austro-Hungarian Occupation of Bosnia and Herzegovina

Austria-Hungary, with Bismarckian Prussia's acquiescence, came to play the dominant role in Bosnia and Herzegovina as Ottoman authority was eliminated there. The Habsburg dynasty did not possess the capability of other imperial powers for overseas expansion because of its weak navy; Austria-Hungary was also unable to acquire any property from the newly unified and strengthened

Germany. Therefore, to obtain captive markets for the disposal of its industrial produce and to procure raw materials cheaply, the Dual monarchy was determined to expand into the Balkans, especially Bosnia and Herzegovina. Equally important was Austria-Hungary's determination to prevent Russia from exerting influence in the Balkans. Finally, the Habsburgs hoped to gain influence in the newly independent Serbia, in part for economic advantage but also to prevent Serbia's annexation of Bosnia and Herzegovina, which could lead to the creation of a South Slav state that would attract Austria-Hungary's Slavic inhabitants.[2]

Not everyone in the Habsburg court was in favor of Austrian occupation of Bosnia and Herzegovina. Hungarian nationalists and German liberals, who were apprehensive that their political strength within the monarchy might be diluted with the addition of more South Slavs, were adamantly opposed and were inclined to provide little funding for the project. Austrian Foreign Minister Julius Count Andrássy feared the exacerbation of already strained national relations within the monarchy if Bosnia and Herzegovina's Slavic population were added to the mix. He also wanted to avoid increased controversy with Russia and therefore recommended moving into Bosnia and Herzegovina "only if it appeared that the Ottoman empire was about to fall apart, or if Serbia were going to pounce upon the area."[3] In the end, Serbia's declaration of war against the Ottoman Empire in 1876 seemed to personify the oppositionists' worst fears that Serbia intended to annex Bosnia and Herzegovina. Serbia, united with Montenegro to attack the Ottoman Empire in order to free Balkan Christians and their land from Turkey, had to be rescued by Russia and could not attain control over Bosnia and Herzegovina. Andrássy then decided to balance the creation of a Russian-influenced autonomous Bulgaria with the Habsburg monarchy's occupation of Bosnia and Herzegovina through the Treaty of San Stefano.[4]

The Congress of Berlin (1878), called the "source of all the unrest in Europe in the following decades and the causes of the first World War,"[5] lived up to its billing in the Balkans. The underlying aim of the congress was to preserve and perpetuate the balance of power that dominated European politics and maintained some measure of peace. Therefore, the popular aspirations for independence expressed by the numerous indigenous revolts in the Balkans endangered the *modus vivendi* engineered by the great powers.

Thus, the congress tried to maintain the status quo while permitting only the minimum necessary alterations to the international order. Montenegro's independent status and Serbia's liberation from Turkey were legitimized, although the independent Serbia became economically dependent on Austria as the price for Habsburg support of its autonomy.[6] The Austro-Russian Treaty of San Stefano was revised to cede Bosnia and Herzegovina to the Habsburgs. The congress formalized Austrian occupation and administrative rights over the province, although the sultan continued to hold formal sovereign rights over Bosnia and Herzegovina until 1908. Despite the argument that many of the inhabitants of that territory were of Serbian nationality, Britain and France were determined to block Russian gains in the Balkans. Bosnian rebel leader Vaso Vidović's petition to the congress that Bosnia be united with Serbia or be granted autonomy within the Ottoman Empire was thus not even read to the delegates.[7]

Habsburg occupation of Bosnia and Herzegovina, touted as a provisional measure until order was restored, was actually intended to prevent Russia, through its South Slav allies Serbia and Montenegro, from acquiring too much influence in the Balkans. However, Dalmatia and its Bosnian hinterland were also economically useful to the monarchy, because Dalmatia's ports would ensure continuation of trade through the Adriatic. The fear that an unfriendly power could interrupt Habsburg commerce by establishing itself on the eastern side of the Adriatic was great enough that the imperial military exerted strong pressure to absorb Bosnia and Herzegovina outright to ensure Dalmatia of greater security.[8]

Bosnia was also valuable in and of itself because of its natural resources: deposits of gold, silver, lead, iron, coal, and iron ore; vast forests; and a large labor force. The labor force, however, suffered from desperate economic conditions before World War I.[9] The stirring of class consciousness during the early development of capitalism in the area was very slight, as befitted the limited industrial production that existed at the time. Nevertheless, even two decades before the actual Austro-Hungarian occupation of Bosnia and Herzegovina, the northeast portion of which formed a wedge into Hungarian-controlled Croatia, Austrian military and diplomatic circles were disposed to acquire the region.[10]

Resistance to Austro-Hungarian Occupation

Immediately prior to the Austro-Hungarian occupation of Bosnia and Herzegovina, the area suffered massive social conflict. There was a total breakdown of order, with various paramilitary groups harassing both each other and ethnic opponents.[11] Not surprisingly, then, at the beginning of the occupation, Bosnia and Herzegovina was an administrative nightmare.

The Habsburg army, under Croatian-born General Josef Philipović von Philippsberg, entered the province fully expecting only slight indigenous resistance to occupation. The feeling was that any recalcitrance would disappear quickly when the superior technological power of the Austrian army was demonstrated. This supposition persisted despite warnings of impending resistance delivered by Austria's Consul-General Wassich, who was based in Sarajevo.[12] The monarchy considered the Bosnians to be "an irrational, volatile people easily tamed by a display of superior firepower but subject to impulses of wild fanaticism."[13] Despite reports that the province was arming itself to repel the occupation troops, the Habsburgs insisted that the population was inferior. Vienna ignored the possibility of irregular warfare and proceeded with a conventional strategy designed to demonstrate overwhelming firepower.[14]

Vienna issued an imperial proclamation designed to reassure the Muslim inhabitants of equal protection under Habsburg law. An official letter to Philipović von Philippsberg in 1878 instructed that "besides the Catholic population attention needs to be directed also to the Muslim population and to give it special protection all the more since the Muslims not only have the largest land ownership but represent the relatively most progressive and most enlightened part of the population."[15]

Despite these overtures and negotiations, much of the Muslim population of Bosnia and Herzegovina was determined to resist occupation by the Christian Habsburgs.[16] The Ottomans aided local preparations for Muslim resistance, leaving approximately 40,000 Turkish troops in Bosnia and Herzegovina and shipping arms and ammunition for the resistance.[17] Thirty of the Turkish battalions were composed of Bosnian Muslims who would eagerly fight against a Christian occupation force.

Estimates of Habsburg troops used to subdue Bosnia range from 150,000 to almost 270,000.[18] The rebels consisted of a formidable but disorganized force of Bosnian Muslim volunteers and Bosnian Muslims from regular Ottoman army battalions, as well as members of former Ottoman gendarmerie units, brigands, and military deserters.[19]

The ferocity of the rebellion, which took the form of guerrilla resistance, necessitated direct Habsburg military governance of the provinces during the first years of occupation, although the worst of the fighting was over by the end of 1878.[20] Austria-Hungary was eventually able to eliminate paramilitary units and brigand bands that had operated with impunity in Ottoman times, although there were flare-ups of socially based (as opposed to ethnically based) conflict during Austro-Hungarian rule in Bosnia and Herzegovina.

In 1879 Austria-Hungary and the Ottoman Empire negotiated the Novi Pazar Convention, which laid out the legal status of Bosnia and Herzegovina and confirmed Ottoman sovereignty and the sultan's rights there as head of the Muslim community. Other important features of the treaty included Austria's recognition of the right of Turkish functionaries to continue in their posts—at least until the indigenous population could be adequately trained—the right of Bosnian Muslims to retain contact with Muslims in the Ottoman Empire and to continue to follow their own customs and traditions, and the continued circulation of Turkish currency in Bosnia. Furthermore, Austria promised that all revenues collected in Bosnia and Herzegovina would be used for provincial exigencies. Although Austria did not strictly follow these conventions, at least they gave a basis for appeal to the Austrian and Ottoman governments when they were violated.

Although Henry Gilfond characterized the Muslims as "quieted and pacified" after their failed resistance efforts, the Serbs and Croats did not peacefully acquiesce to Habsburg rule.[21] In 1881–1882, Serb inhabitants were particularly aroused to full-scale rebellion by the passage of a military law subjecting the entire population of Bosnia and Herzegovina to military obligations for the Habsburgs. Under Turkey, only Muslims had suffered such obligations. The Serb inhabitants feared they were to be mobilized for a war against Serbia and Montenegro. The Bosnian Muslims, too, objected to conscription. As Ottoman subjects (at least nominally, according to Ottoman-Habsburg agreement), the Bosnian Muslims did not want to serve in the military of a Christian state or to acknowledge in that symbolic way permanent Habsburg control over Bosnia.[22]

Only Bosnia's Croatian Roman Catholics welcomed the Habsburgs as liberators, claiming that Bosnia and Herzegovina belonged to Croatia, which at that time was also under Habsburg tutelage. They hoped Croat Catholics and Bosnian Muslims would work together for an anti-Serb policy in a greater Croatia (which would include Dalmatia, Croatia, Slavonia, and Bosnia). The fanatic anti-Austrian reception by the Bosnian Muslims squelched that Croat dream and, in fact, led to negotiations between Muslims and Serbs. The Orthodox Serb inhabitants of Bosnia and Herzegovina particularly wanted political union with Serbia or Montenegro. Their feeling was expressed by Veselin Masleša: "The influence of Serbia proceeds from the thesis that Bosnia is a Serbian land, and that is without discussion."[23]

Austro-Hungarian Administration of Bosnia and Herzegovina

Bosnia's vague legal status challenged Austria-Hungary's administrative expertise. To avoid controversy over the status of Bosnia and Herzegovina, the Joint Imperial Ministry of Finance administered the area, thus making it a crown possession and outside the responsibility of either Austria or Hungary.

The difficulty of obtaining funds from the Delegations (special parliamentary bodies authorized to consider matters concerning both the Austrian and Hungarian parts of the empire) to administer Bosnia and Herzegovina and to funnel Austro-Hungarian capital into the Balkans proved to be a mixed blessing. The lands of Bosnia and Herzegovina were intended to become a colony; however, the monarchy's treasury did not allow sufficient funds to carry out the plan, so Bosnia's administrators were forced to use ingenuity to acquire financial resources from other sources. They did not accept policy direction from the parliament; thus, the monarchy's government gave up its lever for control over administrative policies in Bosnia and Herzegovina. The bureaucrats rather than the politicians made policy in this region. Bureaucratic policy involved paying for military occupation of the area through maximum taxation of the Bosnian population.[24]

The occupation was widely considered to be the prelude to annexation. However, Austria first had to demonstrate its administrative capability to justify permanent control of Bosnia. Austrian officials endeavored to remove some of

the more arcane vestiges of Ottoman rule in Bosnia and Herzegovina by introducing a rational bureaucracy and an impartial judiciary. Baron Benjamin von
Kállay was appointed joint minister of finance in 1882 to bring civil order and
modernization to the area.

Some modernization of Bosnia and Herzegovina did occur under the Dual
monarchy.[25] Communications, transportation, and industry were upgraded,
although Kállay controlled the meager foreign investment that was permitted.[26]
Nevertheless, the results of Habsburg modernization policies were uneven. The
1910 Austrian census demonstrated that even after thirty years of Austrian occupation of Bosnia and Herzegovina, 87 percent of the population was still
engaged in agrarian pursuits for its livelihood.[27] In 1878, Bosnia and
Herzegovina contained six thousand to seven thousand *beys* and *agas* ruling
over approximately eighty-five thousand *kmets,* of which sixty thousand were
Orthodox, twenty-three thousand were Catholic, and two thousand were
Muslim. Nearly all of the almost seventy-seven thousand free peasants were
Muslim.[28] Constituting a little more than a third of the total Bosnian population
(as compared to the Orthodox with over 40 percent and Catholics with approximately 18 percent),[29] the Bosnian Muslims nevertheless accounted for a little
over 50 percent of Bosnia's urban population. The Christians who lived in the
cities followed retail occupations or were artisans. The Catholics were not well
represented in urban occupations during the Austrian years.[30]

In their attempt to bring "rational administration" to Bosnia to replace what
they saw as the chaos and anarchy of the Ottoman era, Habsburg bureaucrats
were generally unpopular, and so Habsburg-connected Croats and other South
Slavs replaced some Ottoman functionaries. Turkish currency disappeared, and
Austrian usage replaced Turkish weights and measures and the postal and customs systems. Military conscription was also introduced. Bosnia and
Herzegovina thus became integrated into the Habsburg Empire to the extent
that Turkish sovereignty "extended little beyond the rights that Moslems possessed of murmuring the sultan's name in prayers and of flying the Ottoman flag
over mosques during prayer time."[31]

Many public matters, particularly the legal issues surrounding conversion,
that had been governed by Islamic law during Ottoman rule were now secular-
ized. Intent upon controlling the Bosnian situation as much as possible, by 1882
the emperor was able to establish agreements with the external supreme heads
of the three major religions in Bosnia that gave him the right to alter and appoint
the Bosnian religious elites.[32] These agreements effectively linked the indigenous hierarchies directly to the Habsburg emperor, who tried to treat the inhabitants not as individual nations but as "only Bosnian speaking Bosnians divided
into three religions enjoying equal rights."[33] However, complaints about Austro-
Hungarian social policy extended to the facts that many foreigners (rather than
indigenous inhabitants) were employed as civil servants in Bosnia and
Herzegovina and that members of the Roman Catholic population were favored

as employees.[34] Furthermore, Bosnian Muslims castigated the Roman Catholic Church for proselytizing, with governmental concurrence.[35]

Thus, political and legal privileges that had devolved only to Muslims when the area was under Ottoman rule were now to be shared by all. The making of the *hajj* (pilgrimage to Mecca) became difficult, and mosques were not always inviolate from state use.[36] Also, Bosnia had one school for each six thousand people, a woefully inadequate number.

The Austro-Hungarian presence eventually won grudging acquiescence from Muslim leaders in Bosnia and Herzegovina by ensuring that those leaders maintained their existing socioeconomic position and way of life, leading a commentator for *Moslem World* to retrospectively describe Habsburg policy as pro-Islamic. Muslims were permitted to retain both their lands and many of their special privileges, including approval of the Bosnian budget by civil and religious officials. *Vakuf* (religious-charitable) funds were not tampered with; nor were the schools.[37]

Although the Muslims acquired little political influence under Austro-Hungarian rule, they remained somewhat quiescent when it became evident that the introduction of Austrian capitalism would not radically alter feudal agrarian relations. The institution of serfdom was thus relatively unchanged, and, in fact, agrarian relations were still based on the Turkish Safer Decree of 1859.[38] Muslim landlords continued to receive their former incomes, and Austrian authorities assisted them in collecting overdue payments. In addition to feudal taxes, *kmets* were also forced to pay various state and local taxes.

Whereas Austria-Hungary did attempt to ease the onerous obligations of the *kmets* to their Muslim landlords by limiting taxes and regularizing their collection,[39] the Christian peasants were still disappointed with Habsburg rule. They had expected the monarchy to champion them over the Muslims through land reform. Although the monarchy encouraged Bosnian peasants to buy their land, agrarian reform plans were quashed, and Bosnian Muslim military officers continued to collect the taxes of those Christian *kmets* who could not afford to purchase their land. Habsburg policy thus ensured a continual flow of taxes without interruption of the structures that were in place.[40]

The disappointment was even greater for Bosnia's Christian peasants because Count Andrássy had promised the Congress of Berlin that he would solve the agrarian problem that had bedeviled the Ottoman Empire in general and Bosnia in particular. Nevertheless, it was in the interest of Austria-Hungary to perpetuate feudalism in Bosnia and Herzegovina so the area could be more easily exploited. The Habsburgs redirected the unhappiness Austrian occupation engendered in the Bosnian population into communal disagreements, especially as South Slav nationalist stirrings took on their own political dynamics. The South Slav discomfort caused by the maintenance of feudal social stratification diluted political activity against Habsburg administration of the area.[41]

In addition to "rational administration," a second prong of Austrian policy in Bosnia was to encourage unification of all Bosnians, no matter what their religion, so they would resist alternative nationalisms. The concept of *bošnjaštvo* (Bosnianism)—one indigenous people living in Bosnia—was officially popularized to supplant separate Serb, Croat, and Muslim nationalistic feelings within Bosnia and Herzegovina. Such Bosnian self-identification was meant to discourage any irredentist challenges on Bosnia and Herzegovina, mounted particularly by Serbia, and to counteract both Serb and Croat nationalistic activism. If the Bosnian Muslims accepted *bošnjaštvo,* Austrian officials believed there was a chance that Bosnian inhabitants of other religions would adopt this identity. To encourage the Muslim elite's acceptance of *bošnjaštvo,* therefore, the monarchy put the issue the elite wanted most to remain the same—that of agrarian relations—into abeyance.

Austrian officials were not averse to allowing Islamic cultural activism in order to pursue Habsburg divide-and-rule tactics. The monarchy hoped the state-supported Muslims could become a counterweight to Serbian nationalists by competing with them both economically and culturally, thereby reducing the political threat the Serbs posed. If the Bosnian Muslims could help to create a territory-based Bosnian "national identity," the Serbs and Croats would be unable to coalesce into a united national unit that included the Muslims, with irredentist aims that would threaten Austrian rule.

For the most part, Bosnian Serbs and Croats were unaffected by *bošnjaštvo,* but scholars differ over the Muslim response. Some claimed *bošnjaštvo* was opportunistically embraced by many Bosnian Muslim elites to avert Serb-Croat rivalry over Bosnia and Herzegovina.[42] However, it is doubtful that *bošnjaštvo* ever truly stirred the Bosnian Muslim community. In fact, Austrian intentions toward the Muslim community may have backfired, as many Muslim leaders increasingly turned instead to conservative Islam. Their religion-based coalescence began to give them a communal self-identification, which helped them to differentiate themselves from the Ottoman-ruled Muslims. Muslims who identified more with the Turks than with Bosnia emigrated to lands ruled by the Ottoman Empire, whereas those who remained under Austrian tutelage were more likely to unite with their fellow Muslims in an attempt to wrest whatever concessions they could from the Habsburgs to make life palatable in Bosnia and Herzegovina.

Thus, ironically, the Austro-Hungarian authorities stimulated a Bosnian feeling of distinctiveness with policies that in the middle to late nineteenth century inevitably encouraged religious differentiation to coincide with ethnic differentiation as nationalism spread to the Balkans. The process of the development of a Bosnian Muslim communal coalition, however, was slow. The aims of the Muslim aristocracy and the Muslim peasantry only gradually coalesced. The high economic status of the Muslim elite under the Ottomans had been essentially perpetuated under the Habsburgs, which secured Muslim elite allegiance to the establishment.[43] Continuing economic disparities ensured that initially the Muslim peasants had difficulty identifying common interests with the Muslim aristocracy. When their desires contradicted those of the Muslim landowners, the peasant interests were sacrificed. This urban-rural dichotomy, a result of Turkish influence in the Balkans, became a lasting and significant element of relations among the various Bosnian peoples.

It was only at the end of the nineteenth century, when an indigenous Bosnian Muslim intelligentsia developed, that the requisite coalition of Muslims from all over Bosnia and Herzegovina began to take shape. Living under a non-Muslim regime and struggling to maintain as many prerogatives as possible against Austro-Hungarian attempts to whittle away at their institutions, the Bosnian Muslims' feeling of distinctiveness and separation—perhaps even a nascent national feeling—grew, differentiating them from Bosnian Christians. Muslim elites engaged in political activity in Bosnia and Herzegovina, evolving into a movement for national liberation. However, the Muslim leaders of Sarajevo, the provincial capital of Bosnia and Herzegovina, maintained a fairly good relationship with the Austrian authorities. Initially, therefore, Sarajevo's Muslim leaders, who were largely landowners and were thus dependent on Austria-Hungary's agrarian policies, confined official protests to rather minor incidents of dissatisfaction.

Meetings were held to formulate petitions that would articulate the economic and religious grievances against Austria-Hungary from all of the regions of Bosnia and Herzegovina. For example, petitions were addressed by a group of Muslim leaders who wanted to protect their cultural institutions from the evils of urbanization. Petitions also dealt with such religious and cultural issues as the regulation of *vakuf* procedures and provision for schools and charitable funds for the underprivileged. Muslims sought to ensure that the Turkish language would continue to be used in the *shari'a* courts. A petition in 1881 by the Sarajevo Muslims protested the abolition of advisory councils through which the Muslim population had previously expressed grievances. They also complained about the "slowness, complexity, and costliness of court litigation under the Austrian regime" and charged that Muslims were insufficiently protected from street bandits.[44] The landlords protested that Austrian authorities were arbitrarily violating laws by not following Ottoman inheritance and land sale regulations, even though they had pledged to continue these practices under Habsburg rule.

Petitions from Travnik centered on alleged hostile treatment of Muslims by government officials. Muslims claimed these government officials made the practice of Islam difficult and that the Austrians allowed the Muslims to be subjected to too much Catholic propaganda. For example, Franciscans were actively attempting to Catholicize the Bosnian Muslims in the 1880s, often under the aegis of Ante Starčević's Croatian Party of Right.[45]

The Muslims from Mostar in Herzegovina, which included a higher proportion of merchants than the Sarajevo contingent,[46] were the first to organize for sustained political action. Mostar was thus considered "the birthplace of the

Muslim movement for cultural and religious autonomy."[47] The initial mobilizing impetus that led them to request greater political representation was an issue similar to others occurring throughout Bosnia and Herzegovina—the problem of conversion of Muslims to Catholicism. Muslims charged that in the absence of a coherent government policy on the subject of controversial religious conversions (the Habsburgs tended to allow adults to choose their own religion, but Muslims considered conversion from Islam to be apostasy), numerous instances of forcible conversion occurred. They claimed this was a result of attacks by the government, in league with Catholic clergy, against the integrity of Islam.

Thus, the questionable conversion in 1881 of Saja Čokić, a fifteen-year-old Muslim girl from a peasant village outside Mostar, engendered activity that was co-opted for political purposes by Mostar's Muslim landowning elites.   Despite the fact that this situation was likely a traditional bride theft,[48] which was practiced interdenominationally within Bosnia, latent anti-Catholic and anti-Austrian feelings filtered to the surface in response to conversion crises such as this. Muslim elites often converted the outrage engendered on the religious plane into protests concerning a wide range of alleged Austrian administrative ill-treatment, particularly regarding religious and cultural autonomy. With Austria-Hungary's rejection of many reform proposals, the bickering among the various Muslim factions was stilled and was replaced by a new, comprehensive Muslim political program that reflected an expanded, increasingly activist constituency. Additional conflicts over conversions of Muslims, particularly by Catholics, increased the level and intensity of activism.[49]

A twelve-member committee of Bosnian Muslim representatives, with two delegates from each region of Bosnia and Herzegovina, convened in August 1900 to draft additional demands. The resulting document contained the seeds of what became the Bosnian Muslim political program throughout the remaining pre–World War I years. The process of developing the petition was an early attempt to create a united front of all Bosnian Muslims and to reconcile differences based on property interests, degree of religious orthodoxy, and other points of contention within the Muslim community.

The Bosnian Muslims complained of noticeable Habsburg neglect and harassment of those who practiced Islam in Bosnia and Herzegovina. Governmental tolerance and even encouragement of aggressive Catholic proselytism; misuse and neglect of Islamic mosques, graveyards, and schools; the absence of truly independent Islamic institutions to administer Muslim affairs; and the lack of genuine religious, educational, and cultural autonomy were cited as the major objections to Austria-Hungary's rule. Expansion of property rights for landlords was also mentioned, but it was not a prominent issue in the 1900 petition. Such agrarian issues emerged later when the Muslim landlords enlarged their role in the movement for Muslim autonomy.

Bosnian Muslim protests and resultant activism against Austrian rule gradually increased, even though the Muslim community remained somewhat disunited about its ultimate goals, reflecting divisions between Muslim elites and intellectuals. Some activists believed the Bosnian Muslims lacked a requisite economic vigor because of their failure to deal with the realities of Austrian occupation. Others demanded a new attitude toward education, since Muslims could not hope to compete with other ethnic groups if they denied their children the education that could be received in either public or Islamic schools. Some promoted cultural consciousness in an attempt to thwart anti-Islamic propaganda aimed at the Muslim youth. Finally, many feared the Muslims in Bosnia and Herzegovina would lose their feeling of communal distinctiveness when faced with rising Serb and Croat nationalist movements.

The latter group of Muslims realized that both the Serbs and the Croats in Austria-Hungary were experiencing a renaissance of economic and cultural vitality. Serbian propaganda attempted to inflame Bosnia's latent anti-Austrian sentiments. Serbophiles within Bosnia and Herzegovina, such as the influential Bosnian Muslim landlord Šerif Arnautović, aided Serbian agitators who were touring Bosnia to advance the goal of Serbian annexation.[50]

Meanwhile, the Croats pursued nationalistic dreams of autonomy within Austria-Hungary that rejected Serbian aspirations for South Slav union. Ante Starčević's popular Party of Right favored the creation of a greater Croatia including Bosnia and Herzegovina. Starčević's integral Croatianism denied the uniqueness of the Serbian nation and considered it part of the Croat nation.

However, for many Croats Starčević's doctrine was superseded by Roman Catholic Bishop Josip Juraj Strossmayer's conception of an all-inclusive Yugoslavism. Under Strossmayer's influence, therefore, some Croats and Serbs began to think seriously of uniting to wrest from Austria-Hungary lands that were inhabited largely by South Slavs. They hoped to acquire the support of Muslim intellectuals so that by common action with the Muslims, the South Slavs could ultimately achieve autonomy from Austria-Hungary. The newly independent Serbian kingdom was an enticing model.

Serb-Croat unity in the anti-Habsburg cause was temporarily frustrated in the 1890s as relations deteriorated over national claims to Bosnia and Herzegovina. Blood was spilled in Zagreb and other cities, and some people demanded "a war of extermination between the two South Slav peoples."[51] In 1902, some Serbs publicly began to question the legitimacy of a separate Croat nation, which, of course, encouraged anti-Serbian feelings among Croats.[52] The Serbs and Croats each sought to increase their power relative to Austria-Hungary by attaining majority status in Bosnia and Herzegovina. Thus, each needed the Muslims in order to become the majority nationality there.

Initially, Serb and Croat politicians had been tempted to ignore the usefulness of the Muslims, considering them a minority that wielded little influence with the ruling Habsburgs. However, the Serbs—who constituted almost 44 percent of the population of Bosnia and Herzegovina—feared an alliance between the Bosnian Muslims, who represented 32 percent of the population, and the Croats with 23 percent. Such an alliance could have impeded the formation of a greater Serbia, to include Bosnia and Herzegovina. The Croat population in Bosnia and

Herzegovina similarly desired Muslim support, in part because of the numbers the Muslims could bring to the Croat side and also perhaps to serve as a buffer between Croatia and the Serbian state.

Thus, both Croatian and Serbian nationalists tried to co-opt the Bosnian Muslims, aggressively attempting to influence the Muslim population to declare itself a part of the Croatian or the Serbian nation, respectively. A wholesale declaration of Serbianism or Croatianism by the Bosnian Muslims would have given that national group a majority in parliament and thus control over Bosnia and Herzegovina. Serb and Croat politicians throughout the Austro-Hungarian and the succeeding royalist and Communist periods similarly tried to achieve this goal and also failed.

Some well-known Muslims, attracted by the military and political success of the independent Serb state, did declare themselves "Serbs of the Muslim faith."[53] Other Muslims were more culturally attuned to Croatia because of their pre-1900 education in the Serbo-Croatian language in Croat state-sponsored schools and identified themselves as "Croats of the Muslim faith."[54] Nevertheless, whereas the majority of declaring Muslims eschewed the anti-Turkish and anti-Islamic orientation of Serb nationalists and followed the Croatian political orientation, which was more complimentary to Muslims,[55] on the whole very few common Bosnian Muslims and relatively few Muslim intellectuals actually declared themselves to be Serbs or Croats, remaining singularly unattracted to the national movements of either group. By continuing to denigrate the Ottoman period, the Serbs were also demeaning the Bosnian Muslims' acceptance of Islam and the entire Ottoman period of their history. Not surprisingly, this evoked little enthusiasm for the principles of the Serb national movement within the Bosnian Muslim population. Croat nationalism, however, was Turcophile and admired the Muslims as good Croats. Many Croats also strongly favored religious pluralism, whereas Serbs thought of the Muslims as fallen followers of the Orthodox religion. Yet although Muslim historical conflicts with Croats were far older and less vividly remembered than those with Serbs,[56] the strong current of "clericalist Croatianism"—which precluded separation of the terms *Croat* and *Catholic*—promoted by Jesuit Archbishop Josip Stadler of Sarajevo, soured many Muslims on the Croatian national movement.[57]

Those Bosnian Muslims who assumed a Croat or a Serb identification did so for practical or political purposes, but they did not discard their Muslim confessional identification or communal membership.[58] National identification in this area of the world escapes the religious factor only with great difficulty. Most Muslims, therefore, did not feel comfortable claiming a national identity that was tied so closely to a church of which they were not members. Thus, whereas many Bosnian Muslims did not acknowledge a Muslim national identity during the Austro-Hungarian period, their communal feeling based on their religious identification allowed them to resist nationalist pressures for self-identification as Serbs or Croats. The nascent socialist movement in Bosnia and Herzegovina was also relatively unsuccessful in attracting Muslim participation in the early twentieth century,[59] a further indication of the lack of interest within the Bosnian Muslim masses toward any noncommunal identity.

Bosnian Muslim loyalty to the monarchy had continued to be divided, because the Austro-Hungarian government was not prepared to grant the Bosnian Muslims the wide confessional and educational autonomy that would have more effectively countered Serb and Croat blandishments. Thus, under the monarchy, Bosnian Muslims had been split in their loyalties between the conservative Austrophile Muslims (called *prdekteri* by native Serbs), who supported the Dual monarchy, and the Muslims who admired the Serb struggle against Austria-Hungary. The *prdekteri* orientation was represented by the literary periodical *Behar* (Blossom), whereas the pro-Serbian orientation was represented by its rival, *Gajret* (Endeavor). The pro-Serbian Muslims, who opposed the divide-and-rule tactics used by the Austro-Hungarians to keep their national minorities in line, were victimized by the *prdekteri*, who were able to persecute with some impunity those Muslims who supported *Gajret*'s views.[60]

Kállay attempted to isolate the Bosnian Muslims from events and trends occurring in other Muslim areas, such as the Ottoman Empire, thereby forestalling any formal or legal links between the Bosnian Muslims and any of the important Islamic leaders outside of Bosnia. This, of course, was contrary to previous agreements between the Ottoman sultan and the Austrian emperor. But Kállay was determined to avoid activities conducive to Muslims in Bosnia considering themselves a nation, as did the Serbs or the Croats.[61]

Kállay also wanted to insulate the Bosnian Muslims from the nationalistic rumblings of the other South Slav lands. At first, he was able to capitalize on dissension among the Bosnian Muslim leaders in the major cities—who, as stated earlier, had their own agendas—to avert serious threats to Austrian control over Bosnia. In the end, however, he did not succeed in isolating Bosnia and Herzegovina from either the autonomy movements or the acquisitiveness of the other South Slav ethnic groups.

In Serbia in 1903, the Austrophile Obrenović dynasty was replaced by the pro-Russian Karadjordjević house. This dynasty, in furtherance of its own ends to reconstruct a greater Serbia, co-opted a version of the concept of Yugoslavism as a political program by which to achieve its goal of becoming a center for the cultural and intellectual activities of all the South Slavs,[62] still a distant dream because of Russian recognition of Austria's occupation of Bosnia and Herzegovina in 1878. Meanwhile, a Croatian party centered in Zagreb encouraged Archduke Franz Ferdinand, when he ascended the Habsburg throne, to consider introducing *trialism*, with South Slav areas—especially including Croatia—becoming the third, purely Roman Catholic Slav state in the monarchy. This third unit would also include Bosnia, which some Croats claimed had been part of the medieval Croatian state.

Despite the separate intrigues regarding the acquisition of Bosnia and Herzegovina, nationalistic Serbs, Croats, and Muslims in that province increased their mutual contacts. Cultural differences between Bosnian Muslims and

Christians had widened as the Christians began to accept some elements of Western European culture. Furthermore, the Christian tendency to consider all Bosnian Muslims as representatives of the Ottoman system without discriminating between peasants and landlords gave the Bosnian Muslims impetus for considering themselves a group apart. At the same time, attitudes within the Ottoman Empire—which later culminated in the reforms of Kemal Atatürk in Turkey—increased cultural differences between the Turks and the Bosnian Muslims.[63] In the end, the Bosnian Muslims and the Christians realized that they shared some common goals, such as wanting religious and educational autonomy.[64] A short time later, some Serbs, Croats, and Muslims comprehended that they shared another mutual aspiration—the establishment of a common South Slav state.

Reflecting the tensions within Bosnia and Herzegovina among the various religious/national groupings, communal conflicts in Bosnia were concerned with the autonomy of the Islamic and Orthodox religious organizations. Catholic autonomy was not at issue, because Catholicism retained a privileged status in the Austro-Hungarian Empire, although William Miller observed attempts by Austro-Hungarian authorities to appear evenhanded in their religious policy.[65] In the political skirmishes to achieve some degree of ecclesiastical autonomy, the Serb and Muslim populations provided mutual support.[66] Incidents of political cooperation between the Muslim and Orthodox populations, however, did not preclude religious tensions between the two communities. The most volatile issue was conversion, which the Habsburg administration eventually regulated through statute, thus averting violent conflicts. Instead, potential communal confrontation was redirected into political protests to the authorities. The frequency of such incidents eventually necessitated the establishment of genuine political organizations to represent the interests of each major religious group.

When Kállay died in 1903, his successor, diplomat István Freiherr Burián von Rajecz (joint finance minister from 1903–1912 and 1916–1918), abandoned Kállay's policies, which had expressed an aversion to indigenous political activity, and inaugurated a more liberal policy. Rajecz considered that the continued absence of Serb and Muslim religious and political autonomy could only worsen the confrontational political mood. The Habsburg regime hoped to encourage the development of moderate political parties that could be manipulated to sympathize with the monarchy's interests. It was hoped that the existence of legitimate parties would undercut the appeal of the genuinely subversive forces existing in neighboring countries that actively threatened the well-being of the empire through terrorism and conspiracy. The security forces would then be free to concentrate on the destruction of these illegal groups.[67]

The result of the new tolerance of political activism in Bosnia was the creation of a rash of ethnically based parties. The *Srpska narodna organizacija* (Serbian National Organization [SNO]), created in 1907, completed the union in the minds of many Christians of Orthodoxy and Serbism. Influenced by nationalists in independent Serbia, the SNO intensified its nationalistic program by claiming Bosnia and Herzegovina as Serbian land and Bosnian Muslims as Serbs who had converted to Islam.[68] To ingratiate themselves with the numerous Bosnian Muslims, without whom they could not dominate Bosnia, Serb politicians were careful to avoid demanding agrarian reform, which would have helped Serb peasants, and instead successfully sought common political ground with the Bosnian Muslim landlords.

Bosnian Catholics were mobilized into two factions: the religiously oriented *Hrvatska katolička udruga* (Croatian Catholic Association [CCA]) and the nationalist *Hrvatska narodna zajednica* (Croatian National Society [CNS]). The party program of the CNS paralleled the Bosnian Serb political program in many ways, claiming that Bosnia and Herzegovina should be unified with Croatia since Bosnia's Muslims were, in fact, Islamic Croats. The Bosnian Croats also sought support for their programs from Bosnian Muslim landlords, albeit less successfully than did the Serbs, and also did not press for agrarian reform to benefit the Christian peasants.

Bosnian Muslim political activism followed a different path from that of the Serbs and the Croats. Muslim struggles for religious autonomy had already attained some degree of political mobilization, and soon after Kállay's death—at least by 1906—the leadership of the Bosnian Muslim autonomy movement was clearly in the hands of the landlords. As they continued to do until the early 1990s, the Bosnian Muslim politicians attempted to participate in stable political coalitions that would protect a multinational environment to counter centrifugal nationalist forces. Inevitably, in such a climate secular interests took precedence over religious interests, a characteristic pattern for Bosnian Muslim politicians that continued until the collapse of post–World War II Yugoslavia in 1992. Whereas these politicians continued to pursue their own class interests, they were also careful to press for cultural, religious, and educational autonomy.

The autonomy movement sought two objectives, which met the Bosnian Muslim needs in general and the Bosnian Muslim elites' needs in particular. First, since the sultan was still considered the head of the Muslim religion, recognition of Muslim autonomy implied that the Habsburg monarchy recognized at least some limited sovereignty by the sultan over Bosnia. Second, autonomy would further legitimate the rule of *shari'a* (Islamic) law in Bosnia. The Muslim landlords intended to appeal to these laws when demanding expanded property rights. [69]

Austria met the Bosnian Muslim demands by pursuing an ethno-religious policy in Bosnia that was meant to limit deleterious political activism. In attempting to frustrate the rising tide of South Slav nationalism, Austria subsidized and actively encouraged religious institutions. The Islamic community created a special challenge for Habsburg policy that was absent in the Catholic and Orthodox religious communities because of the fuzzy line that exists in

Islam between political and religious affairs. The sultan, as head of the Islamic religious community, was also the head of state; any Austrian attempt to change the religious hierarchy in Bosnia was thus an attack on the legal status of Bosnia, which was still de jure, if not de facto, considered part of the Ottoman Empire. Such an attempt would also violate the 1879 Habsburg-Ottoman Novi Pazar Convention, which confirmed Ottoman sovereignty over Bosnia and promised to respect certain Islamic practices, as well as the old social order practiced during the Ottoman period in Bosnia and Herzegovina.

Despite these constraints, after years of negotiations with the Bosnian Muslims over autonomy measures that started under Kállay, the new office of *Reis-ul-ulema* (supreme leader of the Muslim religious community) was created in 1909. This leader of the Muslim community was to be selected by the Habsburg emperor from among candidates chosen by a Muslim nominating body. When the nomination was approved in Istanbul, the process was complete.[70] Under salary to the Habsburg administration, the *Reis-ul-ulema* assumed responsibility for administering in Bosnia the parts of Islamic law that were not inimical to Austrian administrative procedures, protecting *vakuf* administration by Muslim administrators, and advancing Muslim religious and cultural associations in Bosnia and Herzegovina.

To better mobilize and articulate the demands of the Muslim community in Bosnia, the leaders of the autonomy movement formed a political party called the Muslim National Organization (*Muslimanska narodna organizacija* [MNO]) on 4 December 1906.[71] The MNO was to carry on the work of pursuing cultural, educational, and religious autonomy, which represented the aspirations of all Muslims in Bosnia and Herzegovina; but the elites also insisted on achieving their own agrarian goals. Thus, the landowning class protested the 1906 agrarian reforms in Bosnia and Herzegovina, which were very promising for the peasants. The paradox of the situation is clear: The Bosnian Muslim landlords committed the MNO to opposing agrarian reform, which concomitantly delayed solution of the problem of peasant-landlord relations—the problem that greatly undermined cohesion among Bosnian Muslims. MNO leaders easily found the necessary allies and coalitions to prevent land reform: They made common cause with wealthier Serb peasants, who in 1910 composed 6.5 percent of the landlords in Bosnia and Herzegovina,[72] as well as with middle-class Catholics.

The earliest Muslim political party was thus controlled by those who deemed class interests, rather than solely communal interests, to be paramount. Nevertheless, the MNO was widely considered an ethnically based party similar to those created by Bosnian Serbs and Croats. Yet there was a difference. The Serb, Croat, and Muslim parties were significant in the battle for South Slav self-determination in that they were among the first broad-based Bosnian groups to take a provincewide, rather than just a local, view of political crises;[73] however, the Bosnian Muslims lacked the nationalistic outlook encouraged by an autonomous or even a semiautonomous neighboring political entity. Instead, the Bosnian Muslims were courted by Serbs and Croats, who considered them at best an ambiguous national group.

Habsburg Annexation of Bosnia and Herzegovina

The Habsburg occupation of Bosnia and Herzegovina in 1878 had caused widespread social turmoil, especially among the Bosnian Muslims and Serbs. However, the announcement of the outright annexation of the provinces on 7 October 1908 was widely deemed by some to be a diplomatic crisis of epic proportions. Whereas the annexation was merely the de jure recognition of a de facto situation, the actual unilateral announcement of annexation was in fact a formal contravention of the Treaty of Berlin.

The Habsburgs used their obvious success in raising the economic and cultural standards of the population at large in Bosnia and Herzegovina to justify turning their ostensibly temporary occupation into permanent annexation. But the reasons for the change in the legal status of Bosnia and Herzegovina had to do less with domestic Bosnian successes than with external events. Paramount among these was Serbia's increasing economic independence from Austria-Hungary and the ever more blatant expressions of Serbian nationalism, which were infecting Austria-Hungary's Serbian inhabitants. Austria-Hungary was concerned about Serbia's effect on the Orthodox inhabitants of Bosnia and Herzegovina. This fear, coupled with the change of regime in Turkey in 1908, in which the old Ottoman administration was replaced with a more democratic and dynamic regime that might have demanded the return of Bosnia and Herzegovina, convinced the monarchy to legalize its possession of Bosnia and Herzegovina through outright annexation.

Among the South Slav peoples in Austria-Hungary, reaction to annexation was mixed. Some Yugoslav-minded Croats saw annexation as the opening move toward an independent state combining all South Slavs. Other Croat and Slovene politicians joyfully anticipated that annexation of Bosnia and Herzegovina was merely the prelude to the creation of a Roman Catholic South Slav unit within the Dual monarchy, with a status equal to that of Austria and Hungary (the aforementioned trialism). Nationalistic Croats thought that with Bosnia and Herzegovina under direct Habsburg control, they had a better chance to assert their claims to these provinces than they would have had if the territories had remained part of the Ottoman Empire or had become part of Serbia. Some Croats who were unenthusiastic about either trialism or federalism sought instead to pursue a course of union with Serbia, since Hungary's policies of Magyarizing its minority groups only encouraged Croat enmity.

Hungary, however, opposed any kind of Croatian union with Bosnia and Herzegovina. The Magyars feared such union would indeed precipitate trialism, which would proportionately dilute Hungary's power in the monarchy. Relations between Croats and Magyars subsequently deteriorated further over this issue.[74]

Serbia reacted violently to the annexation, which had suddenly caused over 1 million Serbs to become Habsburg subjects. Serbia and Montenegro believed their claim to Bosnia and Herzegovina was more legitimate than that of Austria-Hungary, since Bosnians who considered themselves South Slavs and Serb Orthodox inhabitants formed at least a plurality there. Serbia intended to play on an ethnic affinity with the inhabitants of Bosnia and Herzegovina to acquire at least part of that territory and thus an outlet to the coast.[75] As long as the provinces were administered by the Ottoman Empire, there seemed to be a chance that they could one day be part of Serbia. With the annexation by Austria-Hungary, however, Serbs knew Bosnia was lost to them, and Belgrade was angry—angry enough to underwrite the aforementioned agitators who crossed into Bosnia and Herzegovina from Serbia to incite the South Slavs against Habsburg rule.

Austria-Hungary did not take the Serb reaction lightly, having decided that if Serbia caused untoward trouble over Bosnia, "the kingdom would be sponged off the map."[76] Conversely, certain influential circles within the monarchy had hoped to set up such a strong attraction within the Austro-Hungarian Empire that a centripetal force would be created that would draw all South Slavs to desire incorporation into Austria-Hungary, including even the Serbs.[77] A 1906 memorandum to Emperor Franz Joseph from General Franz Conrad von Hötzendorf, chief of the general staff, expressed his belief that

> The future of the monarchy is to be sought in the Balkans, that moreover the occupation of Serbia and Montenegro must ensue—first of all, to ensure to the monarchy decisive influence in the Balkans; secondly, however, to prevent a sovereign Serbia from becoming a dangerous enemy and a point of attraction for the South Slav territories of the monarchy.[78]

To this end the general, supported by certain influential German circles, favored an expansionist policy and, in particular, a preemptive strike against Serbia to solve the South Slav problem in the monarchy.[79]

As was the case during the early stages of occupation, the Bosnian Muslims initially shared with the Serbs a violent opposition to annexation and were disillusioned by Austria's precipitous announcement of its intent to do so. Whereas the other nationalities in Bosnia and Herzegovina had looked to Serbia, Montenegro, and Russia for backing, the Muslims had depended on their relationship with the Ottoman Turks—a false hope, as it turned out.[80] Without Ottoman intervention the Bosnian Muslims, long used to being the rulers of their area, had been forced permanently into a more subservient role under Austria-Hungary.

Bosnian Muslim feelings toward the Ottoman Empire cooled measurably. The former closeness of Muslims of whatever class or place of origin on the basis of their shared religion now took on public overtones of separatism, because the Bosnian Muslims felt the Ottoman Empire had betrayed their homeland. This was reflected in the way Bosnian Muslim intellectuals referred to themselves and their fellow Muslim citizens. Rather than continuing to use the term *Turčin*, they began to refer to themselves as *Muslimani* (Muslims).[81]

Muslim identity was not easy for the Bosnian Muslims to subordinate, however. They had been willing participants on the side of Turkey in at least 132 military conflicts against Habsburg armies containing soldiers who were Croats, Montenegrins, Serbs, and Slovenes. This could only encourage a feeling of Bosnian Muslim distinctiveness from the rest of the South Slavic peoples. The Christian peasants, moreover, hated the local Muslim landowners because of their exploitative practices and because they represented whichever empire currently dominated at the local level. The seeds of change that undermined this religion-based resentment were planted only during the rise of the national liberation movements; it never truly disappeared, as seen in the contemporary resentment of many Serbs—and Croats—of the Bosnian Muslims.

Bosnian Muslim Gains from Annexation

Initially, the Bosnian Muslims were adamantly opposed to annexation. However, as some Bosnian Muslim elites began to benefit from the formal annexation by the Habsburgs, they changed their stance. For example, the Bosnian Muslim community welcomed the imperial statute of 15 April 1909, which granted autonomy to the Islamic community in religious, educational, and *vakuf* affairs.[82] The statute was negotiated largely through the MNO as the legitimate representative of the Bosnian Muslims. Annexation of Bosnia and Herzegovina mooted the problem of Ottoman sovereignty over the area and removed the main stumbling block in the negotiations for religious and cultural autonomy. The 1909 statute also derailed for a time the development of Yugoslav nationalism among the various ethnic political parties.

A second advantage to the Bosnian Muslims as a result of Habsburg annexation was the implementation in 1910 of a constitution for Bosnia and Herzegovina. The region was finally defined in terms of the remaining parts of the dominion, and its juridical position was no longer vague.

Bosnia and Herzegovina received a representative assembly (*Sabor*), with participation meted out according to the religious affiliation of constituents. Thus, reflecting their percentage of the population in Bosnia and Herzegovina, the Bosnian Muslims had twenty-four delegates in the 1910 *Sabor* (all MNO representatives) compared to thirty-one seats for the Orthodox (all SNO representatives) and sixteen seats for the Catholics (split between the CCA and the CNU [Croatian National Union]).[83] Each of the political parties representing the different religions was forced to pursue consensual tactics, because none had gained an absolute majority. The Habsburg administration encouraged this format, hoping pan-Slavic agitation and Serb nationalism would weaken as a consequence.

Disagreement over land tenure continued to be a major source of tension among and within the various ethnic communities, fractionalizing them and weakening their ability to cause difficulties for the Dual monarchy. The Serb and Croat middle classes favored the repeal of feudalism. The Serb peasants were also in favor of the total repeal of feudalism, but at the same time they felt victimized by the growing Serb middle class, which utilized its burgeoning economic power to charge them high interest rates on loans.[84] Muslim politicians naturally favored the status quo and felt vindicated when the monarchy decided to permit the continuation of feudal relations as represented by the Law on the Voluntary Purchase of *Kmets.*

The Muslim way of life was not tampered with nor even disturbed by the rationalistic policies of the Austrian administration. The continuation of feudal relations, the 1909 Autonomy Statute, and their representation in parliament cemented Muslim politicians' support of the Austro-Hungarian Empire. In fact, Austria-Hungary's Bosnian Muslims were once described as "the last bastion of *Kaisertreue*"[85] because they had become so supportive of Habsburg rule, particularly since annexation had terminated their ability to appeal to the sultan for redress.

Bosnian Serb politicians had refrained from demanding settlement of the agrarian issue as long as there was hope that Serbia might someday control Bosnia and Herzegovina. Austro-Hungarian annexation made this policy untenable, and Muslim support of Austria-Hungary hastened the disintegration of the alliance of interests of the Muslim and Serb politicians in Bosnia and Herzegovina. By 1911, the leadership of the MNO was collaborating in the *Sabor* with the middle-class Croat politicians, a union that put them in the parliamentary majority.[86] Neither of the coalitions the Muslim politicians entered into, however, was based on an acceptance of the Serb or Croat claims to right of possession or control of Bosnia and Herzegovina.

World War I

The assassination of Habsburg heir apparent Archduke Franz Ferdinand on 28 June 1914 by seventeen-year-old Gavrilo Princip—a tubercular Bosnian Serb expatriate studying in Belgrade—five other Bosnian Serbs, and Bosnian Muslim carpenter Mehmed Mehmedbašić [87] served as the pretext for World War I. These young men were a product of the turmoil that reflected Habsburg occupation and was fueled by the Balkan Wars of 1912–1913 throughout the area. Bordering Serbia and Montenegro, Bosnia and Herzegovina was a staging area for anti-Habsburg clashes, and the area was awash with outlaws, peasant rebels, and Serb agitators.

Princip's actions were the culmination of a long process of revolutionary awakening among the secondary-school youth who were impatient with the slow and gradualistic reforms promoted by their predecessors. Princip's group

Mlada Bosna (Young Bosnia) desired decisive action to liberate Bosnia and Herzegovina from Austro-Hungarian rule.[88] Some young Bosnians wanted to unite all of the South Slavs in a federal Yugoslavia; others favored reasserting Serbian territorial demands over that territory. Serb nationalists in particular feared that Franz Ferdinand would seek to fully incorporate Austria-Hungary's South Slav lands into the monarchy under the program of trialism, thus denying Serbia's territorial ambitions to incorporate all Serbs in an independent Serbian state.

Other Bosnians, however, did not share the aspirations of the Bosnian Serbs. They rejected attempts to implant Serbian national identity into the Bosnian Muslim population and would have preferred that Bosnia and Herzegovina remain under Habsburg rule as an autonomous entity. Many Catholic Bosnians also would have opted to remain in Austria-Hungary united with Bosnia and Herzegovina.[89] In fact, Robert Donia reported violent anti-Serb demonstrations in Sarajevo by Bosnian Muslims and Bosnian Catholics, and the Bosnian parliament passed a resolution denouncing the archduke's murder.[90]

The assassination of Franz Ferdinand had devastating consequences for the South Slav population. For Austria, backed by Germany, the assassination was the pretext it had long sought to check Serb pretensions to a larger role in the Balkans. Pan-Serbianism—the rise of which paralleled the blossoming of pan-Slavism in Russia—and the nationalistic foreign policy of Germany's Wilhelm II were troubling Austria-Hungary, particularly when Serbia's territories were enlarged after its victories over Turkey and Bulgaria. The Austrian annexation of Bosnia and Herzegovina, coupled with the previous economic assault of the customs war, was designed to stifle Serbia and its arrogation of the role of the South Slav Piedmont—a role encouraged by the nationalistic rumblings throughout the Balkans. The monarchy was thus disinclined to negotiate a reasonable settlement with Serbia, which, for its part, attempted to be as conciliatory as possible. Instead, taking advantage of its alliance with Germany and the other Central Powers, Austria-Hungary declared war against Serbia. The entangling alliances of the Central Powers versus the Entente (Great Britain, France, and Russia) propelled Europe into World War I.

World War I began in the Balkans, but that area became only a secondary operational theater. The fate of this limited area was tied to the outcome on the main battlefields in northern France and on the eastern front. The Balkan peoples were courted by both sides in the war for the added military strength they could provide. The loyalties of the different South Slav nations were variable, as the Slovenes, Croats, and Serbs of the Austro-Hungarian Empire were drafted to fight against the Serbs and the Allied side. (Croatian-born Josip Broz Tito, post–World War II Yugoslav president, fought for Austria-Hungary during World War I.) Much of the bargaining for Balkan support by both sides appeared to be with offers of land at the expense of Serbian interests. Bulgaria thus entered the war on the side of the Central Powers when it was promised large pieces of the soon-to-be-dismembered Serbia.[91] The Allies promised Dalmatia and Istria to Italy, which would have placed seven hundred thousand South Slavs under the rule of Rome and undercut the possible creation of a Yugoslav state.[92] This was, of course, inimical to Serbia's long-standing aim to unite with other South Slavs living outside the state by serving as the anchor for a strong and independent state. But the South Slav response to World War I did not bode well for the Yugoslavists. Serbs fought on both sides. Croats and Bosnian Muslims were found among Austro-Hungarian divisions, whereas even Bosnian troops of all religions fought on the Serbian side.

In fact, Bosnian Muslims were not united in their responses to the Balkan Wars and World War I. Some pro-Serbian Muslims joined the Serbian side to fight the Turks, volunteering "in the Serbian army on the Salonika front, in the Yugoslav division in Dobrudja, and in the army of Captain Pivko, which was organized in Italy."[93] But by and large,

> Traditional Serbian-Muslim antagonism was aggravated by the First Balkan War. The Muslims were aroused by such ugly scenes as the murder of their co-religionists by Montenegrins, the burning of their villages, forced conversion, and by the flight of the Muslims from the Sanjak of Novi Pazar to Bosnia at the end of 1912.[94]

Many Muslims supported the Austro-Hungarian monarchy simply because it had become an ally of Turkey. They believed the sultan and Franz Joseph had agreed that a victory of the Central Powers would mean that Bosnia and Herzegovina would again become part of the Ottoman Empire. To many Yugoslav Muslims in Bosnia and Herzegovina, therefore, World War I was a sacred war, and the Serbs were their enemy.[95]

Anti-Muslim depredations by the Christian peasants in Bosnia[96] sent many Muslims of fighting age to join local Croats in the Austrian-sponsored *Schutzkorps,* the auxiliary militia formed to hunt down and terrorize Serbian sympathizers. Some may have joined the *Schutzkorps* to avenge Serbian attacks on Muslims in 1914 in eastern Bosnia.[97] Other Bosnian Muslims were recruited into a special counterguerrilla force called the *Steifkorps,* which operated against the Serbian irregulars (*komitas*) who were crossing into Bosnia from Serbia.[98] Some Muslims dealt with their feeling of isolation from the rest of the Islamic world and their repugnance at the thought of living under a Christian ruler by returning to live in the Ottoman Empire. They thereby created large exile communities that were potential sources of support for the Muslims who remained under Austro-Hungarian rule. Meanwhile, pro-Croat Muslims, relatively inactive during World War I, maintained their Croatian orientation.[99] Thus, the Bosnian Muslims were active during World War I, but in keeping with their historical ambivalence, they did not unanimously support one side or the other in the conflict.

One month after World War I was declared, a group of scholars appointed to formulate Serbian war aims envisioned a Yugoslav state containing Serbia,

Croatia, Slovenia, Dalmatia, Macedonia, and Bosnia and Herzegovina (in which a large number of Serbs lived).[100] One of these scholars, Jovan Cvijić, published a brochure entitled "Unity and Psychological Types of the Dinaric South Slav,"[101] with the thesis that "due to its geographical position, as well as ethnic composition, Serbia was predestined to bind or link Western and Eastern Yugoslav lands and tribes." Cvijić also stated the belief that "despite cultural differences, an ethnic entity exists" among the South Slavs. Macedonia was the sticking point because "Macedonian-Slavs are, in regard to their nationality, an undefined ethnic group, placed between Serbs and Bulgars." It was thought, however, that "they would accept the nationality of that state which could absorb them for the longest period of time."[102]

These war aims, which in many ways paralleled the demands of the Yugoslav socialists,[103] were initially unacceptable to the Allies, who did not envision the utter destruction of Austria-Hungary as one of the results of World War I.[104] The Allies were willing only to promise Serbia the possession of Bosnia and Herzegovina and an outlet on the Adriatic.[105]

Croatian politicians and intellectuals from Dalmatia who were living in Western Europe represented another view of the post–World War I South Slav situation through the Yugoslav Committee based in London. Members of the committee initially included Frano Supilo, a leading Croatian politician in the Austro-Hungarian Empire; Ante Trumbić, leader of the Dalmatian Croats; and internationally recognized sculptor Ivan Mestrović. They favored the creation of a South Slavic state from the ruins of the old Habsburg monarchy.

The goals advanced by this committee—dismemberment of the Habsburg Empire and acquisition of territory on the Adriatic—paralleled some of the aims of Serbian Prime Minister Nikola Pašić.[106] Pašić decided to support the émigrés because through their contacts in Western Europe they could describe to the Allies the situation of the South Slavs under Austro-Hungarian rule and make the idea of a South Slav state palatable to the great powers.[107]

Some Bosnian politicians also began to discuss the place of the Bosnian Muslims in the post–World War I world. Some Bosnian Muslims wanted to apply the Wilsonian principle of national self-determination to themselves, and some considered useful a union with other South Slav peoples.[108] Others, however, preferred autonomy for Bosnia and Herzegovina within the monarchy. The president of the Bosnian *Sabor,* Safvet Bašagić, favored some type of union with Croatia under Austro-Hungarian aegis if Bosnia were not permitted to become completely autonomous. Well-known Muslim politician Šerif Arnautović sought to secure the autonomy of a Bosnia and Herzegovina united with Hungary, whereas the Bosnian Muslim spiritual leader *Reis-ul-ulema* Džemaluddin Čaušević favored full autonomy or even union with other South Slavs in their own state.

Bosnian Muslim discussions about their role and fortunes in the post–World War I world demonstrated an increasing political maturity. The experience under Austria-Hungary emphasized certain features of their community that continued to influence their subsequent political fortunes: the transformation of the Bosnian Muslims from ruling cadre in the Ottoman Empire to a position of less influence in Austria-Hungary, their attractiveness to Serbs and Croats who tried to commit them to a national identity few could embrace, and the absence of an ideological stand that encouraged a willingness to go along with the ruling government as long as its policies were not inimical to Bosnian Muslim interests.

South Slav unity was a victim of the Austrian occupation of Bosnia. Serbs, Croats, and Muslims became bitter rivals, a circumstance exacerbated by the Habsburg governors of Croatia and Bosnia. In fact, Austria-Hungary had no intention of permitting the South Slavs to unify into an autonomous unit. Count Andrássy indirectly expressed this sentiment in a speech to the Congress of Berlin:

> The Imperial and Royal Government had to pay close attention to the geographical situation in which Bosnia and Hercegovina would find themselves as the result of the territorial changes brought about by a new demarcation of Serbia and Montenegro. The effect of the closer proximity of the frontiers of the Principalities on the routes of communication with the Orient would be prejudicial to the commercial interests of the Monarchy.[109]

However, the Habsburg Empire was mortally wounded by its acquisition of Bosnia and Herzegovina. An additional 1.2 million South Slavs drastically disturbed the already precarious national balance within the Austro-Hungarian Empire. Furthermore, Austria and Hungary tried to protect their respective commercial interests as the exploitation of Bosnian natural resources and the industrialization of Bosnia and Herzegovina advanced. Hungary questioned Austria's claims to Bosnia and Herzegovina on the basis of Magyar sovereignty over parts of the two provinces during the Middle Ages. So important was the issue of the South Slavs that Archduke Franz Ferdinand may indeed have been seriously considering the adoption of trialism after his accession to the throne, creating a South Slav state unit in the monarchy alongside Hungary and Austria.[110] Instead, Austria-Hungary's collapse after World War I destroyed that option and gave the South Slavs an opportunity to fashion an independent state—the Kingdom of the Serbs, Croats, and Slovenes—which would provide a flimsy structure for uniting them during the interwar period.

NOTES

1. Stephen Burg, "The Political Integration of Yugoslavia's Muslims: Determinants of Success and Failure" (Pittsburgh: Carl Beck Papers in Russian and East European Studies, University of Pittsburgh, 1983), p. 7.

2. Austria-Hungary's commercial and political demands on Serbia were so unpopular and so onerous that Serbian ruler Prince Milan Obrenović had to conduct diplomacy and sign agreements with the Habsburgs without the knowledge or consent of his government.

Branimir M. Janković, *The Balkans in International Relations* (New York: St. Martin's Press, 1988), pp. 91–92. He virtually renounced Serbian claims to Bosnia and Herzegovina and promised to permit no Serbian intrigues against the Dual monarchy. In return, Austria-Hungary pledged to support the Obrenović dynasty and Prince Milan's proclamation of his kingship in Serbia. Charles Jelavich and Barbara Jelavich, *The Establishment of the Balkan National States, 1804–1920* (Seattle: University of Washington Press, 1977), p. 187.

3. Arthur J. May, *The Hapsburg Monarchy 1867–1914* (Cambridge: Harvard University Press, 1951), p. 120.

4. R. W. Seton-Watson chronicled Russian and Habsburg scheming toward this end in "Russian Commitments in the Bosnian Question and an Early Project of Annexation," *Slavonic Review* 8 (March 1930), pp. 578–588. See also Vladimir Dedijer, *The Road to Sarajevo* (New York: Simon and Schuster, 1966), pp. 54–63.

5. Boris Furlan, "The Nationality Problem in the Balkans," lecture delivered at the Hoover Institution, Stanford, California, 20 February 1943, p. 6.

6. May, *The Hapsburg Monarchy*, p. 132.

7. Dedijer, *The Road to Sarajevo*, p. 64.

8. May, *The Hapsburg Monarchy*, pp. 119–120.

9. Salim Ćerić cited Nedim Šarac, *Položaj radničke klase u Bosni i Hercegovini pod austrijskom okupacijom* (Belgrade: 1951), to the effect that the conditions for hired labor were so bad that a large mass protest meeting drew approximately five thousand people. *Ćerić, Muslimani srpskohrvatskog jezika* (Sarajevo: Svjetlost, 1968), p. 167 (note).

10. Robert J. Donia, *Islam Under the Double Eagle: The Muslims of Bosnia and Hercegovina, 1878–1914* (Boulder: East European Monographs, 1981), p. 8. To that end, special units of the Austro-Hungarian military were assigned to the Balkans. Dedijer, *The Road to Sarajevo*, p. 44. Austria even sent military observers masquerading as consular officials to note Turkish troop movements and locations before the Bosnian occupation. P. J. Crampton, "Reviews," *Slavonic and East European Review* 54 (October 1976), p. 615.

11. Three major types of paramilitary units roamed throughout Bosnia and Herzegovina at this time: "Serbian insurgents had organized 'Pandur' corps, militia-like organizations that fought during the uprisings of 1875–78. Moslem 'Zaptie' units, the gendarmerie of the Ottoman era, fought Christian rebels during the rebellion. Deserters from regular Turkish army units also wandered the countryside, looting and plundering." Robert J. Donia, "Imperial Occupation and Its Consequences: The Army and Politics in Bosnia and Herzegovina, 1878–1914," unpublished paper, Ohio State University, Lima (1979), p. 3. The situation prior to Austro-Hungarian occupation appears to have been rather similar to the disposition of forces in the earlier part of the contemporary battle within Bosnia.

12. Arthur J. Evans, "The Austrians in Bosnia," *Macmillan's Magazine* 38 (October 1878), p. 496.

13. Robert J. Donia, "The Battle for Bosnia: Habsburg Military Strategy in 1878," paper presented to the conference "Otpor austrougarskoj okupaciji 1878. godine u Bosni i Hercegovini," Sarajevo, October 1978, p. 3.

14. Evans, "The Austrians in Bosnia," p. 496. See ibid., pp. 7–18, for a description of the battle tactics and the results.

15. Cited in Enver Redžić, *Prilozi o nacionalnom pitanju* (Sarajevo: Svjetlost, 1963), p. 28.

16. See Donia, "Imperial Occupation and Its Consequences," p. 4, for a description of the difference in reactions by the Bosnian Muslim landowners and the lower- and middle-class Bosnian Muslims to the threat of Habsburg occupation. "Radical" lower-class

Muslims were able to overthrow the Ottoman government in Sarajevo—the day before Habsburg troops entered Bosnia.

17. Donia, "The Battle for Bosnia," p. 7. Evans reported that "battalions of Turkish regular troops were fighting in the ranks of the 'insurgents.'" "The Austrians in Bosnia," p. 497.

18. May suggested the lower figure in *The Hapsburg Monarchy*, p. 134. However, in 1913 Theodor von Sosnosky estimated that more than 268,000 imperial troops, led by at least 6,000 officers, were used in combat against the rebels in Bosnia and Herzegovina. *Die Balkanpolitik Osterreich-Ungarns seit 1866*, Vol. 1 (Stuttgart: Deutsche Verlags-Anstalt, 1913), p. 242.

19. Donia, "Imperial Occupation and Its Consequences," p. 6.

20. In a barbed response to U.S. military leaders who expressed reticence to undertake military measures against Bosnian Serbs in the 1990s, Donia and Fine pointed out that "the Austrian success [in pacifying Bosnia] in 1878 is an instructive case of a successful invasion and conquest by a determined foreign foe." Robert J. Donia and John V.A. Fine Jr., *Bosnia and Hercegovina: A Tradition Betrayed* (New York: Columbia University Press, 1994), p. 95.

21. Henry Gilfond, *The Black Hand at Sarajevo* (Indianapolis: Bobbs-Merrill, 1975), p. 46. Baron Emile de Laveleye drew a negative picture of life in Bosnia under Islam and suggested that everyone would be better off under Austria-Hungary in *The Balkan Peninsula* (London: Unwin, 1887), pp. 69–158.

22. Mark Pinson estimated that eight thousand Muslims emigrated to Turkey with the announcement of conscription. "The Muslims of Bosnia-Herzegovina Under Austro-Hungarian Rule, 1878–1918," in Mark Pinson, ed., *The Muslims of Bosnia-Herzegovina: Their Historic Development from the Middle Ages to the Dissolution of Yugoslavia* (Cambridge: Harvard University Press, 1994), p. 94.

23. Veselin Masleša, *Mlada Bosna* (Sarajevo: 1964), cited in Ćerić, *Muslimani srpskohrvatskog jezika*, p. 151.

24. John R. Lampe and Marvin R. Jackson, *Balkan Economic History, 1550–1950: From Imperial Borderlands to Developing Nations* (Bloomington: Indiana University Press, 1982), p. 284. Evidently, Austria-Hungary was at least partially successful in its attempt to draw Bosnia into the modern era, as evidenced by the paean to Kállay's administration of Bosnia in "Baron de Kállay's Achievement," *Spectator* 75 (5 October 1895), pp. 428–429.

25. Ćerić described the strides toward economic modernization made by Bosnia and Herzegovina under Austro-Hungarian tutelage in *Muslimani srpskohrvatskog jezika*, pp. 140–145.

26. Lampe and Jackson, *Balkan Economic History*, p. 307.

27. *Die Ergebnisse der Volkszählung in Bosnien und der Hercegovina vom 10. Oktober 1910* (Sarajevo: Landesdruckerei, 1912).

28. William Lockwood, "Living Legacy of the Ottoman Empire: The Serbo-Croatian Speaking Moslems of Bosnia-Hercegovina," in Abraham Ascher, Tibor Halasi-Kun, and Béla K. Király, eds., *The Mutual Effects of the Islamic and Judeo-Christian Worlds: The East European Pattern* (Brooklyn, N.Y.: Brooklyn College Press, 1978), p. 214. The 1910 Austrian census showed that Bosnia and Herzegovina was composed of 43.5 percent Serbs, 22.9 percent Croats, 32.3 percent Muslims, and 0.6 percent Jews.

29. Pinson, "The Muslims of Bosnia-Herzegovina," p. 93. Pinson also succinctly outlined the difficulty in obtaining firm population statistics for these years, as evidenced by the difference in figures presented by Ivo Banac, who estimated that in 1910 the Muslims com-

posed 32.25 percent of the population, compared with the Orthodox population's 43.49 percent and the Catholic population's 22.87 percent. Banac, *The National Question in Yugoslavia: Origins, History, Politics* (Ithaca: Cornell University Press, 1984), p. 361.

30. Robert J. Donia, "The Urban Sources of Political Success: The Case of the Bosnian Moslem Nobility, 1890–1910," University of Michigan, p. 7.

31. May, *The Hapsburg Monarchy*, pp. 135–136. According to Donia, even those modest rights were doubtful, because the Habsburgs refused to acknowledge even the sultan's limited autonomy over the Bosnian Muslims. *Islam Under the Double Eagle*, p. 161.

32. With the Roman Catholic Church in a privileged position within the Dual monarchy, the major force of this policy was directed at the Serb Orthodox Church. The Orthodox fought a "political war" in 1896 over the issue of autonomy for the Orthodox Church in Bosnia and Herzegovina. Ćerić, *Muslimani srpskohrvatskog jezika*, p. 163.

33. Robin Okey, "State, Church and Nation in the Serbo-Croat Speaking Lands of the Habsburg Monarchy, 1850–1914," in Donal A. Kerr, ed., *Religion, State and Ethnic Groups* (New York: New York University Press, 1992), p. 63. Okey went on to describe how Kállay's policy of religious equality was undermined by power exigencies that required that the Vatican be mollified even at the expense of the feelings of the more numerous Serbs and Muslims. "State, Church and Nation," pp. 64–65.

34. Dedijer, *The Road to Sarajevo*, p. 202.

35. Ibid., pp. 204–205.

36. Charles Jelavich, "Revolt in Bosnia-Hercegovina," *Slavonic Review* 31 (June 1953), p. 422. An observer of the Bosnian area during occupation contradicted reports of obstacles to the hajj, stating that Muslim state officials who left their posts to undertake the hajj did so knowing that their positions would still be available when they returned. W. Miller, "Bosnia Under the Austrians," *Gentleman's Magazine* 61 (October 1898), p. 344.

37. "Islam in Yugoslavia," *Moslem World* 28 (July 1938), p. 309. Modern education was essentially absent in Muslim areas because conservative Muslim leaders hoped to preserve the distinctively Muslim way of life of the Ottoman period. In fact, the education of Muslim women in Habsburg lands remained at its previously abysmal level until World War I at the specific request of Muslim religious and political elites. J. W. Wiles, "Moslem Women in Yugoslavia," *Moslem World* 18 (January 1928), p. 64. Donia, however, cited Sarajevo Muslims' protests concerning the location of a Muslim girls' school in the home of Catholics and their wish that the girls be sent instead to other, Islamic-run institutions. *Islam Under the Double Eagle*, p. 62. For statistics on Muslim religious school enrollments and graduation, see Ćerić, *Muslimani srpskohrvatskog jezika*, pp. 169–171.

38. See Ćerić, *Muslimani srpskohrvatskog jezika*, pp. 145–146, for a description of agrarian relations in Habsburg-administered Bosnia and Herzegovina.

39. For example, taxes to the state were now to be paid in cash rather than in kind, which permitted more accurate accounting and forestalled attempts by owners to cheat the peasants. Landlord claims against peasant harvests were regulated, in part by the creation of an official land registry and recognition of the right to appeal rulings if either side did not agree with the tax appraisal. Overall, however, these measures were minimal in relation to the large financial burdens the *kmets* continued to carry under Habsburg administration. Furthermore, the *kmets* were caught in a price scissors: The manufactured goods necessary for daily life became more expensive, whereas agricultural prices fell. A simultaneous population explosion in the villages only made matters worse.

40. Lampe and Jackson, *Balkan Economic History*, p. 285.

41. Dedijer, *The Road to Sarajevo*, p. 81.

42. See, for example, Banac, *The National Question in Yugoslavia*, p. 360.

43. Traian Stoianovich, "The Social Foundations of Balkan Politics, 1750–1941," in Charles Jelavich and Barbara Jelavich, eds., *The Balkans in Transition: Essays on the Development of Balkan Life and Politics Since the Eighteenth Century* (Berkeley: University of California Press, 1963), p. 314.

44. Donia, *Islam Under the Double Eagle*, pp. 46–47.

45. Pedro Ramet, *Nationalism and Federalism in Yugoslavia 1963–1983* (Bloomington: Indiana University Press, 1984), p. 30.

46. Pinson, "The Muslims of Bosnia-Herzegovina," p. 104.

47. Donia, *Islam Under the Double Eagle*, p. 90. However, the Mostar Muslims were inhibited by their parochialism: They were inordinately concerned about the Austrian tendency to ignore Herzegovina's historical separation from Bosnia. The Herzegovinian protestors thus may have early sacrificed recognition of their aims for autonomy through union with other dissatisfied Muslim groups by frittering away their attention on local problems. Donia, *Islam Under the Double Eagle*, p. 124.

48. Ibid., p. 93.

49. Donia and Fine, for example, described how the conversion of a Muslim girl to Catholicism in 1899 led to Muslim demands for greater educational and cultural autonomy. Donia and Fine, *Bosnia and Hercegovina*, p. 106.

50. May, *The Hapsburg Monarchy*, p. 409; Banac, *The National Question in Yugoslavia*, p. 361; and Donia, *Islam Under the Double Eagle*, p. 107.

51. Jelavich and Jelavich, *The Establishment of the Balkan National States*, p. 255.

52. Paul Garde, "Trois remarques sur la position française," *Le Monde*, (Paris), 18 August 1992, p. 4.

53. Donia, *Islam Under the Double Eagle*, p. 177. Wayne S. Vucinich stated that most Muslims who took sides were pro-Serb "because it was the Serbs who had led the fight against the common enemy, Austria-Hungary." "Yugoslavs of the Moslem Faith," in Robert J. Kerner, ed., *Yugoslavia* (Berkeley: University of California Press, 1947), pp. 267–270. See also his discussion of the genesis of the pro-Serb Muslim society *Gajret*, which became an instrument for the awakening of a nationalist spirit in many Bosnian Muslims. "Yugoslavs of the Moslem Faith," pp. 267–270.

54. Vucinich, "Yugoslavs of the Moslem Faith"; and Burg, "The Political Integration of Yugoslavia's Muslims," p. 11.

55. Fedor Ivan Cicak, "The Communist Party of Yugoslavia Between 1919–1934: An Analysis of Its Formative Process," Ph.D. dissertation, Indiana University (1965), p. 84.

56. Ćerić, *Muslimani srpskohrvatskog jezika*, p. 154.

57. Banac, *The National Question in Yugoslavia*, p. 365.

58. Donia, *Islam Under the Double Eagle*, p. 177.

59. Cicak, "The Communist Party of Yugoslavia Between 1919–1934," p. 86.

60. Vucinich, "Yugoslavs of the Moslem Faith," pp. 267–270.

61. Letter from Kutschera to Kállay, Sarajevo, 8 February 1901, cited in Ferdo Hauptmann, ed., *Borba muslimana Bosne and Hercegovine za vjersku vakufsko-mearifsku autonomiju* (Sarajevo: Arhiv SRBiH, 1967), p. 123.

62. Jelavich and Jelavich, *The Establishment of the Balkan National States*, p. 255. Jelavich and Jelavich also described the tensions in Serbia between those who wanted to achieve greater Serbia and those who supported the Yugoslav idea. *The Establishment of the Balkan National States*, p. 260.

63. For example, Atatürk banished the wearing of the fez in Turkey, a habit that continued in Bosnia.

64. Supporting this contention is the report by Massiau de Clerval, which emphasized that "the common consciousness which can unite those people [the Orthodox, the Catholics, and the Muslims] already exists and only needs to be developed; its indications can be perceived." Cited in Ibrahim Kemura, "Bosna i muslimani u očima jednog posmatrača iz sredine XIX stoljeća," *Glasnik Vrhovnog islamskog starješinstva u socijalističko republici Jugoslaviji* 32 (September–October 1969), p. 419.

65. William Miller, *Travels and Politics in the Near East* (London: Fisher Unwin, 1898), p. 91.

66. Ćerić, *Muslimani srpskohrvatskog jezika*, p. 163.

67. Donia, *Islam Under the Double Eagle*, p. 169.

68. Donia and Fine, *Bosnia and Hercegovina*, p. 102.

69. Donia, *Islam Under the Double Eagle*, p. 172.

70. Burg, "The Political Integration of Yugoslavia's Muslims," p. 10.

71. For a short review of other contemporary Muslim parties, see Atif Purivatra, *Jugoslavenska muslimanska organizacija u političkom životu Kraljevine Srba, Hrvata i Slovenaca* (Sarajevo: Svjetlost, 1974), pp. 20–21.

72. Christian peasants called these feudal lords and moneylenders *kmetoders,* "people who skin the *kmets.*" Ćerić cited Masleša's mention that Petar Kočić (an SNO leader) used the term *kmetoder* to include not only landowners but also the Orthodox middle class as a whole. Masleša, *Mlada Bosna,* cited in Ćerić, *Muslimani srpskohrvatskog jezika,* p. 165.

73. Donia, *Islam Under the Double Eagle*, p. 176.

74. In 1883, the Magyars became so incensed at Croatia's agitation over Bosnia that they abolished the *Nagodba,* the agreement between the Hungarians and Croats that gave the Croats a measure of self-government. Raymond Pearson, *National Minorities in Eastern Europe 1848–1945* (New York: St. Martin's Press, 1983), p. 55.

75. N. Forbes, A. J. Toynbee, D. Mitrany, and D. G. Hogarth, *The Balkans: A History of Bulgaria, Serbia, Greece, Rumania, Turkey* (Oxford: Clarendon Press, 1915), p. 143.

76. May, *The Hapsburg Monarchy,* p. 412.

77. Dedijer, *The Road to Sarajevo,* p. 153. See ibid., pp. 404–424, for a description of the diplomatic machinations of Count Alois Lexa von Aehrenthal, foreign minister of Austria-Hungary, who engineered the annexation. Dedijer detailed the international conditions in the early 1900s that facilitated the beginning of World War I and the importance of the Balkans as "a bridge between Europe, Asia and Africa" in these events. He also described the portents of the aftermath of the war, which inevitably led to World War II. *The Road to Sarajevo,* pp. 18–21.

78. Cited in Dedijer, *The Road to Sarajevo,* p. 144.

79. Ibid., p. 145.

80. Vucinich, "Yugoslavs of the Moslem Faith," p. 268. Austria-Hungary compensated Turkey for abandoning its rights in Bosnia and Herzegovina with $10 million, "nominally compensation for public lands in the lost province." May, *The Hapsburg Monarchy,* p. 420.

81. According to Burg, an additional motive for the altered terminology of self-identification was the fact that "under Austrian rule, to identify oneself as a 'Turk' was perceived by others—and especially by the authorities—as an indication of political opposition to Austrian sovereignty over the province." "The Political Integration of Yugoslavia's Muslims," p. 10.

82. See ibid., for the provisions of this statute.

83. See Donia and Fine, *Bosnia and Hercegovina,* pp. 102–109, for more on the South Slav parties and their programs and alignments during the Austro-Hungarian period.

84. Ćerić, *Muslimani srpskohrvatskog jezika,* p. 166.

85. George Schöpflin, "Nationality in the Fabric of Yugoslav Politics," *Survey* 25 (Summer 1980), p. 9.

86. Purivatra, *Jugoslavenska muslimanska organizacija,* p. 20.

87. See Henry Gilfond, *The Black Hand at Sarajevo,* and Dedijer, *The Road to Sarajevo,* for more on the student society *Mlada Bosna,* of which the assassins were members, and the Serbian Black Hand, which supported and trained the assassins.

88. For an analysis and description of the origins and ideological underpinnings of *Mlada Bosna,* see Wayne S. Vucinich, "Mlada Bosna and the First World War," in Robert A. Kann, Béla K. Király, and Paula S. Fichtner, eds., *The Habsburg Empire in World War I: Essays on the Intellectual, Military, Political and Economic Aspects of the Habsburg War Effort* (Boulder: East European Quarterly, 1977), pp. 45–70.

89. Ibid., p. 59.

90. Donia and Fine, *Bosnia and Hercegovina,* p. 116.

91. Jelavich and Jelavich, *The Establishment of the Balkan National States,* p. 290.

92. Ibid., p. 286.

93. Vucinich, "Yugoslavs of the Moslem Faith," p. 270.

94. Vucinich, "Mlada Bosna and the First World War," p. 59.

95. Vucinich, "Yugoslavs of the Moslem Faith," p. 270.

96. Banac concluded that the anti-Muslim violence of 1918–1919 may have had some class basis but eventually was directed against all classes of Muslims. *The National Question in Yugoslavia,* p. 368.

97. Ibid., p. 149. Banac cited the claim of *Jugoslavenska Muslimanska Organizacija* (JMO) activist Sakib Korkut that the *Schutzkorps* also contained some Serbs. Ibid., p. 367 (note).

98. Vucinich, "Mlada Bosna and the First World War," p. 68 (note).

99. Vucinich, "Yugoslavs of the Moslem Faith," pp. 267–270.

100. Jelavich and Jelavich, *The Establishment of the Balkan National States,* pp. 287–289.

101. Reprinted in *Govori i Rasprave* 2 (Belgrade: 1924).

102. Milorad Ekmečić, "Serbian War Aims," in Dimitrije Djordjević, ed., *The Creation of Yugoslavia 1914–1918* (Santa Barbara: Clio Books, 1980), pp. 21–22.

103. Delegates from the Socialist Parties of Croatia-Slavonia and Bosnia and Herzegovina produced a memorandum in mid-1917 that decried the Austro-Hungarian monarchy for denying Yugoslav self-determination and for its policies that kept the South Slavs poor, ignorant, and divided. See "Memorandum of the Socialist Parties of Bosnia and Herzegovina and of Croatia-Slavonia," in *Memorandum Addressed by the Jugoslav Socialists to the International Socialist Peace Conference in Stockholm* (London: Jugoslav Workmen's Association, 1917).

104. See Alex N. Dragnich, "The Serbian Government, the Army, and the Unification of Yugoslavs," in Dimitrije Djordjević, ed., *The Creation of Yugoslavia 1914–1918,* pp. 40–41, for the reactions of the various Allied states to the problem of the demise of Austria-Hungary. It must also be remembered that the Allies offered inducements to some states—particularly Italy, Romania, Greece, and Bulgaria—to enter the war. Some of that prize was to be Serbian land.

105. Jelavich and Jelavich, *The Establishment of the Balkan National States,* p. 289.

106. Gale Stokes, "The Role of the Yugoslav Committee in the Formation of Yugoslavia," in Djordjević, ed., *The Creation of Yugoslavia 1914–1918,* p. 53.

107. Dragnich, "The Serbian Government," p. 42.

108. Purivatra, *Jugoslavenska muslimanska organizacija,* pp. 23–24.

109. Cited in Dedijer, *The Road to Sarajevo,* p. 58.

110. For more on Archduke Franz Ferdinand's philosophy on ruling the monarchy, see ibid., pp. 118–141.

4

Bosnian Muslims in the Kingdom of the Serbs, Croats, and Slovenes

"A state without social justice is a frame without a picture; a state without justice for its nationalities is a vase without flowers."

—Stjepan Radić[1]

World War I dramatically changed the European landscape, particularly for the South Slavs, who finally gained their own state. However, great power machinations, as well as unresolved tensions from previous historical periods, ensured that the national groups inhabiting the newly constituted South Slav state would not coexist peacefully. Furthermore, the Bosnian Muslims, whose sympathies had largely been with the losing side in World War I, found themselves part of a state ruled by one of the victors of that war. Nevertheless, the Bosnian Muslims, still courted by both Serbs and Croats for their loyalty and national self-identification, were able to convert this interest into a political asset and experience relative political legitimacy within the structure of a South Slav state.

Post–World War I Europe

The 1919–1920 Paris Peace Conference officially ended World War I and established the basis for European political relations during the interwar period. The three great anachronistic autocratic powers that had dominated Eastern Europe for centuries had been eliminated: The Ottoman Empire was reconstituted in 1923 in the form of the Turkish Republic; the Habsburg Empire was dissolved into Austria, Hungary, and parts of other successor states; tsarist Russia was reborn as a revolutionary anti–status quo entity when its internal convulsions ceased.

The responsibility for reconfiguring the new landscape in Europe now lay primarily with Britain, France, Italy, and the United States (the Big Four), since defeated Germany was excluded from the peace talks. In most cases the Big Four would decide who should govern, within what boundaries, and how, especially since the great powers would provide the foreign capital that was needed for the new governments to even begin to assert their authority and make their states viable.

Three overriding concerns guided the disposition of territory in the peace talks. The first was the restoration of the European balance of power, which the war, the subsequent defeat and elimination of the Central Powers, and the revolution in Russia had shattered. The second consideration was the business of balancing the provisions of several secret treaties and promises with the burgeoning demands for self-determination by the various national minorities newly freed from the repression of imperial fetters. The final concern was the awarding of desirable territories from the losing side to the winners of the war and to the war's victim countries.

The restoration of a balance of power in Europe was particularly imperative following the Russian Revolution, which had transformed the former conservative tsarist regime into a center of revolutionary activities and propaganda. France was especially eager to check further German aggression, as well as revolutionary Russia's western designs, by creating a buffer to protect Western Europe. Britain, however, favored a more equitable settlement and a return to normalcy. The creation of the successor states responded more to French than to other interests and in doing so sacrificed principles of national self-determination. The need for an equitable resolution of the problem of national minorities, who composed about one-fourth of the population of Eastern Europe, gave way to economic and strategic concerns. The consequences of this carving up of the empires that had governed Eastern Europe for so many years were felt throughout the twentieth century.[2]

The peace treaties and the treaties between the victorious great powers and the new successor states contained provisions for the treatment of minority populations that were backed by the League of Nations. Nevertheless, the major powers did not give strong consideration to the principle of unity of nationalities or to the civil rights of the population—particularly minorities, who were considered subversive elements—when drawing the new boundaries. Instead, with the backing of one of the victorious great powers, an Allied state could successfully press for territory according to economic, strategic, or historical criteria, no matter how spurious the claim.

Despite the minority rights they had agreed to, the new governments treated their national minorities even worse than they did the alien elements within the national state, much as the new majority populations had been treated when they were conquered peoples. The representatives of many national minorities complained that they had less autonomy after World War I than they had enjoyed under Habsburg rule because of rigid central control and discrimination practiced against them within the newly created European state boundaries. To further exacerbate the mutual distrust between minorities and their new governing regimes, the defeated states were encouraging unrest among ethnic kin in their former territories through propaganda and by reinforcing linguistic and cultural links with the minorities.[3]

Creation of Yugoslavia

The Serbian Karadjordjević royal family favored South Slav union,[4] so with Allied encouragement and its heretofore principal friend, Russia, in revolutionary turmoil, in 1917 Serbia agreed to become part of a Yugoslav state. As one of the victorious states in World War I, Serbia was in a position to secure more favorable borders for Yugoslavia than were the other national groups that had formerly lived under Austro-Hungarian rule. Following British Prime Minister Lloyd George's comment to Serbian Prime Minister Pašić in October 1918 that the structure of postwar Yugoslavia was contingent on whether Serbia was able to occupy certain regions that were under dispute with Italy (such as Dalmatia, which Italy was already beginning to occupy in October 1918), the Serbian army entered the Banat, Bosnia and Herzegovina, Croatia, and other regions that contained South Slav inhabitants,[5] thereby putting those South Slavs under its protection. Other areas with large South Slav (mainly Slovene and Croat) populations were already lost to Italy, Hungary, and Austria. Thus, Slovenia, Croatia, and Bosnia and Herzegovina were forced to coalesce rapidly with Serbia and Montenegro in a South Slav state to forestall the loss of more of their territory.

The lands of the South Slavs had suffered immensely from World War I, during which almost 2 million people died. Communications and transportation were largely destroyed throughout the area, but some regions suffered more than others. Regional differences in the amount of wartime damage sustained encouraged economic disparities and further strained the South Slav union. The Serb economic base—already lagging behind that of Slovenia, Croatia, and Vojvodina—suffered more than was the case in the more industrialized areas.

Territorial variance already existed, primarily in the areas of mineral exploitation, agriculture, and industry. The disparities among regions were further reflected in the differences in lifestyles and standards of living. The northern regions, which had prospered under Austria-Hungary, had already embarked on the process of modernization, whereas the less-developed areas, previously under Ottoman rule, continued to follow a more traditional way of life.[6]

Parliamentary Democracy in the Yugoslav Kingdom

The new Yugoslavia, called the Kingdom of the Serbs, Croats, and Slovenes until 1929, was declared on 1 December 1918. From that time until January 1929, the kingdom was governed as a constitutional parliamentary monarchy, in which all South Slav peoples were constitutionally equal under the Serbian monarchy. Few of the inhabitants of the Yugoslav Kingdom had any experience with such a political form, with the notable exception of pre–World War I Serbia. Serbia and Montenegro entered the interwar period with some able politicians and organized political parties that were practiced in state governance, as well as a political history characterized by independent behavior. The politicians and parties of the nations that had existed under the Austro-Hungarian Empire, on the other hand, were politically astute but were used more to playing the role of opposition than to taking responsibility for government management. Boris Furlan ably summed up interwar Yugoslav political life when he concluded that "with the exception of the Communists and Socialists, all political parties spoke essentially for the middle classes, represented specific ethnic and confessional interests, and lacked reasonably consistent programs and disciplined membership."[7]

At the time the South Slav union was internationally recognized in June 1919, the issue of the exact form of the association—whether unitary or federal—had yet to be settled, except that the kingdom was to be a constitutional, democratic, parliamentary monarchy ruled by the Karadjordjević dynasty. The terms of organization and the enumeration of the legal obligations of the participating groups were vague and thus troublesome. For example, it was unclear whether the state was already legally constituted as a hereditary monarchy before it enacted a constitution or whether the constitution was needed to legalize the king's sovereignty.[8]

The South Slav peoples ("Yug" is the Serbo-Croatian word for south, making Yugoslavia the land of the South Slavs) had no previous history of either territorial or national union, a fact that emphasized the artificiality of a Yugoslav construct in the eyes of its critics. Further, their past associations with the Austro-Hungarian and Ottoman Empires did not provide the South Slavs with a prototype for dealing sensitively with the problems of multinational cohabitation.

The various national groups considered themselves to be distinct peoples, jealously guarding their own cultural identities and clinging to sometimes insignificant linguistic differences. Except for some intellectuals, therefore, few people enthusiastically embraced the idea of Yugoslavism.[9] The old national loyalties and chauvinistic national movements, however, could still inspire devotion among the masses. Especially divisive were the different historical experiences the two largest groups—the Serbs and the Croats—brought to the union.

Croatia's sovereignty had been limited since its 1102 acceptance of the Pacta Conventa with King Koloman of Hungary. Nevertheless, the Croats had a history of federal relationships (with Hungary during the Middle Ages) and some autonomy, at least on paper, within a multinational framework (the Habsburg monarchy). Although its political experience under Austro-Hungarian aegis generally consisted of warding off Hungarian attempts to whittle away its right to maintain its own parliament, Croatia nevertheless supported a partially independent military organization and an independent currency and taxation system.[10] Croat leaders thus expected the Yugoslav Kingdom to be based on an equal partnership with the Serbs and Slovenes in a federal system that would provide for the mutual security of all parties. They resisted the Serb vision of liberation of the South Slavs and incorporation into a Serb-dominated centralized state.[11]

The aspirations of Bosnian inhabitants revolved around the resolution of agrarian relationships. Although most Bosnian Muslim leaders were willing to join a new and independent South Slav state,[12] they were prepared to resist the end of feudal relationships—something Bosnian Serb peasants, for their part, anticipated. The tension between these two perspectives erupted in the form of rural turmoil even before the formal declaration of the Yugoslav Kingdom.[13] Many Bosnian Serbs, anticipating a Serb victory in World War I, stopped paying their landlords and even began attacking them, both physically and verbally.[14] Serbian troops entered Bosnia and Herzegovina, ostensibly to quell the peasant rebellion; in effect they stayed to occupy the territory on behalf of the new administration. Bosnian Muslims responded to these depredations in a variety of ways. Many Muslims emigrated to Turkey in 1919.[15] Others rejected the idea of a South Slav state and continued as they had during World War I to seek some form of autonomy—perhaps in a postwar Austro-Hungarian structure.

Leading Serb politicians were also reluctant at first to pursue a unified South Slav state. They were unwilling to sacrifice the goal of a greater Serbia because they were proud of Serbia's attainment of independence in the nineteenth century and its parliamentary system.

Serbia had a history not only of independence, however, but also of a strong desire to serve as a kind of Piedmont, leading the way to unification for the protection of all Serbs. To the Serb leaders, the creation of Yugoslavia simply represented the succession of the Serbian medieval empire and the culmination of Serbia's successful achievement of independence from the Ottoman and Austro-Hungarian Empires. The exigencies of their new partners were of little importance,[16] because the Serbs insisted on a centralized state. The Serb formulation clashed with the Croat yearning for a European, rather than a Balkan, orientation, which a federation would have better expressed.[17]

An all-Yugoslav election for a Constituent Assembly to fashion the structure of the new state was held in November 1920. The winning parties, both in favor of a unitary or centralized state, were Pašić's Serbian Radical Party (the Radicals), the successor to the prewar Serbian ruling party (ninety-one seats), and the Serbian Democrats, supported primarily by Serbs from the former Habsburg areas (ninety-two seats).[18] Stjepan Radić's Croat Peasant Party (*Hrvatska seljačka stranka* [HSS]) won the largest number of votes in Croatia but refused to participate in drafting the constitution. The Yugoslav Communist Party (CPY) received 198,756 votes, or 12.3 percent of the vote cast,[19] which amounted to fifty-eight seats,[20] one of which was held by a Bosnian Muslim.[21] Although (or perhaps because) the CPY was thus the third largest parliamentary party,[22] it was subjected to harsh repressive measures in late 1920 and was outlawed in early 1921. Muslims secured twenty-four seats, enough to form a substantial bloc of votes, which encouraged Serb and Croat politicians to actively seek their support and loyalty.

Fifteen of the twenty-four Bosnian Muslim delegates to the first Yugoslav Constituent Assembly in 1920 declared themselves to be Croats.[23] Two who favored a centralized Yugoslavia represented the prewar *Gajret* view and identified with the Serbs. However, two Bosnian Muslim representatives called themselves Yugoslavs,[24] in effect not identifying with any nation and representing the desire to maintain Bosnian autonomy within the Yugoslav Kingdom. These Muslim leaders decided that Serb and Croat chauvinism was inimical to the improvement of the economic and social position of the Bosnian Muslims, since it fostered the threat of a partition of Bosnia and Herzegovina, which would make the Bosnian Muslims a permanent and ineffectual minority.[25] Bosnian Muslim actions were in line with the theory of their leader, Mehmed Spaho, that "support for the government, whatever its complexion and policy, would always bring greater benefits to a small minority than pointless defiance."[26]

Deliberations of the Constituent Assembly resulted in the Vidovdan Constitution, which was adopted without the acquiescence of most non-Serb parties on 28 June 1921.[27] Its provisions in effect established for the South Slavs a continuation of the previous Serbian system. The monarch would hold vast powers but would share responsibility for government with the unicameral legislature. The country was divided into thirty-three provinces, whose borders did not—except in the case of Bosnia and Herzegovina—correspond with historical boundaries. Resistance to the provisions of the constitution was such that only 223 of the original 419 elected delegates to the Constituent Assembly participated in the final voting on the formation of the government.

Many of the national groups involved believed the unitary organization legitimated by the constitution deprived them of the rights they deserved within the state. Non-Serbs accused the Serbs of using their status as a victor in World War I to form a greater Serbia out of the South Slav lands and consequently chafed at the high-handed predominance of Serbs in positions of power in the new state.

The Croats in particular were infuriated and protested against forcing members of the Constituent Assembly to take an oath of allegiance to the Serbian monarchy. The Croatian Peasant Party—which favored radical land reform—other Croatian groups, and the Communists withdrew from the assembly in protest against the centralism espoused by the Serbs through the Vidovdan Constitution. This left the Democrats, the Radicals, and representatives of the Bosnian Muslims to accept the constitution.[28]

The Bosnian Muslim representatives, who essentially favored a federal form of government, nevertheless voted for the 1921 centralist constitution. As a result, they won for their constituents increased landlord indemnity for lands lost through agrarian reform, a formal statement of the government's intent to protect the rites and practices of Islam, and the continued geographic integrity of Bosnia and Herzegovina despite the division of the rest of Yugoslavia into small administrative districts that crossed historically defined borders (Article 135, Subsection 3).[29]

Serbia indeed exerted inordinate influence on the governmental process by retaining most of the sensitive government posts for Serbs. There was only one non-Serb prime minister during the interwar period. Patronage appointments ensured that Serbs controlled banking, credit, and other important institutions, particularly the bureaucracy. The Serbs also dominated the police force and the military.[30]

Non-Serbs complained that such widespread Serb control of the bureaucracy and other important levers of power deprived others of legal security and economic freedom, which, coupled with government corruption and the extreme backwardness of the masses, created a difficult situation for the non-Serb population.[31] But the Serbs rejoined that Serbia had been an independent state during the time the other areas were still under the rule of the multinational empires. Whereas the other regions had no real experience with self-government, Serbia had its own well-established military, monarchy, police force, and bureaucracy. In addition, although Serbia had suffered more casualties and economic destruction in World War I than any other South Slav region, the fact that it was on the victorious side gave it added prestige. Serbia had been the driving force in the creation of the new Yugoslav state, and it resisted ceding an inordinate amount of its political independence to that state. Further, Serbia did not want to be at an economic or a cultural disadvantage in relation to the more advanced South Slav areas. The Serbs thus insisted that the Vidovdan Constitution not materially harm their national interests.

Almost completely dominating the political, economic, social, military, and cultural affairs of the Yugoslav Kingdom, Serb leaders also attempted to impose their own view of Yugoslavia on all of its inhabitants. They advanced the theory of the "tri-named nation"—in which the Croats and Slovenes were merely tribes within the Serbian nation. Whereas the Montenegrins considered themselves Serbian and thus were part of the establishment, the Serbs also claimed that the Macedonians were simply another branch of the Serbian nation (South Serbia) and were not Bulgarian or Greek.

This state of affairs was, of course, inimical to the pro-federalism Croats in particular, who believed they were no better off within the Kingdom of the Serbs, Croats, and Slovenes than they had been under Austria-Hungary. The fact that the Orthodox Church was given privileges akin to those of a state church in the Serb-dominated kingdom also riled the Catholic Croats.[32] During the first decade of the new state, Croatia was "virtually in a state of insurrection."[33] With Croat Peasant Party leader Stjepan Radić imprisoned briefly in 1925 for antistate activity, Yugoslav political parties coalesced along ethnic lines even more rigidly than before and provoked constant turmoil during the interwar period.

Had Yugoslavia initially been organized as a federation with greater regional autonomy and recognition of the various national aspirations, according to the plan of Croat intellectuals and politicians, rather than as an asymmetrically Serb-dominated authoritarian state centered in Belgrade, perhaps the non-Serbs would have felt a greater sense of loyalty to the state. However, its rural economy, the multitude of laws and legal systems that reflected the different

experiences of the various peoples who were now united, and other issues dividing the South Slavs ensured that integration of the kingdom would not be easy.[34]
Thus, some Croats were even willing to secede from Yugoslavia to achieve an
independent Croatia if the Serb-dominated Yugoslav Kingdom continued to
ignore their aspirations for greater autonomy.

The Bosnian Muslim delegates who had backed the constitution were quiescent, hoping to better their lot through support of the government. And in fact
they were rather successful in preserving prerogatives for the Bosnian Muslims,
particularly through the skillful political maneuverings of the Yugoslav Muslim
Organization.

The Yugoslav Muslim Organization in Interwar Yugoslavia

Paralleling the increased political activity among the Serbs and Croats within the
Yugoslav kingdom, the Bosnian Muslims began to agitate for more Muslim par-
ticipation in and influence on the government, something their numbers should
have reflected. The Bosnian Muslims constituted a relatively large contingent in
Bosnia and Herzegovina, with 583,000 Muslims reported in the 1921 census.[35]
This was down from the 1910 census organized by Austria-Hungary, in which the
Muslims in Bosnia and Herzegovina numbered 612,000.[36] The drop in numbers
presumably resulted from the emigration of Muslims who preferred to dwell in
Turkey rather than live in a state dominated by Serbs. The Muslims thus consti-
tuted 31.1 percent of the population of Bosnia and Herzegovina, with the
remaining population made up of 43.7 percent Orthodox and 21.3 percent
Catholics.[37] The proportion of Muslims did not change appreciably over the next
two decades; for example, in 1939 the more than 858,000 Muslims in Bosnia and
Herzegovina made up 31.2 percent of the population.[38]

The position of the Bosnian Muslims in the interwar Yugoslav state was
ambivalent. Generally enthusiastic about the creation of a South Slav state, the

TABLE 4.1   Population of Bosnia and Herzegovina by Religion, 1910–1939

	Austrian Census, 1910	*Yugoslav Census, 1921*	*Yugoslav Estimate, 1939*
	Number %	*Number %*	*Number %*
Muslim	612,137 (32.7)	488,137 (31.1)	848,140 (31.2)
Orthodox	824,557 (43.5)	825,390 (43.7)	1,226,991 (44.6)
Roman Catholic	387,707 (22.8)	401,262 (21.3)	595,974 (21.7)

SOURCES: Wayne S. Vucinich, "Yugoslavs of the Moslem Faith," in Robert J. Kerner,
ed., *Yugoslavia* (Berkeley: University of California Press, 1947), p. 263; and Ivo
Banac, *The National Question in Yugoslavia: Origins, History, Politics* (Ithaca:
Cornell University Press, 1984), p. 361.

majority of the Bosnian Muslims recognized the Karadjordjević dynasty and hoped for its protection. During the earliest days of Yugoslavia in 1918 and 1919, before they had coalesced for united political action, Bosnian Muslims experienced widespread violence and intimidation—particularly by the Orthodox population. The attackers—who failed to distinguish among Muslim feudal landlords, small landowners, and free Muslim peasants—thus ironically began the first days of South Slav union by demonstrating some leftover class and national-religious resentment of Orthodox peasants toward their Muslim landlords. As a prime object of Serb-Croat rivalry, however, the Muslims were being pressured to support Serb or Croat separatism or the monarchically instituted centralism.

In response to these threats to their community, the Bosnian Muslims coalesced spontaneously, first into small regional factions and then into larger and more organized groups. However, such small, narrowly focused parties as the Muslim Farm Laborer's Party and the landlord-led Muslim People's Party did not represent the broadest nonclass interests of the Bosnian Muslims and fared poorly in the 1920 parliamentary elections. Muslim elites who had a more inclusive vision of Bosnian Muslim interests responded to the need for unity, as expressed by publicist Sulejman el Syrre Abdagić's 29 January 1919 call for a democratically constituted organization that would "represent *all Muslims* and be a hardened phalanx of our Muslim interests,"[39] by founding the *Jugoslavenska Muslimanska Organizacija* (Yugoslav Muslim Organization [JMO]). Headed by Mehmed Spaho and led mainly by middle-class, urban Muslims, the JMO was created to present a united Bosnian Muslim front in the political arena.[40]

The JMO was founded in Sarajevo on 16 February 1919. It was fairly successful in representing the Bosnian Muslims and in deflecting the worst of the assaults on their community. In return, Bosnian Muslim voting patterns showed consistent widespread support for the JMO, although in its earliest days it was subject to factionalism. In the 1920 elections to the Constituent Assembly, the JMO received 110,895 votes (34 percent) of a total of 328,251 votes cast in Bosnia and Herzegovina.[41] In 1922 two rival groups emerged within the JMO. The faction led by Ibrahim Maglajlić of Tuzla continued to support the Pašić government and the Vidovdan Constitution. The group headed by Mehmed Spaho joined the parliamentary opposition. The latter faction was victorious in the 1923 elections, winning 112,228 votes (eighteen seats) to Maglajlić's 6,074.[42] Interestingly, all of the JMO deputies except Spaho declared themselves Croats.[43]

The JMO focused on unifying Muslim political activity in at least two major areas: agrarian relations and attempted assimilation of Bosnian Muslims by eliciting their identification as either Serbs or Croats. On the agrarian issue, JMO success was mixed. Since Yugoslav agriculture was characterized by "overpopulation, low capital formation, and primitive production technology,"[44] the agrarian issue was among the first to be dealt with by the new Yugoslav government,

TABLE 4.2   Election Results in Yugoslavia, 1920–1927

	Seats			
Political Party	*1920*	*1923*	*1925*	*1927*
Radical	93	109	141	111
Democrat	94	52	37	61
Independent Democrat	—	—	22	22
Croat Peasant	50	71	67	63
Jugoslav Muslim Organization	**24**	**18**	**17**	**18**
Slovene Popular	27	22	20	21
Agrarian	26	11	5	8
Communist	58	—	—	—
Other	6	29	6	11

SOURCES: Nenad Grisagno, *Two Chats On: Yugoslavia Between Two Wars, and Yugoslavia, Italy, and Trieste* (Chicago: Croatian Publishing Co., 1946), p. 57; and Atif Purivatra, *Nacionalni i politički razvitak muslimana* (Sarajevo: Svjetlost, 1970), p. 181.

for both its economic ramifications and its connection to relations among the various South Slav nations.

In February 1919 an Interim Decree was enacted, providing the principles for altering Yugoslavia's agrarian relations. Feudal landholdings and serfdom were abolished, and state-sponsored indemnity was promised to the (mostly Muslim) landlords for the loss of their land. Peasants were to own the land they had tilled, which tended to perpetuate small and inefficient farms. The government promoted this "patronizing neglect" by devoting only 20 percent of its investment to agriculture when 80 percent of its population consisted of peasants.[45]

In fact, the alteration of Yugoslavia's agrarian situation was damaging to the Bosnian Muslim landowners. Compensation to landowners under the agrarian reforms was ruinous to all but the wealthiest landowners.[46] The smaller landowners, who represented the majority, suffered economically as much as their tenants when they worked their own land.[47] The lack of modern agricultural tools and knowledge conspired to keep the Yugoslav peasants at barely the subsistence level.[48] Thus, for example, in 1936, when Dutch farmers were using 311 kilograms of fertilizer per hectare, farmers in Yugoslavia were using only 0.2 kilograms.[49]

Only financiers and banks, which were Serb controlled, profited measurably from Yugoslavia's agrarian policy.[50] Government solutions to the agrarian problem hurt members of all religions financially through confiscation of property and endowments. Agrarian reform was harmful to Muslim and other small land-

holders who received compensation for their lost land in the form of government bonds—not cash—which they usually had to sell below face value. These
landowners were required to partition their estates among the members of their
families, thus yielding numerous small farms that barely provided a subsistence
livelihood.[51] Furthermore, many peasants were no longer needed on the land,
but there was little call for them in alternative employment situations. Historical
conditions militated against rapid industrial development in the Balkans, which
would have absorbed the excess rural population.[52]

Not all Bosnian Muslims suffered equally under the agrarian reforms. The
wealthier landlords salvaged something from the situation. Because of the skillful bargaining of JMO leaders, who traded political votes for economic concessions, their landowners suffered the least.[53] Muslim political leaders supported
passage of a law in 1928 that allotted land to former landholders who, it was officially explained, had been left without the minimum necessary for existence.

Nonagricultural Muslims shared the fate of the non-Muslim population.
Those who were engaged in small businesses or in trade or who were urban
laborers found themselves slowly becoming impoverished, because they were
unable to withstand the competition from those who were better organized.
Small Muslim merchants suffered increasing indigence, as did the other small
merchants. Further, Muslim workers were unable to compete for better jobs.
Whereas 88 percent of the population of Yugoslavia at the time was illiterate and
only one-third of the Bosnian children attended school in 1939,[54] the Muslims
suffered from 95 percent illiteracy[55] (99.68 percent among Muslim women[56]).
The Bosnian Muslims continued to cling to religious institutions for instruction
and did not take advantage of the primary instruction that had been widely
available in their lands since 1911.[57] Their prospects for economic betterment
thus suffered in interwar Yugoslavia, although the prospects were somewhat
attenuated by JMO intervention in the government.

The second focus of JMO policy was on Serb and Croat attempts to win
Bosnian Muslim loyalty by means of Muslims' self-declaration as either Serbs or
Croats. Interwar Yugoslavia maintained and even encouraged this division by
granting official recognition to the major religions. Thus, in the interwar and
World War II periods the Bosnian Muslims were officially treated as a religious
community, and they responded to this treatment by creating the openly confessional political party, the JMO.

However, their refusal to identify themselves as a national group, as had the
Serbs and the Croats, encouraged efforts to elicit Bosnian Muslim individual or
group declarations of Serb or Croat nationhood. Croatian propaganda among the
Muslims emphasized that "the Serbs and the Serb-dominated government were
responsible for their plight and that Muslims were, in fact, Croats."[58] Croat leaders continued the tradition of Croat nationalist Ante Starčević in viewing the
Bosnian Muslims as "the best Croats."[59] Croat chauvinists used this argument to
advance a Croatian claim to the territory of Bosnia and Herzegovina. The Serbs in

turn assiduously courted Bosnian Muslim elites to proclaim themselves Serbs as a gesture that was supportive of the existing political order. However, in general the JMO elites refused the advances of both sides; they were unwilling to anger the Serbs by acquiescing to Croat overtures and were unable to join with the Serbs because of their diametrically opposite position on the agrarian issue. Under these conditions, it is not surprising that some Muslim leaders were still intrigued with the possibility of placing Bosnia and Herzegovina under the tutelage of the Hungarian successor state[60] or with other plans to retain Bosnia's autonomy in order to protect their confessional integrity.

Some Bosnian Muslim elites flirted with the assertion of the Bosnian Muslim nation. They believed the Bosnian Muslims should be recognized as a national group—whether for defensive (anti-Serb or anti-Croat) reasons or because of the belief that Bosnian Muslims were the most "Bosnian" of all the inhabitants of Bosnia and Herzegovina on the basis of their pure and direct lineage from the medieval Islamized Bosnians. Other Bosnian Muslims rejected the notion of a Bosnian Muslim nation out of hand as a contradiction of Islam,[61] and many Serbs and Croats considered the idea unacceptable.

As time passed, however, and the Muslims came under increasing pressure from Serbs and Croats, leaders of the JMO felt compelled to undertake the cause of protection of the religious rights of Muslims in interwar Yugoslavia. The main purpose of the JMO, which was initially to safeguard the position of all Muslims in Bosnia and Herzegovina, slowly turned to representing the position of the Bosnian Muslims, thereby ignoring the position of non-Slav Muslims in Kosovo and Macedonia.[62] The JMO was thus unable to bridge the enormous gap between Bosnian Muslims and other Yugoslav Muslims, even when it concentrated on public policy without religious overtones. Furthermore, the Serbs considered the Muslims in Montenegro and the Novi Pazar district to be Serbs and persuaded the Serb-dominated government in Belgrade to limit JMO political and cultural activity to only Bosnia and Herzegovina. Simultaneously, the Muslim population in Montenegro and the Novi Pazar district was being pressured to "Serbianize" or leave.

The JMO has been branded an expedient, opportunist party, "supporting any Belgrade government that benefitted the Muslims."[63] Since the regime was the only political unit that could dispense such favors in Yugoslavia, it was not surprising that the Bosnian Muslims usually tended to support the central government, although when they deemed it in their best interests they did not hesitate to join the opposition. The Muslim leadership thus frequently bartered the party's parliamentary weight for better treatment of Muslims[64] and, often in concert with the Slovene Clericals, pursued a course appropriate for a small, vulnerable political party.[65]

In 1936, Spaho drew the JMO into a pro-government (and thus pro-Serb) union with the Serbian Radical Party and Anton Korošec's Slovene People's Party to form the Yugoslav Radical Union (*Jugoslovenska radikalna zajednica* [JRZ]). Citing the inability of the JMO to accomplish its goals without supporting Serb

Milan Stojadinović's government, Spaho later defended this action to his Muslim critics, saying that "when the opportunity was extended to us that through the JRZ we could establish a party which would guarantee all that we had fought for in the JMO, we made the decision to enter the JRZ."[66]

The Royal Dictatorship

Croatia's passionate opposition to centralist Serbian control of the government peaked when Stjepan Radić and two other Croats were fatally shot by Montenegrin parliamentary deputy Puniša Račić in 1928.[67] As the country reeled following the homicides, Radić's successor, Vladko Maček, demanded full Croatian autonomy within Yugoslavia and a constitution based on federalism. Increased public unrest and political paralysis and the rambunctiousness of parliament, which threatened the dissolution of the state, encouraged King Alexander to suspend the Vidovdan Constitution and proclaim a royal dictatorship in 1929. Thenceforth, the monarch had both legislative and executive powers, and the legislature was abolished. Political parties were dissolved, and anyone thought to be connected with the CPY—a connection rather loosely defined as critical of the regime—was prosecuted.[68] Although there was no real Communist threat to the Yugoslav Kingdom at the time, perceived revolutionary potential that favored reform was strongly discouraged. The administration of the government was more thoroughly centralized, and the state became in effect a unitary Serb-controlled police state. In this environment, the democratic rights of Serbs fared little better than those of non-Serbs.[69]

In an attempt to impose the concept of Yugoslavism (one South Slav nation) on the rival national groups, the official name of the Kingdom of the Serbs, Croats, and Slovenes became Yugoslavia, stressing the common heritage of the South Slavs. The distinctions between the various nations were officially expunged and were replaced with the concept that Serbs, Croats, and Slovenes were all "tribes" of the unitary South Slav, or Yugoslav, nation. Geographic boundaries based on ethnicity disappeared and were replaced with new administrative districts (*banovinas*) that cut across historical and ethnic lines. For the first time in centuries, Bosnia and Herzegovina was partitioned. It was now part of four *banovinas*—including a portion in the *banovina* of Croatia—each with a Muslim minority.[70] The territorial concessions Bosnian Muslim leaders had won for Bosnia and Herzegovina after World War I were thus eliminated.

Negative reaction to these moves was immediate and widespread, not only in Croatia, Slovenia, and Macedonia but also in some Serbian areas. This attempt at unitarism resulted in a more intense opposition to the monarchy by non-Serb separatists. The Croats suffered greatly at the hands of the Serb-dominated police, as well as from persecution by Serbian nationalists. Croats reacted to this harsh treatment with the creation of the *Ustaše*, an ultranationalistic paramilitary group led by radical Croat politician Ante Pavelić. Armed clashes between Serb and Croat radical groups over nationalist issues were frequent. The Ustaše,

Kingdom of Yugoslavia, 1929, and 1939-1941

Cartographic Services, Department of Geography, Ball State University

went underground and augmented its foreign ties. The JMO, however, pressured by the king and still believing in the efficacy of its role as government supporter and coalition builder, did not speak out against the royal dictatorship.

King Alexander was eventually forced to retract some of the more onerous forms of the unitary government. In 1931 a new constitution was promulgated that provided for a quasi-parliamentary government and allowed more popular participation in national and local affairs. However, legislation could easily circumscribe such participation.[71] A bicameral legislature would serve as a rubber stamp for the actions of the unitary state.

National passions were too inflamed to accept this attempt at placation. On 9 October 1934, King Alexander was assassinated. Having concluded the Balkan

Pact with Greece, Romania, and Turkey on 9 February, Alexander was reviewing other foreign relations. Some have speculated that his murder resulted from his desire to change Yugoslavia's anti-Soviet policy in favor of an alliance that would include France. He died in Marseilles along with French Foreign Minister Louis Barthou, with whom he was going to negotiate this issue.[72] Another theory, however, contended that Alexander was targeted because he was on the verge of dividing Yugoslavia into Serbian and Croatian units in recognition of Croatian demands for greater autonomy.[73] This, too, would have been sufficient cause for enmity toward Alexander by some passionately anti-Croat forces or even pro-Croat forces who sought increased tension in Yugoslavia to further their own desires for autonomy. Still others claimed that Italy, with designs on the Dalmatian coast, encouraged and supported the assassins. Ante Pavelić was involved in planning the assassination from his base in Italy. He induced the terrorist *Vatrešna makedonska revoljuciona organizacija* (IMRO) to supply its operatives to help carry out the murder.[74]

Alexander was succeeded by his minor son Peter. A three-person regency, headed by Alexander's cousin Prince Paul, ruled until his majority. Prime Minister Stojadinović began to disassemble some of Alexander's more onerous policies, attempting to conciliate Croat nationalists, but he was operating under limited political and economic conditions.

Yugoslavia's interwar economic policy mirrored that of the other East European states, which saw the depression destroy the little industrial and agricultural success they had achieved. Yugoslavia joined these states in forging close but patently unequal economic relations with Nazi Germany. In the first economic agreement with Yugoslavia in 1933–1934, for example, Germany agreed to buy Yugoslavia's agrarian surplus in exchange for Yugoslavia's purchase of Germany's industrial goods.[75] Reflecting Yugoslavia's drift toward Germany, a plethora of fascist-type parties arose openly in Yugoslavia, exemplified by the separatist Ustaše.

The increasingly pro-Axis tilt of the Stojadinović government impelled leaders of some of the opposition parties, as well as Prince Paul himself, to explore ways in which to work together toward a democratic regime in Yugoslavia.[76] This united opposition called for decentralization of the state—a kind of "guided democracy"[77]—and solution of the "Croatian problem." Vladko Maček, released from prison through Stojadinović's conciliatory domestic policies, became the vocal leader of this group.

The *Sporazum*

The 1938 Munich agreement and Pavelić's increasingly strident calls for Croats to destroy Yugoslavia impelled the Yugoslav government to try to strengthen internal unity by coming to terms with Croatian demands for autonomy. Stojadinović was replaced as prime minister by Dragiša Cvetković. The outcome of Cvetković's attempts to compromise with the Croats was the ill-timed 1939 *Sporazum* (Agreement), which implicitly indicated government recognition of the fact that the Serbs and Croats were distinct, albeit related, nations.[78] Under the *Sporazum* an enlarged Croatia became an autonomous unit (*Banovina Hrvatska*) and retained most domestic budgetary and administrative functions. The Croatian *banovina* controlled its own Ministry of the Interior and Croatian assembly, to which the king-appointed governor, or ban, was responsible. A constitutional court would settle jurisdictional and other disputes between the *banovina* and the central government.

The *Sporazum,* which federalized Yugoslavia and gave Croatia control over most of its own provincial matters, clearly came too late to placate many Croats, who by this time were too alienated by previous government policies to acquiesce. Many Serbs were also dissatisfied with Croatian autonomy within the monarchy and were displeased that around 850,000 Serbs were included in the territory of the new Croatian *banovina*. Maček may have been trying to win support for the *Sporazum* from the fascist Ustaše by engaging in virulent anti-Serb propaganda within Croatia,[79] but Serbs were clearly worried. The Serbs also propounded vicious anti-Croat propaganda within Serbia. Terrorist actions by extremist groups escalated the tensions.

The initial negotiations regarding the *Sporazum* had been frustrated in part by the disagreement between Cvetković and Maček over the fate of Bosnia and Herzegovina, which was claimed by both the Serbs and the Croats. During the tense days preceding the signing of the *Sporazum,* Mehmed Spaho and most of the Muslim leaders went on record as opposing the partition of Bosnia and Herzegovina between Serbia and Croatia. Spaho thus cleaved to his line of attempting to maintain the indivisibility of Bosnia and to his support of the central government, which alone could assure such indivisibility, when he remarked during preliminary negotiations over the *Sporazum* that "if Bosnia and Hercegovina cannot get autonomy, then we cannot at any price allow the region to be divided, but let the whole of it go to Serbia."[80] Nevertheless, the newly formed Croatia was able to incorporate parts of historical Bosnia and Herzegovina, against Muslim wishes,[81] leaving the rest of Bosnia and Herzegovina still split among three other *banovinas.*

Bosnian Muslim Self-Identification in the Yugoslav Kingdom

The Muslims in Bosnia and Herzegovina thus found themselves in an unenviable position. Exemplifying the tenuousness of the Yugoslav union, both the Serbs and the Croats competitively claimed national kinship with the Muslims to legitimate ancient territorial demands for Bosnia and Herzegovina. The basic issue was related to theoretical possession of Bosnia and Herzegovina: The nation that acquired its loyalty would dominate the South Slav state. Neither a greater Serbia nor a separate Croatia would be viable without this centrally located territory.[82]

Croats claimed that before the medieval Croatian kingdom became a vassal of Hungary in the twelfth century, its territory had included roughly the post–World War II areas of Croatia, Slavonia, Dalmatia, and a large part of Bosnia. Only with the inclusion of Bosnia and Herzegovina could the boomerang-shaped Croatia become a militarily defensible, viable state. Without Bosnia and Herzegovina, Croatian territory—with its large Serbian contingent on the Military Frontier—would eventually be absorbed by neighboring states if that territory should ever become separated from the Yugoslav Kingdom.[83] Serbia, too, asserted historical claims to Bosnia and Herzegovina and resented the carefully neutral position of the Bosnian Muslims, who had become an obstacle to Serbia's dominance of Yugoslavia.[84] However, the Serbs could not afford to totally alienate the Bosnian Islamic community, since its votes were necessary to facilitate Serbian rule in the kingdom during the stormy sessions of the Constituent Assembly and afterward. Negative manifestations of the pressures from both Croats and Serbs included economic discrimination and even open violence.

During the years of the Yugoslav Kingdom, most Bosnian Muslims generally refused to acquiesce to counting themselves as either Serbs or Croats. As was true during the prewar period, some Muslims, mainly of the urban elite and landowning classes, declared themselves Muslim Serbs or Muslim Croats—that is, "a religious minority of the respective national group."[85] In general, however, the majority of Muslims declared no such affiliation, although among those who did, the tendency was toward Croat rather than Serb affiliation.[86] A peculiar but noteworthy case of national ambivalence was exemplified by 1961 Nobel Prize in literature winner Ivo Andrić. Born a Catholic Bosnian, he called himself a Serb after he entered the royal diplomatic corps.[87]

Croat and Serb pressures seemed to stimulate a stronger communal solidarity among Bosnian Muslims in order to increase their abilities to defend the Muslim community. This nascent communal unity was evident even during the chaotic early days of the establishment of Yugoslavia. When peasants were securing the land of their former landlords, Muslim free peasants, as well as Muslim *kmets* and rural poor, had sided with the Muslim feudal landlords,[88] an indication that to some extent the national-religious component was already present among the Bosnian Muslims.

Bosnian Muslim Influence in Interwar Yugoslavia

Despite the ardor with which the Muslims were wooed by Serb and Croat nationalists, Bosnian Muslims were essentially excluded from exercising the political influence their numbers (with the Muslims of the Sandžak they constituted more than 5 percent of the total Yugoslav population,[89] as shown in Table

TABLE 4.3   1931 Census: Yugoslavia

	Total Number (thousands)	*Percentage of Total*
Serbs[a]	5,953	42.7
Croats	3,221	23.1
Slovenes	1,133	8.1
Macedonian Slavs	642	4.6
Bosnian Muslims	729	5.3[b]
Other	2,256	16.2

[a]includes Montenegrins.
[b]thirty-one percent of the population of Bosnia and Herzegovina.

SOURCES: Jure Petričević, *Nacionalnost stanovnišvta Jugoslavije: Nazadovanje Hrvata, manjine napredovanje Muslimana i Albanaca* (Brugg: Adria, 1983), p. 29; Bogoljub Kočović, *Žrtve drugog svetskog rata u Jugoslaviji* (London: Biblioteka *Naše delo*, 1985), p. 146.

4.3) should have ensured. Despite their large numbers in Bosnia and Herzegovina and their willingness to support the standing regime, Muslims were not proportionally represented in any layer of government—not even by those Muslims who declared themselves to be Serbs. Rather, a large number of positions in Bosnia and Herzegovina were filled by Serbs, many of whom were imported from Serbia.[90] For example, the Preliminary Committee of the National Council assigned to Bosnia and Herzegovina eighteen places in the National Council Plenum. Six of the seats should have been held by Muslims because of the size of their population. In the end, however, only two Muslims (Hamid Svrzo and Mehmed Spaho) served on the plenum. On the Central Committee of the National Council, no Muslims were included among the delegates from Bosnia and Herzegovina although two Muslims (Svrzo and Halid Hrasnić) were later co-opted[91] rather than nominated by their coreligionists. Mehmed Spaho became the minister of forests and mining in the first Yugoslav government and later the minister of transportation under Stojadinović.

Muslims were also represented unfairly in the provincial, district, and local governments. The National Council delegation from Bosnia and Herzegovina contained 12 Orthodox, 8 Catholic, and 5 Muslim representatives; the National Government delegation included 7 Orthodox, 4 Catholic, and 1 Muslim member; and in the Sarajevo *opština* (township) there were 13 Orthodox, 13 Catholic, and 9 Muslim members.[92] Of the 273 *pokrajina* (province) positions of state administration, only 17 were filled by Muslims, and Muslims held none of the 54 leading positions.[93]

The Bosnian Muslim community did receive financial and other types of support from the Yugoslav government for battling illiteracy and training and certifying clerics.[94] Thus, a positive result of Bosnian Muslim support of the government was the tolerance with which Islam was treated within Yugoslavia. The rights of the Muslims as a minority religion in the Kingdom of the Serbs, Croats, and Slovenes had been confirmed in 1919 by Article 10 of the Agreement with the Allied powers. Point 7 of the Corfu Declaration and provisions of the later Vidovdan Constitution both stated that the Muslim confession should be given equal treatment with the Orthodox and Catholic religions. This was particularly important to the Bosnian Muslim population in light of its often harsh treatment by Serbian army units in Bosnia and Herzegovina. The military's antagonism was reinforced by the memories of the large number of Bosnian Muslims who had joined the World War I anti-Serb *Schutzkorps*.[95]

The hierarchy of the Islamic religious community continued to protect the religious faith and traditions of the Bosnian Muslims. Religious tribunals settled all juridical matters pertaining to Muslim life except when both parties to a dispute agreed to follow state law and to use state institutions.[96] Whereas the abolition of the caliphate in Turkey had altered the position of Muslims around the world, in the Yugoslav Kingdom the Muslim inhabitants were not sufficiently isolated within the body politic or so resistant to secular matters that the loss of the caliph paralyzed the community. In fact, the further distancing of the Bosnian Muslims from residues of their Ottoman experience encouraged the already extant secularizing tendencies within much of their community. In practice, although this was not publicly admitted, the term *Muslim* was beginning to have a different, less religious meaning in Yugoslavia, as reflected in the distance Muslim communities maintained from each other throughout the country.

The religious organization of the Yugoslav Muslim community was originally divided into three regions. The Muslims of Bosnia and Herzegovina, Croatia, and Slovenia were administered by the *Reis-ul-ulema* in Sarajevo, whereas the Serbian and Macedonian Muslims fell under the jurisdiction of the *Reis-ul-ulema* of Belgrade. The *mufti* (district head) of Stari Bar was the leader of the Montenegrin Muslims.[97] A number of organizations called *tariqas* (*tarikats* in Serbo-Croatian) existed throughout the region to spread and administer Sufism (Islamic mysticism).[98] In 1930, however, as part of King Alexander's centralization program, Muslim religious interests were united in a Supreme Council of the Islamic Religious Community located in Belgrade. Two regional leaderships were maintained, one in Sarajevo and one in Skopje. Then in 1936, the various institutions were merged into one organization based in Sarajevo, and the subsidiary post of *mufti* was abolished.[99]

The creation of one Sarajevo-based Supreme Council did not successfully unify all Muslims in Yugoslavia. In fact, the new organization of the Islamic religious community appears to have reinforced, rather than erased, the cleavages between the Bosnian and other Muslim communities.[100] Yugoslavia's Albanian Muslims were particularly disaffected by what Steven L. Burg termed their "double minority status," namely, their religious domination by the Bosnian Muslims and their political domination by the Serbs.[101] The Bosnian Muslims continued to have their own separate periodicals and newspapers and to run their own schools. Secular trends surfaced, replacing a communal religious focus with an embryonic feeling of national unity.

Conclusion

In summary, the picture of interwar Yugoslavia is one of tension, potential conflict, and widespread dissatisfaction. The new Yugoslav government was faced with border problems and with conflicts inherited from the Austro-Hungarian and Serbian monarchies. Revisionist states such as Austria, Bulgaria, Italy, and Hungary sought to utilize the dissatisfaction of minority peoples throughout the Yugoslav Kingdom to disrupt its functioning. Most of Yugoslavia's frontiers were contested by states that supported the territorial claims of the contentious minorities. Bulgaria confronted the Yugoslav Kingdom over Macedonia, and Italy's resentment of Yugoslavia's existence was coupled with its designs on Albania and the Adriatic. Postwar Italy, as with prewar Austria-Hungary, considered Yugoslavia (Serbia) its main obstacle to economic and political infiltration of the Balkans.[102] Italian enmity was expressed by its persecution of the Yugoslav minority in Italy and its aid to and encouragement of the anti-Yugoslav terrorist group, the Ustaše, as well as of Bulgarian and Albanian irredentism.[103] Hungarian demands on the kingdom were so insistent that Yugoslavia agreed to sign a series of bilateral treaties with Czechoslovakia and Romania that became known as the Little Entente. All three countries were threatened by Hungary's renunciation of territorial changes under the 1920 Treaty of Trianon.

These international concerns only exacerbated Yugoslavia's difficulties as it entered the World War II era. A number of conditions had militated in favor of the unification of the South Slavs. Certain shared linguistic and ancient racial affinities were heightened by the intermixture of the various populations and the identification of common external enemies. The new Yugoslavia, however, was forced into undertaking the almost overwhelming task of trying to forge consensus among three major religious groups—Orthodox, Catholic, and Muslim—and with creating a unified economy composed of grossly underdeveloped regions existing side by side with more industrially developed areas. Such disparities and tensions demanded a higher order of statesmanship than was perhaps attainable by the various concerned parties.

During the interwar period Serbs, Croats, and Muslims continued to lead separate social and cultural existences in Yugoslavia. Political life also continued along separate tracks for the different ethnic groups. The Bosnian Muslims were represented largely by the JMO, which evolved into a legitimate political group. There were also some signs among the Bosnian Muslim community of the expression of a nascent, embryonic national feeling communicated in response to attempts to lure the Muslims into expressions of Serb or Croat self-identification. As a result of the pressures they faced from both Serbs and Croats, the Bosnian Muslim elites decided that their security was best assured within Yugoslavia by supporting the central government from which patronage, protection, and other benefits flowed but not in expressing any strong nationalist identity. This policy of coalition building and support of the central government stood them in good stead throughout the interwar period and even the Tito years. When the Bosnian Muslims abandoned this policy in the 1990s (or, to be more precise, when it was removed as an option), their misfortunes began.

NOTES

1. Cited in Frederic W.L. Kovacs, *The Untamed Balkans* (London: Hale, 1942), p. 129.

2. Michael G. Roskin pointed out that Western Europe had settled similar territorial disputes with heavy fighting during the Middle Ages and the Renaissance, whereas the East Europeans had to wait for the collapse of the last major empire in the region, the Soviet Union, before they could discover "who had the wealth, power, geography, and allies to get and keep what they claimed was theirs." *The Rebirth of East Europe* (Englewood Cliffs, N.J.: Prentice Hall, 1994), p. 35.

3. Robert R. King, "Eastern Europe," in Robert G. Wirsing, ed., *Protection of Ethnic Minorities: Comparative Perspectives* (New York: Pergamon Press, 1981), pp. 80–82.

4. Dusko Doder, "Yugoslavia: New War, Old Hatreds," *Foreign Policy* 91 (Summer 1993), p. 9.

5. Alex N. Dragnich, "The Serbian Government, the Army, and the Unification of Yugoslavs," in Dimitrije Djordjević, ed., *The Creation of Yugoslavia 1914–1918* (Santa Barbara: Clio Books, 1980), p. 47. See Charles Jelavich and Barbara Jelavich, *The Establishment of the Balkan National States 1804–1920* (Seattle: University of Washington Press, 1977), pp. 301–304, concerning Yugoslav land settlements following World War I.

6. Wayne S. Vucinich, "Interwar Yugoslavia," in Wayne S. Vucinich, ed., *Contemporary Yugoslavia: Twenty Years of Socialist Experiment* (Berkeley: University of California Press, 1969), p. 47.

7. Boris Furlan, "The Nationality Problem in the Balkans," lecture delivered at the Hoover Institution, Stanford, California, 20 February 1943.

8. Agnes Headlam-Morley, *The New Democratic Constitutions of Europe: A Comparative Study of Post-War European Constitutions with Special Reference to Germany, Czechoslovakia, Poland, Finland, the Kingdom of the Serbs, Croats and Slovenes and the Baltic States* (London: Oxford University Press, 1929), p. 90.

9. Mihailo Crnobrnja provided a detailed description of the various South Slav players and the groups and positions they represented during the negotiations leading to the creation of the Yugoslav kingdom in *The Yugoslav Drama* (Montreal: McGill-Queen's University Press, 1994), pp. 35–50.

10. Aleksa Djilas, *The Contested Country: Yugoslav Unity and Communist Revolution, 1919–1953* (Cambridge: Harvard University Press, 1991), p. 5.

11. See George Schöpflin, "The Ideology of Croatian Nationalism," *Survey* 19 (Winter 1973), pp. 123–148, for more on the Croatian component of this difficult relationship.

12. Atif Purivatra, *Nacionalni i politički razvitak Muslimana* (Sarajevo: Svjetlost, 1970), p. 134; and Bogdan Krizman, *Hrvatska u prvom svjetskom ratu: Hrvatsko-srpski politički odnosi* (Zagreb: Globus, 1989), pp. 255–257.

13. See Atif Purivatra, *Jugoslavenska muslimanska organizacija u političkom životu Kraljevine Srba, Hrvata i Slovenaca* (Sarajevo: Svjetlost, 1974), p. 44, for a description of some of the arbitrary violence by those *kmets* who did not wait for the official proclamation of the end of feudal relations but declared their own freedom and wreaked vengeance on their erstwhile landlords. Purivatra termed these outbursts not the beginning of an organized peasant revolt but rather "characteristics of an elemental movement of the agrarian masses with elements of violence and anarchical ingredients." *Jugoslavenska muslimanska organizacija*, p. 45.

14. Ivo Banac documented negative characterizations of Bosnian Muslims emanating from Bosnian Serb sources in *The National Question in Yugoslavia: Origins, History, Politics* (Ithaca: Cornell University Press, 1984), pp. 371–372.

15. Ibid., p. 368.

16. Jelavich and Jelavich, *The Establishment of the Balkan National States*, p. 304.

17. Croatian Peasant Party leader Stjepan Radić expressed the yearning of Croats to "Europeanize the Balkans" and not to become Balkanized themselves as the Serbs wished. See Edward James Woodhouse and Chase Going Woodhouse, *Italy and the Jugoslavs* (Boston: Badger, 1920), p. 127.

18. Robert J. Donia and John V.A. Fine Jr., *Bosnia and Hercegovina: A Tradition Betrayed* (New York: Columbia University Press, 1994), p. 125.

19. Paul Lendvai, *Anti-Semitism Without Jews: Communist Eastern Europe* (Garden City, N.Y.: Doubleday, 1971), p. 59. See Paul Shoup, *Communism and the Yugoslav National Question* (New York: Columbia University Press, 1968), pp. 20–21 (note); Ivan Avakumović, *History of the Communist Party of Yugoslavia* (Aberdeen: Aberdeen University Press, 1964), pp. 42–45; and Ivo Banac, "The Communist Party of Yugoslavia During the Period of Legality, 1919–1921," in Ivo Banac, ed., *The Effects of World War I: The Class War After the Great War: The Rise of Communist Parties in East Central Europe, 1918–1921* (Boulder: Social Sciences Monographs, 1983), p. 330, for more data on Communist Party election successes in 1920.

20. George Prpić, "Communism and Nationalism in Yugoslavia," *Balkan Studies* 10 (1969), p. 25. Nevertheless, the CPY remained aloof from the popular outbursts against Serbian centralism. The Communist Party obviously received votes from both Communists and non-Communists, providing its only legal electoral victory in royal Yugoslavia. Presumably, the rationale for non-Communists to cast a vote for the Communist Party was to protest against Serbian domination.

21. Fedor Ivan Cicak, "The Communist Party of Yugoslavia Between 1919–1934: An Analysis of Its Formative Process," Ph.D. dissertation, Indiana University (1965), p. 95.

22. See Banac, "The Communist Party of Yugoslavia," pp. 203–205, and Avakumović, *History of the Communist Party of Yugoslavia*, pp. 49–57, for descriptions of the government's measures to repress the CPY and the CPY responses. One public response was CPY Secretary Sima Marković's statement in April 1921 in the Constituent Assembly that "our Party exists as the Communist Party of Yugoslavia and will continue, despite everything you do to suppress it. You have declared it illegal today, but it will live on. It will grow and thrive in secret, until one day it will re-emerge to sweep you and your like from power and establish the dictatorship of the Proletariat." Cited in S. C., "Political Forces in Yugoslavia Today," *World Today* 2 (November 1946), p. 535. Marković sought ways to legalize the party once again, but the Third International (Comintern) line was hostile to the existence of Yugoslavia. Cominternists argued that the CPY should ally itself with the peasants and that

the Yugoslav state should be broken up into a national republic for each nationality. Avakumović, *History of the Communist Party of Yugoslavia*, p. 72. Marković's faction, however, refused to exploit the revolutionary potential of ethnic conflict in Yugoslavia and sought a unitary, centralized state and party within which to cool off nationalistic tensions so the class conflict could be pursued through trade unionism. In a number of works outlining his theses, such as his *Der Kommunizmus in Jugoslawien* (Hamburg: Verlag der Kommunistischen Internationale, 1922), and *Ustavno pitanje i radnička klasa Jugoslavije* (Belgrade: Narodna Misao, 1923), Marković argued that the national question in Yugoslavia—whether "the Serbs, Croats, and Slovenes are three 'tribes' of one nation or three nations" lacked revolutionary potential. Sima Marković, *Nacionalno pitanje u svetlosti Marksizma* (Belgrade: Narodna Misao, 1923), p. 103. Furthermore, if the nationality question were not solved within the capitalistic framework, then "the class struggle would remain stillborn, overshadowed by the demagogic appeals of competing national groups." Shoup, *Communism and the Yugoslav National Question*, p. 25. Thus Marković, at least initially, defended the idea of a constitutionally reformed but unitaristic state based on maximum autonomy and self-determination for the national groups. Such a policy would satisfy the persistent search for self-determination by these groups. See discussion in Dušan Lukac, "Doprinos revolucionarnog radničkog pokreta urazrešavanju ključnih problema nacionalnog pitanju u Jugoslaviji," *Jugoslovenski istorijske časopis* 4 (1969), p. 168. Marković's position in regard to Yugoslavia specifically was that there was no revolutionary value in pursuing the question.

23. Banac, *The National Question in Yugoslavia*, p. 375.

24. K. F. Cviic, "Yugoslavia's Moslem Problem," *World Today* 36 (March 1980), p. 109.

25. Banac, *The National Question in Yugoslavia*, p. 373.

26. Raymond Pearson, *National Minorities in Eastern Europe: 1848–1945* (New York: St. Martin's Press, 1983), p. 159. Other Muslim leaders criticized Spaho for this. They were particularly incensed by his declaration vowing not to make public statements without prior approval of the National Council. Spaho's critics claimed he was jeopardizing the equal representation of Muslims by signing away the Muslim right to public protest. Purivatra, *Jugoslavenska muslimanska organizacija*, pp. 31–32.

27. The choice of this date to announce the new constitution could not have been more inauspicious. The Serbian defeat by the Turks at Kosovo Polje in 1389 is celebrated on this day, and Archduke Franz Ferdinand was assassinated on this day by a Bosnian Serb patriot. The date was thus suspicious for the non-Serb populace, which saw the constitution as the culmination of pan-Serbianism.

28. Jelavich and Jelavich, *The Establishment of the Balkan National States*, p. 305. According to Jozo Tomasevich, only the Serbian parties in the Constituent Assembly wholeheartedly supported the 1921 constitution. He contended that the votes of the Bosnian and Macedonian Muslims and of a small Slovenian splinter party were "purchased." *War and Revolution in Yugoslavia, 1941–1945: The Chetniks* (Stanford: Stanford University Press, 1975), p. 9. See Vucinich, "Interwar Yugoslavia," pp. 6–8, for a description of the difficulties experienced in the process of drafting the constitution of the Yugoslav Kingdom.

29. Banac, *The National Question in Yugoslavia*, pp. 375–376.

30. In fact, in 1938 more than 95 percent of the generals were Serb. James Gow, "Legitimacy and the Military: Yugoslav Civil-Military Relations and Some Implications for Defence," in Marko Milivojević, John B. Allcock, and Pierre Maurer, eds., *Yugoslavia's*

Security Dilemmas: Armed Forces, National Defence and Foreign Policy (Oxford: Berg, 1988), p. 90. However, M. Deroc provided a detailed description of the ethnic composition of the Yugoslav army in the interwar years that indicated that the entire officer corps was in the process of a dynamic transition toward a more multinational composition. "The Former Yugoslav Army," *East European Quarterly* 19 (September 1985), pp. 363–374.

31. George W. Hoffman and Fred Warner Neal, *Yugoslavia and the New Communism* (New York: Twentieth Century Fund, 1962), p. 61.

32. Donal A. Kerr suggested that this was not a unique phenomenon among new nation-states, which, although proclaiming fidelity to religious liberty, in fact showed less tolerance for minority religions because they detracted from the sovereignty and universal allegiance that were to be devoted to the new state. "Religion, State and Ethnic Identity," in Donal A. Kerr, ed., *Religion, State and Ethnic Groups* (New York: New York University Press, 1992), p. 25.

33. Hoffman and Neal, *Yugoslavia and the New Communism,* p. 60. Vucinich described the events leading up to this phase of the Serb-Croat conflict in "Interwar Yugoslavia," pp. 13–14.

34. Sabrina Petra Ramet provided a nonexhaustive list of Serb actions that agitated their relations with non-Serbs in the Yugoslav kingdom: "During the interwar period the Serbian-dominated government in Belgrade introduced unequal taxation for the various nationality groups, gave preferential treatment to Serbs in military promotions, imposed the Cyrillic alphabet on the Croats, denied the Macedonians schooling in their own language (claiming that they were Serbs), closed all state schools for Kosovo's Albanians and forcibly expelled about 45,000 Albanians from Kosovo province—confiscating their land and turning it over to some 60,000 Serbian 'colonists.'" "War in the Balkans," *Foreign Affairs* 71 (Fall 1992), p. 81.

35. S. M. Zwemer presented a breakdown of the number of Muslims in the various areas of Bosnia and Herzegovina. "Islam in South Eastern Europe," *Moslem World* 17 (October 1927), p. 346. Banac's total of 727,650 Bosnian Muslims included extrapolations of Bosnian Muslims in the diaspora, as well as in other parts of the country. *The National Question in Yugoslavia,* p. 50. See also Wayne S. Vucinich, "Yugoslavs of the Moslem Faith," in Robert J. Kerner, ed., *Yugoslavia* (Berkeley: University of California Press, 1949), pp. 263–264, and G. H. Neville-Bagot, "The Muslims of Bosnia and the Other Autonomous States of Yugoslavia," *Islamic Review* 48 (June 1960), p. 31, for figures showing the number of Muslim inhabitants in Yugoslavia in 1931 according to territorial divisions of the kingdom.

36. Figures from the 1910 and 1921 censuses from N. Kuzmany, "Notes on the Moslems of Bosnia," *Moslem World* 15 (April 1925), p. 177, and Vucinich, "Yugoslavs of the Moslem Faith," p. 263.

37. George G. Arnakis, "The Role of Religion in the Development of Balkan Nationalism," in Charles Jelavich and Barbara Jelavich, eds., *The Balkans in Transition: Essays on the Development of Balkan Life and Politics Since the Eighteenth Century* (Berkeley: University of California Press, 1963), p. 142.

38. Vucinich, "Yugoslavs of the Moslem Faith," p. 263; and Neville-Bagot, "The Muslims of Bosnia," p. 31. In 1939 it was estimated that the Orthodox population in Bosnia and Herzegovina constituted 44.6 percent of the total, with 1.227 million people, and that the Catholic population made up 21.7 percent, with 596,000 members. Vucinich, "Yugoslavs of the Moslem Faith," p. 263.

39. Cited in Purivatra, *Jugoslavenska muslimanska organizacija*, p. 74 (italics in original).

40. The Sandžak, Maćedonian, and Albanian Muslims fought for religious autonomy and preservation of their landholdings through the *Islam Muhafazai Hukuk Džemijet* (Society for the Preservation of the Rights of Muslims). See Banac, *The National Question in Yugoslavia*, pp. 377–378, for a brief discussion of the role, doctrines, and fate of the Džemijet Party.

41. Cicak, "The Communist Party of Yugoslavia Between 1919–1934," p. 92.

42. *Službene Kraljevine Srba, Hrvata i Slovenaca* (March and April 1923). The composition of the 1923 assembly was as follows: 168 Serbs (53 percent of the total), 78 Croat Catholics (25 percent), 25 Slovenes (8 percent), 19 Bosnian Muslims (6 percent), 12 Albanians, 8 Germans, 3 Turks, and 1 Romanian. For a breakdown of the election results, see Ivo Belin, "Malo izborne statistike," *Nova Evropa 7*, no. 11 (11 April 1923), pp. 329–336.

43. Whereas Spaho refused to declare himself either Serb or Croat, his two brothers declared themselves nationally—one a Serb and the other a Croat. Banac, *The National Question in Yugoslavia*, p. 375.

44. Jozo Tomasevich, "Yugoslavia During the Second World War," in Wayne S. Vucinich, ed., *Contemporary Yugoslavia: Twenty Years of Socialist Experiment* (Berkeley: University of California Press, 1969), p. 62.

45. Robin Okey, *Eastern Europe 1740–1980: Feudalism to Communism* (Minneapolis: University of Minnesota Press, 1982), p. 174.

46. Compensation equaled only "the present value of one year's farm rent in kind." Kuzmany, "Notes on the Moslems of Bosnia," p. 179.

47. Ibid.

48. Zwemer, "Islam in South Eastern Europe," p. 347.

49. Okey, *Eastern Europe*, pp. 174–175.

50. Vucinich, "Yugoslavs of the Moslem Faith," p. 275.

51. Ibid.

52. The Jelaviches explained that the Balkan peninsula was not prepared to make good use of the domestic capital available for industrial development or to attract sufficient foreign capital for investment. There was no skilled and disciplined workforce for the factories and no managerial class. The more prosperous classes in Yugoslavia were not drawn to industrial or commercial pursuits. The majority of university students were preparing for careers in government. Jelavich and Jelavich, *The Establishment of the Balkan National States*, p. 323.

53. *Jugoslavia: Basic Handbook*, Part 1: *Pre-Invasion* (London: August 1943), p. 96.

54. Okey, *Eastern Europe*, p. 174.

55. Kuzmany, "Notes on the Moslems of Bosnia," p. 180.

56. Vucinich, "Yugoslavs of the Moslem Faith," p. 273.

57. Ibid. Both Vucinich and J. W. Wiles ("Moslem Women in Yugoslavia," *Moslem World* 18 [January 1928], p. 65), cited the Muslim society *Beogradski Gajret Osman Djikić*, founded in Belgrade in 1923, as a major factor in stimulating and encouraging cultural and educational progress for Muslims, particularly women. The high illiteracy and poor educational situation among the Muslims continued until 1928 when, at the Muslim Congress in Sarajevo, religious and lay intellectuals agreed that the government should be asked to provide public schools in Muslim areas for both sexes. The further liberalization of condi-

tions for Muslim women was encouraged by the 10 July 1928 declaration of the Curia of Khojas, the supreme religious institution. The declaration stated that a Muslim woman could, "when needs require, expose her face, attend all types of public schools, work in stores, and occupy all other offices which are not contrary to the principles of Islamic morality." Vucinich, "Yugoslavs of the Moslem Faith," p. 274.

58. Ibid., p. 271.

59. See Banac, *The National Question in Yugoslavia*, pp. 363–364, for more on Starčević's views on the Bosnian Muslims' relationship to the Croatian nation.

60. Enver Redžić, *Muslimansko autonomaštvo i 13. SS Divizija: Autonomija Bosne i Hercegovine i Hitlerov Treći Rajh* (Sarajevo: Svjetlost, 1987), p. 10.

61. Banac, *The National Question in Yugoslavia*, p. 372.

62. Purivatra, *Jugoslavenska muslimanska organizacija*, pp. 483–493.

63. Matthew M. Mestrović, "The Elections of 1923 in the Kingdom of the Serbs, Croats, and Slovenes," *Journal of Croatian Studies 1* (1960), pp. 50–51.

64. Joseph Rothschild, *East Central Europe Between the Two World Wars* (Seattle: University of Washington Press, 1974), p. 212.

65. *Jugoslavia: Basic Handbook*, Part 1, p. 91.

66. *Pravda* 45, (18 November 1938), XII yr. (Sarajevo), p. 2, cited in Dana Begić, "Akcije muslimanskih gradžanskih političara poslije skupštinskih izbora 1935. godine," *Godišnjak Društva istoričara Bosne i Hercegovine* 16 (1965), p. 183. The dissenting members of the Bosnian Muslim community were assiduously courted by Maček for membership in the Muslim organization of the Croatian Peasant Party. Begić, "Akcije muslimanskih," p. 188.

67. Vatro Murvar alluded to evidence of King Alexander's "absolute responsibility for the massacre in 'parliament.'" *Nation and Religion in Central Europe and the Western Balkans—The Muslims in Bosna, Hercegovina and Sandžak: A Sociological Analysis* (Brookfield, Wis.: FSSSN Colloquia and Symposia, University of Wisconsin, 1989), p. 52.

68. Hoffman and Neal, *Yugoslavia and the New Communism*, p. 60.

69. Tomasevich, "Yugoslavia During the Second World War," p. 61.

70. *Jugoslavia: Basic Handbook*, Part 2: *Post-Invasion*, p. 95. Serbs formed a majority in six of the nine *banovinas*. Donia and Fine, *Bosnia and Hercegovina*, p. 129.

71. Vucinich, "Interwar Yugoslavia," p. 20.

72. Hoffman and Neal observed that "the actual assassination appears to have been arranged by a combination of Bulgarian terrorists, Croatian Ustaše and the Hungarian and Italian governments," each of which had reason for preventing a change in Yugoslav foreign policy. *Yugoslavia and the New Communism*, p. 62. See also ibid., p. 43.

73. Frits W. Hondius, *The Yugoslav Community of Nations* (The Hague: Mouton, 1968), p. 108.

74. Wilhelm Hoettl, *The Secret Front: The Story of Nazi Political Espionage* (London: Weidenfeld & Nicolson, 1953), p. 129.

75. Okey, *Eastern Europe*, p. 178.

76. Hondius, *The Yugoslav Community of Nations*, p. 108. Scholars differed as to the position of Prince Paul regarding Yugoslav fascism. Hoffman and Neal noted that "in foreign policy, Prince Paul and his Serbian ministers pursued a course that took Yugoslavia closer and closer to the Nazis." *Yugoslavia and the New Communism*, p. 62. Vucinich, however, stated that "Prince Paul was critical of the [Stojadinović] government's policy toward the Croats and, like many others, he was alarmed over the open collaboration with Berlin and Rome." "Interwar Yugoslavia," p. 27. Therefore, although Prince Paul was forced to

deal with the fascists and was made to acquiesce to the politics of his semifascist Prime Minister Stojadinović, little evidence exists that Paul himself was sympathetic to fascism.

77. Alex N. Dragnich, *Serbs and Croats: The Struggle in Yugoslavia* (New York: Harcourt, Brace, Jovanovich, 1992), p. 81.

78. Shoup cautioned, however, that "no such general accord existed concerning the remaining Slav groups in the Yugoslav population, nor in respect to the minorities." *Communism and the Yugoslav National Question*, p. 3.

79. Hoffman and Neal, *Yugoslavia and the New Communism*, p. 63.

80. Cited in Vucinich, "Yugoslavs of the Moslem Faith," p. 271.

81. Zoran Batusić, "E Pluribus Unum?" *East European Reporter* 5 (March–April 1992), p. 23.

82. Jelavich and Jelavich, *The Establishment of the Balkan National States*, p. 254.

83. Ibid.

84. Cviic, "Yugoslavia's Moslem Problem," p. 109. See Purivatra, *Jugoslavenska muslimanska organizacija*, pp. 36–39, for a description of Serb machinations to bring about the union of Serbia and Bosnia and Herzegovina. Serb frustration was recently reiterated in a memorial volume dedicated to World War II Serbian guerrilla leader Draža Mihailović. Alija Konjhodzich wrote that "through the sharing of these [few] conscious Serbs of the Moslem faith in all efforts for Serbian liberation and unification, the historical truth of their Serbian origin is more strongly underlined and the Serbian people's rights to two ancient Serbian regions, Bosnia and Hercegovina, where love and unity of the blood brothers has been confirmed and through the joint duels against enemies, is strengthened." These words were written "in memory of Serbians of the Moslem faith who lifted themselves above the backward and nationally unconscious Moslem mass to live and die for their people with whom they share a common blood, tongue and tradition." "Serbians of the Moslem Faith in Chetnik Ranks," in *Draža Mihailović Memorial Book* (Chicago: Organization of Serbian Chetniks "Ravna Gora," 1981), p. 436.

85. William G. Lockwood, "Living Legacy of the Ottoman Empire: The Serbo-Croatian Speaking Moslems of Bosnia-Hercegovina," in Abraham Ascher, Tibor Halasi-Kun, and Béla K. Király, eds., *The Mutual Effects of the Islamic and Judeo-Christian Worlds: The East European Pattern* (Brooklyn: Brooklyn College Press, 1978), p. 217.

86. George Schöpflin, "Nationality in the Fabric of Yugoslav Politics," *Survey* 25 (Summer 1980), p. 9.

87. Cviic, "Yugoslavia's Moslem Problem," p. 109.

88. Purivatra, *Jugoslavenska muslimanska organizacija*, p. 45.

89. Lenard J. Cohen, *Broken Bonds: The Disintegration of Yugoslavia* (Boulder: Westview Press, 1993), p. 13.

90. Purivatra, *Jugoslavenska muslimanska organizacija*, pp. 58–59.

91. Ibid., p. 30. Purivatra also discussed the exclusion of Muslims from the state apparatus in Bosnia and Herzegovina; ibid., pp. 55–65.

92. Ibid., p. 33.

93. Ibid., p. 62. Father Anton Korošec, leader of the Slovenian Populist Party, reported to Prince Paul on 28 January 1940 that Džafer-beg Kulenović, Spaho's JMO successor, had complained that despite Muslim cooperation with the government, Yugoslavia's Muslims were not receiving a fair share of patronage appointments. Kulenović also demanded that the Muslim Sandžak and parts of Bosnia and Herzegovina not already swallowed by Croatia be consolidated into a separate *banovina* with the same rights of home rule as the

Croats enjoyed and, it was rumored, as the Serbs and the Slovenes would soon obtain. Jacob B. Hoptner, *Yugoslavia in Crisis 1934–1941* (New York: Columbia University Press, 1962), pp. 198–199.

94. Zwemer, "Islam in South Eastern Europe," p. 348.

95. Enver Redžić, "Nacionalne manjine u jugoistočnoj evropi," *Pregled* 70 (October 1980), pp. 1294–1295.

96. For more on the rights of the Islamic and other religious communities in the 1931 constitution and related documents, see Ivan Lazić, "The Legal and Actual Status of Religious Communities in Yugoslavia," in Zlatko Frid, ed., *Religions in Yugoslavia: Historical Survey, Legal Status, Church in Socialism, Ecumenism, Dialogue Between Marxists and Christians etc.* (Zagreb: Binoza, 1971), pp. 46–47.

97. Steven L. Burg, "The Political Integration of Yugoslavia's Muslims: Determinants of Success and Failure" (Pittsburgh: Carl Beck Papers in Russian and East European Studies, University of Pittsburgh, 1983), p. 15.

98. Ibid., pp. 16–17.

99. For more detail on the organization of the Muslim community, see ibid., p. 16, and Steven L. Burg, "Islam in Yugoslavia," pp. 309–310.

100. Burg, "The Political Integration of Yugoslavia's Muslims," p. 19.

101. Ibid., p. 18.

102. Boris Furlan, "The Nationality Problem in the Balkans," lecture delivered at the Hoover Institution, Stanford, California, 20 February 1943, p. 6.

103. Vucinich, "Interwar Yugoslavia," p. 47.

5

Bosnian Muslims in World War II

"The friendship of Germany toward the Yugoslav people is not only spontaneous; it has gained its depth and permanence in the midst of the tragic confusions of the World War. The German soldier then learned to prize and respect his extraordinarily courageous foe. I believe that this feeling was reciprocated. This mutual respect is strengthened through common political, cultural, and economic interests. So . . . we form the hope that the German-Yugoslav friendship may also in the future further develop and ever grow closer."

—Adolf Hitler at a reception for Prince Paul, 1 June 1939

World War II proved to be another watershed period in the history of Yugoslavia, as it was for the rest of Europe. During the conflagration, Yugoslavia ceased to exist as a unified political entity. More than 1 million Yugoslavs died during the war,[1] most of them victims of the savagery that pitted South Slavs against South Slavs—much like the conflicts in the 1990s. The many and varied factors that allowed Yugoslav nations to inflict such barbarism upon one another during the war arose from the unhappy society in interwar Yugoslavia. A brief outline of some of the underlying factors that exposed the area to German blandishments, invasion, and subsequent civil war follows.

Economically, Yugoslavia's problems were shared by most of Eastern Europe. These overwhelmingly agrarian societies were paralyzed by the price-scissors phenomenon, a severe depression of agricultural prices in relation to industrial prices. Peasant indebtedness spiraled and canceled the effects of modest economic expansion. Inefficiency grew as too many peasants occupied too little land. In 1921, one hundred hectares of cultivable land were inhabited by 131 peasants; in 1938, up to 144 peasants were living on the same amount of land.[2] East European countries could not spark the industrial development that would have enticed people from the overpopulated rural areas to the urban settings. These underdeveloped countries also lacked the technological and educational skills, as well as the credit, to boost their productivity and market their goods.[3]

Extremist movements on both the left and the right flourished in the political vacuum caused by the inability of centrist peasant movements to solve the agrarian problems. Stalin's repudiation of East European Communist Party cooperation with all other movements in the early 1930s changed in 1935 when

117

fascism became a threat. Communist parties were suddenly encouraged to join with all democratic forces, particularly social democrats, in a popular front against fascism.

The Nazis were determined to gain a secure footing in Eastern Europe, which they considered to be Germany's traditional sphere of influence. Germany absorbed much of the agrarian surplus throughout the region with its willingness to forgo hard currency in favor of bartering with the poorer countries. In view of its extensive trade relationships with Eastern Europe, Germany was in a position to encourage the politics of nationalism as manipulated by indigenous fascists. Of course, there was a profound difference between the Nazi brand of nationalism and that of Eastern Europe, although the brutality of the one did not always exceed that of the other.[4] Nevertheless, the revisionist states of Eastern Europe, bent on making territorial changes, welcomed the aid of Nazism against the status quo powers.

In league with Stalin between 1939 and 1941, Germany was able to move massively into Eastern Europe, gaining the region's implicit acquiescence with German designs, as well as its economic contribution to the Axis war effort. Germany and Italy were able to utilize the mutual antagonisms and competing territorial claims of the East European states to forestall any united front these states might form against German and Italian imperialism.

Yugoslavia's Entry into World War II

Yugoslavia first allied itself officially with the Axis powers when Germany forced it to sign the Axis Tripartite Pact on 25 March 1941. However, Yugoslavia's ties to Germany had been forged earlier. In 1934, France refused to use its influence with Italy to stem Rome's oppression of its Yugoslav minority and its financing of the Croatian Ustaše. France was less concerned about its friendship with Yugoslavia than it was with building an anti-German buffer to include Italy. As a result, some Yugoslavs began to consider Germany to be a potential bulwark against Italian imperialism,[5] an outlook bolstered by Hitler's assurance that Germany had no territorial designs on the Balkans. In 1936, Germany did intercede in both Budapest and Rome in favor of Yugoslavia in exchange for economic concessions.[6] Yugoslavia's foreign policy thus shifted from one of reliance on France and on its Balkan partners through the Balkan Pact and the Little Entente to a policy of "neutralism" in which it would maintain its nonbelligerent status, at least until its military was battle ready.

Yugoslavia's leaders attempted to extract concessions from Germany in return for their participation in the Tripartite Pact. When the pact was signed after difficult negotiations, German Foreign Minister Joachim von Ribbentrop had agreed to Yugoslavia's demands that Germany respect Yugoslavia's sovereignty and territorial integrity and that Yugoslavia not be required to provide military assistance or to suffer passage of Axis troops through its territory. The Italian government, in its turn, was required to take into account Yugoslavia's security interests and its desire to possess an outlet to the Aegean Sea.[7] This last promise, Anthony Eden stated in his memoirs, was to be fulfilled by the Yugoslav possession of Salonika.[8]

Both domestic and international anti-Axis protest demonstrated the unpopularity of the Tripartite Pact, even though by signing the agreement the Yugoslav government had successfully avoided military involvement. Allied against the pact within Yugoslavia stood the royal officer corps.[9] Air Force General Dušan Simović on several occasions attempted to dissuade Prince Paul from signing the pact, warning him that the officer corps harbored anti-Axis sentiments.[10]

When Prince Paul finally acceded to the pact,[11] Air Force officers, led by generals Simović and Bora Mirković, overthrew the government nonviolently on 26 March 1941.[12] Prince Paul went into exile, and Alexander's minor son was crowned Peter II. General Simović became prime minister; Vladko Maček, a Croat, and Slobodan Jovanović, a Serb, became deputy prime ministers.

Universal Serb approval greeted the Belgrade coup and the multinational composition of the new government. Serbs, Croats, Slovenes, and the JMO representative from the deposed government, Džafer-beg Kulenović, headed the new regime. Interestingly, however, some Croats believed the putsch was engineered by the Serb-controlled army against Croatian autonomy in Yugoslavia. Other people responded to the Nazi propaganda that was rife in Yugoslavia at that time. Articles appeared accusing Serbia of selling out its brother Slavs to England and emphasizing German friendship toward Croats, Macedonians, and Slovenes. Propaganda pamphlets distributed in Croatia played on Serbo-Croat tensions and German sympathies for the Croat position.[13]

Belgrade's fevered diplomacy in the intervening days between the coup and Yugoslavia's involvement in World War II attempted to improve Yugoslavia's precarious position both internally and externally. The leaders of the new Simović government tried to placate Germany and their Yugoslav constituents in an attempt to gain time for their own military preparations by not openly suspending the pact but not ratifying it either.[14] Having turned to a traditional friend for help, Yugoslavia was disappointed when Stalin, still bound to Germany through the 1939 Nazi-Soviet Pact, did not respond to a request for military assistance. Although on 6 April 1941 Stalin did sign a rather lukewarm friendship agreement with Yugoslavia, the Soviet Union proceeded to ignore those obligations.

Internally, the new Yugoslav government attempted to "circle its wagons." As Maček responded ambivalently to vague Axis overtures concerning an autonomous Croatia,[15] Germany cultivated relations with more pliant Croats, especially the Croatian extremists. Amid anti-Axis demonstrations in various parts of Yugoslavia, Maček agreed to occupy a position in the Yugoslav government with the provisos that the 1939 *Sporazum* giving Croatia greater independence within Yugoslavia would be honored, that Yugoslavia would engage in negotiations with the Germans, and that no activities should take place that would justify Axis intervention or invasion.

To placate the Germans, the new Yugoslav government assured them that Yugoslavia would remain neutral and would otherwise recognize the previously negotiated Tripartite Pact.[16] These assurances, however, did nothing to assuage Hitler's rage over the sudden replacement of Prince Paul, with whom he had successfully negotiated.[17] Hitler had counted on an alliance with Yugoslavia to protect Germany's right flank from an Allied attack and to keep Turkey out of the war in the Balkans,[18] so that through Operation Marita Germany could intervene in Greece.[19] He was determined to destroy Yugoslavia "in a lightning-like operation [so that] Turkey would be sufficiently deterred and the subsequent campaign against Greece would be influenced in a favorable way."[20] Hitler's Directive no. 25 stated that "the military Putsch in Yugoslavia has changed the political situation in the Balkans. Even if Yugoslavia at first should give declarations of loyalty, she must be considered as a foe and therefore must be destroyed as quickly as possible."[21] Germany intended to smash both militarily and politically this small, poorly armed and poorly led, only partly mobilized, politically disunited, psychologically paralyzed, and almost completely surrounded country.[22]

Defeat of Yugoslavia

On 6 April 1941, the massive and brutal Axis invasion of Yugoslavia began. Germans, Italians, Hungarians, and Bulgarians made up the invasion forces against the only half-mobilized Yugoslavia. Hitler fielded a tremendous battery against Yugoslavia so that the destruction of the South Slav kingdom would not force a further postponement of his invasion of Russia.[23]

Despite the haste with which Germany's invasion of Yugoslavia was prepared, the collapse of Yugoslavia was not altogether surprising. Yugoslavia was defeated because of the military rout but also because of the disaffection of the population and the disintegration of the fabric of the country.[24] The Germans bombed Belgrade and overwhelmed the poorly equipped and organized Yugoslav army. On 17 April Yugoslavia unconditionally surrendered to Germany. The king and the government leaders had left Yugoslavia in exile on 15 April.

Upon Yugoslavia's defeat, Germany made Zagreb the capital of the newly declared fascist Independent State of Croatia (*Nezavisna država Hrvatska* [NDH]). Various parts of this territory were protected by either Germany or Italy. The NDH was headed by Ustaše leader Ante Pavelić, because the legitimate Maček government refused to collaborate with the fascists. It was nominally ruled as a kingdom by the Italian duke of Spoleto.[25] Although he never set foot in Croatia, he was known as King Tomislav II, the first Croat king since the thirteenth century. The territory of Bosnia and Herzegovina was added to Croatia proper, as were Srem and Slavonia. Germany also controlled part of Vojvodina and the economically important areas of Slovenia, leaving a small portion to Italy. By taking the most economically advanced areas of Yugoslavia, as well as those that contained strategic raw materials, Germany was able to exploit

German-Occupied Slovenia

Hungarian-Occupied Slovenia

Hungarian-Occupied Serbia

Italian-Occupied Slovenia

Independent State of Croatia

German-Controlled Serbia

Italian-Occupied Dalmatia

Italian-Occupied Montenegro

Italian-Occupied Kosovo

Italian-Occupied Albania

Bulgarian-Occupied Macedonia

Partitioned Yugoslavia 1941

Miles

0   40

Cartographic Services, Department of Geography, Ball State University

Yugoslav economic capabilities, labor, and raw materials. Occupied Yugoslavia further aided the Axis war effort by providing a line of communication with Greece.[26] Italy annexed a large portion of Dalmatia, all of Montenegro, and the Adriatic islands. Bulgaria and Italian Albania received parts of Macedonia, and Albania took over much of Kosovo.

Germany controlled rump Serbia and soon appointed General Milan Nedić, former Yugoslav war minister, to head the government. Although he was a collaborator, Nedić has not gained quite the historical opprobrium as that of the genocidal Ante Pavelić. In fact, Nedić may have cooperated with the fascists out of loyalty to Serbia and the king in an attempt to moderate Serbia's danger.[27] The fact that the Serbian quisling government was never as trusted by the Germans as was the Ustaše regime in Croatia bolsters that view. Whereas Croatian military forces peaked at about 250,000, the Serbian puppet regime was never permitted to command more than about 20,000 troops.[28]

Bosnian Muslims Under Fascist Rule

In a July 1938 directive to the Ustaše, Ante Pavelić declared that Bosnia and Herzegovina was not considered a country in its own right. A clear statement of the Croat geopolitical position appeared in a declaration issued by a rightist student group in Zagreb in April 1939:

> It is sufficient only to look at the map of our historic provinces to see how Croatia without Bosnia and Hercegovina from a geopolitical viewpoint—which here is of decisive importance—cannot survive, develop and generally be a politically capable and more permanent unit. Without Bosnia and Hercegovina between the two outstretched legs of Croatia there would yawn a fatal abyss.[29]

In the wake of the German invasion of Yugoslavia, the Ustaše claimed Bosnia and Herzegovina as part of Croatia based on geopolitical, historical, linguistic, and ethnic factors.

From the Ustaše point of view, one could also not correctly distinguish "the Muslims from the Croatian nation, because Bosnia is the heart of the Croatian state, and the Muslim tribes part of the Croatian nation."[30] On the first anniversary of the establishment of the NDH, Pavelić was photographed wearing a fez, symbolic of Croatian unity with the Muslims.[31]

The Ustaše view was simply that the Bosnian Muslims were Croats, and therefore their land was Croatian. The Bosnian Muslims accordingly were to be treated as brothers and allies, the "purest of all Croats."[32] Islam was honored for salvaging the spirit of Croatia from the past. *Bošnjaštvo* (Bosnianism) was "Croatianism" preserved by Islam, but it was an Islam divorced from the Middle East and thus simply another Croatian religion.[33] On the same occasion in 1941 in which he had foretold that a third of the eight hundred thousand Serbs in Bosnia and Herzegovina[34] were to be expelled, a third killed, and a third converted to Catholicism, Mile Budak, the minister of education, proclaimed that the NDH was to become a nation of two religions, Catholicism and Islam.[35]

The Orthodox, Jewish, and Gypsy populations were to be eliminated, but Islam was to be honored. The importance of Islam to Croatia was emphasized when Pavelić chose as his vice premier first Osman Kulenović and then his brother Džafer-beg Kulenović, Spaho's successor in the JMO.[36] The latter Kulenović was a longtime protagonist of Bosnian autonomy but nevertheless seemed prepared to acquiesce to the Croatian version of history, which held that the Bosnian Muslims were part of the Croat nation. Thus, Kulenović had obligingly declared himself a Croat prior to joining Pavelić's government in November 1941,[37] as had a number of Muslims during the interwar period. NDH officials and Ustaše members included more than 12 percent Muslims,[38] whereas ironically the Muslims apparently were not represented officially in the Yugoslav government-in-exile in London.[39]

The Ustaše declarations about Islam were motivated by more than feelings of brotherhood. In reality, the "Croatization of Islam," when coupled with the annihilation of the Serbs in Croatia, would rid the NDH of ethnic diversity and thus justify the joining of Croatia with Bosnia and Herzegovina.[40] To this end, NDH officials counted both Croats (23 percent) and Muslims (37 percent) when they calculated that Croats made up almost 60 percent of the population of Bosnia and Herzegovina.[41] The Ustaše may have also hoped that Croatia's acquisition of Bosnia and Herzegovina would assuage Croat anguish over the Ustaše surrender to Italy of Dalmatia and the Adriatic islands[42] or at least that it would further the interests of economic circles in Zagreb.[43]

The Muslim masses and leadership, lay as well as religious, did not seem to be united on the question of their origins or on their degree of commitment to the Yugoslav idea. At least initially, primarily upper-class Muslims seem to have responded surprisingly well to domination by the Ustaše regime, perhaps expecting that it would enforce a rule of law. This was not to be, however, and the Bosnian Muslims in the larger cities issued a series of protests through their clergy.[44]

Nevertheless, to the Muslim villagers the Ustaše was less feared than the resistance movements that were operating in their area. The Ustaše even sent arms to the villagers for their self-defense.[45] Some Muslims were induced to participate in anti-Serb and anti-Jewish massacres staged by the Ustaše.[46] In fact, JMO leaders initially proclaimed unity and full collaboration with the Ustaše movement[47] and did not discourage anti-Serb terrorism by some Muslims. The JMO leaders did not foresee that these anti-Serb measures would earn the Yugoslav Muslim community the enmity and distrust of the surviving post–World War II Serb community.

In courting the support of the Muslim masses in Bosnia and Herzegovina, Pavelić finally agreed to permit them religious and educational autonomy as presented in a plan drawn up by Hakije Hadžić, a radical pro-Croat Muslim leader and Pavelić appointee, in August 1941.[48] The Ustaše, however, was prepared to grant this measure of autonomy only if the Muslims did not insist on ethnic differentiation from the Croats.[49] Some Muslims, particularly those representing the autonomist movement, insisted that the Bosnian Muslims did not share the same ethnic origins as the Serbs and the Croats. They made their beliefs known to NDH and German officials,[50] but neither group responded positively.

Nevertheless, the Pavelić regime did exert itself to retain the support of the Muslims and their leaders, Osman and Džafer-beg Kulenović, by promising to give increased attention to Muslim material, educational, and religious aspirations. Accordingly, an art gallery in Zagreb, which had housed the sculptures of

Ivan Mestrović, gained three minarets and became a mosque for the use of the Muslims of the Independent State of Croatia.[51]

One result of the Bosnian representations to the Germans was a determination to utilize already formed Muslim legions to aid German military strategies in Bosnia and Herzegovina. In 1943, in response to an order by Heinrich Himmler that Bosnian Muslims should become more involved in the NDH and thus be denied to the resistance groups, a division of Bosnian Muslims was commissioned to be attached to the Nazi SS in Croatia. The Grand Mufti of Jerusalem, Haj Amin el-Husseini, encouraged the Bosnian Muslim clergy to join the pan-Islamic struggle against European colonialism by aiding in the recruitment of the Thirteenth SS, Handžar (Scimitar), division by the Prinz Eugen SS division.[52] After extensive training outside of Bosnia, in 1943 the Handžar division of twelve thousand Muslim volunteers returned and participated in bloody anti-Serb actions.[53]

Pavelić did not welcome the formation of the Bosnian Muslim SS division because he thought its creation too greatly differentiated the Bosnian Muslims to substantiate his claim that they were simply Islamized Croats. The Muslim religious and political leaderships' collaboration with the NDH also failed to ensure their influence in the Ustaše regime.[54] In fact, despite declarations to the contrary, the Muslim position in the NDH was really little better than it had been in the Yugoslav kingdom. To emphasize that Croatia and Bosnia and Herzegovina were to be irrevocably united into a greater Croatian unit, the *Ustaše* divided Bosnia and Herzegovina into eleven provinces, with a concomitant dilution of specifically Muslim political influence.[55] Therefore, some Muslims—especially those allied with Uzeiraga Hadžihasanović, a JMO leader from Sarajevo—sought autonomy in a special relationship with the Third Reich.[56] They feared that Pavelić's embrace of them meant they would eventually be expected to accept Catholicism.[57]

The Muslim political leadership admired the Germans more than they did the Ustaše.[58] Some Bosnian Muslims even claimed that racially the Bošnjaks were not Slavs but were descended from the Germanic Goths who entered the Balkans in the third century "under the name 'Bosni' in the period of the Roman Illyrian provinces."[59] Those Bosnians craved German protection and, in fact, proposed that Bosnia and Herzegovina be made an autonomous institution under the benign rule of Germany, much as some Muslim elites had previously encouraged an autonomous Bosnia within Habsburg Hungary.[60] They counted on Bosnia and Herzegovina becoming a German protectorate to evade what was a smothering relationship with the Ustaše government. German protection could conceivably empower the Muslim leaders, at least to the level they had enjoyed as property owners under Austro-Hungarian tutelage.[61] However, in the end the Muslim autonomists were rebuffed by Germany, which feared its client, the NDH, would find insupportable the removal of NDH influence over Bosnia and Herzegovina.

Even with all the blandishments by the NDH, the Bosnian Muslim community suffered divided loyalties. Many did not follow the ultraconservative religious and political leadership into collaboration with the Ustaše, especially when Germany refused to make Bosnia and Herzegovina a direct German protectorate. In fact, on 12 October 1941 some Sarajevo Muslims explicitly and officially rejected those Muslims who had committed crimes and atrocities against Serbs. A resolution of the Muslim clergy's annual general assembly on 14 August 1941 expressed a similar repugnance.[62] Rather than be swallowed by the Ustaše government of the NDH, many Bosnian Muslims participated in the antifascist resistance.[63] Unlike most of the other Yugoslav national groups, Bosnian Muslims could be found in the Ustaše, in home-guard units, in purely Muslim militias,[64] in multinational Yugoslav (Partisan) units, and—in small numbers— in the Serb (Četnik) resistance forces.[65] This situation, of course, meant that on occasion Muslims killed Muslims.

The Ustaše was aided by some Muslims in an orgy of massacre of Serbs, as well as Jews and antifascist Croats, within Croatia. Muslim villagers were reluctant to join Ustaše units, however, because anti-Serb actions called forth devastating reprisals by Četnik units. Četnik cooperation with Germans and Italians against the Partisans and similar agreements between Četniks and the Ustaše may have been the factors that initially galvanized the Bosnian Muslims to join the multinational Partisans. Eventually, at the beginning of May 1942, a Muslim Partisan unit was created in liberated territory in Herzegovina.[66] Other Muslim Partisan units, even battalions and brigades, were formed subsequently.

After the war, Zajim Šarac, former Yugoslav minister of commerce, described what he felt were the sentiments of the mass of Bosnian Muslims living in the NDH during World War II:

> The majority of the ruling circles placed itself at the service of the fascist invaders. . . . The circles of the high *Ilmia* [*ulema*, or Muslim religious leaders], among whom Reis-ul-Ulema Spaho, gave their blessings to German arms and together with the treacherous politicians described the occupation as being the liberation of the Moslems.

Claiming that the fascist policy in Yugoslavia was to increase the mutual hatred among the Yugoslav peoples, Šarac contended that

> In Bosnia and Hercegovina, especially, the enemy intended with the help of Moslems and Croats to threaten the national existence of the Serbian people. With the help of Moslem traitors the German and Italian fascists formed armed bands composed of the worst social scum, which committed the worst terror and murder of the innocent population in order to spread the flames of fratricidal war.[67]

As a result of these actions, the Bosnian republic suffered more deaths than any other Yugoslav republic (668,000) and, after Montenegro, the highest percentage of wartime deaths in Yugoslavia, losing as much as 20 percent of its population.[68]

Resistance During World War II

The Četniks

Nationalistic Serbian guerrilla units, called Četniks after Serbian anti-Turk guerrillas during the Ottoman era,[69] were formed in Bosnia soon after the German invasion of Yugoslavia. Composed mainly of Serb and Montenegrin remnants of the former Yugoslav royal army and Serb peasants they had recruited, the Četniks were led by a general staff colonel, Draža Mihailović. Eventually recognized by the Yugoslav government-in-exile as a general and as its minister of war, Mihailović attempted to gather a force that would be ready to seize political power and reinstate the prewar regime in Yugoslavia when the Germans withdrew from the Balkans. Until then, he would protect the Serbian population and interests for his monarch.[70] Mihailović supporters claimed that his decisions to limit his military actions to occasional sabotage and small skirmishes and to take no measures to attack or provoke German occupation forces were attempts to limit German reprisals toward the general population and to preserve his meager forces.[71]

The Četniks primarily targeted the Bosnian Muslims[72] as the contemporary manifestation of Serbia's age-old enemy "the Turks," thus illustrating continuing resentment of the Orthodox peasants toward the Muslim landlords.[73] Serbs also resented the Bosnian Muslims because many Muslims had become allies of the Ustaše. The bestiality of the Muslim SS Handžar division against the Serbs called forth equal brutality against Muslims.

The anti-Muslim zealotry of some Serbs was exemplified by calls for the creation of Serbian hegemony in the Balkans,[74] primarily by creating a "homogeneous Serbia"—that is, a Serbia "cleansed" of Croats, who would be sent to Croatia, and Muslims, who would go to Turkey or Albania.[75] However, even before the ideological basis was stated, a series of massacres in southeastern Bosnia in December 1941 and January 1942 claimed the lives of more than two thousand Muslims. In other massacres in 1942 and 1943 ten thousand Muslims were killed.[76] Vladimir Dedijer recounted in *Dnevnik,* his wartime diary, that "one night [in Rogatica] the Chetniks took their revenge on the Moslems. They slaughtered every Moslem who stood taller than a rifle."[77]

The Četnik atrocities against the Croatian and Muslim populations were at least in part a reaction to the preceding Ustaše-inspired Muslim terrorist activities,[78] although a Četnik conference in July 1942 recommended that only Muslims proven guilty of crimes should be held culpable.[79] Thus, there were opportunistic collaborators between Četnik units and Muslims in certain areas. Nevertheless, the fact that the Četniks did not always discriminate between Muslims who willingly collaborated with the Pavelić regime and those who were quietly sympathetic to the Serbs or were members of other antifascist resistance groups[80] in its turn estranged many Muslims from the Serbs and their greater Serbian program. As a result, the Četnik ranks contained few Muslims[81] and, in fact, were termed "anti-Muslim" in a report by Živko Topalović, a leading Četnik.[82] Četnik brutality against the Bosnian Muslims often resulted in enhanced Muslim recruitment into Ustaše legions,[83] but more often they joined Partisan units.

The anti-Muslim terrorism continued until mid-1943, at which time the Četniks recognized that the Muslims of Bosnia and Herzegovina and the Sandžak might materially aid the furtherance of the Četnik's political aims.[84] Mihailović evidently concluded that to legitimize the postwar claims of the Karadjordjević dynasty, he, as the monarch's representative, needed to build up his reputation as a Yugoslav, not just a Serb, leader. Mihailović thus made some overtures to Croats and Slovenes, as well as to Muslims.

The Partisans

The Partisans, the multiethnic resistance force, were commanded by CPY leader Josip Broz Tito. He had been sent from the Soviet Union back to Yugoslavia, the land of his birth, by Stalin in the mid-1930s to reorganize the badly frayed CPY. Prior to World War II, despite the electoral success of representatives to the Constituent Assembly, the Yugoslav Communists had experienced a particularly difficult time establishing any political influence within the Yugoslav Kingdom, barely surviving factionalism and the rigors of protecting the cells of their countrywide underground movement. Following the 1929 imposition of dictatorship, the CPY virtually collapsed under the suppression.[85] However, King Alexander's assassination in October 1934 ended the dictatorship. This event and the rise of Nazism permitted the Communist Party to recover during the mid-1930s. Tito, who succeeded Milan Gorkić as head of the CPY in 1937, proceeded to build a party that became increasingly attractive to members of all national groups. The CPY appeared to be regime supportive during the chaos accompanying the rise of Nazism and Stalin's policy of anti-Nazi popular fronts in Europe.[86] With the deterioration of Soviet-German relations, the CPY dropped the previous Stalin-inspired policy of calling for a breakup of Yugoslavia in favor of a Balkan federation. Instead, the party publicly stressed the need for Yugoslav unity against foreign aggression and dropped its antiwar agitation. The CPY also attempted to develop a position on the national problem to enhance its contention that it was the only party able to defend the rights of all Yugoslav nations equally.[87]

The Nazi-Soviet Pact interrupted the CPY's patriotic line, eliciting a new program that called for neutrality among Communists in regard to the emerging fascist versus antifascist groups. Tito expressed great enthusiasm for the pact, calling it a contribution to peace, in an article in the Comintern journal.[88] Coincidentally, the beleaguered Prince Paul rewarded the supportive Communist Party with a reduction of police harassment, thereby handing the CPY a golden opportunity to increase its membership.[89]

When the Soviet Union was attacked by Germany in June 1941, the CPY was absolved of the previous Soviet-imposed restraints against anti-Axis involvement. The CPY, about twelve thousand strong at the time, was the only Yugoslav group not heretofore discredited by petty nationalism. In fact, in contrast to Yugoslavism, the unitary position on nationalism adopted by royal Yugoslavia and its representatives, as well as the greater Serbianism or greater Croatianism adopted by the Četniks and the Ustaše, respectively, the Partisans broadcast the theme of *Bratstvo i jedinstvo* (brotherhood and unity). The Partisans stood for equality of all the various national groups throughout Yugoslavia, which helped their recruitment for simultaneously ridding the country of occupation forces and carrying out a social revolution.

The role of the CPY during the first months of Yugoslavia's occupation is still obscure.[90] The CPY's silence and refusal to work with any other antifascist resistance group until the Soviet Union was drawn into the war smacked of opportunism, if not the collaborationism of which some have accused it. The CPY's war record was attacked, with accusations of acquiescence in the dismemberment of Yugoslavia. However, the CPY denounced dismemberment in favor of a common stand of all Yugoslav nationalities against the fascists.[91]

The Partisans were joined by people from each of the national groups, who were more responsive to the message of patriotism and internationalism than to the narrow, chauvinistic postures of the Ustaše and the Četniks. Nevertheless, initially the Partisan movement was peopled mainly by Serbs from the Šumadija in Herzegovina, where the Partisan uprising had begun, and it continued to be dominated by Serbs who were being driven into the hills by Ustaše terrorists.[92]

The Partisan campaign against the fascist occupation began in earnest in July 1941. The Partisans started by appealing for a united popular front to resist the occupation. A call for insurrection was addressed to members of all nations and nationalities of Yugoslavia. It began with this telling exhortation: "Peoples of Yugoslavia: Serbs, Croats, Slovenes, Montenegrins, Macedonians, and Others!"[93]

According to the appeal, all national groups willing to work under the leadership of the CPY were welcomed into the resistance. It is revealing that initially the appeal did not specifically include the Bosnian Muslims, a fairly numerous and identifiable group in Yugoslavia,[94] although the CPY District Committee did distribute leaflets to the Bosnian Muslims exhorting them to become the masters of their own fate and to resist the "dead end" the NDH would produce for them.[95] This sentiment reflected the continued CPY reluctance to term the Bosnian Muslims a national group equal in status to the Serbs, Croats, and others. It was, however, implicitly promised that after the war the Muslims would be fully recognized as a separate national group.[96] In fact, in July 1940 the issue of the ethnic distinctiveness of the Bosnian Muslims was on the CPY agenda. Although the issue was treated at the CPY's Fifth Provincial (*Pokrajinske*) Conference for Bosnia and Herzegovina and later at the CPY's Fifth Territorial Conference in Zagreb in November 1940,[97] the future status of the Bosnian Muslims was still undecided.[98]

Partisan ranks grew to eight hundred thousand by 1944.[99] The Partisans were able to draw on the large mass of peasantry for human resources and economic sustenance, because the defenders of Yugoslavia offered the South Slavs the promise of a better future than did the Četniks, whose greater Serbian outlook was attractive only to the Serbs. Interestingly, many Serbs and almost all of the fighting Montenegrins did not respond well to the Četnik view of a greater Serbia and joined the Partisans in large numbers.[100] Even today, many consider Serb forces—particularly those from eastern Herzegovina who had spontaneously risen against the invading Germans in the first days of the invasion of Yugoslavia—to have been the linchpin of Partisan defenses.

The people who joined the Partisans were not forced to become Marxists or to join the CPY, and the CPY-Partisan leadership welcomed everyone into the struggle against the occupier. Religious officers were present in all Partisan battalions and brigades, and clergy of all faiths participated at various levels of the Partisan forces, including the organs of the provisional national government.[101] Non-Communists occupied leadership positions, although none could command more than a platoon.[102] The CPY was careful, however, to maintain tight control of the Partisan organization. People's committees were formed in liberated territories under local rule, but they were also under the watchful eye of the CPY leadership.

The Partisans were very careful in their dealings with the general population. Looting was forbidden, and they acted with restraint toward the populace, unlike the other resistance movements or occupying forces.[103] The Partisans also attempted to dampen interethnic tensions within their ranks among those who could not help being affected by Muslim and Catholic (Ustaše) and Orthodox (Četnik) atrocities against coreligionists.[104]

A second significant difference between the Partisans and the other Yugoslav resistance groups was seen in their treatment of women. From the beginning, the Partisans treated women as equals of men, both militarily and economically. Many wartime Communist leaders agreed that "without this mobilization of women they could have never won the war and the revolution."[105] And Milovan Djilas noted that the women performed their wartime tasks more bravely than the men.[106]

Initially, the Partisans and the Četniks attempted to cooperate in anti-Axis maneuvers (from July through November 1941).[107] Tito rated Partisan-Četnik cooperation in eastern Bosnia as smooth "for quite some time."[108] However, the Četniks perceived Partisan insistence on establishing national liberation committees in territories they liberated as a threat to the postwar return of the royal government, which they represented. The two forces thus became open and bitter enemies.

Furthermore, the Četnik resistance to pitched battle differed from the Partisans' enthusiasm. The Četnik reticence toward combat did not apply to those whom the Četniks deemed indigenous enemies, however. They specifically attacked Tito's Partisans, because Mihailović believed the Partisans were a greater threat to his goal of reestablishing the Yugoslav monarchy than were the fascists, a belief that may have justified in their eyes their uneasy union with the Ustaše and German forces at various times.[109] Thus, a confidential 1944 Allied Forces Headquarters handbook on the Četniks claimed that

> The role of the Četniks was not so much to contribute to the direct destruction of the Partisan forces in pitched battles—this was left to the Axis and quisling troops—but to clean up the territory from which the Partisans had been expelled and to hunt down any who remained behind or any who were known to sympathise with them. This function was carried out in the main by a system of "trojkas," teams of three men traditionally employed in the art of assassination and terrorism.[110]

Četnik action against the Partisans on occasion equaled that of the fascist occupiers. The Četniks considered their role to be to protect Serb interests in Yugoslavia so that when the war ended the monarchy would be reestablished "but with an even stricter Serbian domination to prevent any future repetition of the Croat 'betrayal' of 1941."[111] Therefore, Mihailović (also at Eden's request) was determined to husband Četnik military strength until fascism waned and Allied intervention in the Balkans was imminent. Četnik engagement of the fascist enemy was therefore rare,[112] which, according to Kenneth Macksey's account of European guerrilla warfare, ironically seemed to parallel the policy of Churchill and the Special Operations Executive (SOE) —the "evasion of battle and conservation of strength for a supreme moment."[113]

The Partisans, on the other hand, did not shrink from direct combat with the fascists, as is revealed in their casualty figures: 350,000 killed and 400,000 wounded during World War II. Only one quarter of the 12,000 Yugoslav Communists in the Partisans were alive at the end of the war.[114]

The Partisans engaged the enemy militarily knowing of the strict German policy of reprisals against the population.[115] Hitler ordered the execution of one hundred hostages from "all classes of the population" for every German soldier killed by the resistance and of fifty hostages for every German soldier injured. In fact, the Četniks claimed the Partisans went out of their way to provoke reprisals, because in this way "the people were reduced to a state of hopelessness and thus encouraged to enlist under the Partisan banner."[116] Četnik sympathizers believed German reprisals threatened the survival of the Serbian nation if the number of hostages became excessive.

Of course, the argument the Partisans made is also compelling. The Axis occupation had to be resisted. German retaliation was unfortunate, but resistance could not be halted simply to end German executions. Fortuitously, the German retaliations drove more people into the hills to escape the atrocities, where they could be recruited for the resistance. Thus, the brutality of the Axis regimes fed the ranks of the Partisans and other rebels. Axis preoccupation with the imminent invasion of Russia did not permit a meticulous pacification of Yugoslavia. The consequence of the hasty and brutal occupation program backed by insufficient forces was the swelling of the Yugoslav resistance.[117]

Critics of the Četniks charge that Mihailović's troops occasionally aided the Axis forces by attacking the Partisans.[118] The Četniks signed cooperative agreements with both the Italians in Herzegovina and the Ustaše in Bosnia, which helped the Četniks avoid a two-front war in their battle against the Partisans but, incidentally, also left the Muslims in the region without protection from Četnik terrorism.[119] Lower echelons of both the Italian and German armies operating in Yugoslavia regularly cooperated with and even armed the Četniks.[120] On this basis, the Četniks' Yugoslav credentials were suspect to a large number of Yugoslav inhabitants. And in fact, many former Četniks who wanted to help Yugoslavia shake off its fascist shackles joined the Partisans.[121]

Citing evidence of Četnik collaboration with the Axis forces to smash the Partisans,[122] the Allies switched sides and channeled moral and material support to the Partisans after the Teheran Conference in 1943.[123] Others, however, have suggested that Mihailović might have been sacrificed to protect the Anglo-Soviet deal regarding Yugoslavia's postwar status.[124] Whatever the rationale, the Allies gave the Partisans the status of an allied force and considered them "one of the few nations of Fortress Europe in which a broad-based resistance did contribute significantly to the obstruction of the Axis military effort."[125] Ultimately, even the Yugoslav government-in-exile was forced to reject Mihailović's Četniks as its representative in the field.

The nucleus of what later became the Yugoslav national government was formed in fall 1942. Fifty-four representatives of the National Liberation Movement from every area (except Slovenia and Macedonia, who were unable to attend) met in Bihać on the Bosnian-Croatian border and constituted themselves into the Antifascist Council of National Liberation of Yugoslavia (AVNOJ), the political organ of the National Liberation Front. Representatives to AVNOJ included a few prominent members of the prewar political parties, but members of the CPY were in the majority. During the second session, held in Jajce the following year, Tito was named president of the National Liberation Committee (the executive arm of AVNOJ), and Ivan Ribar, a prewar speaker in the Constituent Assembly, was chosen president of AVNOJ. At this session on 29 November 1943, AVNOJ was declared to be the "supreme legislative and executive organ of Yugoslavia and the supreme representative of Yugoslav sovereignty."[126]

The royal government-in-exile was thenceforth denied legitimacy in representing Yugoslavia both at home and abroad, and King Peter II was forbidden entrance to Yugoslavia until a plebiscite of all Yugoslavs after the war determined what form of government they desired. Furthermore, Yugoslavia rejected the

1941 dismemberment and declared that "the country would be thenceforward organized on democratic federalist principles as a state of equal nations."[127] Five Yugoslav nations were recognized at this time: Serbs, Croats, Slovenes, Montenegrins, and Macedonians. Each would have its own republic.

The lack of a unique numerically dominant nation in Bosnia and Herzegovina posed a problem for the Partisans.[128] A number of solutions for creating pure national units were proposed and ultimately rejected.[129] But in the meantime Tito decided to use Bosnia and Herzegovina to solve some problems faced by the interwar Yugoslav regime. He precluded the overwhelming economic preponderance of Croatia within Yugoslavia by separating Bosnia and Herzegovina from the former Independent State of Croatia, despite Croatia's designation of Bosnian Muslims as Islamicized Croats. Further, despite Spaho's energetic statement of preference for Serbian union, that area could not be united with Serbia because of the widespread fear of Serbian hegemony, also expressed by the reduction of Serbia's direct control over Vojvodina and Kosovo. Instead, Bosnia and Herzegovina was to become the sixth republic in Yugoslavia, with the constituent communities of Serbs, Croats, and Muslims to share control of the republic equally.

In hindsight, many consider the declarations made at Jajce to be at least an implicit recognition of a distinct Bosnian Muslim national identity. Although some Bosnian Muslims were clearly linked to the occupying fascist powers, the remaining Bosnian Muslim population was not necessarily compromised. The Jajce declaration could be seen as essentially a pledge of faith in the loyalty of most of the Bosnian Muslim population to Yugoslavia and, therefore, as an attempt by the Yugoslav Communists to deal with the recurrently dangerous issue of the Bosnian Muslims and their relationship to the Serbs and Croats in the context of their solution of the Yugoslav national problem as a whole.

NOTES

1. Bogoljub Kočović, *Žrtve drugog svetskog rata u Jugoslaviji* (London: Biblioteka *Naše delo*, 1985), p. 125.

2. Wayne S. Vucinich, "Interwar Yugoslavia," in Wayne S. Vucinich, ed., *Contemporary Yugoslavia: Twenty Years of Socialist Experiment* (Berkeley: University of California Press, 1969), p. 37.

3. Robin Okey, *Eastern Europe 1740–1980: Feudalism to Communism* (Minneapolis: University of Minnesota Press, 1982), p. 175. Despite all of these desperate economic problems, however, Vucinich offered a picture of an interwar Yugoslavia that might have been able to overcome its enormous problems and eventually pull itself into some semblance of prosperity if World War II had not decimated its advances. See ibid., pp. 56–58.

4. "Nazism horrifies by the enormity of its wickedness; the bad side of East European nationalism was more a matter of selfishness, pettiness and parochialism." Okey, *Eastern Europe*, p. 179.

5. Vucinich, "Interwar Yugoslavia," p. 47.

6. Ibid., p. 48.

7. Ibid., pp. 53–54. For a detailed description of the diplomatic moves required to nego-tiate Yugoslavia's adherence to the Tripartite Pact, see Ronald L. Krimper, "The Diplomatic Prelude to the Destruction of Yugoslavia, January to April 1941," *East European Quarterly* 7 (Summer 1973), pp. 125–147.

8. Anthony Eden, *The Memoirs of Anthony Eden, Earl of Avon: The Reckoning* (Boston: Houghton Mifflin, 1965), p. 265. Wilhelm Hoettl detailed the Ciano-Pavelić agreement whereby Croatia would cede to Italy a large part of the Dalmatian coast. *The Secret Front: The Story of Nazi Political Espionage* (London: Weidenfeld and Nicolson, 1953), p. 137.

9. According to Vucinich, this sentiment was also shared by a diverse group composed of Communists, students, and pro-Western Yugoslavs. "Interwar Yugoslavia," p. 54.

10. Ibid., p. 53; Hoettl, *The Secret Front,* p. 143; and an interview with Simović in H. R. Madol, *The League of London: A Book of Interviews with Allied Sovereigns and Statesmen* (London: Hutchinson, 1942), p. 106.

11. Cecil Parrott, an intimate of the Yugoslav royal family, stressed that Prince Paul was not pro-Axis in a letter in the *London Times Literary Supplement,* 2 January 1981.

12. Jozo Tomasevich suggested that this coup was "amply prodded by the British ser-vices" in "Yugoslavia During the Second World War," in Vucinich, ed., *Contemporary Yugoslavia,* p. 67. See also M.R.D. Foot, *Resistance: An Analysis of European Resistance to Nazism 1940–1945* (London: Eyre Methuen, 1976), p. 188; Mihailo Crnobrnja, *The Yugoslav Drama* (Montreal: McGill-Queen's Press, 1994), p. 63; and Donald Hamilton-Hill, *SOE Assignment* (London: Kimber, 1973), p. 102. Nora Beloff defined "amply prodded" as, at the minimum, helping "to create the false impression that an anti-German rising could pro-duce positive results." *Tito's Flawed Legacy: Yugoslavia and the West Since 1939* (Boulder: Westview Press, 1985), p. 64. On the scene in Belgrade as assistant naval attaché for the British Embassy during the coup, Alexander Glen was "convinced that the coup was much more spontaneous and deep-rooted than the speculation suggests and, whether we may have had influence or given encouragement, that events on 27 March would have taken the course they did with or without the British." *Footholds Against a Whirlwind* (London: Hutchinson, 1975), pp. 63–64. Eden's memoirs revealed his authorization to Britain's Yugoslav Minister Sir Ronald Campbell for "any measures that you may think it right to take to further change of Government or regime, even by *coup d'etat." The Reckoning,* p. 264.

13. Krimper, "Diplomatic Prelude," p. 141.

14. Eden, *The Reckoning,* p. 269. Still, Tomasevich asserted that not only did "all belliger-ence" leave the new government once it was in office, but "it was as anxious as the old one not to offend or provoke Hitler, and therefore proceeded slowly in improving the country's defenses. . . . There is little doubt that it was paralyzed by fear of Germany as much as the previous government had been, or more so as the invasion now became imminent." "Yugoslavia During the Second World War," p. 68. Steven K. Pavlowitch's study of this period cited a Churchill telegram and other unsuccessful efforts to induce the Simović govern-ment to counter Germany by attacking Albania and capturing equipment there. "Yugoslav-British Relations 1939–1941 as Seen from British Sources," *East European Quarterly* 12 (Fall 1978), p. 335. But Simović declared that this plan was foiled by the swift-ness of the German attack. Madol, *The League of London,* p. 107. Germany's allies may have been as astounded by the Yugoslav coup and as fearful of its consequences as the Yugoslavs were fearful of Germany. Italian Foreign Minister Ciano attempted to mediate

between Yugoslavia and Germany to prevent war between them and also because "the Italians, too, despite their long-standing desire for a Balkan sphere, were totally unprepared for a war with Yugoslavia." Matteo J. Milazzo, *The Chetnik Movement and the Yugoslav Resistance* (Baltimore: Johns Hopkins University Press, 1975), p. 3. Others have contended, however, that Mussolini's goal of attacking Greece and then Yugoslavia in summer 1940 had been postponed to October 1940 only upon Hitler's request. See, for example, Krimper, "Diplomatic Prelude," p. 125.

15. Hoettl, *The Secret Front*, pp. 136–138.

16. Tomasevich, "Yugoslavia During the Second World War," p. 68; George W. Hoffman and Fred Warner Neal, *Yugoslavia and the New Communism*, (New York: Twentieth Century Fund, 1962), p. 64. Anthony Eden, however, did not mention this in his memoirs; he indicated only that Yugoslavia sought to renew its contacts with Germany and Italy. *The Reckoning*, p. 274.

17. "Conflict and Conflict Resolution in Yugoslavia: A Conference Report, Discussion from Dialogues on Conflict Resolution: Bridging Theory and Practice," 13–15 July 1992 (Washington, D.C.: United States Institute of Peace, 1993), p. 6; and Vucinich, "Interwar Yugoslavia," pp. 54–55.

18. Vucinich, "Interwar Yugoslavia," p. 54.

19. Krimper, "Diplomatic Prelude," p. 128.

20. "Minutes of a Conference Regarding the Situation in Yugoslavia, Berlin, 27 March 1941," in U.S. Department of State, *Documents on German Foreign Policy, 1918–1945*, Series D 12, no. 217 (1941), (Washington, D.C.: U.S. Government Printing Office, 1962), p. 373.

21. "Führer's Directive no. 25, 27 March 1941," in U.S. Department of State, *Documents on German Foreign Policy 1918–1945*, Series D 12, no. 223 (1941) (Washington, D.C.: U.S. Government Printing Office, 1962), p. 395.

22. Tomasevich, "Yugoslavia During the Second World War," p. 74.

23. U.S. Department of State, "Minutes of a Conference Regarding the Situation in Yugoslavia," pp. 373–374. For alternative interpretations, however, see Jacob B. Hoptner, *Yugoslavia in Crisis 1934–1941* (New York: Columbia University Press, 1962), p. 267, and Dragiša N. Ristić, *Yugoslavia's Revolution of 1941* (University Park: Pennsylvania State University Press, 1966).

24. Some analysts blame a Croatian fifth column for weakening Yugoslavia and aiding Germany's advance. See, for example, W. Victor Madej, ed., *German Operations in the Balkans (Spring 1941–1944)* (New Martinsville, W. Va.: Game Marketing, 1979), p. 71. Tomasevich, however, suggested another view: "It was the system of hegemonism by Serbian ruling groups characteristic of the state during the interwar period. This made of Yugoslavia a state ruled by few for the few, in which the non-Serbian nations and broad strata of population in general had no stake and for which they would not fight." "Yugoslavia During the Second World War," p. 74.

25. See Milazzo, *The Chetnik Movement*, pp. 6–19, for more on Italy's role in designating Pavelić to head the wartime Croatian regime and on the gradual estrangement between Mussolini and the Ustaše in favor of closer Ustaše ties with Germany.

26. Kenneth Duke, "German Foreign Policy in S. and S.E. Europe, 1942–1945," *South Slav Journal* 4 (Spring 1981), p. 7.

27. Hoffman and Neal, *Yugoslavia and the New Communism*, p. 65.

28. Tomasevich, "Yugoslavia During the Second World War," p. 80.

29. Quoted in Fikreta Jelić-Butić, "Bosna i Hercegovina u koncepciji stvaranja Nezavisne Države Hrvatske," *Pregled* 12 (December 1971), p. 667, from a later publication of the declaration by T. Mortidija in *Hrvatski Narod*, 24 December 1941.

30. Jelić-Butić, "Bosna i Hercegovina," p. 664. See also Stella Alexander, *Church and State in Yugoslavia Since 1945* (Cambridge: Cambridge University Press, 1979), p. 22.

31. Hoettl, *The Secret Front*, p. 162. But the Vatican representative's disdain for Islam in interwar Yugoslavia was emphasized in Ante Trumbić's negative answer to the following question: "Is it possible for our people to put Mohammedanism and the other Christian confessions on the same footing?" See Dragan Bartolović, "Political Tendencies in the Church," in Erich Weingartner, ed., *Church Within Socialism: Church and State in East European Socialist Republics* (Rome: IDOC International, 1976), p. 231.

32. Jozo Tomasevich, *War and Revolution in Yugoslavia, 1941–1945: The Chetniks* (Stanford: Stanford University Press, 1975), p. 105.

33. "Krv nije zatajila," *Ustaša*, 9 November 1941, cited in Jelić-Butić, "Bosna i Hercegovina," p. 670 (note). Ante Starčević, founder of the pre–World War I Croatian Party of Right, first presented the idea that the Bosnian Muslims were an integral part of the Croatian nation.

34. There were also seven hundred thousand Muslims and five hundred thousand Croats in Bosnia and Herzegovina. Dinko Tomašić, "Croatia in European Politics," *Journal of Central European Affairs* 2 (April 1942), p. 81 (note).

35. *Hrvatski Narod*, 26 June 1941, cited in Alexander, *Church and State in Yugoslavia Since 1945*, p. 22. Viktor Gutić, governor of western Bosnia, emphasized that Croatia should be "thoroughly cleansed of Serbian dirt" shortly after Budak's speech. Cited in Andrew Bell-Fialkoff, "A Brief History of Ethnic Cleansing," *Foreign Affairs* 72 (Summer 1993), p. 116.

36. *Jugoslavia: Basic Handbook*, Part 2: *Post-Invasion* (London: August 1934), p. 18.

37. K. F. Cviic, "Yugoslavia's Moslem Problem," *World Today* 36 (March 1980), p. 109. See also Enver Redžić, *Muslimansko autonomaštvo i 13. SS divizija* (Sarajevo: Svjetlost, 1987), p. 14, for a discussion of Kulenović's participation in the NDH government.

38. *Jugoslavia: Basic Handbook*, Part 2, p. 37. Other sources put the number of Muslim *Ustaše* at 20 percent. See, for example, "Conflict and Conflict Resolution in Yugoslavia," p. 6.

39. Redžić, *Muslimansko autonomaštvo*, p. 60.

40. Mile Konjević, "O nekim pitanjima politike ustaša prema bosanskohercegovačkim muslimana 1941. godine," *Pregled* 12 (December 1971), p. 674.

41. Tomasevich, *War and Revolution in Yugoslavia*, p. 105. Redžić claimed Muslims represented 12 percent of the population of the NDH. *Muslimansko autonomaštvo*, p. 29.

42. Jelić-Butić, "Bosna i Hercegovina," p. 669.

43. Konjević, "O nekim pitanjima," p. 673.

44. Redžić, *Muslimansko autonomaštvo*, pp. 16, 30.

45. Ibid., p. 24.

46. *Jugoslavia: Basic Handbook*, Part 2, p. 30.

47. Konjević , "O nekim pitanjima," p. 678, citing an article in *Hrvatski Narod*, 15 August 1941.

48. Ibid., p. 677.

49. Ibid., p. 682.

50. See Redžić, *Muslimansko autonomaštvo*, pp. 71–79, for a discussion of the Memorandum of the National Committee of 1 November 1942 addressed to Hitler.

51. Slobodan Stanković, "Arab Countries Finance Construction of a Mosque in Zagreb," *Radio Free Europe Research*, RAD Background Report no. 176 (Yugoslavia), (31 August 1982), p. 2; and Alexander, *Church and State in Yugoslavia Since 1945*, p. 22.

52. Redžić, *Muslimansko autonomaštvo*. Hoettl suggested that Germany raised the Muslim SS division to attract Muslim sympathies and perhaps to influence Turkey to adopt a more benevolent attitude toward Germany. *The Secret Front*, pp. 162–163. See also Bogdan Denitch, "Religion and Social Change in Yugoslavia," in Bohdan R. Bociurkiw and John W. Strong, eds., *Religion and Atheism in the U.S.S.R. and Eastern Europe* (Toronto: University of Toronto Press, 1975), p. 374; and Milovan Djilas and G. R. Urban, "The End of the Bolshevik Utopia," *World Today* 47 (October 1991), p. 176. Djilas and Urban revealed that the former members of the Muslim SS Handžar brigade the postwar authorities were able to find were summarily shot.

53. Data from a report by the Grand Mufti of Jerusalem, Haj Amin el-Husseini, cited in Redžić, *Muslimansko autonomaštvo*, p. 100.

54. Ivica Mlivončić, "Crkve i religija u vrijeme narodno-oslobodilačke borbe," *Naše teme* 11 (1967), p. 1107.

55. Ivo Banac, *The National Question in Yugoslavia: Origins, History, Politics* (Ithaca: Cornell University Press, 1984), p. 377.

56. Redžić, *Muslimansko autonomaštvo*, p. 21.

57. The Croat ambivalence toward Muslims was made explicit in a telegram in which NDH Chief Assistant Ademaga Mešić asked Minister of Internal Affairs Andrija Artuković whether Serb Orthodox inhabitants who converted to Islam were to receive similar privileges as those who converted to Catholicism. Redžić, *Muslimansko autonomaštvo*, p. 19 (note).

58. A special study by General Oberst von Vietinghoff of the XXVII Army Corps entitled "Balkan Campaign 1941" claimed the Muslim civilian population in Sarajevo welcomed the invading German forces. Milazzo, *The Chetnik Movement*, p. 5, cited the study. See p. y, 14–15, in U.S. Army, European Command, Historical Division, *Guide to Foreign Military Studies*, MS no. B-334, and Redžić's citation of a report by el-Husseini regarding the enthusiastic Bosnian Muslim reception of German troops in March 1943 in *Muslimansko autonomaštvo*, p. 100. Other Muslim deputations from western Bosnia requested Italian occupation forces to help subdue national tensions. Redžić, *Muslimansko autonomaštvo*, p. 50.

59. From the Memorandum of the National Committee to Adolf Hitler, 1 November 1942, cited in Redžić, *Muslimansko autonomaštvo*, p. 73.

60. Ibid., pp. 10, 21 (note).

61. Ibid., p. 10.

62. "The October 12, 1941, Resolution of the Sarajevo Moslems," *South Slav Journal* 6 (Autumn 1983), pp. 37–39. Similar sentiments appeared earlier in "The September 22, 1941, Resolution of the Mostar Moslems," *South Slav Journal* 5 (Summer 1982), pp. 31–33.

63. See, for example, Konjević, "O nekim pitanjima," p. 678. *The National Liberation Movement of Yugoslavia: A Survey of the Partisan Movement, April 1941–March 1944* (P.I.C.M.E., 1944) listed a number of prominent Bosnian Muslims among the Partisan ranks, although Bosnian Muslims were, not surprisingly, reluctant to join what they considered an atheistic army led by Communists; p. 107.

64. Redžić described the attitude and actions of the Muslim Volunteer Legion, led by Muhamed Hadžiefendić, in *Muslimansko autonomaštvo*, p. 68.

65. Ibid., p. 21. However, Redzcaronić claimed that "only the worst Muslim rabble" joined the Ustaše and that in Yugoslavia Muslim reconciliation with the Četniks was impossible. Ibid., p. 76. Thus, the Četnik initiative to form a Muslim division came to naught, as it was determined that such a division would cause more harm to the Serb nation than good for the Serb war effort. Ibid., p. 84.

66. Ibid., p. 52, citing *Zbornik NOR-a* IV, Document no. 2, p. 12.

67. Zajim Šarac et al., *Yugoslav Muslims' Message to India* (Bombay: People's Publishing House, 1947), p. 10. See also *Jugoslavia: Basic Handbook*, Part 2, p. 30; and Redžić, *Muslimansko autonomaštvo*, pp. 18–19.

68. Kočović, *Žrtve drugog svetskog rata u Jugoslaviji*, p. 183.

69. The authors of *German Operations in the Balkans* (see note 24) claimed, in fact, that a major goal of the Četniks was to annihilate Yugoslavia's Muslim population; p. 195. See also Hoffman and Neal, *Yugoslavia and the New Communism*, p. 70; Tomasevich, "Yugoslavia During the Second World War," pp. 81–83; Milazzo, *The Chetnik Movement;* and *The Četniks: A Survey of Četnik Activity in Yugoslavia, April 1941–July 1944*, G-2 (PB), A.F.H.Q. (September 1944). The latter work also provided a brief description of Mihailović's organizational plans as described by Colonel Žujović, Mihailović's representative for Dalmatia. *The Četniks*, pp. 7–8.

70. The Simović government in London sent directives to the Četniks to that effect. Milazzo, *The Chetnik Movement*, p. 17.

71. Hoffman and Neal, *Yugoslavia and the New Communism*, p. 70. Foot sympathetically recounted Mihailović's motives for the lack of Četnik enemy engagement in *Resistance*, p. 190. *The Četniks* chronicled Mihailović's reluctance to lead an uprising; pp. 8–9.

72. Tomasevich, *War and Revolution in Yugoslavia*, p. 257.

73. For example, "The Montenegrins and the Serbs around Bileća, Herzegovina, were far more harsh toward the Muslims than toward the small Croatian community." Milazzo, *The Chetnik Movement*, p. 53.

74. "Projekat Stevana Moljevića, 30. Juni 1941," in Vladimir Dedijer and Antun Miletić, eds., *Genocid nad muslimanima, 1941–1945: Zbornik dokumenata i svjedočenja* (Sarajevo: Svjetlost, 1990), p. 12.

75. "Pismo Stevana Moljevića—Dragiši Vasiću, februar 1942," in Dedijer and Miletić, eds., *Genocid nad muslimanima*, p. 34.

76. Tomasevich, *War and Revolution in Yugoslavia*, p. 258. Radoje L. Knežević described a Četnik clash with armed Bosnian Muslims right after the fall of Yugoslavia. Radoje L. Knežević, ed., *Knjiga o Draži*, Vol. 1 (Windsor, Canada: Srpska narodna odbrana, 1956), pp. 9, 25.

77. Cited in C. L. Sulzberger, *Unconquered Souls: The Resistentialists* (Woodstock, N.Y.: Overlook Press, 1973), p. 157.

78. Tomasevich, *War and Revolution in Yugoslavia*, p. 259. See Bell-Fialkoff, "A Brief History of Ethnic Cleansing," pp. 116–117, for a glimpse of the scope of *Ustaše* massacres during World War II.

79. Redžić, *Muslimansko autonomaštvo*, p. 59.

80. Hoffman and Neal, *Yugoslavia and the New Communism*, p. 70.

81. Wayne S. Vucinich, "Yugoslavs of the Moslem Faith," in Robert J. Kerner, ed., *Yugoslavia* (Berkeley: University of California Press, 1947), p. 272. Tomasevich chronicled the existence of some Croats, Slovenes, and Muslims in the Četnik ranks, but only a few. "Yugoslavia During the Second World War," p. 83. Mustafa Mulagić was the leading Muslim

Četnik and a member of Draža Mihailović's National Council. Vucinich, "Yugoslavs of the Moslem Faith," p. 272. On the other hand, Alija Konjhodžich claimed there were "thousands of Moslems in the Chetniks." The most well-known were Sarajevo's Chief of Police Fehim Musakadić, Ismet Popovac, Hamdija Cengić, and Skopje's Chief Judge Derviš Secerkadić. "Serbians of the Moslem Faith in Chetnik Ranks," in *Draža Mihailović Memorial Book* (Chicago: Organization of Serbian Chetniks "Ravna Gora," 1981), p. 439.

82. Živko Topalović, *Pokreti narodnog otpora u Jugoslavija 1941–1945* (Paris: 1958), cited in Tomasevich, *War and Resistance in Yugoslavia*, p. 175. Mihailović stated in a speech on 28 February 1943 that the Partisans, Ustaše, and Muslims were his chief enemies and that only the Italians supported him steadfastly. *The Četniks*, p. 17. Documentary evidence exists, however, that Četniks did attempt to create Muslim Četnik formations. "Muslimana istočne Bosne povodom pokušaja četnika da stvore muslimanske četničke formacije," *Zbornik NOR-a* IV, Document no. 32, p. 94, cited in Redžić, *Muslimansko autonomaštvo*, p. 39.

83. The historical overview of the conference report "Conflict and Conflict Resolution in Yugoslavia" described the allegiance of the Muslims in Foča after a Četnik massacre there; p. 6.

84. Tomasevich, *War and Revolution in Yugoslavia*, p. 257; Redžić, *Muslimansko autonomaštvo*, p. 59.

85. George Prpić estimated that in 1932 the CPY had approximately five hundred members. "Communism and Nationalism in Yugoslavia," *Balkan Studies* 10 (1969), p. 26. Stevan K. Pavlowitch estimated that by 1940 there were only six thousand members. *Tito: Yugoslavia's Great Dictator: A Reassessment* (London: Hurst, 1992), p. 26. See Ivan Avakumović, *History of the Communist Party of Yugoslavia*, Vol. 1 (Aberdeen: Aberdeen University Press, 1964), pp. 60–92, for a description of what he called the CPY's "semi-legal" years (1921–1928) and the party's relationship with international communism.

86. Avakumović, *History of the Communist Party of Yugoslavia*, p. 179.

87. Paul Shoup, *Communism and the Yugoslav National Question* (New York: Columbia University Press, 1968), p. 50.

88. *Die Welt* (20 November 1939), cited in Avakumović, *History of the Communist Party of Yugoslavia*, p. 175. See also Tito's article in the Comintern journal *Die Welt* (30 November 1939), cited in Stephen Clissold, ed., *Yugoslavia and the Soviet Union 1939–1973: A Documentary Survey* (London: Oxford University Press, 1975), p. 6.

89. Beloff, *Tito's Flawed Legacy*, pp. 60–62.

90. Some, for example, claimed Yugoslav Communists deserted from the army when Hitler first attacked Yugoslavia. Alexander Jevremovich, *The Bolshevization and the Soviet Economic Exploitation of Yugoslavia* (Washington, D.C.: National Committee for a Free Europe, 1953), p. 10. See also Desimir Tochitch, "Titoism Without Tito," *Survey* 28 (Autumn 1984), p. 3.

91. The minutes of a CPY meeting reflected the party's position "opposing the breakup of Yugoslavia, asserting the right of the Yugoslav Party to jurisdiction throughout the territories of the former Yugoslav state, and even claiming the Italian portions of the Julian region for Yugoslavia." In Jovan Marjanović, *Srbija u Narodnooslobodilačkoj borbi* (Belgrade: Nolit-Prosveta, 1964), p. 79. Shoup described this occasion as one on which the CPY (and Tito in particular) showed it was not above concealing some of its actions from the Soviet Union, particularly concerning local matters. Thus, the CPY, when describing this meeting and its resolutions, failed to inform the Comintern that the Macedonian Communist Party had not been represented because through its leader it had allied itself

with the Bulgarian Communist Party. Shoup, *Communism and the Yugoslav National Question,* p. 62. For more on the Macedonian flight from the CPY, see Shoup, *Communism and the Yugoslav National Question,* pp. 51–54. Tito insisted that the Nazi attack on the USSR only accelerated and did not inspire the Communist-led uprising. Cited in Hoffman and Neal, *Yugoslavia and the New Communism,* p. 71. Vladimir Dedijer argued also that the CPY had been planning its resistance ever since the fall of Yugoslavia but needed the intervening time to bring its plans to fruition. *Tito* (New York: Simon and Schuster, 1953), p. 150. It was also suggested that the Partisans deferred an early strike in order to concentrate on training, since "premature insurrection might be fatal to future chances." Kenneth Macksey, *The Partisans of Europe in the Second World War* (New York: Stein and Day, 1975), p. 61. Of course, this statement by Tito, which appeared in *Borba,* 24 May 1972, called into question these views of Yugoslavia's position: Tito acknowledged that for Yugoslavia World War II was also "a civil war. But we did not want to speak about it during the war, because it was of no use to us." Cited in Tochitch, "Titoism Without Tito," p. 4 (note 6). Tito confirmed in approximate terms that Serbs composed 44 percent of the Partisans' National Liberation Army, Croats 30 percent, Slovenes 10 percent, Montenegrins 4 percent, Muslims 2.5 percent, and others 6 percent. *Borba za oslobodjenje Jugoslavije,* pp. 194, 197. Cited in Atif Purivatra, *Nacionalni i politički razvitak muslimani* (Sarajevo: Svjetlost, 1970), p. 72.

92. *The National Liberation Movement of Yugoslavia,* p. 23.

93. "Call of the Central Committee of the Yugoslav Communist Party to Insurrection," *Yugoslav Information Bulletin* (March 1975), pp. 14–15. This was also reproduced as "Peoples of Yugoslavia: Serbs, Croats, Slovenes, Montenegrins, Macedonians and Others! (Proclamation of the Central Committee of the CPY to the Peoples of Yugoslavia—Call for an Uprising)," in *Josip Broz Tito: Military Thought and Works: Selected Writings (1936–1979)* (Belgrade: Vojnoizdavački zavod, 1982), pp. 72–74.

94. Koca Jončić attempted to explain away this and other notable exclusions of the Muslims with the fact that the national minorities also received short shrift. The CPY was setting up an integrated National Liberation Movement under "extremely intricate conditions" and with often "inadequate coordination" and communication with central organs of the CPY. Jončić, "The Yugoslav Nationalities and the Decisions of AVNOJ," *Socialist Thought and Practice* 23 (December 1983), pp. 91–92.

95. Proclamation of the Provincial Committee for the CPY for Bosnia and Herzegovina "To the Muslims of Bosnia and Herzegovina," December 1941, p. 222, cited in Redžić, *Muslimansko autonomaštvo,* p. 35.

96. For a discussion of the Communist Party's attitude toward the national identity of the Bosnian Muslims as seen through official proclamations of the National Liberation Army, see Purivatra, *Nacionalni i politički razvitak,* pp. 65–129.

97. Atif Purivatra, "Stav komunističke partije Jugoslavije prema nacionalnom pitanju u Bosni i Hercegovini," in Milan Petrović and Kasim Suljević, eds., *Nacionalni odnosi danas* (Sarajevo: Univerzal, 1971), p. 190.

98. *Yugoslavia 1962–1991* (2d ed.), p. 177.

99. Hoffman and Neal, *Yugoslavia and the New Communism,* p. 73.

100. According to Milazzo, "Even the Partisans . . . were an overwhelmingly Serb movement until well in 1943, and there is considerable evidence that they often expanded their ranks by appealing to national sentiments which had little to do with allegiance to the Yugoslav idea." *The Chetnik Movement,* p. 186. Fred Warner Neal also dismissed a popular Yugoslav national ideal in the interwar period, except for a few intellectuals and political

leaders. "From Particularism to Unity: The Kaleidoscope of Nationalism(s) in Yugoslavia, *American Universities Field Staff,* Southeast Europe Series 2 (1954), p. 8.

101. Mlivončić, "Crkve i religija," pp. 1117–1119.

102. Foot, *Resistance,* p. 192.

103. Hoffman and Neal, *Yugoslavia and the New Communism,* p. 72.

104. For example, to win over some Muslims who had abandoned their homes upon the approach of the Partisans, "the Partisan unit secured the deserted homes against plundering and placed the peasants' stock under the care of persons who had remained in the locality; the Moslems, upon hearing this, returned to their villages, and the Partisans seized the opportunity to lecture them on the aims of their struggle." Shoup, *Communism and the Yugoslav National Question,* p. 65. On occasion, however, the Partisans failed to protect the population adequately. For example, Shoup reported how a Muslim village that laid down its arms at the behest of the Communist police chief was slaughtered by Serb Četniks seeking revenge. *Communism and the Yugoslav National Question,* p. 65.

105. Tomasevich, "Yugoslavia During the Second World War," p. 97. Barbara Jancar described the participation of Yugoslav women in the resistance during World War II in "Women in the Yugoslav National Liberation Movement: An Overview," *Studies in Comparative Communism* 14 (Summer–Autumn 1981), pp. 143–164.

106. Milovan Djilas, *Wartime* (London: Martin Secker and Warburg, 1977), p. 210.

107. Tomasevich, "Yugoslavia During the Second World War," p. 88. Tito may even have taken part in Četnik actions against the invaders in 1941. Richard Cavell Fattig, "Reprisal: The German Army and the Execution of Hostages During the Second World War," Ph.D. dissertation, University of California–San Diego (1980), p. 143. Tito's version of Četnik-Partisan relations and meetings with Mihailović in August and November 1941 is documented in "The Struggle of the Peoples of Subjugated Yugoslavia," in Josip Broz Tito, *Selected Works on the People's War of Liberation* (Bombay: Somaiya, 1969), pp. 170–171. See also Basil Davidson, *Partisan Picture* (Bedford: Bedford Books, 1946), pp. 91–92.

108. Tito, "The Struggle of the Peoples of Subjugated Yugoslavia," p. 177.

109. Antun Miletić discussed one example of Četnik collaboration in "O saradnji komandanta četničkih odreda istočne Bosne Jezdimira Dangića sa nemcima (avgust 1941–april 1942)," *Vojnoistorijski glasnik* 23 (May–August 1972), pp. 135–147.

110. *The Četniks,* p. 15, contains an order regarding troika recruitment and training signed by Petar Bačević on 6 August 1943.

111. Dennison Rusinow, *The Yugoslav Experiment 1948–1974* (London: Hurst, 1977), p. 10.

112. *The Četniks,* pp. 8–9, chronicled Mihailović's reluctance to lead an uprising.

113. Macksey, *The Partisans of Europe,* p. 63.

114. *Borba,* 20 June 1950, cited in Jevremovich, *The Bolshevization,* p. 2. As admirers of the Partisan struggle during World War II, Hoffman and Neal remarked that "it is difficult to portray adequately in words the drama of the Partisans' blood, suffering, courage and infinite faith in their cause." *Yugoslavia and the New Communism,* p. 74. See Tomasevich, "Yugoslavia During the Second World War," pp. 97–109, for a detailed description of the offensives against the Partisans and their resulting military situation. Nora Beloff was apparently underwhelmed by the Partisan sacrifice, claiming they lost most of their people in the civil war against the Četniks and the Ustaše rather than through fighting the Germans, Italians, and other occupiers. *Tito's Flawed Legacy,* pp. 82, 98, 122.

115. Tomasevich, "Yugoslavia During the Second World War," p. 90. See also Fattig, "Reprisal," for documented treatment of the German hostage and reprisal system.

116. Hoffman and Neal, *Yugoslavia and the New Communism,* p. 71 (note). Fattig also observed that German officers stationed in Serbia did not believe these measures commanded by Hitler would be effective, because guerrillas sought increased reprisals against the nonguerrillas to swell their own ranks. "Reprisal," p. 57.

117. Milazzo, *The Chetnik Movement,* p. 1. The Partisans have not been totally absolved from the charge of deliberately provoking Axis retaliation against the population. The Partisan strategy may indeed have been to "remove the party underground from the cities to the poorly supervised rural areas, seek support in the villages and among the roving groups of refugee Serbs, and create enough disorder to stimulate German reprisal actions, which would further radicalize the civilians and create more recruits for the Partisans." Milazzo, *The Chetnik Movement,* p. 21.

118. Major Radoslav Djurić, a close collaborator of Mihailović who subsequently defected to the Partisans, stated that on 3 December 1941 Mihailović ordered all Četnik units to attack the Partisans. Cited in ibid., p. 10. "While Mihailović seems to have stood aside from collaboration personally, his chief lieutenants repeatedly joined forces with the Axis in his name." Hoffman and Neal, *Yugoslavia and the New Communism,* p. 73. See also Hoettl, *The Secret Front,* p. 158. A pamphlet written by Vaso Trivanovitch entitled "Mihailovich's Treason: Documentary Evidence" (Ridgefield, Conn.: Acorn, 1946), purported to prove Mihailović's willful collaboration with the fascists. Milazzo recounted Mihailović's unsuccessful attempts to obtain weapons from the Germans for an attack on Partisan headquarters in Užice. *The Chetnik Movement,* pp. 35–38. Tomasevich concurred, stating that "the goal, as Chetnik documents prove again and again in general and specific orders, was nothing less than the complete destruction of the Partisans." *War and Revolution in Yugoslavia,* p. 259. Paul Leverkuehn supported this thesis based on materials gathered on the war experiences of Germany's Brandenburg Division in the Balkans. *German Military Intelligence* (London: Weidenfeld and Nicolson, 1954), pp. 152–153.

119. Redžić, *Muslimansko autonomaštvo,* p. 49.

120. Duke, "German Foreign Policy," p. 8; Leverkuehn, *German Military Intelligence,* p. 152.

121. *The Četniks,* pp. 81–82; Fattig, "Reprisal," p. 159.

122. Evidence continues to mount that Tito, too, contacted the Germans with an eye to collaboration in case of Allied invasion, which would have ensured the reenthronement of the Karadjordjević monarch. Nevertheless, in the end little came of these contacts. Hoettl, *The Secret Front,* p. 171; Djilas, *Wartime,* pp. 231–237.

123. Milazzo contended that the embattled Serbian Četniks "decided to go underground by attaching their troops to Nedić's legalized formations in order to carry on the war against the Serbian Partisans under official protection. They could thus avoid being captured by the Germans and continue fighting the Communist resistance without directly compromising Mihailović's position with the Allies." *The Chetnik Movement,* p. 40. See *The Chetnik Movement,* pp. 33–35, for a description of British contacts with Mihailović.

124. See, for example, John O. Iatrides, "Review of K. St. Pavlovich, *Razgovori sa Slobodanom Jovanovićem 1941–1945,*" *Balkan Studies* 12, no. 1 (1971), p. 308.

125. Milazzo, *The Chetnik Movement,* p. vii (source of quote); J. F. Brown, *Nationalism, Democracy and Security in the Balkans* (Aldershot: Dartmouth, 1992), p. 3. Tomasevich

speculated that by providing the Partisans with military aid, the Allies may have planned for the Partisans to tie down a large number of German troops and even force Germany to withdraw some troops from France before the Overlord invasion. "Yugoslavia During the Second World War," p. 104. Beloff, however, recorded that far from tying down German forces in Yugoslavia, the Nazis left Hungarian, Romanian, Bulgarian, Italian, and Ustaše units to administer Yugoslavia while German troops went to the Eastern Front. *Tito's Flawed Legacy,* p. 73.

126. Tomasevich, "Yugoslavia During the Second World War," p. 103.

127. Ibid.

128. In 1948, the Serbs in Bosnia and Herzegovina represented 44.7 percent of the population, the Muslims 30.9 percent, and the Croats 23.9 percent. Pedro Ramet, *Nationalism and Federalism in Yugoslavia 1963–1983* (Bloomington: Indiana University Press, 1984), p. 145.

129. See Hamdija Pozderac, "The National Question and the Formation of the Yugoslav Federation," *Socialist Thought and Practice* 23 (December 1983), p. 44.

6

Growth of Bosnian Muslim Nationalism Under Tito[1]

"It has been said that this war was a just war and we believed it to be so. But we are also looking for a just end to the war; we demand that everyone should be master in his own land; we do not want to settle other people's accounts; we do not want to be a bargaining counter for other peoples; and we do not want to be mixed up in any policy of spheres of influence.... This Yugoslavia is not for bargaining or trading."

—Tito, in *Borba*, 28 May 1945

"We should rather go hungry and barefoot than sacrifice our independence."

—Tito[2]

The Bosnian Muslims emerged from World War II in an ambivalent position. Whereas many Bosnian Muslims acquitted themselves honorably in the Partisans, the notorious Handžar Brigade, which continued to operate until the end of 1944, was linked in the popular mind with the Bosnian Muslim community. Nevertheless, the Bosnian Muslims came to play an increasingly important role in the politics of Yugoslavia and even in the foreign policy aspirations of Tito. In this chapter I explore these developments and their influence on the Bosnian Muslims from the end of World War II until the late 1970s. I also examine Tito's national policy, focusing on the change in Bosnian Muslim national identity and the significance it had for both domestic and foreign policy in Yugoslavia and for the Bosnian Muslims themselves. After analyzing the theoretical basis of Yugoslavia's national policy, I examine its application and implications for the Bosnian Muslims.

Post–World War II Yugoslavia

It was almost a foregone conclusion as the war began to wind down that the CPY, led by Tito, would dominate post–World War II Yugoslavia. Many South Slavs had rejected the wartime London-based Yugoslav government-in-exile, with its strong Serbian orientation, as a vehicle for the postwar unification of Yugoslavia. The other interwar political parties had been unable to act effectively to preserve Yugoslavia's interests or to rise above narrow nationalist or religious identifications. These parties were simply not compatible with or relevant for a country that had just fought a war of liberation from foreign invasion and simultaneously experienced a social revolution and a civil war. Furthermore, most of the compromised chauvinistic interwar leaders had been killed or exiled during and immediately after World War II as Tito moved to consolidate Communist control over Yugoslavia. Thus, the alternative to Tito and the Communists might well have been further brutal civil war.

Tito's prescription for turning post–World War II Yugoslavia into a viable nation-state was certainly credible. As Dimitrije Djordjević pointed out, Tito sagaciously avoided the mistakes of earlier Yugoslavists. Unlike the luminaries of the nineteenth century, Tito recognized the multiple national identities of the South Slavs and allowed them national self-determination within a uniform political order. He established a federal state but tapped the CPY, which became highly centralized immediately after World War II, to exercise complete control of Yugoslav society.[3] Following the declaration of the new Yugoslav federation in 1945, the 1946 constitution provided for six republics, five of which were known by their titular national groups. The sixth, Bosnia and Herzegovina, was recognized as a multinational conglomerate of Serbs, Croats, and the a-national Bosnian Muslims, retaining borders similar to those under the Ottoman and Austro-Hungarian regimes.

Tito also attempted to attenuate some of the other complaints that had made the Yugoslav Kingdom vulnerable. For example, immediately after World War II had ended, the agrarian issue was addressed. No one could own more than thirty-five hectares of land, which ended control by Bosnian Muslims and other landlords over large tracts of land. In Bosnia and Herzegovina, this policy also encouraged an urban movement, particularly among the wealthier Muslims who had not already moved to the cities to escape the ravages of war.

Furthermore, to Serb consternation, Tito drastically weakened their potential for dominating the federation by creating from traditional Serb territory the independent republic of Montenegro, the inhabitants of which considered themselves Serbia's closest relatives, and the independent republic of Macedonia. Tito also sought to reassure Yugoslavia's national minorities within Serbia by delineating within its borders the autonomous regions of Kosovo-Metohija (later called Kosovo) and Vojvodina, which would have some independent decisionmaking power within the federation, although less than the republics. As a result of these jurisdictional alterations, many Serbs watched with dismay as Tito in effect dismantled Serbia, taking lands the Serbian army had conquered in the early twentieth century.

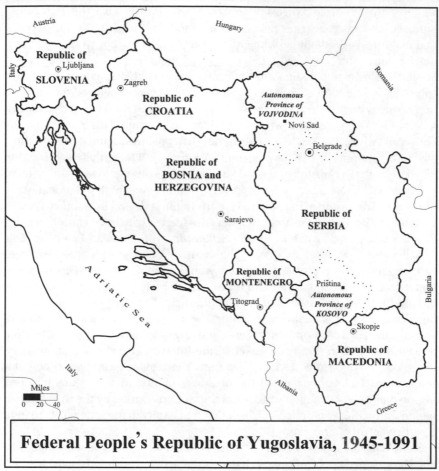

Austria

Hungary

Italy

Republic of
⊙ Ljubljana
SLOVENIA   Zagreb
                    ⊙

Romania

Republic of
CROATIA

*Autonomous
Province of
VOJVODINA*
■ Novi Sad

⊙ Belgrade

Republic of
**BOSNIA and
HERZEGOVINA**

⊙ Sarajevo

Republic of
SERBIA

A d r i a t i c   S e a

Republic of
MONTENEGRO

Pristina ■
*Autonomous
Province of
KOSOVO*

Titograd ⊙

⊙ Skopje

Bulgaria

Italy

Republic of
MACEDONIA

Albania

Greece

Miles
0   20   40

Federal People's Republic of Yugoslavia, 1945-1991

Cartographic Services, Department of Geography, Ball State University

   Finally, the often mutually exclusive claims of Serbia and Croatia to the lands between them were denied altogether. Control of Bosnia and Herzegovina would have clearly made Serbia or Croatia overwhelmingly predominant both economically (especially in the case of Croatia[4]) and politically within the new federation—something Tito was reluctant to allow. Instead, Bosnia and Herzegovina became a separate republic, designed to be a multinational unit dominated by none of the three major constituent groups—Serbs, Croats, or Muslims. In fact, some conservative party members—including Serbian Aleksandar Ranković, vice president of Yugoslavia, chief of security, and presumed heir apparent to Tito—may have viewed the indigenous Bosnian Muslims as a potential core around which a hypothesized "Yugoslav" nation could evolve. Like the Habsburgs, Ranković and his colleagues believed that since the Bosnian Muslims were a-national (that is, unidentified with either Serbs or Croats), they would be a magnet for those who possessed a more universal and less parochial vision of the South Slavs as members of a multireligious but nevertheless ethnically unified tribe.[5] Tito's definition of Yugoslav federalism, however, recognized the limits to homogeneity among the South Slavs: "The lines between the federated states in a federal Yugoslavia are not lines of separation, but of union. This is a community house, one whole, but inside, each must be master of himself and develop culturally and economically in a new federative Yugoslavia."[6] Nevertheless, this vision failed for both the Habsburgs and the later Yugoslav conservatives.

Yugoslavia's federal policy was dependent upon resolving the national question—the relationship of the national groups to the state and its resources and to each other. Tito and his Communist associates made a concerted effort to replace the various South Slav national *weltanschauungs* with Marxism-Leninism. This socialist vision assumed that an equitable distribution of economic resources with an emphasis on economic equality would erase the worst excesses of ethnonationalism and, indeed, eventually of national self-identification. Memories of World War II's nationalistically inspired atrocities would fade as all Yugoslav peoples dwelled in economic and political security. But to achieve this sense of security, the Yugoslav Communists were initially determined to follow the same ill-conceived notion that had weakened the interwar Yugoslav Kingdom. They, too, sought to unite Yugoslavia by creating a Yugoslav value system throughout the country. The assimilation of the members of all national groups into one overarching Yugoslav nation would heal the wounds caused by the war's mutual national atrocities while encouraging individual loyalty to the state rather than to a particular "tribe" or nation.

Some national groups perceived more benefits from Tito's policies than others. Thus, some Serbs and Croats chafed at the restrictions imposed by the CPY, which suggested an evenhanded approach to both nations. However, some of the newly enfranchised groups, such as the Macedonians and the Bosnian Muslims, and some formerly oppressed groups, such as the Kosovar Albanians, found their opportunities for access to the system's rewards enhanced.

Yugoslav National Policy

Yugoslavia's national policy was originally based on the Leninist theory of nationalities, which was developed by Stalin.[7] The three basic principles of this Soviet theory were the right to national self-determination (which included the right to secede from the federation), the territorial autonomy of nationalities, and the full equality of nationalities. Stalin was able to solve the apparent contradiction between the rights of self-determination and secession and the need for the Soviet Union to maintain rigid control over all the territories that historically belonged to Russia with the theory "national in form, proletarian in content." The right to national self-determination was a proletarian right that was not applicable to the bourgeoisie. The right to secession, which was part of national self-determination, was likewise a proletarian right. If a region were indeed proletarian, however, it would not want to exercise the right to secede from the Soviet Union, the fatherland of socialism. Any territory that expressed the desire to secede was thus tainted by bourgeois thinking. Stalin explained the policy in this way:

> There are occasions when the right of self-determination conflicts with ... the higher right—the right of a working class that has assumed power to consolidate its power. In such cases—this must be said bluntly—the right to self-determination cannot and must not serve as an obstacle to the exercise by the working class of its right to dictatorship. The former must give way to the latter.[8]

The national policy of the CPY demonstrated a similar ambivalence toward its own national entities. On the one hand, Yugoslav leaders feared the power of aroused nationalism in one form or another for the future of a viable, united Yugoslavia. On the other hand, they realized that nationalism had been a very sensitive and tenacious factor throughout the history of the various South Slav peoples and that it would continue to be important until it could be subsumed by some other compelling force.

The national question had bedeviled the CPY since it was founded as the first truly Yugoslav party in April 1919. The CPY's position was as ambivalent as that of other Yugoslav political parties;[9] it did not distinguish itself with a clear, concise, and workable—much less revolutionary—solution to the Yugoslav national problem. Italian Communist Party leader Palmiro Togliatti expressed the Communist International's irritation when he accused the Yugoslav Communists of "being temperamentally unable to take a united position on the national question, or on any other issue, because of their disputatious Balkan temperament."[10]

Even Marx did not guide the Yugoslav Communists regarding a solution to the national question. And Engels described the South Slavs as "refuse of a thousand year old ethnic development."[11] Marx and Engels, decrying pan-Slavism as reactionary, wrote in Horace Greeley's *New York Tribune* that the Serbs and Croats, among other Slavs, were "ethnic garbage" who were "retrogressive and counterrevolutionary elements."[12] It was left to later practitioners such as Stalin to attempt to create a socialist-Communist policy regarding the nationalities.

Stalin's influence on the national question may have been felt early in the Balkans, since the CPY undertook an energetic consideration of the nationalities issue in Yugoslavia as early as 1922. With the triumph of the ideological line of the Comintern at the Second Party Conference,[13] many Communists adhered to the recommendation that Yugoslavia should be broken up into its component parts[14] so it could become part of a Balkan federation. Only Balkan union would bring Balkan peace. A resolution of the Fourth Congress of the CPY in 1928 echoed the proposal that Yugoslavia's constituent parts should be formed into independent states.[15] Sima Marković, secretary general of the CPY during its formative years, doubted, however, that the national problems in the Balkans would be soluble until the proletariat had broken its chains[16] and engaged in an ideological duel with Joseph Stalin over the revolutionary character, or lack thereof, in the national movements of the various Yugoslav nations.[17]

During its early years, the party served as a rallying point for those who opposed the creation of any type of Yugoslav state, those who opposed the way Yugoslavia had already been established, and those who opposed certain Yugoslav (Serb-dominated) institutions.[18] It is doubtful, however, that even a fully united and committed Communist party could have gained much support from a statement of policy in regard to the nationality issue because so many different views were held so strongly by the various intellectuals within the country.

The argument raged between Yugoslav Communists who wanted a gradual approach to changing Yugoslavia's structure and those, particularly Croats, who supported the Comintern position, which concentrated on the interests of the international Communist movement as interpreted through the prism of Soviet interests. With the rise of Nazism, however, in 1937 the Comintern altered its position on Yugoslavia. It no longer argued for weakening Yugoslavia through exploitation of the national problem. Instead, the previous policy of encouraging the secession of disgruntled minorities was now seen as encouraging fascism, Stalin's newfound nemesis. The new Communist policy advocated cooperation with all other antifascist political groups (the Popular Front) and supported a unified Yugoslavia. The CPY refused to abandon its search for a revolutionary solution to the national problem, but it acknowledged that these changes could occur within the framework of the Yugoslav state.[19]

In late 1937 the Comintern chose Josip Broz Tito, a Croat by nationality and a metalworker by trade, to become general secretary of the CPY after the Stalinist purge of the former CPY leadership. His handpicked lieutenants, both during and after World War II, represented most of the Yugoslav nationalities and were Tito's, rather than Stalin's, followers. The purges had removed all those who might have had any prestige that rivaled Tito's. Under Tito's guidance, the CPY began to act like a truly Yugoslav party rather than simply a Soviet offshoot.[20] Nevertheless, it is not surprising, given the Yugoslavs' loyalty to Stalin and their strong ideological ties to Stalin's brand of Marxism-Leninism, that in the immediate post–World War II period Yugoslav national policy still closely followed the Stalinist model—even after the 1948 conflict between Tito and Stalin, which removed Yugoslavia from the Soviet sphere of influence. The Yugoslavs continued to retain certain Soviet-style forms, such as the establishment of a formally federal state structure, recognition of cultural autonomy, and a centralized party to transcend national divisions and bind the country.

Yugoslav national policy mimicked Soviet policy in form in a second, very intriguing way. It recognized new nations, based on historical or cultural factors, to circumvent real or potential national conflicts. Thus, the Yugoslav Communists recognized the Macedonian nation and its attendant national institutions, which undercut Bulgarian and Greek claims to that area and its population and circumscribed Serbian control over the region. Tito took this action (and created the two autonomous areas of Kosovo and Vojvodina within Serbia) to allow national expression by the major groups within Yugoslavia. A second reason, however, according to Milovan Djilas, was that he was "afraid of Serbian nationalism because he thought that the Serbs were an expansionist race with hegemonistic ambitions, way beyond their numbers and power."[21]

Tito's other attempt at nation building was undertaken more than twenty years after the end of World War II, when he officially recognized the Muslims of Bosnia and Herzegovina as a separate and equal nation within Yugoslavia. As has been pointed out in earlier chapters, throughout history the Bosnian Muslims were importuned by both Croats and Serbs to declare themselves as belonging ethnically to one or the other group. The national group that claimed the Bosnian Muslims would demonstrate a numerical majority in Bosnia and Herzegovina and thus would exercise the right to control decisionmaking and the distribution of resources there. The Bosnian Muslims were eventually recognized as a separate nation with all of the attendant rights and privileges of that status, including their own independent power base. The process of achieving this status, as is detailed later, raised many perplexing and fascinating questions.

Politicization of Bosnian Muslim Consciousness

The elevation of the Bosnian Muslims to the status of a nation was not seriously considered immediately after World War II. In the immediate postwar era, because of their ambiguous loyalties during World War II, the Muslims of Yugoslavia—most of whom lived in Bosnia and Herzegovina—were in an even more uncomfortable position than the Croats in Bosnia who had also been tainted by their World War II support of the Axis powers. The Bosnian Muslims were considered a unique but a-national group within Yugoslavia.

The Communist government was particularly leery about the organization *Mladi Muslimani* (Young Muslims). Founded informally in 1939 and officially in 1941 by a group of Muslim youth, the organization was intended to help young people grapple with the role of Islam during the immediate pre–World War II era. Muslims in Bosnia and Herzegovina and the Sandžak were particularly unhappy with the establishment of the Croatian *banovina*, which split their community into different governing units.[22] The Muslim youth in this organization thus prepared to defend the Islamic community and to show a united Islamic front.[23] During World War II, many members of *Mladi Muslimani* undertook charitable and social work to aid refugees from the war while attempting to avoid Ustaše, Četnik, and Partisan clashes. However, other members favored a more active and militant role in the conflict and joined various of the existing military groups, including the *Domobrani* (Home Guards) and the Handžar division.[24] They also organized Muslim youth in cities as well as villages into cultural, social, and religious activities.

After World War II ended, *Mladi Muslimani* intensified its activities as the Communist government began to close Muslim places of study and worship.[25] Members of *Mladi Muslimani* feared the policies of the Communist government endangered those who practiced Islam in Yugoslavia.

During the post–World War II persecution of religion in Yugoslavia, Islam fared as badly as, if not worse than, other religions in many ways, although its practice was not forbidden. The Yugoslav state had taken over the education, religious taxation, and judicial functions heretofore reserved for the Islamic community leaders. Mosques and other religious institutions, as well as schools for teaching Islam and the Koran, were often closed or converted to other purposes, and children could not openly be taught their religion. The training of Muslim teachers was circumscribed, as was the publication of Islamic books. *Vakuf* property was nationalized or otherwise removed from the control of the Muslim community, and many of the mosques that had been damaged in the war remained unrepaired or were officially converted to other uses. The Islamic religion did not regain any form of self-regulation until the passage of the 1954 law on the freedom of religion. Muslim practices, such as women wearing veils, were outlawed.

The *Reis-ul-ulema* who was elected in 1947 and his newly appointed subordinates functioned—with the consent of the CPY—primarily as a state representative body, explaining and implementing the new regulations that touched the Islamic community.[26] They had been enjoined to encourage acceptance of the new constitution of the Islamic community promulgated in that year.

These measures to secularize and socialize Yugoslavia were not aimed exclusively at Islam, as the other religions suffered similar hardships. In fact, the Muslims were not perceived to be the most pernicious religious community by the Communists. The new regime conducted a much more intense battle against both the Roman Catholic Church and, to a lesser extent, the Serbian Orthodox Church.[27]

Mladi Muslimani members also feared government designs on their national self-determination. They resented the fact that despite the contribution of Bosnian Muslims to the Partisan war effort and despite wartime declarations to the contrary, the postwar government seemed to expect Muslims to declare themselves either Serbs or Croats.[28] And in 1945 People's Deputy Husaga Ćišić complained that Yugoslavia's federal constitution did not mention Muslims as a constituent national group.[29]

Beginning in 1946, the Yugoslav government moved against *Mladi Muslimani*, imprisoning many of its leaders. Alija Izetbegović, known today as president of Bosnia and Herzegovina, received a six-year sentence.[30] As a result of the government crackdown, the organization went underground,[31] but its leadership was decimated when the *Uprava državne bezbednosti* (UDBa) (secret police) moved against the organizations in Sarajevo, Mostar, Zagreb, and the smaller towns and villages.[32] Liberal Muslim elites who had joined the Partisans seized on the Communist suppression of religion and ambivalence toward the Bosnian Muslims to encourage the Bosnian Muslim community toward secularization and thus perhaps toward an amalgamation with other Yugoslavs. Muslimness would serve as an ethnic-identifying, but not all-encompassing, personal marker. The liberal Bosnian Muslim leaders encountered opposition from religiously conservative anti-Communist Bosnian Muslims, who mounted resistance to the new Communist-dominated government. When Islamic institutions such as the Vakuf Assembly adopted a more supportive attitude toward Tito's government, Islamic institutions were legitimated under the Communist regime, and the *vakuf* system in particular was permitted to support Bosnia and Herzegovina's major Islamic cultural institutions.

The Yugoslav censuses since World War II illustrate the evolution of official, as well as Bosnian Muslim, recognition of the national identification of Bosnian Muslims, as well as the domestic and foreign influences on that development.[33] The immediate postwar years were a time of slavish replication of the Soviet model in Yugoslavia, intending to show that the Yugoslavs were orthodox Communists. Although Yugoslavia recognized nationalist distinctions following its World War II promises, the Soviet-style withering away of chauvinistic nationalism was encouraged. Promoting that policy, in the 1948 census the Bosnian Muslims were permitted to declare themselves as Serb-Muslims, Croat-Muslims, or nationally "undetermined" Muslims, revealing the stance of Communist leaders that held that Muslims were correctly identified nationally as either Serbs or Croats but did not possess their own separate national identity. The Bosnian Muslims could view themselves as a distinct community, but the recognition of a new ethno-religious group as constituting a distinct national unit was considered unconstructive. Reflecting their reluctance to identify themselves nationally as Serbs or Croats, 778,403 Bosnian Muslims in Bosnia and Herzegovina marked the "undetermined" category, whereas a little more than one-tenth of that number marked the Serb (71,991) or Croat (25,295) designation.[34] Slavic Muslims in Serbia, Croatia, and Macedonia demonstrated no such ambivalence: A full 83 percent of Serbian Muslims declared Serb nationality, more than 70 percent of Muslims in Croatia identified themselves as Croat, and 95 percent of the Muslims in Macedonia called themselves Macedonian.[35]

Yugoslav orthodoxy in national policy was mirrored by orthodoxy in other areas, such as the insistence on agricultural collectivization, which the Soviet

Union had vigorously pursued. When it became obvious that collectivization was causing more enmity and dislocation than social benefits, however, Yugoslav leaders began to see the limited value of Stalinism for Yugoslavia. Instead, they sought a new model to inspire the party and the population.

The concept of economic self-management, introduced in the 1950s as the Yugoslav alternative to Soviet socialism (part of Yugoslavia's concept of *separate roads to socialism*), had interesting implications for Yugoslavia's national policy. Conceptually, self-management was meant to introduce direct democracy into the workplace to attenuate worker alienation from the productive process. Self-management thus signified decentralization and worker self-government through workers' councils in the economic sphere, but it also became established in the political arena through gradual decentralization. Whereas separate national economies—noncentralized economies controlled by the republics—could be established, republics and local units of government would also receive expanded political control at the expense of the federation. The success of self-management was considered necessary for the achievement of equality and concord among the national groups, particularly as a large disparity existed in economic development among the national groups (the Slovenes, Croats, and Hungarians in Vojvodina had a much higher standard of living than most other national groups in Yugoslavia).

The reality did not conform to the conceptual goal of self-management. Increasing liberalization of the economic and political systems under self-management failed to reach the logical conclusion of the introduction of a market economy or a multiparty political system, because these would have entailed a significant loss of control by the League of Communists of Yugoslavia (LCY, formerly CPY). Instead, the myriad reforms introduced transformed the Yugoslav economic and political systems and created a new set of significant domestic political actors. One would no longer necessarily encounter all of the most influential players at the federal level. Regional, district, and local administrators and legislators entered the competition for the resources of economic development. These battles over the federally controlled means of development were inevitably perceived as matters of interest for the national groups, and the individual protagonists at the republic, district, and local levels and in the various enterprises took on the mantle of defenders of their national group.[36]

Bosnia and Herzegovina was a winner of sorts in the decisions to liberalize the economy and to proceed with enhanced economic development of the country. Bosnia became Yugoslavia's center of heavy industry and weapons production, raising the standard of living tremendously in that republic (as well as increasing pollution levels and other negative effects of industrialization). Bosnia had abundant natural resources, and, as was proved during World War II when it was Tito's major base for guerrilla operations, its mountainous terrain protected Yugoslavia's industry from invasion from the east.

The political and economic changes occurring as a result of self-management were enshrined in the new constitution, the Fundamental Law of 1953. These changes resulted in some new opportunities for the Bosnian Muslims, particularly as the Islamic community was able to utilize the 1953 federal law on the "legal position" of religious communities to expand their religious opportunities. The election of a new, activist *Reis-ul-ulema*, Hadži Sulejman ef. Kemura, in 1957 ensured that the Islamic community would control its own spiritual and material affairs to the greatest extent possible. Thus, Kemura reorganized the Islamic community's institutions to consolidate functions into four regional Islamic councils, headquartered in Sarajevo, Priština, Titograd, and Skopje. He also expanded religious instruction and the availability of religious materials[37] and sanctioned sermons in Serbo-Croatian, which, an observer reported, contributed to "an awakening of Islamic consciousness" within the Muslim community.[38]

Although the Bosnian Muslims were able to translate the more liberal religious laws to their own advantage, their access to the political system remained limited. The Serbian Communist Party lost control over Bosnia and Herzegovina with the creation of a separate Bosnian Communist Party in 1949,[39] but the Bosnian Muslims were still unable to wield the kind of clout their numbers should have allowed. Individual Bosnian Muslim politicians could hold office and garner economic or political rewards in the newly decentralized system. But the community as a whole, which was not recognized as a corporate national group in the census or through any other mechanism, was denied the access to the republic and federal levers of power that other national groups in Bosnia and Herzegovina, particularly the Serbs, enjoyed.

Self-management recognized, indeed enshrined, politics based on narrowly perceived national interests at all levels of the federation. Factories founded because of political motives arose that were located in economically irrational areas (far from resources, consumption, or distribution centers) to boost employment in depressed areas. Economic and political cooperation across republic borders also resulted. However, actors who possessed no national group legitimacy could not be influential players in the game. Bosnian Muslims, therefore, could only have gained influence at the local, republic, or federal level by cooperating with or being considered Croats or Serbs.

The withdrawal from Stalinism and the search for a specifically Yugoslav form of socialism were also reflected in the changing Yugoslav view of nationalism. Although it still wanted ethnic particularism to fade, the Yugoslav leadership was aware of the sensitivities of the various national groups and sought to nudge them toward less defensiveness. The leaders introduced the concept of *Jugoslovenstvo* (Yugoslavism—one Yugoslav nation).

Mindful of the overtones of chauvinistic Serbianism recalled from the Yugoslav Kingdom's attempt to impose *Jugoslovenstvo*, the Yugoslav Communists were careful to introduce a somewhat similar policy as an option rather than a demand. During the ideological campaign for *Jugoslovenstvo* in the 1950s, the 1953 census reflected this policy by introducing the category "Yugoslav undetermined." With the elimination of the category nationally "undetermined" Muslim in that census, the "Yugoslav undetermined" category surged, presumably used mostly by Bosnian Muslims who did not want to declare themselves as either Serbs or Croats, as well as by members of mixed marriages and those who were repelled by the idea of national self-determination after the nationalistically motivated horrors of World War II. Thus, the lack of Bosnian Muslim legitimacy was reflected in that census, in which there was still no Muslim category as such. "Muslim" was still considered a religious rather than a national preference. Atif Purivatra estimated that a considerable number of Bosnian Muslims who had declared themselves Serbs or Croats in the previous census switched to the "Yugoslav undetermined" category (wrongly encouraging those who, like the Austro-Hungarian von Kállay, looked to the a-national Bosnian Muslims as a core around which a larger nationalism—whether Bosnian or Yugoslav—might be built).[40]

Slavic Muslims in areas other than Bosnia and Herzegovina again felt no compunction about declaring themselves to be members of the major national group in their region. The Bosnian Muslims, however, continued to identify themselves for census purposes by whatever designation would permit them to demonstrate a separation from Yugoslavia's dominant national groups.[41] It would not be unrealistic to assume that this is one indication of the early self-differentiation of the Bosnian Muslims from other Yugoslav Muslims and that it is the basis for the rationale of a distinctive national status for the Bosnian Muslims. (See Table 6.1 for census data.)

The Bosnian Muslims' situation was also affected by the interplay of exogenous and endogenous factors. The domestic conception of decentralization through self-management was mirrored in Yugoslav foreign policy through the policy of nonalignment. With the death of Stalin, aggressive Soviet hegemony appeared to recede. The concomitant growth of national communism within the Communist bloc was paralleled in the West by the creation of new national states as western colonialism also retreated. Yugoslavia's separate roads to socialism, which rejected Soviet economic and political colonialism, inspired Communist-bloc national communism. And its independent foreign policy, beholden to neither the Communist nor the capitalist bloc, inspired the former colonial countries of Asia and Africa. Tito was recognized, along with India's Jawaharlal Nehru and Egypt's Gamal Abdel Nasser, as a founder of nonalignment. Tito's resulting prestige in the nonaligned movement increased the salience for him of world affairs. Nonalignment in general and Yugoslavia's involvement with Middle East elites in particular gave Yugoslavia a high profile in international politics. Concomitantly, Tito's interest in the fortunes of the Bosnian Muslim community increased, since a large contingent of the nonaligned countries was Muslim.

TABLE 6.1   Population of Bosnia and Herzegovina by Census, 1948–1991

Year	Muslims	Serbs	Croats	Yugoslavs	Total Population
1948	788,403[a]	1,136,116	614,142	—	2,563,764
1953	—	1,264,372	654,229	891,800[b]	2,847,459
1961	842,248[c]	1,406,057	711,665	275,883	3,277,948
1971	1,482,430	1,393,148	772,491	43,796	3,746,111
1981	1,629,924	1,320,644	758,136	326,280	4,102,783
1991	1,905,829	1,369,258	755,892	239,845	4,364,574

[a] Called nationally "undetermined" Muslims.
[b] Called "Yugoslav undetermined."
[c] Steven L. Burg suggested this number might be too low, since there were many self-identified Serbs, Croats, Yugoslavs, and others who adhered to Islam. "The Political Integration of Yugoslavia's Muslims: Determinants of Success and Failure" (Pittsburgh: Carl Beck Papers in Russian and East European Studies, University of Pittsburgh, 1983), p. 39.

SOURCES: Atif Purivatra, *Nacionalni i politički razvitak muslimana* (Sarajevo: Svjetlost, 1970), p. 33; Mushtak Parker, *Muslims in Yugoslavia: The Quest for Justice* (Toronto: Croatian Islamic Centre, 1986), p. 15; "The National Composition of Yugoslavia's Population, 1991," *Yugoslav Survey* 33 (1992), pp. 4–5.

Tito first signaled official interest in encouraging the expression of the separate group status of the Bosnian Muslims by changing the census designation of Muslims starting in the early 1960s. The first step toward official recognition of the Bosnian Muslims as an integral secular group in Yugoslavia was taken in the 1961 census with the addition of the category "Muslim (ethnic membership)." Although "ethnic membership" did not possess quite the prestige of "nation" (which dignified the Serbs, Croats, and others), this Bosnian Muslim secular self-identification attracted almost 850,000 adherents in the 1961 census.

An interesting and perhaps unwelcome phenomenon occurred, however, as a result of the appearance of this new census designation. The category "Yugoslav undetermined" was a major loser to the Muslim category, indicating that many citizens had used the former category to reject being placed in a repugnant national box (either Serb or Croat). But even more arresting is the fact that "most of these remaining 'Yugoslavs' (87 percent) were still recorded in Bosnia-Herzegovina," and 84 percent of those were Muslims.[42] Apparently, a substantial proportion of nonreligious Slavic Muslims regarded Muslim as a religious rather than a national category.

As the previous census showed, members of mixed marriages and others who were repelled by narrow ethnic labels following World War II shared this feeling. However, the full integration of the Bosnian Muslims into Yugoslav society was made more difficult by the fact that Ranković, who favored centralization of authority and centralized planning, seemed anxious to abet Serb interests in Bosnia to the detriment of the Croats and Muslims living there. Centralism naturally favored the most numerous nation in Yugoslavia, the Serbs, so regardless of

TABLE 6.2   Changing Population Ratios in Bosnia and Herzegovina, 1948–1991

	1948	1953	1961	1971	1981	1991
Bosnia and Herzegovina	100.0	100.0	100.0	100.0	100.0	100.0
Serbs	44.3	44.4	42.9	37.2	32.0	31.4
Muslims	30.7	31.3	25.7	39.6	39.5	43.7
Croats	23.9	23.0	21.7	20.6	18.4	17.3
Yugoslavs	—	—	8.4	1.2	7.9	5.5
Montenegrins	0.1	0.3	0.4	0.3	0.3	n.a.
Albanians	0.0	0.1	0.1	0.1	0.1	n.a.
Slovenes	0.2	0.2	0.2	0.1	0.1	n.a.
Macedonians	0.0	0.1	0.1	0.1	0.0	0.0
Other	n.a.	n.a.	0.9	0.8	1.5	2.1

n.a. = not available.

SOURCE: Jure Petričević, *Nacionalnost stanovništva Jugoslavije: Nazadovanje Hrvata, manjine napredovanje Muslimana i Albanaca* (Brugg: Adria, 1983), p. 115.

whether Ranković's policy choices stemmed from Serb nationalism or simply from a strong belief in centralization, the outcome of increased Serbian influence was the same. Only after Ranković's forced departure in July 1966,[43] which spelled the defeat of conservative, antireformist forces within the party, were the Bosnian Muslims and various heretofore powerless groups able to secure more influence within Yugoslav society as it started to decentralize. Muslim leader Avdo Humo echoed Bosnian Serb leader Cvijetin Mijatović's admission that the Bosnian Croats and Muslims had a difficult time in post–World War II Yugoslavia when he described the Bosnian Muslim view of the Ranković era and the effects of centralization in Bosnia and Herzegovina:

> The worst treated were the institutions of the Croat and Moslem people. Those people were nationally oppressed and under strong pressure from the unitarist-centralist authorities. In the policy of assimilation and decentralization of the Moslems there was always present an attempt by the authorities to turn the Moslem national institutions into Serbian Moslem institutions.[44]

After the fall of Ranković, additional economic and political reforms were introduced and implemented in Yugoslavia, accelerating the economic boom that extended from the 1950s through the mid-1970s. As a result, Yugoslavia was the first East European country to become associated with West European trade blocs.

The reformers clung to the classic Marxist theory that economic equality would eliminate national tensions and nationalism. Chauvinistic nationalism would wither if funds and patronage were no longer centralized. Vetting for elite recruitment was removed from the security organs, formerly controlled by

Ranković, and central party organs were no longer charged with the enlistment of participants. Republic and provincial organs of the LCY were to take over the selection of their own officials. Personnel decisions for the management of enterprises, although they still considered political criteria, also took into account technical and managerial skills. The principle of collective leadership in party and state became the alternative to Tito's one-person rule after his demise.

The 1967–1968 and 1971 constitutional amendments enshrined the reformers' victory by legitimizing decentralization of decisionmaking at all levels and in all areas of life. However, the reform program simply reflected and institutionalized previous decentralizing tendencies. For example, even before 1966, although the constituent Communist parties were subordinated to the central party apparatus and leadership, most Communist functionaries preferred to serve only in their own republics, which allowed for a certain republic esprit de corps. This narrow republic focus, which prior to 1966 began to be manifested in the common republic responses to the central party, flourished after the institution of the latest reforms.[45]

Less than a decade after the Ranković affair, the consequences of the reformist program disturbed the seeming equanimity of Yugoslav politics. Chauvinistic nationalism emerged into full view in Yugoslavia in the 1970s, taking advantage of the new direction in policy to express dissatisfaction with the functioning of the Yugoslav system—economically as well as politically. De-etatization (the withering of the state's economic role) occurred only at the federal level. Regional and enterprise etatism continued to thrive and encouraged a regional and local drive for self-sufficiency and a consequent economic politicization.[46] These conditions of economic irrationality and local autarky also encouraged ethnic overreactions.

Nationalistic Croatian politicians within the LCY attempted to use the modernizing and pluralistic fever in the country to gain more advantages for their republic and to squelch permanently the centralists, formerly represented by Ranković. They were incensed that the economic and accompanying political reforms were being implemented too slowly and complained that the more developed republics were being discriminated against in federal economic policies. Croats resented being forced to contribute what they considered to be an oversized share to the federal coffers for programs that did not specifically benefit their republic. Furthermore, they complained, Croatia was able to control only a fraction of the foreign currency it brought into Yugoslavia. Its contributions were being used for capital investment in backward areas of the country, which would bring less return than funds reinvested in Croatian enterprises.

The immediate goal of these Croats was to further decentralize both the LCY and the rest of society through a greater devolution of power away from the central government and a relaxation of the principle of democratic centralism, according to which minority opinions were less readily acceptable. Greater participation by mobilized citizens in the distribution of enterprise earnings and in direct and competitive elections would be encouraged, accompanied by a purge of the older and more resistant Communists.[47]

Croatian Communists were supported by some voluble Croatian nationalists who complained about Serbian cultural domination and agitated for the recognition of Croatian as a separate language.[48] Croatian demands for "decentralization, de-etatization, depoliticization, and democratization" also found allies in wealthy and modern Slovenia, as well as among those Macedonians who feared the Serbian designs against their newly recognized nationhood. Croats in Bosnia and Herzegovina also responded positively to the anticentralist tone of the Croatian leadership when it became evident that they were underrepresented in decisionmaking units throughout their republic.[49] Croatian dissatisfaction with Yugoslav policies was spreading to the Serbo-Croatian competition for influence in Bosnia and Herzegovina.

Most worrisome for Tito, the complaints from every quarter were couched in national terms. Croatian nationalists centered particularly in *Matica Hrvatska* (the Croatian cultural-literary society) complained about Croatian treatment in Bosnia and Herzegovina. Still considered by many diehards to be part of Croatia, Bosnia and Herzegovina was targeted for Croatian nationalist agitation. Eventually, Croatian nationalists concluded that the only way to protect Croatian rights in the area was to annex certain areas of western Bosnia and Herzegovina that contained a large proportion of Bosnian Croats to Croatia proper.[50] The more radical Croatian demands, punctuated occasionally with Ustaše symbols, were reminiscent of the pre–World War II Croatian ambitions for greater autonomy from interwar Serbian domination and were forcefully condemned by the leaders of other republic party organizations, including the Bosnian Party.

When Serbs in Croatia began arming themselves,[51] Tito intervened in December 1971. He sensed that the Croatian Communist Party leaders were becoming more Croatian national representatives than leaders of the LCY representing the Croatian republic. This feeling was being transmitted to the general public, producing a greater frequency of nationalist excesses. As a consequence, Tito massed a show of force around Zagreb and was able to deflate student strikes and other manifestations of defiance against the LCY. He blunted the attack against the integrity of Yugoslavia by the nationalists. Later, in fall 1972, the purge that had removed all those who had endangered Yugoslavia with their nationalist appeals in Croatia, Macedonia, and Slovenia was extended to other republics. In the climate of excessive pluralism and a lesser political role for the party, some Serbs were also indicted for "seeking economic hegemony as a substitute for the political hegemony which they had lost with the dismantling of a unitary State."[52] The Bosnian party elite seem to have escaped the Titoist purges that followed the Croat crisis. And the Bosnian Muslims appeared to emerge in a stronger position than ever, increasing their percentage in the League of Communists of Bosnia and Herzegovina (LCBiH) from 26 percent in 1969 to at least 30 percent in 1972. The absolute number of Bosnian Muslims in the LCBiH continued to increase throughout the 1970s.[53]

The series of purges of liberals and nationalists that extended to all areas in Yugoslavia during the early 1970s was meant to reunite the LCY and reinstitute democratic centralism. The republic and provincial parties (the provinces were counted as republics in all but name[54]) were once again to be accountable to the federal party. As Robin Alison Remington pointed out, however, Tito's reforms "represented more of a flirtation than a 'return' to Leninism,"[55] because Tito acquiesced to some of the demands made by Croats in the early 1970s. But he also took steps to preclude the recurrence of such nationalistically motivated rebellious actions.

The reform was blamed for reducing party influence to an advisory role. The resurgence of chauvinistic nationalism was being used by local, nationalistic politicians to forward their own rather than a Yugoslav agenda. Other groups demanded that the reforms be permitted to proceed to their logical conclusion—the economic, political, and social liberalization of Yugoslavia. During the ensuing crackdown, the LCY was enjoined to control more closely personnel appointments to all important political and nonpolitical positions. Furthermore, at the Eighth Trade Union Congress in November 1978, Tito called for sharply limited terms of office for party and government heads at all levels, from district to republic.

Tito sought to curtail all challenges to his personal authority and to the dominance of the LCY with his cleansing of tainted cadres. In the process of quashing the upsurge of chauvinistic nationalism, he also undertook an official Yugoslav counterattack against Muslim nationalism and pan-Islamism as early as 1972 with the dismissal from their party posts of two alleged proponents of these aberrations, Avdo Humo and Osman Karabegović.[56]

Yet at the same time the Communists were squelching nationalist challenges, the Bosnian Muslims were being encouraged to identify themselves in a national rather than a religious sense. With the replacement of the 1953 federal constitution with a new constitution in 1963 and the end of officially endorsed Yugoslavism soon thereafter, the national identification of the Bosnian Muslims became a popular issue in the mid-1960s.[57] The new republic constitution had avoided the problem of national identification of the inhabitants by stating that Bosnia and Herzegovina was inhabited by "Serbs, Moslems, and Croats allied in the past by a common life."[58] Nevertheless, the Twelfth Conference of the Central Committee of the League of Communists of Bosnia and Herzegovina concluded on 17 May 1968 that "the Muslims are a distinct nation."[59] In 1969, at the Fifth Congress of the LCBiH, the Yugoslav leadership explicitly and publicly supported the separate national identity of the Bosnian Muslims.[60]

Henceforward, the Bosnian Muslims were to be in a position of equality in terms of rights and privileges with the other five nations (*narodi*) of Yugoslavia. The question of whether the claim to separate nationhood on the basis of historical and cultural factors was based on reality seems to have been of secondary importance to both the Bosnian Muslims and the federal government, which had officially recognized their separate national status. Since many Bosnian Muslim intellectuals believed in their distinctiveness, they worked to raise the consciousness of the Bosnian Muslim population. The feeling of distinctiveness became an integral component of their feeling of nationhood.

The national recognition of the Bosnian Muslims emphasized that Tito's endorsement of "organic Yugoslavism," with its tolerance of cultural and national distinctiveness bound together by the World War II Partisan experience, had replaced Ranković's concept of "integral Yugoslavism," which had emphasized the universality of Yugoslavism for all of Yugoslavia's South Slavs. The intention was to finally end the artificial debate over the ethnogenesis of the Bosnian Muslims by showing that their experience in national self-determination before the late nineteenth century was similar to (although not as rapid as) that of the Serbs and Croats, who had identified themselves communally first on the basis of their religion and later on the basis of nationalism. Bosnian Muslim Communists were particularly eager to encourage the Bosnian Muslim community to follow this path and thus become a "prophylaxis against competing national claims both from within the Republic and from without."[61] These Communists fully expected that the Bosnian Muslim community, paralleling the Serbs and Croats, would go beyond the religious elements of self-identification and serve its own political and economic interests within Bosnia and Herzegovina.

The expectations of the Bosnian Muslim politicians were met to a certain extent in succeeding years. The Muslim designation in the 1971 census— "Muslims in the sense of nationality"—still waffled, causing a large number of Muslims to remain in the "Yugoslav" category.[62] Nevertheless, more than 1.7 million people throughout Yugoslavia chose the Muslim category. According to the census, the Bosnian Muslims were the third largest national group in the country and constituted the largest nation in Bosnia and Herzegovina.[63]

Bosnian Muslim demographics became vitally important as the new constitution, promulgated in 1974, turned Yugoslavia into a de facto confederation. The republics (and Vojvodina and Kosovo) consequently received the bulk of decisionmaking power (except for foreign policy, defense, and a few other areas). Federal decisionmaking was dependent on a fragile consensus, which could be frustrated by the veto of any of the constituent units. Administrative and legislative personnel decisions became lodged at the republic level, where obligation and responsiveness lay. The careful application of the criterion of ethnicity became even more necessary. Local and republic positions were considered more desirable because of the power they wielded than were the relatively impotent federal jobs.[64]

Because most high-ranking jobs in the republics, as well as in the federal government, were filled according to an *ethnic key* (apportionment according to the proportion of the national group in the population), the fact that the Bosnian Muslims were accorded national status opened important avenues of access to levers of influence. Furthermore, the percentage of declared Muslims indicated the number of jobs Bosnian Muslims would receive at all levels and the importance of those jobs. Therefore, the recognition of the Bosnian Muslims as a nation was of vital importance to their decisionmaking capabilities.

Despite Tito's attempts to reimbue the LCY and the federal system with greater authority, it became obvious that the provisions of the 1974 constitution had turned Yugoslavia into a confederation, with overtones of consociationalism. Nevertheless, the changes described here did not obviate problems in Yugoslavia. The Yugoslav system still suffered from "party interference, apathy, inefficiency, lack of initiative, and corruption,"[65] all of which were compounded by Yugoslavia's deteriorating economic situation. Although the standard of living generally rose, the differential in incomes between the more-developed and less-developed republics also increased.[66]

The 1974 constitution has been blamed for the disintegration of the Yugoslav market and the consequent mutual dissatisfaction of the various ethnic groups.[67] The confederalism it imposed at the time seemed more likely to maintain a unified political system through its emphasis on rotation of officials and their appointment according to the ethnic key, as well as on the republics' ability to veto federal legislation. However, the new system encouraged the republics and even the localities to shoulder much of the decisionmaking heretofore reserved for the federal government. This forced the regions and localities to go head-to-head for the limited resources of the Yugoslav state. Such unremitting conflict could only exacerbate ethnic particularism. Furthermore, the LCY was abdicating power to the republic parties, which in effect turned Yugoslavia into a multiparty political system, with each republic controlled by its own party organization.

The question is, who controlled multiethnic Bosnia and Herzegovina? The reforms strengthened the republics to the detriment of the central government just as the Bosnian Muslims were in the process of finally being recognized as a separate Yugoslav nation, with all the prerogatives that were attached to that designation. This, of course, meant the Bosnian Muslims became "more equal" to the other South Slav nations than ever before; thus, for the first time they became truly influential within Yugoslavia. One might argue that their existence within the Ottoman Empire constituted their golden age, because they were considered part of the ruling class. However, Bosnian Muslim prestige was intrinsic to the Ottoman Empire and, to a certain extent, was dependent upon and constrained by the privileges extended to them by the Porte in Constantinople. When the Ottoman Empire collapsed, the Bosnian Muslims' influence in the region also collapsed. Therefore, Yugoslav recognition of the Bosnian Muslims as a nation equal to the other Yugoslav nations in prestige and advantages meant that for the first time in post-1878 history they were part of the "in crowd," true players with real access to a significant proportion of Yugoslav prerogatives and privileges.

The flaws in the Yugoslav resolution of its national problem were illustrated markedly by the Bosnian Muslim situation. Initially, according to Jovan Djordjević, the preeminent Yugoslav constitutionalist, in Yugoslavia the republic was not considered "the state of a nation."[68] However, the 1974 constitution recognized the sovereignty of the nations and nationalities, as exercised through the republics and autonomous provinces, and explicitly referred to them as "states." Although in theory all inhabitants, regardless of their national origin, had a right to equal representation and participation in the sovereign republics, in reality each republic was dominated by the representatives of the majority constituent nation. All of the republics, except for Bosnia and Herzegovina, had in effect become the national territories of their own nations and, as such, were able to represent the interests of those nations. Bosnia and Herzegovina, lacking a dominant nation, did not have the same kind of clout in terms of resource allocation and political decisionmaking.

Now that the Bosnian Muslims had become an officially recognized nation with a plurality of the population in Bosnia and Herzegovina, many Bosnian Muslim leaders deemed it logical that Bosnia and Herzegovina should be considered their national territory, imbued with the capability of fighting for the interests of Bosnia and Herzegovina on a more level field of conflict. Although it was not officially implied by word or deed that recognition of the Bosnian Muslims as a nation signified that their plurality in Bosnia and Herzegovina entitled them to control the republic as their "homeland," one could understand why some Bosnian Muslims jumped to that conclusion. After all, the Bosnian Muslims, as indigenous Slavic Muslims, had no other homeland, whereas most Bosnian Serbs and Bosnian Croats lived in areas contiguous to the Serb and Croat homelands.

The aspirations of Bosnian Muslim politicians to increase their power within the republic and those of some Bosnian Muslim nationalists to create a Muslim homeland in Bosnia and Herzegovina were challenged by a third point of view, represented by an activist Muslim clergy buoyed by an unexpected surge of Islamic religious identity among some Bosnian Muslims. This was not supposed to happen in a Communist country, where religion was discouraged, and within a community as notoriously nondevout as the Bosnian Muslims. Recognition of their nationhood was expected to have only secular implications, since previously the Bosnian Muslims had shown little religious predilection. However, when they gained national recognition and began to increase their communal self-identification as a nation, their religiosity was concomitantly asserted as a main part of their national self-identification and differentiation.

Official Yugoslav policy toward the various religious groups was generally affected by the attitude of the religious hierarchies toward nationalism.

Furthermore, the policy toward a specific national group depended on the official attitude toward that nation's religion.[69] Whereas the LCY did not, in fact, practice a neutral and evenhanded policy toward each religion and nation, nevertheless it did consistently reject involvement by any religious organization in interethnic relations. For the LCY, the churches were to influence only the strictly ritual sphere; religion was to have no legitimate position in public life.[70]

The fact that Islam is a universal religion made it different from the other religions and, conceivably at least, more threatening to Yugoslav unity in the eyes of official Communist Yugoslavia. There was evidence, however, of a policy of official partisanship toward certain religious organizations of "favored nationality groups" that was akin to the Soviet favoritism of the Russian Orthodox Church over other religions.[71] Pedro Ramet, in fact, observed an "escalation of church-state functions in cases where the church retains the role of defender of its nationality group"—for example, the Macedonian Orthodox Church.[72]

At least for a time, the Bosnian Muslims may have held the position of a "favored," although closely watched, religious group. The political efficacy of the Bosnian Muslim community in short-circuiting Serb-Croat wrangling over control in Bosnia and Herzegovina endeared the Islamic Religious Community (IVZ) to the Bosnian government. In fact, the Bosnian government contributed significantly to the IVZ's budget.[73] But the IVZ viewed the Bosnian Muslim situation differently than did the secular Bosnian Muslim leaders, resenting what seemed to be a double standard in the Bosnian Muslim feelings toward nation and religion. An observation by a Bosnian Muslim religious leader illustrates this difference:

> Unfortunately, attempts have been made to challenge us, and understandably we must not become reconciled with them. We are aware that the small "m" [Muslim religion] represents the foundation of the big "M" [Muslim *narod*] without which it would signify an empty name. The forces representing the big "M," in this process, are not justified in their case. The steadfastness of the muslim masses and their stubbornness to remain what they are is the greatest contribution to the recognition of the new status of Muslims in the Socialist Republic of BiH.[74]

Following the example of the religious hierarchies of the other Yugoslav nations, the IVZ expected to begin to hold a position within Bosnia and Herzegovina analogous to that of the Orthodox Church in Serbia and the Catholic Church in Croatia. This condition would also have been more in line with the Muslim view of the world, whereby Muslims should be ruled as much as possible by their own people through their own Muslim institutions. Indeed, as soon as the nationhood of the Bosnian Muslims was officially recognized, the religious hierarchy began to pursue a more active and public role in the lives of Bosnian Muslims, seeking to play the role of intermediary between them and the rest of Yugoslav society and to be the spokesperson for the Muslim community and its interests.

However, the Yugoslav leadership was not about to permit the Islamic religious hierarchy to adopt the role such a hierarchy would normally play in a Muslim-dominated society. Hamdija Pozderac, a Muslim member of the LCY Presidium since 1979, publicly attacked Muslim proponents of a plan for a Muslim republic in an article in *Borba* on 11 May 1978.

In 1979 the staff of the Sarajevo Islamic weekly *Preporod,* the organ of the Association of Islamic Clergy in Bosnia and Herzegovina, was fired for its alleged overreaction to a book by former Partisan Derviš Sušić. Sušić, a Muslim, had published extracts of the book in a series of articles entitled "Od Vidovdanskog ustava do Pavelićevog kabineta" ["From the Vidovdan Constitution to Pavelić's Cabinet"] in the Sarajevo newspaper *Oslobodjenje* in August and September 1979. The extracts were critical of Muslim religious and political leaders before and during World War II. The answering storm of protest articles in Islamic journals expressing antagonism toward Sušić's work, particularly in *Preporod,* was anathema to the LCY. The book had likely had at least nominal approval by Yugoslav officials.[75]

Rationale for Bosnian Muslim National Recognition

The status of nation meant Bosnian Muslims would begin to receive a fair share in the allocation of personnel positions throughout the republic's state and party bureaucracies. As the largest nation in Bosnia and Herzegovina, they could also expect to have a greater voice in decisions about resource allocation within both the republic and the country.

There are at least four different levels on which to investigate the significance of Bosnian Muslim national recognition. First, recognition was supposed to attenuate the problem of separating explicitly nationalist arguments from purely regional economic or political interests. The coincidence of the economic unit of major resource allocation and decisionmaking (the republic and autonomous province) with national boundaries made this separation difficult. The addition of the Bosnian Muslims to the equation would make it easier for the representatives of the genuinely multinational Bosnian republic to make more rational economic and political decisions.

But the republic's economic, much less its political, problems were not easily solved. Bosnia and Herzegovina was an overwhelmingly agrarian republic immediately after World War II, which should have qualified it as an underdeveloped area in postwar Yugoslavia and a special target for development assistance. Indeed, for a short time, when Tito feared Soviet intentions to limit Yugoslav independence, he located strategic industries in Bosnia and Herzegovina to take advantage of the geostrategic isolation provided by its mountainous terrain.[76] The post-Stalin years, however, reduced the strain on Yugoslavia and simultaneously reduced the need to maintain those factories "established in splendid isolation from markets, roads or skilled manpower."[77] Thereafter, Bosnia and Herzegovina's development was given lower priority. During the period 1952–1968 the republic experienced an average annual growth of only 4.2 percent, much lower than the Yugoslav average of 6.4 percent.[78] Its economic condition continued to deteriorate until the 1971–1975 economic plan braked its slide somewhat. However, Bosnia and Herzegovina was unable to catch up with the advanced republics or even to narrow the gap with the economic average of Yugoslavia as a whole.[79]

Furthermore, the recognition of the legitimacy of the Bosnian Muslim voice in decisionmaking made the attainment of a political consensus within Bosnia and Herzegovina even more difficult to achieve. Tito had considered that 1968 was the right time to confer upon the Bosnian Muslims an enlarged decisionmaking role in society to demonstrate that Yugoslavia gave even its smaller and historically abused groups the right to full self-realization. He considered the Muslims in Bosnia to be a good example with which to illustrate this benefit of life in Yugoslavia.

The Bosnian Serbs in particular resented the fact that they had lost the capacity to dominate the republic and to control the political and economic life of the region, because the Muslims and Croats had traditionally cooperated when Serbian attempts to manipulate Bosnian (as well as Yugoslav) policymaking became too blatant.[80] This resentment flared up dangerously when the controls exerted by Tito's personal touch disappeared. Robert J. Donia and John V. A. Fine Jr. pointed out, however, that through the LCBiH, the three national groups in Bosnia and Herzegovina were often able to present a common front regarding Bosnian issues in federal and party structures,[81] and, in fact, as a whole they became perhaps the most conservative of the republic party organizations.

On a second level, the rise in Bosnian Muslim national consciousness might have had elements of a response to the gradual increase in international Islamic activism, which had become steadily more aggressive since the end of World War II. Pan-Islamism originated in the 1870s when the Turkish sultans attempted to mobilize the Muslim world to support and ally with the weak and impoverished Ottoman state. This feeling of Islamic unity has been exploited since that time to increase international political efficacy by governments wanting to promote their own political interests, as well as by radical figures attempting to implement a revolutionary social doctrine without government backing.[82]

Ramet has suggested that "Muslim nationalism in Yugoslavia predated the worldwide Islamic revival by several years,"[83] thus precluding the theory that militant international Islam was the spark that first ignited Bosnian Muslim nationalism. However, neither the genesis of the Islamic revival nor the moment when the Bosnian Muslims began to consider themselves a nation rather than merely a religious group can be precisely dated. Perhaps the Bosnian Muslim awakening was influenced in some measure by the same forces that were in the process of creating the Islamic revival even as the awakening was lending its impetus to strengthening the force of worldwide Islam. Bernard Lewis cautioned, however, that international pan-Islamism has had much less success than more local manifestations of Islam. Nevertheless, even the basest attempts at international pan-Islamism have "already gone very much further than anything comparable within the Christian world, and have occasionally had diplomatic consequences," except among the Muslims of the Soviet Union, Eastern Europe, and China,[84] before that part of the world was shaken by the collapse of communism.

Recognition of Bosnian Muslim nationhood was a way to co-opt the potential for indigenous Muslim response to the siren song of militant international pan-Islamic activism. Since Islam had not yielded to the antireligious pressures of the Yugoslav Communist society, it seemed to have a stronger hold than ever on its adherents. Although the Bosnian Muslim leaders appeared able to fulfill their dual roles as state employees and representatives of the interests of their constituents, nevertheless Islamic religious practices appeared to have lost little ground to the secular ideology of Yugoslav communism.[85]

On the contrary, Islam seemed to have been fully involved in the religious revival among Yugoslav youth, which had cut across all religious groups. Regarding the rise and development of Islam in Yugoslavia, Boris Vušković noted that Islamic "fundamentalism" made progress in Yugoslavia because "obviously certain great ideologies in the world have somehow found themselves in a crisis. On the other hand, we [the Communists] have been propagating certain things in a way that did not make us attractive enough."[86] For example, some Islamic religious leaders claimed the Communists had become obsolete for Yugoslavia and should be replaced by a leadership sensitive to influence by the religious establishments.[87]

To counter this kind of threat, some Yugoslav party leaders favored identifying religion with nationalism, thus tying the religious leaders to the political workings of the state. In so doing in the case of the Bosnian Muslims, however, Yugoslav leaders encountered the paradox of having recognized a new nation from a religion even as they felt forced to suppress the national-religious demands that were destined to arise from that situation. Dušan Dragosavac thus termed this equalizing of religion and nation "a boon to clericalism," which is clearly anathema to a socialist regime.[88]

Recognition of the distinctiveness of the Bosnian Muslim nation gave the traditional Muslim leaders a new weapon in their attempt to keep the faithful from straying. The desire to cultivate those old traditions that set the Bosnian Muslims apart from other Bosnians apparently increased the appeal of Islam to the Muslim masses from a religious and even a political point of view.[89] Muslim religious leaders, taking advantage of the new religiosity, thus joined the ranks of those lambasted by Dragosavac: "The clericalists from church ranks cannot make peace with the secularization resulting from the division of church, state and school. They continue to interfere in worldly problems, including national ones, by stirring up intolerance among nations and fomenting numerous kinds of nationalism."[90] The official worry, therefore, was that Islamic content might overrun the boundaries implicitly set by the Communists and form a severe counterforce to the attempt to create socialism in Yugoslavia.

A third level for analyzing Bosnian Muslim nationhood was that of the apparently happily coincidental meeting of the needs of both the Muslims in Bosnia and Herzegovina and the Yugoslav federation. The Bosnian Muslims received national recognition, and the Yugoslav leadership was able to capitalize on the foreign policy aspect of this situation. The elevation of the Bosnian Muslims to national status endeared Yugoslavia to Middle Eastern and North African Arabs, who were discovering increased power through worldwide Islamic activism. The nonalignment movement was composed of many influential Muslim leaders, as well as those non-Muslims who maintained close ties with the nonaligned Muslim states. Tito hoped that at least the moderate nonaligned Muslim leaders would be more amenable to his foreign policy suggestions within the framework of the nonalignment movement, since Yugoslavia had raised the official status of a heretofore unrecognized and fairly impotent Muslim society. The greater status for Yugoslavia such an action engendered among the nonaligned Muslims might have increased Tito's leverage in the movement at a time when he most needed it—when he was attempting to prevent Castro from co-opting the nonaligned movement for Cuban imperialism masquerading as representation of the socialist commonwealth.[91] In furtherance of Yugoslavia's foreign policy aims, Yugoslav delegations to Islamic states usually included a Muslim representative from Bosnia; foreign Islamic leaders were frequently taken to Sarajevo for a visit with local Muslims.[92] In all, Tito cleverly used "his Muslims" to advantage by acting as if Yugoslavia were "the second-strongest Moslem country in Europe, after Turkey."[93]

Because Tito needed firm friendships in the Middle East and other Muslim-dominated areas to succeed in his policy of nonalignment, Bosnian Muslims were courted by Tito and his colleagues and were given privileges within Yugoslavia that in many ways were equal to those of the Serbs, Croats, and other nations to show that Muslims were not only tolerated but were valued. Their prestige and power within Yugoslavia grew accordingly.

The fourth level on which to examine the development of Bosnian Muslim nationalism, and perhaps the most important, was that recognition of the Bosnian Muslim nation removed from the ongoing Serb-Croat antagonism one issue over which there was likely to be no compromise: to which nation (Serbia or Croatia) did Bosnia and Herzegovina by right belong. Even with the Muslims having been declared a viable third nation in the republic, however, the problem did not totally disappear during the 1980s, as witnessed in this peroration by expatriate Serb Alija Konjhodzich:

Today, our country is ruled by atheistic Communism, which pronounces all faiths as the "opiate of the people," where Serbianism is extinguished through all possible means, where the Moslems are proclaimed a new nation of some sort, solely in order that they do not declare themselves Serbs, as they always have, and to end this national determination of the Moslems. They did not succeed nor will they. The most informed Serbian Moslem writers, journalists, authors have declared themselves Serbs. They write Serbian and of Serbianism. Broz calls them "Serbian Chauvinist," and prohibits their work. This alone indicates the intense Serbianism of the Bosnian-Hercegovinian Moslems who reject Broz's "Moslem Nation."[94]

Conclusion

In summary, the recognition of the Bosnian Muslims as a nation was a recognition of their need for self-realization. But it was also a political decision made to solve national conflicts within Yugoslavia and to enhance Yugoslavia's international prospects with the nonaligned world. The manipulation of the Bosnian Muslims, therefore, met a wide variety of needs. The implications of this decision for the unity of Yugoslavia and Bosnia and Herzegovina in the post-Tito period belied the motives for which the move was apparently undertaken. Political and economic exigencies became intermixed, which heightened the nationalistic feelings of those who felt economically deprived and those who felt economically robbed. The Bosnian Muslims, given access to decisionmaking levers, were never quite able to create lasting coalitions with other Bosnian groups that might have stabilized the political scene. Without Tito to quell nationalistic outbursts and with the political monopoly of the LCY unchallenged during the 1960s and 1970s by the failure to introduce truly democratic institutions within which to work out conflicts and achieve recognition of human rights and economic liberalization, the Bosnian Muslims had no political cover when the Titoist institutions that were meant to protect them and the other peoples of Yugoslavia failed.

NOTES

1. This chapter, as well as the following chapters, draws heavily from research undertaken to produce my chapter entitled "The Bosnian Muslims: The Making of a New Nation in the Former Yugoslavia," in Jill Irvine, Carol Tilly, and Melissa Bokovoy, eds., *From Partisans to Politics* (New York: St. Martin's Press, forthcoming).

2. Cited in Leo Mates, *Nonalignment: Theory and Current Policy* (Dobbs Ferry, N.Y.: Oceana, 1972), p. 207.

3. Dimitrije Djordjević, "Three Yugoslavias—A Case of Survival," *East European Quarterly* 19 (January 1986), p. 387.

4. According to Sabrina Petra Ramet, a Croatia that retained its NDH boundaries, which included Bosnia and Herzegovina, would have controlled approximately two-fifths of

Yugoslavia's population (by the 1948 census), land, and hydroelectric capability; three-fourths of its coal; three-fifths of its petroleum; and the advantage of Croatia's industrial potential to utilize these assets. *Nationalism and Federalism in Yugoslavia, 1962–1991* (2d ed.) (Bloomington: Indiana University Press, 1992), p. 177.

5. Ibid.

6. From a speech on 22 May 1945 in Zagreb, cited in Frits W. Hondius, *The Yugoslav Community of Nations* (The Hague: Mouton, 1968), p. 180.

7. Ramet provided a discussion of the eight major components of Yugoslav national policy in *Nationalism and Federalism in Yugoslavia*, pp. 54–58.

8. Joseph Stalin, "Report on National Factors in the Development of the Party and the State," from a report delivered at the Twelfth Congress of the Russian Communist Party, 23 April 1923, in Joseph Stalin, *Marxism and the National Question: Selected Writings and Speeches* (New York: International Publishers, 1942), p. 158.

9. Dušan Lukac chronicled the tortuous argumentation in 1923 preceding the CPY's rejection of integral Yugoslavism and acceptance of the distinctiveness of the Yugoslav nations in "Doprinos revolucionarnog radničnog pokreta u razrešavanju ključnih problema nacionalnog pitanja u Jugoslaviji," *Jugoslovenski istorijske časopis* 4 (1969), pp. 163–170. See also Fedor Ivan Cicak, "The Communist Party of Yugoslavia Between 1919–1934: An Analysis of Its Formative Process," Ph.D. dissertation, Indiana University (1965), pp. 171–175.

10. Cited in Paul Shoup, *Communism and the Yugoslav National Question* (New York: Columbia University Press, 1968), p. 13.

11. Cited in Robert A. Kann, *The Multinational Empire: Nationalism and National Reform in the Habsburg Monarchy 1848–1918*, Vol. 2: *Empire Reform* (New York: Columbia University Press, 1950), p. 44.

12. See Bogdan Raditsa's review of Franjo Tudjman, *Velike ideje i mali narodi*, in *Balkan Studies* 10 (1969), p. 463. For a further explication of how Marx and Engels regarded the South Slavs, see Hermann Wendel, "Marxism and the Southern Slav Question," *Slavonic Review* 2 (December 1923), pp. 289–307.

13. Aleksa Djilas charged that this policy toward Yugoslavia was influenced by the Comintern, "which was nursing a special animosity towards Yugoslavia as nothing more than an artificial creation of British and French 'imperialists.'" "Communists and Yugoslavia," *Survey* 28 (Autumn 1984), p. 27.

14. At the Fifth Conference of the Comintern (June–July 1924), the Resolution on the National Question in Yugoslavia recommended a new action program for the CPY that included "the disassociation of Croatia, Slovenia, and Macedonia from the structure of Yugoslavia and the creation by them of independent republics." Cicak, "The Communist Party of Yugoslavia Between 1919–1934," p. 172. A similar resolution passed in Belgrade in 1923, however, emphasized the national unification of these three nations. Cicak, "The Communist Party of Yugoslavia Between 1919–1934."

15. See Edvard Kardelj's acknowledgment of the shortsightedness of this policy in *Political and Military Strategy: Creative Role of Josip Broz Tito in the National Liberation Uprising and Socialist Revolution in Yugoslavia* (Belgrade: Socialist Thought and Practice, 1977), p. 42.

16. Ivan Avakumović, *History of the Communist Party of Yugoslavia* (Aberdeen: Aberdeen University Press, 1964), p. 68.

17. Cicak, "The Communist Party of Yugoslavia Between 1919–1934," pp. 173–175.

18. Avakumović, *History of the Communist Party of Yugoslavia,* p. 47.

19. Jovan Raičević, "Savez komunista Jugoslavije i nacionalno pitanje," in *KPJ-SKJ: Razvoj teorije i prakse socijalizma: 1919–1979* (Belgrade: "Savremena administracija," 1979), p. 232, cited in Ramet, *Nationalism and Federalism in Yugoslavia,* p. 49.

20. Shoup, *Communism and the Yugoslav National Question,* p. 47.

21. Milovan Djilas and G. R. Urban, "The End of the Bolshevik Utopia," *World Today* 47 (1991), p. 177.

22. Sead Trhulj, *Mladi Muslimani* (Zagreb: Globus, 1992), p. 10.

23. Ibid.

24. Irfan Sijerčić, "The Activities of the 'Young Moslems' at the End of the War 1944–1945," *South Slav Journal* 8 (Spring–Summer 1985), p. 66. In this article, reprinted from *Bosanski Pogledi* 2 (May 1961), Sijerčić documented his exploits as a Young Muslim, as well as the fate of other Muslims he knew at the hands of the Ustaše and the Partisans.

25. Trhulj, *Mladi Muslimani,* p. 12.

26. Steven L. Burg, "The Political Integration of Yugoslavia's Muslims: Determinants of Success and Failure" (Pittsburgh: Carl Beck Papers in Russian and East European Studies, University of Pittsburgh, 1983), pp. 24–25.

27. Ivan Lazić, "The Legal and Actual Status of Religious Communities in Yugoslavia," in Zlatko Frid, ed., *Religions in Yugoslavia: Historical Survey, Legal Status, Church in Socialism, Ecumenism, Dialogue Between Marxists and Christians etc.* (Zagreb: Binoza, 1971), p. 75.

28. Trhulj, *Mladi Muslimani,* p. 12.

29. Selim Arnaut, "Izmedju priznavanja i negiranja," *Danas* (30 January 1990), p. 40.

30. Milan Andrejevich, "Bosnia-Herzegovina: Yugoslavia's Linchpin," *Report on East Europe* 1 (7 December 1990), p. 23.

31. Trhulj, *Mladi Muslimani,* p. 14.

32. Ibid., p. 20.

33. Jovo Paripović and Fahrudin Radončić emphasized the political importance of census figures in "Igre za granice," *Danas* (2 April 1991), pp. 22–23. See also Ruža Petrović, "Brojčane promene etničkih grupa," *NIN* (29 March 1991), pp. 34–36.

34. Atif Purivatra, *Nacionalni i politički razvitak muslimana* (Sarajevo: Svjetlost, 1970), p. 33. Data from Yugoslav statistical accounts for 1948, 1953, 1961, and 1971 can also be found in George Schöpflin, "Nationality in the Fabric of Yugoslav Politics," *Survey* 25 (1980), p. 13, and Dennison I. Rusinow, "Yugoslavia's Muslim Nation," *Universities Field Staff International Reports* (Europe) (1982), pp. 4–5.

35. Burg, "The Political Integration of Yugoslavia's Muslims," p. 21.

36. Dennison I. Rusinow, "Nationalities Policy and the 'National Question,'" in Pedro Ramet, ed., *Yugoslavia in the 1980s* (Boulder: Westview Press, 1985), p. 134. See also Dijana Pleština, *Regional Development in Communist Yugoslavia: Success, Failure, and Consequences* (Boulder: Westview Press, 1992), for a discussion of the importance of inter-regional economic disparities in interethnic rivalries.

37. See Burg, "The Political Integration of Yugoslavia's Muslims," pp. 25–28, for a description of the organizational structure of the Islamic Religious Community.

38. Ibid., p. 29. A study by sociologist Esad Ćimić reported increasing lay and clerical activity during the early 1960s. *Socijalističko društvo i religija* (Sarajevo: Svjetlost, 1970).

39. Robert J. Donia and John V.A. Fine Jr., *Bosnia and Hercegovina: A Tradition Betrayed* (New York: Columbia University Press, 1994), p. 171.

40. Purivatra, *Nacionalni i politički razvitak Muslimana*, p. 33.

41. Burg, "The Political Integration of Yugoslavia's Muslims," p. 22.

42. Z. Jahović, "Neither Serbian nor Croatian, but Bosnian!" *Oslobodjenje* (27 March 1991), p. 6, in Joint Publication Research Service–East Europe Region, 1991, no. 68 (JPRS-EER-91-068) (20 May 1991), p. 27. See also ibid., pp. 48–49, for an estimate of the demographics of the population claiming Yugoslav national status.

43. The Ranković affair showed that only vigilance would keep Titoism on its pragmatic but socialistic path. Increasing pressures by the coincidentally non-Serb and more advanced areas of the country for more economic liberalization and less centralized (that is, Serbian) control had produced the reforms that began in 1965. The reforms established a more consumer-oriented economy with decentralized investment, freer prices, and a more receptive climate for foreign capital. When the marketplace, rather than patronage or theory, was permitted to dictate which enterprises should continue in business, many formerly inefficient enterprises folded. "Political investment," that is, capital investment for political rather than economic motives, ended. This, of course, meant the economically backward areas of Yugoslavia (Serbia, Montenegro, Bosnia and Herzegovina, Macedonia, and Kosovo) received less investment capital and suffered a consequent rise in unemployment and decline in living standard. See William Zimmerman, *Open Borders, Nonalignment, and the Political Evolution of Yugoslavia* (Princeton: Princeton University Press, 1987), for an analysis of the importance of Yugoslavia's policy of open borders for its political and economic development.

At the LCY Central Committee meeting in 1966, Ranković's excesses were brought to the attention of the party. Not only was he accused of using the secret police both to spy on party and government officials and for intimidation to increase his control within the party; Ranković had also apparently flaunted his pro-Serb orientation by diverting investment funds from individual enterprises to federal investment in the Serbian republic. See Ilija Jukić, "Tito's Legacy," *Survey* 77 (Autumn 1970), pp. 95–98, for a description of Ranković's attempted obstruction of the reforms.

Desimir Tochitch set forth the provocative thesis that "the 1966 public disgrace of Ranković, who could never do anything except with Tito's agreement, became necessary for Tito in order to provide evidence of the sacrifice of a reactionary scapegoat in the cause of the reforms, and to appease local Party leaders." Thus, Ranković's political demise did not measurably change the workings or effectiveness of the organs of repression—the centralized Serb-dominated police and the armed forces. Desimir Tochitch, "Titoism Without Tito," *Survey* 28 (Autumn 1984), pp. 10–11. Also see *Borba*, 8–14 December 1964.

Because in the eyes of his opponents Ranković was linked not only to Serbian but also to conservative centralist interests within the party that opposed the reforms, the threat he posed was deemed severe enough to expel him from his party positions and to institute a purge of his followers. These moves, which signaled the official separation of federal government and Serbian interests, benefited the reformers, who gained more party support for their programs.

44. *Vjesnik*, 5 July 1971, cited in K. F. Cviic, "Yugoslavia's Moslem Problem," *World Today* 36 (March 1980), p. 110.

45. April Carter, "The Republics and the Party," *Government and Opposition* 19 (Summer 1984), p. 386. Carter continued, "The Slovene and Croatian Parties in fact appear to have closed ranks successfully against the intervention of Ranković well before 1966. After 1966 the previous centralizing elements—loyalty to Tito, common experience in and immediately after the war, a habit of old style party centralism and discipline—broke down. A younger generation of republican leaders was coming to the fore, impatient of 'the old man.'" "The Republics and the Party," p. 386.

46. Rusinow, "Nationalities Policy and the 'National Question,'" p. 136.

47. Dennison I. Rusinow, *The Yugoslav Experiment 1948–1974* (London: Hurst, 1977), p. 248.

48. See Ramet, *Nationalism and Federalism in Yugoslavia*, pp. 98–106, for a discussion of actions perceived by Croats as threatening the viability and unity of their republic after the fall of Ranković. Kosta St. Pavlovich's *Razgovori sa Slobodanom Jovanovićem, 1946–1958* (Windsor, Canada: Avala, 1972) presented a firsthand account of the Serb and Croat positions on the form of a post-Tito Yugoslavia.

49. Ramet, *Nationalism and Federalism in Yugoslavia*, p. 124.

50. Ibid., p. 125. In a portent of the 1990s, Ramet further pointed out that the Serbian nationalists responded to Croatian nationalist demands for parts of Bosnia and Herzegovina not with outrage at the carving up of a discrete republic unit but with a demand to attach parts of southeastern Bosnia and Herzegovina to Serbia.

51. Dusko Doder, "Yugoslavia: New War, Old Hatreds," *Foreign Policy* 91 (1993), p. 13.

52. Rusinow, *The Yugoslav Experiment*, p. 323.

53. Burg, "The Political Integration of Yugoslavia's Muslims," pp. 45–46.

54. Provisions of the 1974 constitution created an anomalous position for Serbia, which festered throughout the 1970s and 1980s. The endowment on Kosovo and Vojvodina of political equality with the republics in effect weakened Serbia's control within its republic boundaries and permitted those provinces veto power over constitutional changes that would have righted the situation in Serbian eyes. Later, Slobodan Milošević used this issue to attempt to force the other Yugoslav republics to redress the political balance more in Serbia's favor. See Mihailo Crnobrnja, *The Yugoslav Drama* (Montreal: McGill-Queen's University Press, 1994), pp. 93–97, for more on the Serb situation resulting from the 1974 constitution.

55. Robin Alison Remington, "The Politics of Scarcity in Yugoslavia," *Current History* 83 (November 1984), p. 370.

56. Ramet, *Nationalism and Federalism in Yugoslavia*, p. 185. See also *New York Times*, 8 April 1974, p. 2, for more on official response to religious overtones of Muslim nationalism.

57. Fuad Muhić, "Paranoične ideje o 'muslimanskoj republici,'" *Borba*, 30 April–1–3 May 1983, p. 13.

58. Cited in Zachary T. Irwin, "The Islamic Revival and the Muslims of Bosnia-Hercegovina," *East European Quarterly* 17 (January 1984), p. 443.

59. Purivatra, *Nacionalni i politički razvitak Muslimana*, p. 30.

60. Ramet, *Nationalism and Federalism in Yugoslavia*, p. 179. See also Burg, "The Political Integration of Yugoslavia's Muslims," p. 40. At the Central Committee meeting of the League of Communists of Serbia in May 1968, Dobrica Ćosić and Jovan Marjanović strongly condemned this concept as "senseless," but they were subsequently expelled from the party. See Jukić, "Tito's Legacy," p. 101; Ramet, *Nationalism and Federalism in Yugoslavia*, p. 179. According to Rusinow, a Bosnian Jewish Communist, Nisim Albahari,

first proposed that the Bosnian Muslims should be granted official national status. "Yugoslavia's Muslim Nation," p. 7 (note).

61. Irwin, "The Islamic Revival," p. 445.

62. Jahović, "Neither Serbian nor Croatian, but Bosnian!" p. 27.

63. In Bosnia and Herzegovina in 1971, 39.6 percent of the population was Muslim, 37.2 percent Serb, 20.6 percent Croat, and 2.6 percent other. Schöpflin intimated that the attainment of a Muslim plurality in Bosnia and Herzegovina in the 1971 census was the result of a statistically significant Muslim switch in national self-determination from Serb to Muslim. "Nationality in the Fabric of Yugoslavia," p. 9.

64. Rusinow, "Nationalities Policy and the 'National Question,'" p. 137.

65. Andrew Borowiec, *Yugoslavia After Tito* (New York: Praeger, 1977), p. 6.

66. N. L. Karlović's presentation of data on regional standards of living discounted the oft-repeated hypothesis that Croats in general enjoyed a higher standard of living than Serbs. He thus contended that "the level of social development *per se* does not play a major role in the Croat-Serb conflict, as most studies would suggest." He noted that a correct calculation of personal income for both regions showed that overall, Serbs and Croats had achieved an equal standard of living. Nevertheless, there appeared to be no increased sense of "convergence of interests and policies based on socio-economic criteria" because Croatia had become the subordinate member of a core-periphery relationship with the Serb-dominated core. "Internal Colonialism in a Marxist Society: The Case of Croatia," *Ethnic and Racial Studies* 5 (July 1982), pp. 283, 284–286. Andrew Borowiec captured the mood of the 1970s when he wrote that "the statistical Yugoslav lives better than ever before; at the same time, statistics can't measure his increasing frustration: contact with the West has convinced him that under a different system he could have done much better." Ibid., p. 6. On the other hand, a 1986 poll conducted by the Institute for Sociological Research at Belgrade University's Department of Philosophy found that 43.1 percent of the respondents preferred a "Western market economy," whereas 53 percent were satisfied with the Yugoslav system of self-management. Mihailo Popović, "Beogrdjani o socijalizmu," *NIN* (7 September 1986), p. 18.

67. See, for example, LCY Central Committee member Milo Djukanović's statement that "the 1974 Constitution permitted the prerequisites for the rise of nationalism, because it inaugurated national states, national economies, national histories, etc." Cited in Dragan Gavrilović, "Sudbinska veza naroda Crne Gore i Srbije," *Intervju* (10 November 1989), p. 6. See also Milorad Vučelić's interview with Slobodan Vučetić, member of the Presidium of the Serbian Socialist Alliance of Working People, entitled "Izbori i demokratija—federacija i srbija," *NIN* (26 November 1989), pp. 14–15. An earlier statement of this position appeared in *Borba*, 12–15 October 1984, as reported in JPRS-EER (1 November 1984), p. 120.

68. Jovan Djordjević, "La République Socialiste," in *Le Fédéralisme Yougoslave* (Paris: Librairie Dalloz, 1966), p. 115.

69. Pedro Ramet divided the religious organizations of Yugoslavia into three categories: those that "have acted as the cultural guardians of their respective peoples for more than a millennium" (the Roman Catholic and Serbian Orthodox churches); those ethnic churches that are "linked with particular groups but [are] lacking the claim to historical guardianship" (the Czech Brethren, Slovak Evangelical, Hungarian Evangelical, and Old Catholic churches); and those newer, nonnational churches that deny "the importance of national culture as part of their ideology" (Seventh Day Adventists, Baptists, Jehovah's Witnesses).

"Religion and Nationalism in Yugoslavia," in Pedro Ramet, ed., *Religion and Nationalism in Soviet and East European Politics* (Durham: Duke University Press, 1989), p. 149. Ramet considered the Macedonian Orthodox Church, which became autocephalous in 1967, and the Islamic community to be special cases. He argued that the Islamic community "is distinct both because its institutional organization is looser and less politically conscious, and because the enveloping Islamic culture (that is, in today's Yugoslavia, taken to be constitutive of a distinct Muslim nationality) is perhaps entirely a product of the synthesis of the peculiarly religious element (i.e., Islam as a way of life) and of Turkish culture (i.e., the culture of a conqueror whose very conquest was inspired in large part by the drive to spread Islam)." Ramet, "Religion and Nationalism in Yugoslavia," p. 150.

70. Ibid., p. 150.

71. David Kowalewski, "The Religious-National Interlock: Faith and Ethnicity in the Soviet Union," *Canadian Review of Studies in Nationalism* 9 (Spring 1982), p. 98.

72. Ramet, "Religion and Nationalism in Yugoslavia," p. 151.

73. Muhamed Hadžijahić, Mahmud Traljić, and Nijaz Šukrić, *Islam i muslimani u Bosni i Hercegovini* (Sarajevo: 1977), p. 163.

74. Cited in Irwin, "The Islamic Revival," pp. 446–447.

75. The issue of the role of religious institutions during World War II remained, however. For example, in 1985 Lieutenant Colonel Milia Stanišić, retired, charged that "the church institutions of all three main religious confessions with substantial standing and influence on the people inflamed nationalistic revanchism." Quoted in Velizar Zečević, "Otkuda toliko kvislinga," *NIN* (28 November 1985), p. 22.

76. Rusinow, *The Yugoslav Experiment,* p. 100.

77. Ibid.

78. Ramet, *Nationalism and Federalism in Yugoslavia,* p. 143.

79. Ibid., p. 144.

80. Milan Andrejevich, "The Future of Bosnia and Herzegovina: A Sovereign Republic or Cantonization?" *Report on Eastern Europe* 2 (5 July 1991), p. 30.

81. Donia and Fine, *Bosnia and Hercegovina,* p. 181.

82. Bernard Lewis, "The Return of Islam," *Commentary* 61 (January 1976), p. 45.

83. Ramet, *Nationalism and Federalism in Yugoslavia,* p. 186.

84. Lewis, "The Return of Islam," p. 46.

85. Sabrina P. Ramet reported that in post–World War II Yugoslavia, whereas religiosity had declined in general, the Islamic community was the least affected. *Balkan Babel: Politics, Culture, and Religion in Yugoslavia* (Boulder: Westview Press, 1992), p. 140.

86. Quoted in Fuad Muhić, *Politika* 10 (18 April 1985), cited in Slobodan Stanković and Zdenko Antić, "Situation Report," *Radio Free Europe Research* (7 June 1985), p. 412.

87. Ibid.

88. Dušan Dragosavac, "Present-Day National Problems," *Socialist Thought and Practice* 23 (October 1983), p. 18.

89. Sabrina Ramet suggested that this phenomenon occurred "when a new generation, educated to think of the Bosnian Muslims as a national group and encouraged by contacts with a renascent Middle East, began to look to Islam as a basis for political mobilization." *Nationalism and Federalism in Yugoslavia,* p. 185.

90. Dragosavac, "Present-Day National Problems," p. 17.

91. I am grateful to Robin Alison Remington for suggesting this point to me.

92. Cviic, "Yugoslavia's Moslem Problem," p. 110.

93. Slobodan Stanković, "Tito's Successors Fear 'Moslem Nationalism,'" RAD Background Report/82 (Yugoslavia), *Radio Free Europe Research* (18 April 1983), p. 3.

94. Alija Konjhodzich, "Serbians of the Moslem Faith in Chetnik Ranks," in *Draža Mihailović Memorial Book* (Chicago: Organization of Serbian Chetniks "Ravna Gora," 1981), p. 442.

7

Bosnian Muslims and the Dynamics of Post-Tito Politics[1]

"Let us not forget we are in the Balkans, where lies and deceit are the highest moral values."

—Viktor Zakelj, Socialist Party deputy, Slovenian Parliament, 1991[2]

"You cannot tie the fate of a land in which several nations live to the fate of only one of them. That is a residue of the past."

—Muhammed Tunjo Filipović[3]

The Muslims entered the post-Tito era in a more equitable position in Bosnia than they had enjoyed since they lost their status as part of the ruling class in the Ottoman Empire. They coped well under socialism, having become an officially recognized nation, a status that carried certain rights and privileges. They were no longer thought of in vague terms in regard to the other Yugoslav national groups. Instead, before Yugoslavia dissolved into internecine conflict, Bosnia and Herzegovina seemed to have fulfilled many of the highest aspirations expected of it. The seemingly well-integrated population heartened those who hoped the Serbs and Croats had tempered their mutual antagonism over control of Bosnia and Herzegovina, as the Bosnian Muslims claimed national status in Yugoslavia and thus had a share in decisionmaking and the distribution of resources.

Viewing the hapless situation of the Bosnian Muslims in the 1990s, however, one can see that the legacy of past local and global wars, which left the aspirations of some groups unsatisfied, came back to haunt the Balkans in response to the ravages of the general deterioration of Yugoslavia during the 1980s and the transition to a market economy. The Bosnian Muslims were not spared these problems and indeed were not exempt from the antitotalitarian backlash that followed Tito's death and that released much of the anger kept bottled up since the 1945 Communist takeover of Yugoslavia. The question is why? Was there a countrywide perception and acceptance of the Bosnian Muslims as a legitimate, equal nation within Yugoslavia, deserving of the accompanying prerogatives?

Were the Bosnian Muslims indeed masters of their fate within Yugoslavia in the 1980s? Could they have pursued different strategies to avoid the savagery directed against them in the next decade? And finally, if not most important, what happened to the seeming elite consensus and the machinery set up throughout the Titoist years to prevent just this sort of deterioration into ethno-national conflict that led to the killings in the 1990s?

Yugoslavia After Tito

The post-Tito era boded well for Yugoslavia. By the end of the 1970s Yugoslavia's industrial output was twelve times larger than it had been twenty-five years earlier. In a social sense, the changes were also remarkably favorable. Yugoslavia had begun to urbanize, and the population structure had changed. There were many "worker-peasants" who engaged in part-time agriculture to supplement income from a major urban job. Consumerism increased, and mortality and birth rates approached those in the West. Yugoslavia's formerly agrarian economy had gradually industrialized and modernized.

Bosnia and Herzegovina shared in and contributed to the prosperity in Yugoslavia. As an industrializing area, Bosnia and Herzegovina became more urbanized, and, as would be expected, the larger cities swelled and became more cosmopolitan. The increasing desirability of the larger urban areas lured many from the rural regions. Inevitably, the traditional ethno-religious separation of the rural setting gave way to the conglomeration and intermingling of various groups in high-rise housing, schools, the workplace, and various social arenas. By 1990 around 40 percent of urban Bosnian marriages involved mixed ethnonational backgrounds.[4] Ethnonational particularism seemed to be giving way to a supranational Yugoslav or even Bosnian allegiance, as von Kállay during the Austro-Hungarian period and conservative Yugoslavs during the early post–World War II period had desired. Eventually, the urban perspective would have begun to penetrate the still traditional rural attitudes, which were yet governed by some ethnonational differentiation.

But the steady urbanization of Yugoslavia and the accompanying changes such urbanization elicited coincided with other important innovations in Yugoslav society. The death of Tito in May 1980 meant the end of the era of strong Titoist control. Even before his death, problems with the economy had arisen, as inflation and foreign debt and trade deficits rose precipitously during the 1980s and productivity declined just as precipitously. Clashes between leaders of the various republics were becoming more and more apparent, which made cooperation in solving these problems and reforming the political system difficult to achieve.[5] Tito had tried to provide for political and economic continuity by creating a rotating collective presidency, supported by a multinational army, to be the supreme arbiters in case of interrepublic strife. No single leader would assume his mantle after his death. However, his passing meant the end of the Yugoslav federation, for his personal attention was the glue that bound the federation together cross-nationally and ensured some degree of consensus governance. Tito's "revered charisma as well as his feared dictatorship," as former Yugoslav Ambassador Cvijeto Job put it[6]—combined with his territorial, economic, and political manipulation of Yugoslav lands and ethnic groups—provided the safety valve that kept the separate nations from arguing openly over prerogatives, resources, and territory, as well as over the interpretation of their history.

The other three domestic institutions that bound Yugoslavia together under Tito began to change after his death until they and the concealed mechanisms on which they were based, which had promoted societal stability, eventually disappeared. The LCY lingered throughout the 1980s, but for all intents and purposes it was splintered into republic-centered parties; it succumbed to republic competition in early 1990. The federation lost much of its power and in effect was superseded by republic-controlled decisionmaking in which coalition building and competition between republics controlled Yugoslav politics. As of this writing, all that is left of Yugoslavia is the jury-rigged "rump Yugoslavia," composed of Serbia and Montenegro, which has not attained universal recognition or approval as the successor to the post–World War II Yugoslav federation. Finally, the federal army, which was once considered to be the only truly Yugoslav-oriented multinational force in Yugoslavia, lost its cohesive focus with the dissolution of the Yugoslav federation, which it was sworn to defend. The Yugoslav People's Army (YPA) favored continued centralism within Yugoslavia and a unified party structure, which Slobodan Milošević—current president of rump Yugoslavia, whose policies led to the breakup—also supported. Thus, with its traditionally large number of Serb and Montenegrin officers and a policy orientation like Serbia's, the YPA was eventually transformed into a Serbian force with the breakup of Yugoslavia in mid-1991.[7]

The perceived weakening of the Soviet Union under Gorbachev was the final blow to Yugoslav unity in any form, for the fear of a potential Soviet resurgence and a concomitant attempt to reintegrate the old Communist bloc disappeared. With the destruction of the ideology that had long bolstered their power, the Communist rulers of Yugoslavia had to scramble for a new legitimizing factor so they could remain in power. Nationalism was the legitimizing factor widely chosen throughout Eastern Europe, but nowhere did the rejection of supranationalism have more unfortunate and bloody consequences than in the former Yugoslavia.[8]

How did the South Slavs, who, with the exception of the four years during World War II, lived together for almost fourteen centuries without mutual bloodletting now come to be at each other's throats? What political dynamics caused this mutual dislike to peak in Bosnia and Herzegovina after Tito's death? A series of missed opportunities for Bosnia and Herzegovina to build a strong consensus over its fate among its three major constituent ethnic groups and a series of unfortunate actions taken by many actors in and around the Yugoslav arena weakened the institutions that could have preserved Bosnia—and Yugoslavia—in the post-Tito era.

Bosnian Muslim Status in Yugoslavia during the 1980s

The 1981 census demonstrated that Yugoslav officialdom had come to grips and felt as comfortable with the Bosnian Muslims as an equal nation as had many of the Bosnian Muslims themselves. The designation, which had become simply "Muslim," drew 2,000,034[9] Muslims, or 8.9 percent of the total Yugoslav population (up from 5.1 percent in 1948[10]), to choose that category—still the third largest Yugoslav ethnic group. (See Table 7.1) This classification was used by Serbo-Croatian-speaking Muslims of Slavic origin who were born or lived in Bosnia and Herzegovina, the Sandžak, or Montenegro "and [were] in general oriented towards Bosnia."[11]

Apparently, there was still some vacillation within the Muslim community regarding its proper designation and position in Yugoslavia. This is exemplified by the fact that in Yugoslavia the designation *Muslim* must be carefully defined. *Muslim* with an initial capital letter signifies the name of an ethnic group, whereas *muslim* with an initial lower-case letter denotes a religious group.[12] The logical consequence of such a designation is that the unusual term *Muslim muslims* was used in Yugoslavia to identify persons belonging to the Muslim nation and following Islam. In the face of such ambiguities and uncertainties, some

TABLE 7.1   Ethnic Composition of Yugoslavia by Percentage of Total Population, 1948–1981

National Group	1948	1953	1961	1971	1981
Serbs	41.4	41.7	42.1	39.7	36.3
Croats	24.0	23.5	23.2	22.0	19.8
Slavic Muslims	5.1	n.a.	5.2	8.4	8.9
Slovenes	9.0	8.7	8.6	8.3	7.7
Macedonians	5.1	5.3	5.6	5.8	6.0
Montenegrins	2.7	2.8	2.8	2.4	2.6
Albanians	4.8	4.4	4.9	6.4	7.7
Hungarians	3.2	3.0	2.7	2.3	1.9
Yugoslavs	n.a.	6.0	1.7	1.3	5.4
Other	4.6	7.7	5.9	5.6	3.6

sources: Paul Lendvai, *National Tensions in Yugoslavia* (London: Institute for the Study of Conflict, 1972), p. 2; Gordon C. McDonald et al., *Area Handbook for Yugoslavia* (Washington, D.C.: Department of the Army, 1973), p. 76; Richard F. Nyrop, ed., *Yugoslavia: A Country Study* (Washington, D.C.: U.S. Government Printing Office, 1982), p. 277; George S. Schöpflin, "Nationality in the Fabric of Yugoslav Politics," *Survey* 25 (Summer 1980), p. 13.

TABLE 7.2 Distribution of Ethnic Muslims in Yugoslavia by Republic, 1948–1991

Republic–Autonomous Province	Number of Muslims by Census (thousands)					
	1948	1953	1961	1971	1981	1991
Bosnia and Herzegovina	788	892	842	1,483	1,630	1,905
Serbia	*	*	*	215	237	*
Serbia proper	6	64	84	125	151	*
Kosovo	10	6	8	26	59	*
Vojvodina	1	11	2	3	5	*
Montenegro	1	6	30	70	78	90
Macedonia	2	2	3	1	39	**
Croatia	1	16	3	19	24	48
Slovenia	0	2	1	3	13	27

*Figures unavailable.
**Macedonian Muslims included in designation "Other."

SOURCES: Slobodan Stanković, "Danger of Pan-Islamism in Yugoslavia?" *Radio Free Europe Research* (26 August 1982), p. 3; "The National Composition of Yugoslavia's Population, 1991," *Yugoslav Survey* 33 (1992), pp. 3–24; Jure Petričević, *Nacionalnost stanovništva jugoslavije: Nazadovanje Hrvata manjine napredovanje muslimana i albanaca* (Brugg: Adria, 1983), p. 47.

Muslims did not opt for the "Muslim" category in the 1981 census, identifying themselves otherwise on the census form.

For the Bosnian Muslims, "Yugoslav undetermined nationality" and even "undecided Muslim" would not express as well what the category "Muslim" would if "Muslim" were indeed understood to mean Bosnian Muslim as a nation and not merely adherence to the Islamic religion. However, a commentator who noted that the 1981 census recorded a large rise in the number of "Yugoslavs" in Bosnia and Herzegovina—from 44,000 in 1971 to 326,000 in 1981—suggested that most of that figure was composed of Bosnian Muslims who "do not care for the formal identification of religion and nationality."[13] The "Yugoslav" designation was also chosen by members of mixed marriages and their offspring, as well as by Serbs and Croats (and others) who did not want to identify themselves ethnically as anything but Yugoslavs or who, living in a republic not dominated by their national group, felt safer so declaring.

As discussed in Chapter 6, the recognition of the Bosnian Muslims as a nation was intended to have four major effects on the political affairs of Yugoslavia, three domestic and one international. During the 1970s, it appeared that on many fronts the expectations of Yugoslavia's leadership were fulfilled. After Tito's death, however, disturbing signs that the Bosnian Muslim position was not overly solid began to appear.

First, historically Bosnian Muslim national identification had been a bone of contention between Serbs and Croats. National recognition of this group meant the Bosnian Muslims would no longer be the targets of attempts by Serbs and

Croats to force allegiance toward either national group. Tito had expected that this move would quell the nationalist passions and aspirations of the Serbs and Croats for Bosnia and Herzegovina and provide a mediating force between these two quarrelsome groups. To accomplish this, however, the Bosnian Muslims would have to possess some independent power so they could confront Serbs and Croats as equal players.

During the 1970s, the Bosnian Muslims seemed to attain a larger proportion of important jobs and influence within the Bosnian republic. This situation signified their increased prestige in Bosnia and Herzegovina, particularly since the bulk of important decisionmaking regarding economic, social, and other concerns resided in the local and republic bodies. This followed Tito's acknowledgment that to prosper, Yugoslavia had to loosen its central controls over economic, party, and state decisionmaking. The results of this acknowledgment were embodied in the 1974 constitution, which made Yugoslavia a confederation. Federal decisionmaking was limited essentially to foreign policy and national security concerns. One result of this redirection of decisionmaking was the new status and power that came with an appointment to republic and local LCY and state organs.

On the state level, during the late 1970s and early 1980s the regime appeared to be consciously recruiting elites on the basis of an *ethnic key,* which determined representation in top party and government positions, as well as some key positions in security and the armed forces, in proportion to a nation's distribution in the population. Thus, one would have expected to see the nationally recognized Bosnian Muslims represented significantly in the ethnic key, because Tito wanted to cement their position and prerogatives as soon as he recognized them.

After Tito's death, the Bosnian Muslims strove to maintain and even increase their representation in the many areas of political life in which they seemed to be underrepresented.[14] For example, despite the fact that in 1971 the Muslims made up 39.6 percent of the population of Bosnia and Herzegovina, they only made up 33.9 percent of the total LCBiH membership.[15] (See Table 7.3) This situation did not improve dramatically during that decade, as the estimated Bosnian Muslim party membership was 31.1 percent in 1973 and 33.9 percent in 1978.[16] Even more telling was the fact that the Muslim party elite in Bosnia constituted approximately 31 percent of the total during the 1970s. Statistics on total Muslim membership in the LCBiH for 1981 demonstrate that the situation began to improve at the beginning of that decade, with Muslims holding 35.1 percent of the memberships.[17] Figures obtained from a 1985 study by Boris Vušković indicated that ethnic Muslims had attained party membership approximately equal to their proportional representation in the population at large.[18]

Muslim state elites in Bosnia in the 1970s totaled approximately 42 percent, slightly over the percentage of Muslims in Bosnia and Herzegovina. Noting a similar correlation in other heterogeneous areas of Yugoslavia, Lenard Cohen

TABLE 7.3 Ethnic Composition of the League of Communists of Bosnia and Herzegovina, 1971 Census

Nation	Number	%	Party Members	%
Muslims	1,482,430	39.6	86,869	33.9
Serbs	1,393,148	35.0	120,438	47.0
Croats	772,491	20.0	30,493	11.9
Other	300,000	7.5	18,450	7.2
Total	3,746,111	100.0	256,250	100.0

SOURCES: George S. Schöpflin, "Nationality in the Fabric of Yugoslav Politics," *Survey* 25 (Summer 1980), p. 16; *Popis stanovištva i stanova 31. III 1971: Nacionalni sastav stanovništva po opštinama,* Statistički bilten, nr. 727 (Belgrade: Savezni zavod za statistiku, 1972), p. 6.

observed that "in each multiethnic region [Croatia, Bosnia, and Kosovo] Serbs are more overrepresented in the party elites . . . while the principal ethnic group of each region has a 5–10 percent better representation in the state elite."[19]

In 1981 the percentage of Bosnian Muslim members of the party was roughly equal to their total percentage in the general population, a distinct improvement from the figures for 1971.[20] Nevertheless, when tallying the number of persons from Bosnia and Herzegovina with obviously Muslim names holding party and government leadership positions in 1983, Muslim underrepresentation on the federal level was obvious.[21]

Despite the expectation that each republic would select the members of its own delegations to central organs taking the proportion of ethnic representation in the republic into account, the Bosnian Muslims in fact were not represented in leadership positions in relation to their population in Bosnia and Herzegovina after Tito's death. In the 1981 census, the Muslim category (signifying Bosnian Muslims) registered 1,999,890, or 8.9 percent, of the total Yugoslav population.[22] The Muslims from Bosnia (or at least those with obviously Muslim names) in the Federal Assembly totaled at most only 20 percent of the 30 representatives from Bosnia and Herzegovina in 1983.[23] In 1985, there were 4 Bosnian Muslims (recognizable by name) of 30 representatives from Bosnia and Herzegovina in the Federal Chamber of the Federal Assembly and 2 or possibly 3 Muslims (according to name) among the 12 representatives of Bosnia and Herzegovina in the Federal Assembly's Chamber of Republics and Provinces.[24] Furthermore, in 1983 of 162 members of the Council of the Federation, only 5 had noticeably Muslim names. Their republic of origin was not given, so some of the representatives may have been from Macedonia, Montenegro, Kosovo, or elsewhere.

In 1979 a Bosnian Muslim, Hamdija Pozderac, was elected to the LCY Presidium. Prior to that there had been only one Muslim in the LCY Presidium—from Kosovo[25]—and there were no Muslims on the 9-member State Presidency.[26] A head count of individuals with Muslim names in high positions from 1983 to

1986 also provided the following statistics: Of 14 federal secretaries in 1983 there was one with a Muslim name; of 30 members of the Federal Executive Council in 1983, one had a Muslim name. In 1985, there was one Muslim from Bosnia in the LCY Presidency out of 14 members.[27] Finally, the proportion of Muslim apparatchiks in the LCY in 1982 was 8 percent, close to the 8.9 percent total of Muslims in Yugoslavia.[28]

In addition to the representation being skewed against them in party and government positions, Bosnian Muslims were underrepresented in the military and security services, which traditionally contained high levels of Serbs and Montenegrins. Thus, although Muslims as a national group made up 8.4 percent of the total Yugoslav population in 1970, in the YPA only 3.2 percent of the general officers and only approximately 4.0 percent of the officer corps were Bosnian Muslim (some data utilize the title Slavic Muslims).[29] In 1972, the Serbs constituted 40.5 percent of the total population of Yugoslavia and 60.5 percent of the YPA officers; 46.0 percent of the generals were of Serb origin. Similarly, in 1972 the Montenegrins, with 2.9 percent of Yugoslavia's total population, made up 8.0 percent of the officers and 19.0 percent of the generals of the YPA.[30] (See Table 7.4) An article in the journal *NIN* in 1976 pointed out the discrepancies and announced that there is "no reason why there is not a larger number of Muslims from Bosnia-Hercegovina among military officers,"[31] although the situation did not change substantially during the next decade.

During the 1970s and 1980s the Bosnian Muslims were underrepresented according to their numerical strength in the population in other areas, too. For example, in 1971 only 5.6 percent of the functionaries of party and mass organi-

TABLE 7.4   Ethnic Composition of Officer Corps by Percentage of
Population, 1970, 1972, 1991

Nation/ Nationality	Generals		Entire Officer Corps				Total Population		
	1970	1972	1946	1970	1972	1990	1948 Census	1971 Census	1991 Census
Serb	46.7	46.0	51.0	57.4[a]	60.5	60.0	41.4	39.7	36.2
Croat	19.3	19.0	22.7	14.7	14.0	12.6	24.0	22.1	19.7
Slavic Muslim	3.2	4.0	1.9	4.0	3.5	2.4	5.1	8.4	10.0
Slovene	6.3	6.0	9.7	5.2	5.0	2.8	9.0	8.2	7.5
Albanian	0.0	0.5	n.a.	1.2	2.0	0.6	4.8	6.4	9.3
Macedonian	3.9	5.0	3.6	5.6	6.0	6.3	5.1	5.8	5.8
Montenegrin	19.3	19.0	9.2	10.3[a]	8.0	6.2	2.7	2.5	2.3
Hungarian	0.4	0.5	n.a.	0.6	0.5	0.7	3.2	2.3	1.6
Yugoslav	n.a.	n.a.	n.a.	n.a.	6.7	n.a.	n.a.	n.a	3.0
Other	0.9	0.0	1.9	1.0	0.0	1.6	4.6	4.6	n.a.

[a]Estimate.

SOURCES: Ivan Babić, *U.S. Policy Towards Yugoslavia: Illusions and Reality* (New York: Croatian National Congress, 1979), p. 13; *Economist* (21 August 1977): Richard F. Nyrop, *Yugoslavia: A Country Study* (Washington, D.C.: Headquarters, Department of the Army, 1982), p. 275; *Balkan WarReport* 17 (January 1993), p. 6; Lenard J. Cohen, *Broken Bonds: The Disintegration of Yugoslavia* (Boulder: Westview Press, 1993), p. 182; and "The National Composition of Yugoslavia's Population, 1991," *Yugoslav Survey 33* (1992), p. 12

zations and legislative and government personnel, 4.6 percent of managerial personnel and the technical intelligentsia, 2.7 percent of natural scientists, 0.3 percent of physical scientists, and 3.1 percent of the literary and artistic intelligentsia were Bosnian Muslims. In sum, on average, only 4.1 percent of Bosnian Muslims were part of the elite in Yugoslavia in the early 1970s despite their 8.4 percent share of the Yugoslav population.[32]

The educational level and training of Muslim students did not rise substantially during this era; for students in institutions of higher education, the Bosnian Muslims' progress in relation to other groups was uneven. In areas preparatory for government work, the Bosnian Muslims had a greater proportion of seats on economic faculties in Yugoslav universities than on political faculties, where the Serbs were overrepresented. Muslims made up only 1.4 percent of the students of the LCY Political School in 1979, whereas the Serbs constituted the overwhelming majority of students with 62.2 percent.[33] There was less ambiguity in the Bosnian higher administrative schools, which were considered an alternative training ground for government work. Whereas Muslims constituted nearly 40.0 percent of the total population of Bosnia and Herzegovina in 1971, the Serbs held 54.0 percent of the places, the Muslims 20.3 percent, Croats 14.0 percent, and Yugoslavs 4.4 percent.[34]

Although these figures demonstrate that Muslims were underrepresented in most areas of the elite, Lenard Cohen cautioned that "because a large number of the group identified as 'Yugoslavs' are actually Moslems (who have not chosen to adopt 'Moslem' as an ethnic affinity although that is now officially encouraged), their underrepresentation has not been as great as it first appears, particularly in the political sectors."[35] In 1982 Cohen summarized the picture of lopsided ethnic elite representation in Yugoslavia as follows:

> The Serbs are overrepresented in the political elite*. . . especially in the party and mass organizations, and the Croats underrepresented, with the two groups having their "fair" proportions of the nonpolitical sectors. The Moslem contingent is particularly underrepresented in what is regarded officially as their own republic, but it is only over the last decade that Moslem ethnic and regional consciousness has been encouraged. Most of the self-defined "Yugoslavs" are Moslems, but some are also Serbs who prefer a no longer officially encouraged, but still more neutral, form of identity. . . . The Serbian elite predominance is only absent in literary and artistic circles. It is the only sector in which Moslems outnumber Serbs (especially when the large "Yugoslav" contingent is added) and is the sector in which the Croats of Bosnia have their highest level of representation.[36]

The second effect Tito strove for in recognizing the Bosnian Muslims was to attempt to mobilize their leadership to actively support Yugoslavia to garner for their own community any gains accruing to Bosnia and Herzegovina from a more cohesive Yugoslavia. This point arose from the 1974 constitution's assignment of sovereign rights to each nation and nationality in its own republic or autonomous region: All titular nations had their own republics, including Serbs and Croats. Since the Bosnian Muslims had become an officially recognized nation, at least some of their population could logically have concluded that whereas Bosnia and Herzegovina represented all of its inhabitants, in certain respects it had become "their" republic. To protect their new status and perhaps an implicit "homeland," the loyalty of Bosnian Muslims to the Yugoslav federation would only deepen.[37]

Indeed, upon the public recognition of their nationhood—especially as manifested in the census categories—the Bosnian Muslims' religious hierarchy became energized during the late 1960s and early 1970s to counter the threat to their identity posed by Serb and Croat nationalism. Bosnian Muslims immediately sought to present a historical record equal to that of the Serbs and Croats.[38] To promote a Muslim national separation from the Bosnian Serbs and Croats, during the 1980s Bosnian Muslim historians were busily attempting to prove beyond all doubt that Bosnian Muslims had always possessed some sense of their distinctiveness. They stressed that official recognition of its nationhood was simply recognition of an already extant Bosnian Muslim national identity, not merely of a religious affiliation. Sociologist Esad Ćimić's data indicated that in the Bosnian Muslim community national identification was entwined with religious identification. Therefore, he concluded, the Bosnian Muslim—more often than the Serb and the Croat—followed his religion not "from religious impulses, but [from] the aspiration of forming *his own* national distinctiveness, individuality" (italics in original).[39]

Like other newly recognized nations, the Bosnian Muslims attempted to forge a new and perhaps more modern national identity to accompany their newly acquired national status. In their desire to bring into sharper focus their unique national character, they emphasized what made their nation different from that of their neighbors. Historians pointed to many of the shared experiences and events, which have been alluded to in earlier chapters, as proof of the virtually constant communal identity of the Bosnian Muslims throughout their history. They emphasized particularly the common Muslim response to the foreign interference to which their area was subjected.

Inevitably within nations experiencing a national awakening, the feeling of differentiation evokes an initial paranoia that what they have only recently achieved will be taken away. For the Muslims, the threat revolved particularly around pan-Serbianism,[40] which, coincidentally, was experiencing its own reawakening. A 1986 memorandum issued by the Serbian Academy of Sciences and Arts signaled a more aggressive Serbianism by decrying the victimization of Serbs by the Yugoslav system—particularly the 1974 constitution, which confederalized Yugoslavia and in doing so dramatically weakened Serbia. Serb nationalists considered this document by Dobrica Ćosić[41] (former president of the contemporary rump Yugoslavia) and others to be the ultimate statement of Serbian aspirations. The memorandum expressed Serb anger over the loss of control in Kosovo as a result of a burgeoning Islamic population and a large outflow of

Serbs who felt unwelcome in traditional Serb lands, as well as of other Titoist policies designed to whittle away at Serbian power and the denial of a Serbian entity that included all Serbs. One of the features of this Serbian nationalism was the open expression of anti-Islamic sentiments—primarily toward the Kosovar Albanians, who had pretensions to equality within Yugoslavia, but also toward the Bosnian Muslims.

It is not unusual that Bosnian Muslim paranoia might have evolved into a felt need for wide recognition of communal identity, expressed perhaps in new territorial or status acquisition. Bosnian Muslim historians thus emphasized the contemporary secularization of a previously religious view of the Muslim community that had evolved into a national identity within Yugoslavia. These intellectuals were in the mainstream, akin to other interpreters of European history who characteristically justified present activities by reference to a heroic past whose flow had been interrupted by avaricious outsiders.

The Bosnian Muslim intellectuals initially advanced a theory that did not threaten the identity or authority of other nations within Yugoslavia. The concept of the Muslim nation in Yugoslavia was carefully defined to exclude all Yugoslav Muslims except Serbo-Croatian-speaking Slavic Muslims in Bosnia and Herzegovina and the old Sandžak of Novi Pazar and a small number in Kosovo.[42] This sensitivity to the borders of the Bosnian Muslim nation made the historians' theory more widely palatable and served in some measure to identify the Bosnian Muslims in a secular rather than a religious manner.

The third reason Tito had elevated the status of the Bosnian Muslims was to end the Serb-Croat squabbling over resource distribution within Bosnia and Herzegovina. He had hoped that by adding a third, perhaps mediating group, more rational, less nation-based policies would be developed within the republic and even perhaps at the federal level. However, the addition of the Bosnian Muslims to the equation did not erase national arguments over purely regional economic or political decisions in Bosnia and Herzegovina.

The figures seemed to point to the prominent, if not dominant, position of the Serbs within most regional structures and in the federal elite structure. Nonetheless, care should be exercised in this area. The gradual confederalization of politics in Yugoslavia indicated that although the Serbs had not lost their dominance in many traditional areas of their control, other groups were making inroads into their quasi-monopoly of power and influence. But could a non-Serb group actually make policy, or would it be able only to thwart the execution of Serb-initiated policy?

Confederalization as promoted by the 1974 constitution altered the way the Yugoslav market operated and even changed the characteristics of Yugoslavia's state sovereignty. When Tito was alive, procedures worked well enough in that he remained the ultimate arbiter and until his death all power except his was relative. But no one was truly satisfied with his system, a fact that was revealed after his death. The onus of much economic and political decisionmaking moved to the republics and localities, which were now expected to confront each other in seeking the state's limited resources. The federal government's ability to ameliorate regional conflict lessened with its declining influence at all levels of decisionmaking, an influence centralization had previously conferred. This change in emphasis was coupled with the rise of a new generation of republic-level politicians with a republic focus and power base. The end product of this confluence of factors was the exacerbation of national particularism in regard to both political and economic decisions. The federal government, led in the late 1980s by Ante Marković, provided no viable challenge.

The weakened LCY, too, had virtually abdicated power to the republic parties—the real locus of influence—and became more a forum for those parties. In effect, then, Yugoslavia came to have a multiparty political system with the elites of each republic vying for influence and resources for their own party structure. This, too, encouraged ethnonationalism. Increasingly, then, party and state decisionmaking was based on ethnonationalism rather than on coherent, federally conceived initiatives.

In Bosnia and Herzegovina, because of the power-sharing conditions established by Tito when he inserted the Muslims into the equation, coalitions drove decisionmaking. The Bosnian Muslims, of course, had been forced to play the role of perpetual coalition partner throughout their history, which detractors denigrated as opportunism. Nevertheless, during the 1980s the Bosnian Muslims began to widen their power base and legitimacy within the republic and the federation at the expense of the formerly dominant Serbs. The Serbs' growing frustration at having to play coalition politics in Bosnia and Herzegovina was given freer rein in the post-Tito era. And indeed much mistrust of the federation existed at least in part because leadership positions and staffing of Yugoslav political institutions as a whole depended on ethnic definition rather than on more ascriptive elements. The heterogeneity of most regions of the country was in conflict with politically supported national particularism, a volatile mixture whose possible outcome was ethnonational conflict.

Finally, with an eye on the international scene, Tito hoped to co-opt potential Bosnian Muslim enchantment with the militant international pan-Islamic movement. With a stake in what was happening at home, Tito wanted to encourage the Bosnian Muslims to abjure international ties that were inconsistent with Yugoslav foreign policy. This course also fit with Tito's foreign policy orientation favoring nonalignment. His attempts to woo Muslim leaders in the nonaligned movement with the status of his own Muslims made him a popular leader among those elites. However, before Tito's death the nonaligned movement was becoming fractionalized by Castro's attempt to radicalize it. Furthermore, it became evident that religion was becoming an increasingly important element for the Bosnian Muslim community, which sensitized the Bosnian Muslims to trends in the external Muslim world. Thus, simultaneous with the numerical growth of Bosnian Muslims and contrary to the secular aims of Bosnian Muslim intellectuals, a growth of religious identification and sentiment occurred within the Bosnian Muslim community.

It is difficult to determine whether increasing Bosnian Muslim religious identification was a genuine reflection of deeper religiosity—as appeared to be occurring in the general, worldwide Islamic community—or whether it was the growth of a Muslim national identity that subsumed Islam as a religion into a broader cultural and political doctrine.[43] Few reliable data exist that specifically measure the number of faithful and the intensity of religious beliefs among the Bosnian Muslims, although a 1983 article in the *Jerusalem Post* estimated that around three thousand Yugoslav Muslims made the hajj yearly, a figure that differs significantly from figures published by Yugoslav sources (see Table 7.5).[44] A slow but steady rise in the degree of Muslim affiliation in the Yugoslav population at large was noted in the mid-1960s.[45] This tendency reflected the liberal atmosphere in Yugoslavia in the late 1960s. However, the Belgrade weekly magazine *NIN* found that the proportion of young Yugoslavs who claimed to be religious dropped 14 percent in 1983 from the 1969 total of 40 percent.[46] These contradictory findings suggested no "recent increase in the number of faithful in Yugoslavia, but an increase of the number of those who freely express their religious beliefs."[47]

Perhaps the cultural and social openness of the 1980s dispelled some of the fear about expressing religious beliefs that the former climate of secularism had initially created. Yugoslav sociologist Esad Ćimić studied religious manifestations in Herzegovina and concluded that in contrast to Herzegovinian Serbs and Croats, Muslims

Have a consciousness in which the national and the religious are often intertwined and complement each other (more explicitly than for the other groups). Because of that, one sometimes does not belong to this confession from religious motives, but aspiring to establish *his own* national distinctiveness, his individuality.[48]

The more open political and social climate of the 1980s also permitted the flowering of religious institutions in Yugoslavia. For example, in 1977 *Reis-ul-ulema* Hadži Naim Effendi Hadžiabdić reported that "the material position of our religious employees has never been better. All imams are covered by health, pension and invalid insurance. A large number of very beautiful mosques have been built—there are more than 500."[49] In fact, more than one thousand mosques and buildings dedicated to Islamic education had been built in Yugoslavia between 1945 and the mid-1980s.[50] Furthermore, Yugoslavia was the only European country during that time that could boast an Islamic theological school, three thousand mosques, and several Islamic middle schools, as well as a number of Muslim periodicals.[51]

A rash of rebuilding and refurbishing of Islamic institutions occurred during the 1970s; funding came almost entirely from the contributions of Muslim believers, with some subsidy from the leadership of the Bosnian LCY. In 1977, it was

TABLE 7.5   Yugoslav Muslims Taking the Hajj, 1967–1983

Year	Bosnian Muslims	Total Yugoslav Muslims
1967	344	1,539
1968	346	1,317
1969	—	1,554
1970	—	1,517
1971	695	2,211
1972	—	18 (suspect figure)
1973	—	2,077
1974	766	2,077
1975	—	1,048
1976	—	855
1977	—	1,115
1978	424	953
1979	501[a]	1,320
1980	—	1,260
1981	—	899
1982	—	995
1983	—	868

[a]Also includes Muslims from Croatia and Slovenia.

SOURCES: H. Hfz. Husein Mujić, "Ovogodišnje putovanje na hadž," *Glasnik VISa* 30 (May–June 1967), p. 233; H. Alija Kusturica, "Osvrt na ovogodišnje hodočašće," *Glasnik VISa* 31 (April–May–June 1968), p. 237; David Edwin Long, *The Hajj Today: A Survey of the Contemporary Makkah Pilgrimage* (Albany, N.Y.: State University of New York Press, 1979), p. 134; H. Hfz. Sinanuddin Sokolović, "Hadž 1971, godine (2211 (hadžija iz SFRJ)," *Glasnik VISa* 34 (March–April 1971), p. 135; Ibrahim Lisovac, "Ovogodišnje putovanje na hadž," *Glasnik VISa* 37 (May–June 1974), p. 224; Zejnil Fajić, "Putovanje na hadž u 1398./1978, godini," *Glasnik VISa* 41 (November–December 1978), pp. 632–634; Merzuk Vejzagić, "Put na hadž u 1979./1399, godini," *Glasnik VISa* 42 (November–December 1979), p. 627; and Kingdom of Saudi Arabia, Ministry of Finance and National Economy, Central Department of Statistics, *Statistical Yearbook.*

reported that the Commission for Religious Questions had funneled what amounted to 10 percent of the Islamic community's religious budget to the Bosnian Islamic leadership. The Bosnian LCY also subsidized the dissemination and preparation of manuscripts of interest to the Islamic community in the Arabic, Turkish, and Persian languages. Two-thirds of the cost of restoring the Gazi Husrefbeg Mosque was absorbed by the republic government and the city of Sarajevo.[52] Interestingly, the cooperation evidenced between the official Islamic religious hierarchy and the Bosnian political leadership was assisted by the secular Muslim intelligentsia, which retained active contacts with both groups.[53]

Whereas the Bosnian Muslims seemed to become increasingly more integrated into the Yugoslav community of nations, they were also experiencing more contacts and links with foreign Muslims. For example, the Bosnian Islamic Council, which supervised all affairs of the Islamic Religious Community in its region, began to distribute literature discussing general Islamic concerns, as well as Arabic-language literature from the Middle East. Hajj figures largely from Yugoslav sources indicated an active but variable participation of Bosnian Muslims in the pilgrimage to holy places (see Table 7.5).

Furthermore, because the resources for training and educating the future religious leaders were still somewhat weak in Bosnia, students went to universities in the Islamic Middle East and Asia.[54] For example, in 1978 almost 150 Yugoslav Muslim students pursued their Islamic education abroad[55] with subsidies from the host governments (Egypt, Iraq, Kuwait, Libya, Morocco, Saudi Arabia, and the Sudan). This figure continued to increase during the 1980s. The Bosnian Islamic community, however, still suffered from a paucity of qualified clergy because many of these students did not return to Yugoslavia but remained in the Arab countries in which they studied to serve as translators for Yugoslav enterprises.[56]

Rising Islamic activism among the Bosnian Muslims was viewed uncomfortably by the LCY,[57] which feared the Muslims would begin to pursue their political interests more as members of a Muslim religious community than as a secular part of Yugoslavia. This feeling was spurred by reports of Bosnian Muslim youths returning from study abroad in Muslim lands who "had ceased to be Communists and had become instead fanatic Moslems, not only in the ethnic sense, but, what was even more dangerous for the regime, in the religious sense as well."[58] Although the characterization of fanaticism was extreme, it does appear that the increasing religiosity of the Bosnian Muslim community was a source of concern to official Yugoslavia.

The Yugoslavs were caught in a contradiction by recognizing a nation whose "primary determinant" was religion,[59] an anti-Marxist paradox to say the least. The Muslim national challenge was thus taken very seriously in Yugoslavia throughout the 1980s. Islam was a total ideology-theology that could, like (or instead of) Marxism, regulate the entire life of its citizens, with its cradle-to-grave and sunrise-to-sunrise prescriptions of how to live and its centrality and universality in the lives of Muslims. Even more than Marxism, "Islam from the lifetime of its founder *was* the state. [Thus,] the identity of religion and government is indelibly stamped on the memories and awareness of the faithful from their own sacred writings, history, and experience."[60] Marxists considered a resurgent and aggressive Islam to be dangerous in that for Muslims there was no difference between religious and political authority. Therefore, although the Yugoslav leaders were bound to give the Bosnian Muslims as many privileges and as wide a latitude as possible in coming to their self-realization, officials were determined to prevent any pan-Islamic manifestations from arising within the Bosnian Muslim community during the 1980s that could injure national relations in Yugoslavia.

Rise of Nationalism in Bosnia and Herzegovina

Until Tito recognized the national status of the Bosnian Muslims, "*republic* nationalist manifestations were not severe" in Bosnia and Herzegovina.[61] Tito's acknowledgment of their nationhood in his pursuit of a political agenda, however, opened up a new front for nationalist conflict in Yugoslavia. Alexandre Bennigsen illustrated a similar dilemma in Soviet relations with their Muslims. Although the Soviet Muslim leadership cooperated with the Soviet government by taking every opportunity to praise the life of Muslims under Soviet Communist rule, the price was steep: "The Soviet regime must pay . . . for any action by the Muslim leaders in its favor—by immediate and important concessions such as the slowing down of antireligious propaganda, the opening of new mosques, or the publication of religious literature."[62] As both the former Soviet Union and Yugoslavia discovered, there was no small paradox in a Communist country taking steps to ease the plight of a religious group to obtain its cooperation in achieving other, political goals.

Several distinct factors pointed toward the potential for a new Yugoslav arena for ethnonationalistic conflict in Bosnia and Herzegovina. For example, the old concept of Bošnjak was again proposed to serve as a national label for all residents. However, only the Muslim Bošnjak Organization demonstrated enthusiasm for this name, and only a small number of Muslims used it for self-identification.[63] Also, some Bosnian linguists continued to suggest that *Bosanski,* Serbo-Croatian with a liberal sprinkling of Turkish loanwords spoken in some areas of Bosnia, should be recognized as a separate and distinct Yugoslav language.[64]

A more threatening factor, particularly to Serbs, was the approach of the time when the Bosnian Muslims would constitute an absolute majority, rather than merely a plurality, of the population in Bosnia and Herzegovina. This situation would have been potent ammunition to further Bosnian Muslim nationalism. Serb leaders sounded the alarm. Orthodox priest Žarko Gavrilović, for example, speculated on whether Serbian interests might be threatened in Bosnia and Herzegovina, saying "we are sincerely disturbed about the burgeoning anti-Serbian mood in Yugoslavia, including Bosnia, and we are inclined to believe that it is groundless and dangerous. . . . Is Bosnia and Hercegovina becoming another Kosovo for Orthodox Serbs and Serbian priests?"[65] Increasing Serb distrust of Bosnia and Herzegovina was a definite factor in the Serbian internal security service's decision to intensify operations in Bosnia and Herzegovina without official Bosnian knowledge or approval, a fact that came to light only in 1989.[66]

Despite the value for Yugoslavia of Bosnian Muslim nationalism, there were warnings of the dire consequences of encouraging it. In May 1986, for example, Hrvoje Istuk, a member of the LCBiH Presidium, criticized the fact that Muslim nationalism "recently has joined to its idea about the Muslims as the sole bearers of the statehood of Bosnia and Hercegovina a unitaristic thesis about annexing the Sandžak to such a Muslim state."[67]

The charges of burgeoning "Khomeini-like fundamentalism" leveled increasingly against offending Muslims might have covered what really concerned Yugoslav authorities: These Muslim nationalist manifestations may have been the prelude to the formation of a radical Muslim, and thus anti-Marxist, bloc that would appeal to both Bosnian and Albanian Muslims. This was unlikely, because the political, religious, social, and similar needs of the Albanian and Bosnian Muslims coincided very little. Nevertheless, if all the Muslims of the former Yugoslavia were to feel threatened *as Muslims* by a common (anti-Muslim) enemy, it was conceivable that a Muslim front, united despite different exigencies, might fight against the Serbs or others.

Thus, following the rather lukewarm attempts to control Bosnian Muslim nationalism in the 1970s, the Yugoslav leadership launched a major salvo, starting on 10 April 1983, against what was perceived to be chauvinistic Bosnian Muslim nationalism. Thirteen Muslims, including Alija Izetbegović, were arrested and in July were tried in the Sarajevo District Court on charges of "hostile and counter-revolutionary activities."[68] The majority of the defendants were well-educated, professional people twenty-six through sixty-one years of age. They included two imams, two lawyers, two teachers, and four engineers. Two of the defendants were women; one defendant was a former party member and another a former Partisan.[69] The defendants were described as "active Muslims" who had used Muslim nationalism "to do the criminal deed of hostile propaganda directed to the destruction of nations and brotherhood and unity, and the equality of the nations and nationalities in the SRBiH [Socialist Republic of Bosnia and Herzegovina] and SFRJ [Socialist Federated Republic of Yugoslavia]."[70] Their alleged crimes included the fact that they

> Described communism as a threat to Islam, welcomed anti-Yugoslav turmoil in Kosovo, criticized Yugoslav nationalities policy as aimed at the Serbianization of the Muslims, plotted to eliminate the Serbian and Croatian populations in Bosnia-Herzegovina, and manipulated the religious feelings of others in an effort to mobilize support for a militant Islam.[71]

Furthermore, they were accused of developing illicit links with reactionaries abroad and spreading hostile propaganda within Yugoslavia. The latter claim dealt in particular with the dissemination of a document written by Izetbegović in 1970 called *The Islamic Declaration: A Programme for the Islamization of Muslims and the Muslim Peoples*.[72]

Careful inspection of the declaration reveals some elements Yugoslav authorities might indeed have considered provocative. For example, Izetbegović wrote that

> Just like an individual, a people that has accepted Islam is thereafter incapable of living and dying for any other ideal. It is unthinkable that a Muslim should sacrifice himself for any king or ruler, no matter who he might be, or for the glory of any nation or party, because the strongest Islamic instinct recognizes in this a kind of paganism and idolatry.[73]

The leaders of Yugoslavia during the 1980s were well aware of the precarious future of their country, even as it appeared that the Soviet Union under Gorbachev had forsworn foreign military adventures. Yugoslavia valued its role as a nonaligned country, but it also appreciated its precarious position between East and West and would not have welcomed the provocation that held that a part of the Yugoslav population could disregard the exigencies of fighting in the Yugoslav People's Army in case of aggression. However, the declaration did include the proviso that "Muslim minorities within a non-Islamic community, provided they are guaranteed freedom to practice their religion, to live and develop normally, are loyal and must fulfil all their commitments to that community, except those which harm Islam and Muslims."[74] The question of who would define those interests and what circumstances would be considered harmful to Islam and Muslims was unspecified but provocative. Would the Bosnian Muslim faithful be permitted by their faith to defend Yugoslavia against any aggressors, including those with close connections to fellow Muslims? The following scenario would have given Yugoslav leaders pause at that time: an aggressive Soviet Union utilizing military units composed of Central Asian Muslims to persuade Yugoslavia's Muslims not to fight against them.

A second example of rhetoric potentially unsettling to Yugoslav authorities was the declaration's blunt statement that "there can be neither peace nor coexistence between the Islamic religion and non-Islamic social and political institutions. . . . By claiming the right to order its own world itself, Islam obviously excludes the right or possibility of action on the part of any foreign ideology on that terrain."[75] Presumably, Marxism could only be considered by Muslims to be merely one additional foreign ideology.

Furthermore, the declaration appeared to sanction the overthrow of non-Islamic governments by Muslims: "*The Islamic rebirth cannot begin without a religious revolution, but it cannot be successfully continued and completed without a political one.*"[76] And "the Islamic movement should and can start to take over power as soon as it is morally and numerically strong enough to be able to overturn not only the existing non-Islamic government, but also to build up a new Islamic one."[77] Such words would indeed have sounded threatening to the protectors of Marxist Yugoslavia, although the Yugoslav Muslim conquest of Yugoslavia was inconceivable even if *all* the Yugoslav Muslims could overcome their differences and consolidate.

Finally, the declaration stated that "a natural function of the Islamic order [was] to gather together all Muslims and Muslim communities in the world . . . [into] a great Islamic federation from Morocco to Indonesia, from tropical Africa to Central Asia."[78] The declaration did not explicitly exclude countries that contained Islamic minorities. Nationalism was to be discarded as useless to Islam, since "Pan-Islamism has always sprung from the very heart of the Muslim people, while nationalism has always been imported goods."[79] The declaration thus denigrated the possibility of attaining a future national Yugoslavism.

The declaration was not particularly complimentary toward the established Islamic community, for it criticized in very strong terms

> The class represented by the *hajjs* and sheikhs who, in contrast to clear dictates on the nonexistence of a clergy in Islam, have emerged as an organized class which has preempted the interpretation of Islam and set itself up as an intermediary between man and the Qu'ran. . . . [These theologians and priests are] narrowminded and backward people, whose deathlike embrace has strangled the still living Islamic idea.[80]

The defendants denied that the treatise referred particularly to Yugoslavia,[81] and indeed there were no references in it to Yugoslavia or to Bosnian Muslims in particular. Proof of the other major charge also remained elusive. The allegation of illegal links with foreign reactionaries was based on the claim that some of the accused had secretly visited an Islamic state in January 1983.[82] An article in the *South Slav Journal* speculated that the Islamic state could only have been Iran, something, however, that was not mentioned in open-court proceedings.[83] One of the defendants, writer Melika Salehbegović, concluded that in the eyes of Yugoslav officials, the visits to Iran by herself and some of the other defendants and her unsent letter to Khomeini represented a threat that Bosnian Muslims would endanger Yugoslavia with such contacts.[84] Prosecutors treated the declaration and the subterfuge of the trip as proof that the defendants were conspiring to create "an ethnically pure Moslem Bosnia-Herzegovina."[85]

In their enthusiasm over the successes of the Khomeini revolution, the argument went, the conspirators had become members of the Young Muslims, emulating the pre– and post–World War II group of that name. The goal of the contemporary Young Muslims was alleged to be to overthrow the Yugoslav constitutional order, in partnership with some anti-Yugoslav exile organizations, to purify Bosnia[86] and make it a pan-Islamic state called Islamistan.[87] The *Islamic Declaration* was allegedly prepared to further this purpose.[88]

The prosecutors' arguments against the accused were not terribly credible for at least one important reason. If indeed widespread admiration for the Khomeini revolution existed among Bosnian Muslims, one would expect that this admiration was for the fact that it had occurred at all rather than for the goals it had achieved, since Yugoslavia's Bosnian Muslims were mainly Sunni and, as such, were bitter rivals of Khomeini's Shiites.

Aside from the fact that most Muslims in Yugoslavia were not stirred to action by the publication of the declaration, the document "became obsolete after the Islamic revolution in Iran in 1979."[89] Nevertheless, even a whisper of such thoughts and actions must have stunned the Yugoslav leadership. The fragility of the ethnic balance in Yugoslavia had become even more delicate with the burgeoning of Bosnian Muslim nationalism. The fact that such nationalism could occur in a national-religious form reminiscent of the Serb and Croat variants would appear doubly dangerous to Yugoslav authorities. In fact, Fuad Muhić, described as "an ardent defender of the Moslem nationality in Yugoslavia,"[90] felt Muslim nationalism was the most dangerous nationalism of all, because the Muslims had created "a sort of spiritual union with Moslems all over the world, 'from Gibraltar to Indonesia,'" based on the Koran.[91] Milan Kangrga, an academic from Zagreb, emphasized that "the danger of Islam lies not in itself, as such, but rather in the tendencies contained within it, which do not shrink from openly and militantly advocating that Marx's science (which is European par excellence) be replaced by the Islamic religion and the Koranic way of life."[92]

In August 1983, the Muslim defendants received sentences ranging from six months to fifteen years[93] on charges of counterrevolutionary activity, hostile propaganda, and Muslim nationalism. Hasan Čengić, a Muslim theologian, was given a ten-year sentence that was later reduced to six and a half years.[94] Izetbegović, sentenced to fourteen years in prison for wanting to create a Muslim republic in Yugoslavia, was released in 1988 in a general amnesty along with three other Muslims who had gone to prison for "pan-Islamic" activities.[95]

The entire incident of the arrest and conviction of the Bosnian Muslims for hostile propaganda was only one in a series of campaigns against nationalism that were undertaken throughout the late 1960s and the 1970s after the purge of Ranković in 1966. As illustrated by the trial of Bosnian Muslim activists, Bosnia was particularly aggressive against any form of nationalism that might threaten multinational cooperation in Bosnia and Herzegovina. Vojislav Šešelj, a Bosnian Serb, was also prosecuted and convicted of nationalist excesses, including advocating the dismemberment of Bosnia and Herzegovina and its annexation by Serbia and Croatia, in 1984. Further Yugoslav-wide campaigns had been launched against Albanian, Serbian, and Croatian nationalism, as well as "punk nationalism."[96] The Muslims, however, had every reason to be paranoid with regard to their potential persecution within Yugoslavia—particularly since the death of Tito, who had been regarded as the guarantor of their national prerogatives and security.[97]

Indeed, secular Muslim leaders were able to regain some degree of influence over the Bosnian Muslim community in the wake of the crackdown against increased Muslim religiosity and the accompanying nationalism. Looking back on this period after the passage of two decades, academician Muhammed Tunjo Filipović charged that

> Accusations [of Muslim fundamentalism are] a form of political, moral, and cultural terrorism . . . the last form of resistance to the fact that Muslims are becoming an equal historical and cultural factor both in our country and in the world. That attack on Bosnia and Herzegovina had the function of political and psychological preparation of pressure on Muslims, which culminated in the well-known trial of the "fundamentalists" in Sarajevo.[98]

However, the position of some of the most influential Bosnian Muslim secular elites was shaken by their involvement in the Agrokomerc scandal in 1987. The former chicken-farming business turned agricultural mega-enterprise, led by Fikret Abdić, was headquartered in northwest Bosnia in Velika Kladuša. With strong ties to Bosnian federal government leaders and widespread connections to much of Bosnia's economy, Agrokomerc pursued an aggressive growth strategy without the requisite collateral to back the promissory notes it issued to banks throughout Yugoslavia. Although this was not an uncommon practice, it became a scandal during the contemporary anticorruption drive. The lack of financing for the more than $500 million involved[99] caused mass impoverishment in a large portion of northwestern Bosnia when neither the enterprise nor the state could save the corporation from its folly.

Many Muslims believed the Agrokomerc scandal had been manipulated by Serbia to limit the influence of Bosnian Muslim elites, since the brunt of the punishment fell on Bosnian Muslim party, political, and economic leaders and their families. The highest-ranking Bosnian Muslim politician, Hamdija Pozderac—scion of one of the families that had built up the unsecured debt— was forced from his position as federal vice president right before he would have become president of Yugoslavia on the next rotation of the Federal Presidency. Abdić, also a member of a deeply involved Muslim family, lost his seat on the Bosnian LCY's Central Committee but retained local popularity, which he parlayed into an electoral victory in 1990 and then into a seat on the Presidency of Bosnia and Herzegovina.

The Serbs believed there was a good reason to crack down on Bosnian Muslim nationalism—to prevent the Croats and the Bosnian Muslims from making common cause based on shared geographic and economic interests, as well as what some considered strong historical, ethnic, and linguistic connections.[100] The two groups' coalescence would have created a union of 60 percent of Bosnia and Herzegovina's population. The Serbs would obviously have been nervous about such an eventual counterweight to Serbian power,[101] particularly in light of the onset of Milošević's program of Serbian nationalism.[102] There are signs that some Croats may indeed have had such a plan in mind for the future as is seen, for example, in the inclusion of Muslim authors in the 1989 *Bibliography of Croatian Writers of Bosnia-Herzegovina Between the Two Wars,* to the outrage of Yugoslavia's Islamic community.[103]

Despite the appearance of Serbian nationalism and paranoia, the position of the Bosnian Muslims improved in some ways during the 1980s following the brief postwar days of militant atheism and Yugoslavism. Muslims seemed to have been simultaneously integrated into Yugoslav life while developing a new sense of religiosity or national consciousness. The Islamic Religious Community no longer appeared to lack influence in the decisionmaking spheres of the government and at the beginning of the 1990s seemed to have attained a new self-confidence and even activism on its own behalf.[104] However, as we shall see in Chapter 8, the gains of the Bosnian Muslim community were more limited than they appeared to be.

Tito had carefully crafted a set of institutions to take his place after he was gone. The institutions were created to ensure as much continuity and as much pressure to maintain the unity of the federation as he could build in without undermining his own power. But Tito, although he was president for life, could not guarantee that after his death the institutions he had so carefully fashioned would do their jobs.

Indeed, after his death the working of the institutions had begun to encourage ethnonational rather than Yugoslav aspirations. The complexities of the issues and the ramifications of the decentralization and liberalization of the LCY, the burgeoning economic discontent between the poorer and richer republics, and the fissures developing in the political system were just becoming apparent to some extent at Tito's death. Gradually throughout the 1980s, however, the dynamics of the machinery not surprisingly produced policies based on distinctions among nations (and nationalities). When the political unit for economic and political decisionmaking (the republic or the autonomous province) coincided fairly strongly with national boundaries, it was inevitable that economic and political decisionmaking would be infused with ethnonationalism—to the detriment of both the economic and political systems, as well as of various republics at various times.[105]

Finally, the system undercut the only group of people who had a stake in the continuation of Yugoslavia as a whole—those who thought of themselves as only Yugoslavs without hyphenation. But when political and economic decisionmaking and personnel decisions became based entirely on national identification and the national key, "Yugoslavs" became an unrepresented group. It was potentially more rewarding, then, to declare oneself a Bosnian Muslim or other recognized nation than to hold fast to any obviously undervalued self-identification as Yugoslav. The political dynamics of the post-Tito era were thus a far cry from what Tito had intended when he altered the system in the 1970s.

Throughout the 1980s, this situation worsened until it culminated in the 1990s with the ultimate breakdown of Yugoslavia into constituent parts and the mutual bloodletting among formerly united South Slavs. Chapter 8 details the final days of the Yugoslav state and the ultimate collapse of the Titoist machinery and consensus.

NOTES

1. This chapter draws on findings first reported in Francine Friedman, "Ethnic Conflict in Yugoslavia: The Rise of Tribalism," paper presented at the Annual Meeting of the Midwest Political Science Association, Chicago, Illinois, 16 April 1994.

2. David Olive, *Political Babel: The 1,000 Dumbest Things Ever Said by Politicians* (New York: Wiley, 1992), p. 161.

3. Manojlo Tomić, "Na dva brvna niz reku," *NIN* (26 April 1991), p. 25.

4. Robert J. Donia and John V. A. Fine Jr., *Bosnia and Hercegovina: A Tradition Betrayed* (New York: Columbia University Press, 1991), p. 186.

5. Sharon Zukin argued that Tito's death had less of an impact on Yugoslav attitudes than did the inflation and resulting austerity measures that occurred after his death. "Self-Management and Socialization," in Pedro Ramet, ed., *Yugoslavia in the 1980s* (Boulder: Westview Press, 1985), p. 76.

6. Cvijeto Job, "Yugoslavia's Ethnic Furies," *Foreign Policy* 92 (Fall 1993), p. 58.

7. Patrick Moore, "Where Is Yugoslavia Headed?" *Report on Eastern Europe* 2 (6 September 1991), p. 35.

8. For an incisive and detailed description of the 1992 Bosnian crisis, see Paul Shoup, "The Bosnian Crisis in 1992," in Sabrina Petra Ramet and Ljubiša S. Adamović, eds., *Beyond Yugoslavia: Politics, Economics, and Culture in a Shattered Community* (Boulder: Westview Press, 1994), pp. 155–187.

9. A 1986 publication of the Toronto-based Croatian Islamic Centre claimed that the 1981 census deliberately undercounted Yugoslavia's Muslims. See Mushtak Parker, *Muslims in Yugoslavia: The Quest for Justice* (Toronto: Croatian Islamic Centre, 1986), p. 14.

10. Jure Petričević, *Nacionalnost stanovništva jugoslavije: Nazadovanje Hrvata manjine napredovanje muslimana i albanaca* (Brugg: Adria, 1983), p. 75.

11. Darko Tanasković, "Muslims and muslims in Former Yugoslavia, Part 1," *East European Reporter* 5 (May–June 1992), p. 14.

12. Ibid.

13. Viktor Meier, "Yugoslavia's National Question," *Problems of Communism* 32 (March–April 1983), p. 55. As early as 1982, Dušan Bilandžić, a sociologist from Zagreb, asserted that the phenomenon of Yugoslavism would probably be short-lived; rather, he presciently suggested that the post-Tito era would see an increasing nationalistic assertiveness by the Yugoslav nations and nationalities. See "High Tide of Declared Yugoslavs," interview in *Vjesnik* (Zagreb), 8 May 1982.

14. Pedro Ramet pointed out that the Croat nationalists made a similar charge about their conationals in Bosnia and Herzegovina in 1971. *Nationalism and Federalism in Yugoslavia, 1963–1983* (Bloomington: Indiana University Press, 1984), p. 131.

15. George Schöpflin, "Nationality in the Fabric of Yugoslav Politics," *Survey* 25 (Summer 1980), p. 16.

16. Lenard J. Cohen, "Regional Elites in Socialist Yugoslavia: Changing Patterns of Recruitment and Composition," in T. H. Rigby and Bohdan Harasymiw, eds., *Leadership Selection and Patron-Client Relations in the USSR and Yugoslavia* (London: Allen and Unwin, 1983), p. 124.

17. Ramet, *Nationalism and Federalism in Yugoslavia*, p. 132.

18. Cited in Jelena Lovrić, "Nacionalna karta partije," *Danas* (10 December 1985), p. 5. Vušković further stated that the Serbs and Montenegrins were overrepresented in the LCBiH, the Croats and "Yugoslavs" were underrepresented, and the Muslims were almost evenly represented. Lovrić, "Nacionalna karta partije," p. 8.

19. Cohen, "Regional Elites in Socialist Yugoslavia," pp. 123–124. Boris Vušković noted that "Muslims . . . have a share in the LC [League of Communists] membership in Banja Luka, Mostar, and Tuzle that is far higher than their share in the population. . . . Indeed this is far higher than their average share at the level of the B-H CC [Central Committee of the LCBiH] . . . in Sarajevo. . . . Muslims have a slightly smaller share in the LC membership from their share in the population, and this is almost identical to the republic situation." "Nacije u SKJ: Nacionalna struktura članstva Saveza komunista u većim gradovima republika i pokrajina," *Naše Teme* 30, no. 3–4 (1986), p. 380.

20. From Wolfgang Höpken, "Party Monopoly and Political Change: The League of Communists Since Tito's Death," in Ramet, ed., *Yugoslavia in the 1980s,* p. 46.

21. See *Directory of Officials of the Socialist Federal Republic of Yugoslavia: A Reference Aid* (Washington, D.C.: United States Central Intelligence Agency, Directorate of Intelligence, December 1983), CR 83-11848; *Directory of Yugoslav Officials: A Reference Aid* (Washington, D.C.: United States Central Intelligence Agency, Directorate of Intelligence, December 1985), CR85-16320; Slobodan Stanković, "Appendix: Who's Who," in *The End of the Tito Era: Yugoslavia's Dilemmas* (Stanford: Hoover Institution Press, 1981), pp. 121–140; "East European Leadership List," *Radio Free Europe Research* 23 (January 1985), pp. 31–33.

22. "The National Composition of Yugoslavia's Population, 1991," *Yugoslav Survey* 33 (1992), p. 12.

23. *Directory of Officials.*

24. *Directory of Yugoslav Officials.*

25. *Directory of Officials.*

26. Stanković, *The End of the Tito Era,* p. 65.

27. *Directory of Yugoslav Officials.*

28. Slobodan Stanković, "On the Eve of the 12th Yugoslav Party Congress," *Radio Free Europe* (25 June 1982), p. 4.

29. A. Ross Johnson, *The Role of the Military in Communist Yugoslavia: An Historical Sketch* (Santa Monica, Calif.: Rand, 1978), p. 19. See also Schöpflin, "Nationality in the Fabric of Yugoslav Politics," p. 15.

30. Bogdan Denitch, *The Legitimation of a Revolution: The Yugoslav Case* (New Haven: Yale University Press, 1976), p. 114.

31. Sava Stajčić, "Koje naš oficir," *NIN* (14 March 1976), p. 16.

32. *Popis stanovništva i stanova 31. III 1971: Aneks uz statistički bilten 727* (Belgrade: Savezni zavod za statistiku, 1972), p. 5.

33. Schöpflin, "Nationality in the Fabric of Yugoslav Politics," p. 18, citing *Komunist* (11 January 1980); and Lenard J. Cohen, "Balkan Consociationalism: Ethnic Representation and Ethnic Interaction in the Yugoslav Political Elite," paper presented to the Northwestern Political Science Association, Portland, Oregon, March 1979, p. 42.

34. One could compare the situation for Muslims in 1930–1931 when only 1.7 percent of all the students in Yugoslavia were Muslim (by religion). See Cohen, "Balkan Consociationalism," p. 42.

35. Ibid., p. 34.

36. Ibid., p. 36.

37. Hamdija Pozderac, the Muslim president of the Central Committee of the LCBiH, equally decried both the Bosnian Muslim nationalists, who considered Bosnia and Herzegovina to be the national state of Yugoslav Muslims, and Serb and Croat nationalist attempts "to deny the national and state identity of Bosnia-Herzegovina." *NIN* (10 April 1983), cited in Slobodan Stanković, "Tito's Successors Fear 'Moslem Nationalism,'" *Radio Free Europe Research* (18 April 1983), p. 4.

38. These activities should be placed within the context of the national revivals of the other Yugoslav nations during this time. Sabrina Ramet chronicled the reawakened interest in historical and cultural themes among the other Yugoslav national groups, illustrating that unanimously their focus was on their own nation and not on the generic Yugoslav

people. *Balkan Babel: Politics, Culture, and Religion in Yugoslavia* (Boulder: Westview Press, 1992), p. 29.

39. Esad Ćimić, *Socijalističko društvo i religija* (Sarajevo: Svjetlost, 1970), p. 258.

40. Fuad Muhić, "Paranoične ideje o 'muslimanskoj republici,'" *Borba*, 30 April–1–3 May 1983, p. 13.

41. Cited in Sabrina Ramet, "War in the Balkans," *Foreign Affairs* 71 (Fall 1992), p. 92.

42. Steven L. Burg, "The Political Integration of Yugoslavia's Muslims: Determinants of Success and Failure" (Pittsburgh: Carl Beck Papers in Russian and East European Studies, University of Pittsburgh, 1983), p. 42. In 1990, Alija Izetbegović reiterated this definition of Bosnian Muslims, which emphasized regional group rather than only religious affiliation, when he expressed concern for "all three million Muslims" in Yugoslavia. This figure equaled the Muslim population of Bosnia and Herzegovina and excluded many Albanian, Macedonian, and other Yugoslav Muslims. Cited in Dusko Doder, "Yugoslavia: New War, Old Hatreds," *Foreign Policy* 91 (1993), p. 13.

43. Ćimić believed this to be so from the study he made of Herzegovina. *Socijalističko društvo i religija.*

44. *Jerusalem Post*, 9 June 1983, cited in Nenad Ivanković, "Podno tisuću minareta," *Danas* (27 March 1984), p. 14.

45. Sergej Flere, "Denominational Affiliation in Yugoslavia 1931–1987," *East European Quarterly* 25 (June 1991), p. 154.

46. Slobodanka Ast, "Yjed Andžela," *NIN* (29 July 1984), p. 18.

47. Ćimić, *Socijalističko društvo i religija*, p. 125.

48. Ibid., p. 258 (emphasis in original).

49. "Muslims in Yugoslavia: Adaptation and Accommodation," *Impact International* 7 (24 June–7 July 1977), p. 14.

50. "Anti-Moslem Feelings Denied," *Yugoslavia: Situation Report, Radio Free Europe Research*/1 (Yugoslavia) (30 November 1984), p. 29.

51. Ivanković, "Podno tisuću minareta," p. 14.

52. Burg, "The Political Integration of Yugoslavia's Muslims," p. 47.

53. Ibid.

54. Ivan Ceranić, "Religious Communities in Yugoslavia," in Zlatko Frid, ed., *Religions in Yugoslavia: Historical Survey, Legal Status, Church in Socialism, Ecumenism, Dialogue Between Marxists and Christians etc.* (Zagreb: Binoza, 1971), p. 29.

55. Burg, "The Political Integration of Yugoslavia's Muslims," pp. 32–33; Ahmed Smajlović, "Muslimani u Jugoslaviji," *Glasnik VISa* 41 (November–December 1978), p. 562.

56. Burg, "The Political Integration of Yugoslavia's Muslims," p. 33.

57. See, for example, Ramet, *Balkan Babel*, p. 170.

58. Stanković, "Tito's Successors Fear 'Moslem Nationalism,'" p. 3.

59. Schöpflin, "Nationality in the Fabric of Yugoslav Politics," p. 9.

60. Bernard Lewis, "The Return of Islam," *Commentary* 61 (January 1976), p. 40 (emphasis in original).

61. Fred Warner Neal, "Yugoslav Approaches to the Nationalities Problem—The Politics of Circumvention," paper presented at the annual meeting of the American Association for the Advancement of Slavic Studies, Washington, D.C., 16 October 1982, p. 11 (emphasis in original).

62. Alexandre Bennigsen, "Soviet Muslims and the World of Islam," *Problems of Communism* 29 (March–April 1980), p. 46.

63. Tanašković, "Muslims and muslims in Former Yugoslavia, Part 1," p. 14.

64. Z. Jahović, "Neither Serbian nor Croatian, but Bosnian!" *Oslobodjenje* (27 March 1991), p. 6, in JPRS-EER-91-068 (20 May 1991), p. 28; Ramet, *Nationalism and Federalism in Yugoslavia*, p. 185.

65. "'Injustices' Against Serbs, Church in Bosnia Protested," *Pravoslavlje* (1 April 1986), pp. 10–11, in JPRS-EER-86-107-115.

66. Reported in Ramet, *Balkan Babel*, p. 33.

67. Cited in Mila Štula, "Licem u lice s partijom," *Danas* (20 May 1986), p. 21.

68. A partial listing of the defendants and their professions appeared in F. N., "Pritvoreno jedanaest nacionalista," *Borba* (Zagreb) 61, 11 April 1983, p. 15.

69. "The Trial of Moslem Intellectuals in Sarajevo," *South Slav Journal* 6 (Spring 1983), p. 55.

70. F. N., "Pritvoreno jedanaest nacionalista," p. 15.

71. Ramet, *Nationalism and Federalism in Yugoslavia*, p. 186.

72. The declaration appeared in the *South Slav Journal* 6 (Spring 1983), pp. 56–89. It was republished in Sarajevo in 1990. Alija Izetbegović, *The Islamic Declaration: A Programme for the Islamization of Muslims and the Muslim Peoples* (Sarajevo: 1990). Quotations were taken from the 1990 version, which differs somewhat in translation, although not in thrust, from the 1983 publication.

73. The *Islamic Declaration*, p. 6.

74. Ibid., p. 50.

75. Ibid., p. 30.

76. Ibid., p. 43 (emphasis in original). Passage repeated in ibid., p. 51.

77. Ibid., p. 56.

78. Ibid., p. 60.

79. Ibid., p. 64.

80. Ibid., p. 9.

81. "Dr. Izetbegović's Address at the 1983 Sarajevo Trial," *South Slav Journal* 8 (Spring–Summer 1985), p. 95.

82. Slobodan Stanković, "Anti-Moslem Feelings Denied," in "Situation Report: Yugoslavia," *Radio Free Europe Research* (30 November 1984), p. 1, citing *Večernje Novosti* (29 July 1983).

83. "The Trial of Moslem Intellectuals in Sarajevo," p. 55. Stanković cited a Croat leader in Sarajevo, Branko Mikulić, who stated that those arrested also were connected with the Muslim Brotherhood, which he characterized as a terrorist organization. "Campaign Against 'Khomeini-Inspired' Moslems in Yugoslavia," RAD Background Report/119 (Yugoslavia), *Radio Free Europe Research* (24 May 1983), p. 2, citing *Tanjug* (18 May 1983).

84. Cited in Parker, *Muslims in Yugoslavia*, p. 40.

85. "The Trial of Moslem Intellectuals in Sarajevo," p. 55.

86. Stanković, "Tito's Successors Fear 'Moslem Nationalism,'" p. 2, citing *Oslobodjenje* (Sarajevo) 11 April 1983. In a different article, Stanković quoted a Muslim party official, Nijaz Durković, to the effect that *Mladi Muslimani* "had been used by Hitler's Third Reich, which hoped to create on its basis an 'independent Islamic state and an ethnically pure Bosnia.'" "Campaign Against 'Khomeini-Inspired' Moslems in Yugoslavia," p. 2, citing *Komunist* (13 May 1983).

87. Slobodan Stanković, "Further Attacks Against Yugoslavia's 'Young Moslems,'" RAD Background Report/102 (Yugoslavia), *Radio Free Europe Research* (10 May 1983), p. 1, citing Djuro Kozar, "Errors of 'Fighting Islam,'" *Borba* (Zagreb), 19 April 1983.

88. Slobodan Stanković, "Yugoslav Communists Versus 'Militant Islam,'" p. 2, *Radio Free Europe Research* (1 August 1983), citing *Vjesnik,* 16 July 1983.

89. Muhić, "Paranoične ideje," p. 13.

90. Stanković, "Campaign Against 'Khomeini-Inspired' Moslems in Yugoslavia," p. 3.

91. Muhić, "Paranoične ideje," p. 13.

92. In Stanković, "Tito's Successors Fear 'Moslem Nationalism,'" p. 4, citing *Filozofska Istraživanja,* nos. 4–5 (April–May 1982).

93. The original sentences and their later alterations appeared in *South Slav Journal* 6 (Autumn 1983), p. 54.

94. Complaints of his mistreatment in prison were published in *Die Weltwoche* (14 August 1986), p. 7, reported in JPRS-EER-86-144-91.

95. Patrick Moore, "The Islamic Community's New Sense of Identity," *Report on Eastern Europe* 2 (1 November 1991), p. 20.

96. Stanković, "Tito's Successors Fear 'Moslem Nationalism,'" p. 3, citing *Vjesnik,* 11 April 1983.

97. Muhić, "Paranoične ideje," p. 13.

98. In Mustafa Mujagić, "Da, ja sam fundamentalist," *Danas* (9 January 1990), p. 14.

99. Branka Magaš, *The Destruction of Yugoslavia: Tracking the Break-up of 1980–92* (London: Verso, 1993), p. 111.

100. See, for example, the peroration of the Croatian National Congress concerning official attempts to prevent the Bosnian Muslims from publicly claiming their Croatian heritage. *Violations of Human and National Rights of the Croatian People in Yugoslavia: Memorandum Submitted to the Madrid Review Conference on Security and Cooperation in Europe* (New York: Croatian National Congress, 1980).

101. K. F. Cviic, "Yugoslavia's Moslem Problem," *World Today* 36 (March 1980), p. 112.

102. See Stephen Engelberg "Carving out a Greater Serbia," *New York Times Magazine,* 1 September 1991, pp. 18–21, for more on the spectacular rise of Slobodan Milošević.

103. Ramet, *Balkan Babel,* pp. 172–173.

104. Ibid., pp. 173–174.

105. Ivo Jakovljević reported a severe degeneration in the Yugoslav economy in every republic, with Bosnia and Herzegovina showing the least precipitous decline and Montenegro the worst. "Kolika cijena samostalnosti," *Danas* (4 December 1990), p. 18.

8

Collapse of Yugoslavia and the Fate of the Bosnian Muslims

Remember how the unbelievers
plotted against you,
to keep you in bonds,
or slay you,
or expel you from your home.
They plot and plan
But Allah also plans
And the Best of Planners is Allah.

—Al-Anfal (8):30[1]

Why this sudden bewilderment? This confusion?
Why are the streets and squares
emptying so rapidly
Everyone going home, lost in thought?
Because night has fallen,
and the Barbarians have not come!
And some of our men, just in from the border,
Say there are no Barbarians any longer.
Now what's going to happen to us
without the Barbarians?
They were, those people, after all,
A kind of solution.

—Constantinos Kavafis[2]

"Everybody in former Yugoslavia wants to be a majority,
even if they are in a minority."[3]

The disintegration of Yugoslavia was a result of many failures and missed opportunities. However, in the end the inherent contradiction between Slovene and Croat aspirations for autonomy and Serbia's desire to regain its interwar hegemonic position felled the Yugoslav union. The Yugoslavs could not rise above these opposing demands and their deep-rooted attacks on the nascent political pluralism of the post-Tito era. Instead, many activist elites succumbed to the lowest common denominator of politics—ethnonationalism. The pursuit of national sovereignty in this context necessarily excludes national minorities— not to mention democrats, critical intelligentsia, and other vulnerable groups— whose interests are sacrificed to elite aspirations for political legitimation and nationalistic aggrandizement.[4]

As has become evident, the breakup of Yugoslavia spelled the demise of a stable, multicultural Bosnia and Herzegovina. Initially, it appeared that Bosnia and Herzegovina might escape the chaos throughout Eastern Europe resulting from the collapse of communism. In this situation of ethnonational particularism, the challenge for Bosnia and Herzegovina was to steer a course that would recognize the needs of all of its constituent nations and political forces. However, the options of the Bosnian Muslims became increasingly circumscribed as their main protector, the LCY, disintegrated and communism was replaced by nationalism as a legitimating ideology in Yugoslavia. Further, the international arena was unable—or unwilling—to take on the role of protector of the Bosnian Muslims. In the end, the Bosnian Muslims' homeland fell victim to clashing ethnonationalistic aspirations.

Yugoslavia's Democratic Elections and Their Aftermath

The first democratic elections in a Western sense held in Yugoslavia since World War II seemed to be part of the democratic upsurge experienced by Eastern Europe in the wake of the implosion of the Soviet Union. Thus, in spring 1990, truly competitive multiparty elections were scheduled in Slovenia and Croatia. However, reflecting the increasingly vicious politics of nationalism pursued throughout the country during the 1980s, the winning candidates represented national rather than Yugoslav or even socialist points of view, with disastrous results for the cohesion of Yugoslavia and the future of the federation. Similarly, Slobodan Milošević's Socialist Party of Serbia retained control of the Serbian government in the December 1990 elections.[5] Milošević appealed to nationalist and populist Serbs with his rescinding of Kosovo's autonomy the previous year and his call to redraw Yugoslavia's boundaries to include all Serbs within a reconstituted Serbia if recentralization of Yugoslavia could not be realized.[6] In a bid to restore the ethnocentric nationalism of bygone days,[7] he also stirred up Croatian Serb fears of the ruling Croat nationalists.

The newly elected republic leaders squabbled among themselves about the future configuration of Yugoslavia.[8] The Slovenes were pushing the boundaries of the Yugoslav federal arrangement in an attempt to enhance Slovenia's sovereignty by regulating its republic borders and denying other federal government decisionmaking power. Slovene conflict with Serbia over the form of the Yugoslav state undercut any consensual possibilities. Slovenia and Croatia in particular saw Serbia's tightening control over Kosovo under martial law as a direct threat of Serbian expansionism and drew appropriate conclusions about their own future prospects in a Serb-controlled Yugoslavia. Milošević's open encouragement of Serb chauvinism and ethnic conflict in Croatia[9] and his demand that Yugoslavia become more centralized under the Serb-dominated LCY and central government threatened the vision of confederalism treasured by Slovene and Croat elites. Meanwhile, nationally aroused Croats ignored the rights of the more than six hundred thousand Serbs living in Croatia and essentially excluded them from the political process[10] by subordinating their status from one of "brotherly unity" with Croats, as mandated in the Croat republic constitution,[11] to the reality of minority status. Following the Slovene lead, nationalist Croats called for increased confederalization of the country,[12] in which enlarged republic authority would protect their prerogatives and their land against Serb encroachments. They also demanded greater control over their own economies, which they believed the Serb-controlled federal bureaucracy was recklessly draining and endangering.[13]

Ironically, Bosnia and Herzegovina and Macedonia attempted to mediate this conflict by proposing plans that embraced elements of Slovenia's proposed confederation but allowed the federal government to retain some important powers.[14] However, neither side would budge from its national program. Both sides raised the tension level as a Serb versus Croat media war began in an attempt to mobilize a population that seemed interested in pursuing personal economic advancement rather than political objectives.[15]

Into the fray jumped the Bosnian Croat prime minister of Yugoslavia Ante Marković. Having become prime minister in 1989 at a time when the economy was experiencing a severe downturn, Marković had turned his admirable economic and political savvy to building broad-based political support for his economic reform program. Marković's regime succeeded in temporarily lowering inflation from 2,600 percent to 120 percent shortly after assuming office,[16] but his "shock treatment" program for stabilizing the economy also resulted in the fall of manufacturing by 17 percent.[17]

Amid the increasingly nationalistic appeals in the republics, Marković attempted to take advantage of his limited success to create an all-Yugoslav non-ideological (that is, nonsocialist) party, with a platform of political democratization and economic reforms, to pursue a market economy.[18] The party, named the Alliance of Reform Forces, was formed on 29 July 1990 in Bosnia and Herzegovina. The symbolism of the locale, the republic with the largest number of declared "Yugoslavs," was marked.[19] However, Marković's party was notably unsuccessful in encouraging citizens to "think federation." The party became active only *after* the Slovene and Croat elections, and its legitimacy and competitiveness were compromised. Instead, politics became increasingly the possession of the republics, and the alliance was able to garner only 50 of the 735 contested seats in the four republic elections in which it participated.[20] Marković resigned at the end of 1991.

The politics of ethnonationalism had won. As the republics argued over Yugoslavia's future, the presidency of the federation became weaker and less able to make decisions, arguing even over the venue for its meetings.[21] The elections thus had emboldened the victorious republic parties, which became stronger and demanded more prerogatives for their own republics and conationals. This situation became increasingly dangerous, with the heads of the republics spouting nationalistic expressions while ignoring political guarantees for ethnic minorities.

The atmosphere became increasingly conflictual, despite ongoing interrepublic negotiations between December 1990 and June 1991.[22] Weapons may have been acquired by Serbs and Croats as early as 1991, if not sooner,[23] and the first armed clash between Serb and Croat forces began at Plitvice National Park on 1 April. The atmosphere was poisoned even more when the Serbs refused to recognize the normal rotation of the federal presidency, which would have made the Croat Stipe Mesić president of Yugoslavia in May 1991, on the grounds that his program constituted the creation of an independent Croatia and the destruction of Yugoslavia. At that point, with the federal presidency paralyzed and unable to fulfill its constitutional duties, Slovenia and Croatia used this situation and Milošević's increasingly heavy-handed violations of human rights in Kosovo to indicate the end of the normal functioning of the Yugoslav federation. They opted for independence.

In referenda, the citizens of both republics had voted overwhelmingly for independence if outstanding issues of the future shape of Yugoslavia were not satisfactorily settled (December 1990 in Slovenia and May 1991 in Croatia). On 25 June 1991, with the requisite decisions still not made, the Croat and Slovene governments obeyed the popular mandates and openly broke with the federation. They nullified the Yugoslav constitution and federal legislation relevant to their territories and declared their independence from Yugoslavia, thus unilaterally transforming Yugoslavia's internal administrative borders into international frontiers.

The Yugoslav federation declared the republics secessionary and their bid for independence illegal.[24] The YPA response, paralleling the Serb-Montenegrin desire to maintain an integrated Yugoslavia, was to enter Slovenia[25] to preserve the existing Yugoslav borders. However, Slovenia's territorial defense troops, which were part of the network of secondary defense Tito created in every republic during the Cold War to protect against Warsaw Pact aggression, were able to secure significant amounts of weaponry and were not intimidated. Slovenia's fledgling army successfully defended its independence, as the YPA demurred against an all-out invasion.[26] After a ten-day rout and subsequent negotiations on withdrawal, the YPA left Slovenia. With a homogeneous citizenry containing few Serbs, Slovenia was not a target for the greater Serbian aspirations shared by many YPA officers.[27]

Meanwhile, Croatia's Krajina (the old Austrian Military Frontier) was ablaze as aroused Serbian irregular forces attempted to take control of territories with large Serbian populations and clashed with Croatian military units. Throughout the post-Tito period, Croatian nationalists had pursued an undemocratic and insensitive rejection of legitimate status for their Serb minority. Altering Croatia's constitution to exclude anyone but Croats as citizens, Croatian nationalists secured massive layoffs of Serb apparatchiks[28] and expropriated Serbian land and property that had often been part of a family's patrimony for centuries.[29] Croatian nationalists refused to consider the sensitivities of the Serbs in Croatia with the adoption of historically charged symbols Serbs associated with the new state's Ustaše past, such as the *šahovnica* (a red and white checkerboard shield featured on Croatia's flag)[30] and the *kuna* as the new monetary unit. Later, extremist Serb forces in Croatia—which had grown increasingly influential—united with the adjacent Bosanska Krajina portion of Bosnia and Herzegovina, proclaimed the "Serbian Autonomous Region of Krajina," and demanded annexation by Serbia.[31] In the end, between July 1991 and January 1992 Croatia lost almost 30 percent of its territory and suffered many casualties.

Neither individual European states nor multilateral European bodies exerted themselves to pressure Croatia to ensure civil and human rights guarantees to the large Serbian minority still living in Croatia. In fact, the European Community (EC) gave official imprimatur to the breakup of Yugoslavia by recognizing the independence of Croatia and Slovenia on 15 January 1992,[32] after the failure of the EC-sponsored Hague Conference on Yugoslavia chaired by British politician Lord Carrington.[33] Serbs in Croatia vigorously protested the EC action. Bosnian and Macedonian officials, too, had opportuned the West to withhold recognition until the situation stabilized.[34] At the Hague Conference, attended by federal and republic leaders from Yugoslavia in September 1991, they reiterated alternative proposals for the solution of the crisis, such as the creation of a union of sovereign Yugoslav states with central control over a national army, a common currency, a common market, and a joint parliament and collective presidency. These proposals were similar in many respects to Ante Marković's December 1990 eleven-point program.[35]

The Bosnian Muslims in particular needed the security of a multinational Yugoslavia; they could not resist being swallowed by Serbia or Croatia or both without federal protection or at least an internationally brokered agreement that the Croats and Serbs would not make claims to the lands of Bosnia and Herzegovina.[36] However, the sanctity of borders had already been breached with the secession of Slovenia and Croatia, which became a dangerous precedent for Bosnia.[37]

Many analysts fault Germany for breaking ranks with standing EC policy, which was reflected in the recommendations of the Arbitration Committee of the European Community's Conference on Yugoslavia. The Badinter Commission, named for French constitutional lawyer Robert Badinter who headed the five-member group, declared that no new state should be recognized in Europe that forcibly altered frontiers (including internal borders) or that failed to formally ensure the protection of the rights of its ethnic minorities and demon-

Cartographic Services, Department of Geography, Ball State University

strate popular consensus for independence. Croatia clearly did not fit that profile, prompting elites in Bosnia and Herzegovina and Macedonia to request in
early December 1991 that West European leaders withstand German pressure to
recognize Croatian and Slovenian independence until the objections of Croat
Serbs—who from a fully enfranchised nation had been relegated to a minority
with less rights, including that of self-determination—could be mitigated and
the fighting in Croatia halted.[38]

Former Yugoslav ambassador to the EC Mihailo Crnobrnja suggested that
Germany believed its recent reunification through an alteration of borders
by means of self-determination of its peoples would serve as a model for
Yugoslavia.[39] The ingenuousness of likening a fairly homogeneous area with

the multiethnic Yugoslavia, underpinned by the Western view of the nation-state relationship, which was not the same as the East European version—especially in regard to what that difference in relationships meant for national self-determination—undercuts this explanation, however. It further suggests that the German policy may have responded to other factors, such as domestic pressures from Germans who frequented Croatia and Slovenia as tourists, as well as the numerous Croat guest workers in Germany. Ironically, the same German argument of "preventive recognition" could have been applied to Bosnia and Herzegovina, but it was not, which also suggests German ulterior motives.

Whatever its reasons, Germany's precipitous recognition of Croatia and Slovenia with the argument that such a policy would lead to a permanent cease-fire also forced the EC and even the United States to recognize their independence without sufficient diplomatic preparation or insistence upon Croatian abandonment of menacing actions against its Serbian minority. German, EC, and U.S. recognition prior to the realization of a comprehensive political agreement for the entire Yugoslav state that would take into consideration the status of all the republics of the former Yugoslavia, as well as the position of the various nations in multiethnic Bosnia and Herzegovina, in effect encouraged Croatian chauvinism. Premature recognition of Slovenia and Croatia also weakened any leverage the international community might have had to bring the Yugoslav problem to a more peaceful conclusion through the threat of nonrecognition. By preempting any homegrown Yugoslav solutions, the international community effectively frustrated the development of a modus operandi whereby the involved parties could create mechanisms for conflict resolution. Like the Concert of Europe in the nineteenth century, the international community took it upon itself to create the conditions for peace with little input from an engagement of the involved actors.

The United States was also roundly criticized for diplomatic tactlessness, which may have exacerbated the situation. In June 1991, during a visit to Belgrade, Secretary of State James Baker expressed U.S. interest in maintaining the status quo in Yugoslavia, despite the fact that Slovenia and Croatia had already indicated their preference for independence. Baker's position was that if the Yugoslav nations decided to sever their political connections and seek independence, political settlements of the major issues separating the various parties would have to be negotiated first to avoid civil war.[40] Slovenia and Croatia were bluntly warned that unilateral secession from Yugoslavia would not be recognized by either the United States or its European allies; nor would they receive economic assistance. At the same time, Baker suggested that Milošević should consider a looser federal structure to satisfy the recalcitrant republic leaders. Baker's posture, however, encouraged Serbian pretensions to continued Yugoslav unity despite forceful dissent from other republics. Serb boldness and refusal to consider weakening the central government even in the face of Baker's requests were also boosted when General John Calvin, commander of the North Atlantic Treaty Organization (NATO), categorically stated that NATO would not intervene in Yugoslavia, which did not lie within NATO's security zone.[41]

Opponents of U.S. policy also accused the Bush administration of encouraging European failure in the solo handling of the first major crisis since union by ensuring that European leaders were indubitably sensitized to the necessity of continued U.S. engagement in Europe.[42] If that was indeed the U.S. intention, it was undoubtedly a failure, because the United States ended up pursuing what seemed to the rest of the world to be a vague and reactive policy. Indeed, eventually the United States found its options constrained and was forced to cleave to the European line[43] rather than provide the kind of strong and decisive leadership the Yugoslav tragedy required.

In this atmosphere of flawed domestic and international decisionmaking, even multicultural Bosnia and Herzegovina was not able to withstand the siren call of ethnonationalism. In the winter 1990 elections to the Bosnian Assembly,[44] the three nation-based parties representing the Serbs, Croats, and Muslims of Bosnia and Herzegovina won almost 90 percent of the 240 available parliamentary seats. The issue-based parties were rejected by the voting populace. The *Hrvatska demokratska zajednica* (Croatian Democratic Community [HDZ]), led by Sarajevan Stjepan Kljuić but founded by and dependent on Croat nationalist Franjo Tudjman, won 44 seats to represent the Bosnian Croats; the *Srpska demokratska stranka* (Serbian Democratic Party [SDS]), headed by Montenegrin-born Radovan Karadžić, with 72 seats, would speak for Bosnian Serbs.

The Muslim *Stranka demokratske akcije* (Party of Democratic Action [SDA]), which garnered 86 seats, initially attempted to represent as many elements within the Bosnian Muslim community as possible. The SDA was described by one observer as "a movement of religious dissidents (like Izetbegović), former apparatchiks, Communist entrepreneurs and intellectuals who all, however, agreed that Bosnia must be indivisible."[45] Thus, the party leadership included such disparate personalities as Adil Zulfikarpašić—a Muslim dissident—academician Muhammed Tunjo Filipović, and Fikret Abdić, a highly popular businessman from Bihać. However, this coalition later split apart. Zulfikarpašić and Filipović rejected the SDA's self-image as "a centrist party influenced by Islam and highly sensitive to Muslim religious, political, and cultural rights."[46] They thus left the SDA to form a different party, the Bosnian Muslim Organization, an avowedly secular party that rejected any hint of Bosnian Muslim religiosity. Abdić, who had already clashed with Izetbegović in the preelection period, withdrew from the SDA and later challenged Izetbegović on the battlefield.[47]

If less blatantly nationalistic parties had emerged to lead the republic out of the Titoist era, Bosnia and Herzegovina might have survived the succeeding storms. Elites who concentrated on support for individual rather than national rights and on democracy and a market economy were noticeably lacking in the winning parties' leaderships. The fact that the three dominant parties had almost mutually exclusive constituencies[48] strained the already widely stretched lines of tension within the republic. Inauspiciously, the number of parliamentary seats each party won closely coincided with the proportion of that nation's population in Bosnia and Herzegovina, demonstrating the deep divide within the polity. The electoral breakdown reaffirmed that much of the voting followed national-religious identification, although one-third of eligible voters had abstained and one-third of those voting had supported parties that lacked nationalist programs.[49] Nevertheless, the large percentage of SDA voters demonstrated that the Muslims were becoming as nationally conscious as the Serbs and Croats. The SDA's informational proclamation to Bosnian Muslims encouraged this tendency by describing in detail how to answer census questions. Bosnian Muslims were reminded that their national affiliation was Muslim, their mother tongue Bosnian, and their religion Islam.[50]

Without a clear majority party, postelection governance of Bosnia and Herzegovina was conducted by multinational coalition. SDA head Izetbegović became the first president of the republic's presidency, which was to rotate among the parties every two years. Momčilo Krajišnik of the SDS became president of the National Assembly. The prime minister was a Croat, Jure Pelivan, representing the HDZ. The three major national groups were also represented on the seven-member Bosnian State Presidency (two each from the SDA, HDZ, and SDS and the remaining seat for "others"), in the Parliament, and as heads of various ministries.[51] Thus, the minister of the interior was from the SDA, the minister of defense from the HDZ, and the minister of information from the SDS.[52] However, a lack of programmatic unity among the three parties, as well as "political purges" of ethnic rivals by members of all three parties in various government institutions,[53] short-circuited structural arrangements designed to produce consensual government.[54] Negotiations among the three nation-based parties broke down over the issue of the future structure of Bosnia. The Muslims and Croats favored Bosnian sovereignty over Serb domination in a truncated Yugoslavia. However, the Bosnian Serbs did not relish minority status in an independent Bosnia and Herzegovina. Tensions over this issue increased such that apparently many Bosnians were arming themselves by 1991, if not earlier,[55] although Izetbegović allowed the YPA to disarm Bosnia's Territorial Defense Units in early 1992,[56] leaving them defenseless when the fighting began in earnest.

Perhaps it is too much to have hoped that the decades of goodwill built up by the peaceful coexistence of the various nations were enough to withstand the chauvinistic storms blowing around the borders of Bosnia and Herzegovina.[57] This is not to say that some people did not openly aspire to and work for a peaceful solution. On 5–7 April 1992, for example, approximately two hundred thousand demonstrators[58] assembled before the Bosnian Parliament building to demand peace in Bosnia and Herzegovina, the resignation of the government

(Prime Minister Jure Pelivan did resign) and new elections, the dismantling of paramilitary units, and YPA defense of Bosnia and Herzegovina—not just of Bosnian Serbs.[59] But the demonstration was shattered when snipers dispersed the gathered Serbs, Croats, and Muslims, killing and wounding indiscriminately.[60] This incident was merely one more showing that the aspirations of the Serb—and Croat—nationalists had fatally splintered the already weakened Bosnian decisionmaking apparatus. Greater Serb aspirations had become the inclinations of many Bosnian Serbs, who invited Serbia's authority over Bosnian territory they occupied. An independent Croatia, including Croat-dominated territories in Bosnia and Herzegovina, was pushed by Bosnian Croats. These aspirations were translated into a conflict within the land of Bosnia and Herzegovina[61] between Bosnian Serbs and Croats supported by their "mother countries" (Serbia and Croatia).[62]

The increasing tensions and the proximity of interethnic conflict to its borders impelled Bosnia and Herzegovina's leaders in July 1992 to follow the constitution's direction to center much of the republic's legislative and executive decisionmaking powers in the presidency rather than in a system of division of powers and checks and balances, which had been provided for in nonwartime conditions. Nevertheless, the Constitutional Court of Bosnia and Herzegovina issued an urgent call to continue to maintain inviolate Yugoslavia's and Bosnia's constitutional order.[63] In spite of this effort, the conjunction of negative trends—increased political and military tensions, lack of tolerance for multiculturalism, use of national quotas for state and social organization, and the increasing absence of democratic procedures—that had destroyed Yugoslavia also weakened Bosnia and Herzegovina's ability to respond constructively to the 1991 secession crisis and succeeding catastrophes.

Croat President Franjo Tudjman and Serbia's Milošević seemed fairly close in their desires to utilize ethnonationalism to advance their own power.[64] Tudjman has been called racist, whereas Milošević has been deemed Machiavel-lian. Yet both were able to see opportunity in the chaos accompanying the fall of Yugoslavia. Like their interwar predecessors Maček and Cvetković in 1939, Tudjman and Milošević conspired together in the turmoil to carve up Bosnia and Herzegovina without Muslim input.[65]

Meanwhile, in the ongoing interrepublican negotiations, Bosnian President Izetbegović—supported largely by the multinational urbanized population in Bosnia and Herzegovina—argued for a new vision for Bosnia and Herzegovina, based on tolerance for multiculturalism in a specifically Bosnian rather than Yugoslav construct.[66] He proposed restructuring Bosnia and Herzegovina along regional rather than purely ethnic lines.[67] However, many Bosnian Serb and Croat nationalists would not accept that concept. They supported a Bosnia and Herzegovina legitimized by its constituent national groups—the kind of corporate pluralism instituted by Tito—as opposed to liberal pluralism, which is legitimized by the people as individual citizens. They would not accept the possibility of a Bosnian Muslim president, despite public assurances by Izetbegović that the Bosnian Muslims recognized a multiethnic Bosnia and did not demand the institution of Islamic radicalism or even an Islamic state.

Izetbegović, who resigned from the SDA leadership, was supported publicly in his primarily secular view of the future of Bosnia and Herzegovina within Yugoslavia by the head of the Yugoslav Islamic Religious Community, Hadži Jakub Effendi Selimoski. Selimoski considered the realization of anything but a secular state to be a mistake.[68] Furthermore, Selimoski stated that he "categorically reject[ed] altering borders [in] the one place in Europe where Muslims have achieved religious and political freedom."[69]

Some Bosnian Serbs, however, demanded the right of self-determination. They were caught up in the possibility after so many years of realizing the dream of Serb hegemony over all Serbs and the lands they occupied. They argued that recognition of the independence of the former Yugoslav republics meant the international community was accepting the borders mandated by Tito, which gratuitously excluded one-third of the Serbian population from Serbia proper and left Serbs as minorities in both Croatia and Bosnia and Herzegovina.

Bosnia and Herzegovina, which provided a natural land bridge to Serbs in Croatia and whose population was about 30 percent Serb, should be ruled at least in significant part by the Serbs. To further their plans to keep Bosnia and Herzegovina within the newly constituted Yugoslavia and forestall Izetbegović's independent action, the Serbs dredged up the 1970 Islamic Declaration discussed in Chapter 7 ("The Rise of Nationalism in Bosnia and Herzegovina"), charging that Izetbegović, a "fundamentalist Muslim," would use it as a blueprint for a Muslim Bosnia and Herzegovina.[70]

To protect themselves from the feared Muslim hegemony, in September 1991 Bosnian Serbs had formed themselves into four Serbian autonomous regions in northern and western Bosnia and requested YPA protection. To better pursue its war against Croatia, the YPA had transferred much of its military equipment from Croatia to preexisting military bases and airfields in Bosnia and Herzegovina. Furthermore, Bosnia and Herzegovina contained a significant percentage of Yugoslavia's remaining military industries.[71] The increasingly Serbianized YPA troops[72] thus responded to the Bosnian Serb request. The YPA became concentrated in Bosnian territory in September 1991, eager for a rationale to use Bosnia as a launching pad for an attack on Croatia—to the consternation of the Bosnian population, which was not sympathetic to the nationalist Serbs.[73] At the same time, Croat army and paramilitary troops moved into western Herzegovina.[74] A Helsinki Watch report also claimed that YPA and Serbian irregular troops attacked Croatia from Bosnian territory,[75] but the increased YPA presence throughout Bosnia and Herzegovina was one sign of YPA preparations for war inside Bosnia as well. Another sign was the YPA demand that Bosnia and Herzegovina disarm and demobilize its territorial defense forces, whereupon the weapons were given to Serbian militias.[76]

In the wake of international recognition of Croatia and Slovenia and the ensuing diplomatic intervention that ended in a cease-fire and U.N. peacekeeping
between Croatia and Serbia, the war in Croatia moved to Bosnia and
Herzegovina. Two military operations—*Drina*, to connect Serb-controlled lands
in eastern Herzegovina with northeastern Bosnia and with Serbia proper, and
Most, to link Bosnian Krajina to Serbia by way of a bridge over the River Sava—
were to be implemented.[77] Bosnia and Herzegovina was faced with a terrible
dilemma.[78] The Yugoslavia of which Bosnia and Herzegovina was a constituent
republic had disappeared with the declarations of independence by Slovenia
and Croatia. The remainder, Serbia and Montenegro, styled itself as Yugoslavia,
but Bosnia and Herzegovina would have become a Serbian land under these circumstances—a situation that was contrary to history and to the wishes of a
majority of its inhabitants. Groups of Bosnian Serbs rejected the option of
Bosnian self-determination and declared autonomy from Bosnia, bolting from
the Bosnian Parliament. Although they realized that war would be likely if
Bosnia also sought independence from Yugoslavia, the remaining delegates in
Bosnia's Parliament also feared Bosnia and Herzegovina would otherwise be at
the mercy of a chauvinistic Serbia in which Muslim and Croat human rights
were not likely to be respected. In November 1991, therefore, the Bosnian government requested U.N. peacekeeping forces.

Into the domestic maelstrom in Bosnia and Herzegovina were thus inserted
the indecision and flawed decisionmaking of the international community.
International attention might have halted the conflict before too much damage
was done, but, as has been the case throughout history, the major powers—acting out of perceived self-interest—merely inflamed the volatile situation.
Various analysts have freely apportioned blame for the ensuing conflict in
Bosnia and Herzegovina.[79] The international community was absorbed in dealing with the ramifications of the sudden implosion of the Communist system, as
well as with Saddam Hussein's challenge in the Persian Gulf. It responded to the
crisis with a Security Council–mandated arms embargo on all Yugoslav parties in
September 1991. This action favored the Bosnian Serbs, who were supported by
the military and weaponry of the Serb-controlled YPA, whereas the Bosnian
Muslims had little weaponry and no legal access to any weapons.

Thus, deprived of international protection as a republic within the collapsing
Yugoslavia, the Muslim-led Bosnian government pursued EC recognition. On 15
October 1991, the Bosnian Parliament declared its sovereignty, beating the 23
December 1991 deadline for recognition of independence for any of the six
Yugoslav republics that requested it. The Badinter Commission concluded in
January 1992 that Slovenia and Macedonia met all of the human rights and
minority rights prerequisites for EC recognition but that Bosnia and
Herzegovina and Croatia would have to ensure that the human rights of Serbian
residents would be fully respected before they would meet the criteria for recog-

nition. Bosnia's Serbs had expressed in a variety of forums their disagreement with the move for Bosnian independence; nevertheless, the Badinter Commission recommended that Bosnia and Herzegovina hold a plebiscite to determine the popular will.[80] On 29 February and 1 March 1992, 62.68 percent of Bosnia and Herzegovina's population voted overwhelmingly (99.7 percent of ballots cast[81]) for independence. Many Bosnian Serbs boycotted the referendum, as urged by Radovan Karadžić and by pamphlets dropped by the Yugoslav air force,[82] preferring to belong to the Serb Republic proclaimed on 21 December 1991 and thence to be incorporated into the newly formed Yugoslavia.

In this environment of miscues and missed opportunities, Yugoslavia became an intra-European and cross-Atlantic football. The United States was reluctant to intervene, hoping to enter the post–Cold War period with an emphasis on spending less for military and security policy and investing in domestic economic and social policy to ensure domestic political benefits. Europe, however, seemed eager to belie its almost passive foreign policy role in the Gulf War in an attempt to lessen U.S. influence on European affairs.

Western diplomats had already determined that Bosnia and Herzegovina met all EC criteria for an independent state, including no forcible border changes, respect for the rights of national minorities, and a referendum to express the public will—the final tally of which favored independence. Izetbegović's government, having thus followed the West's dicta, declared Bosnia and Herzegovina independent on 3 March 1992. Following Germany's lead, the international community mistakenly thought that—as in Croatia previously—recognition of Bosnia and Herzegovina as an independent state would forestall conflict over that region, stop its disintegration, and protect its borders and territorial integrity.[83]

Other analysts have hinted at a Saudi role in the process, suggesting that Saudi Arabia exerted significant pressure on the United States to support Bosnian independence in return for Saudi considerations with regard to the Middle East peace process. The Saudis sought U.S. support because Bosnian Muslims were deemed to be moderate, much like those Muslims the United States was counting on to solve the Arab-Israeli conflict.[84] However, the United States and the European states that recognized its independence did not permit Bosnia to acquire weaponry to defend its sovereignty. Thus, whereas the Bosnian Serbs were amply supplied with weaponry and YPA technology, the Bosnian Muslims were limited to what they could beg, borrow, steal, or slip past the embargo. The West's "plague on all your houses" attitude in reality was a policy that encouraged battlefield superiority of the Bosnian Serbs.

The EC recognized the independence of Bosnia and Herzegovina on 6 April, and U.S. recognition of independence of Bosnia and Herzegovina (as well as of Croatia and Slovenia) came one day later. Serb demands for self-determination in Bosnia and Herzegovina were waved aside.[85]

According to a Helsinki Watch report, fighting broke out almost immediately.[86] Bosnia and Herzegovina, without material Western support for its independence, was being torn apart by hostile neighbors and internal opponents.[87]

The West tried mediation to ameliorate the damage its policies had created. In February 1992, the EC had invited representatives of Bosnia's Serbs, Croats, and Muslims to Lisbon to negotiate a peaceful solution to the Bosnian crisis. A vague "cantonization" agreement emerged that proposed an ethnic-based division of Bosnia and Herzegovina. This plan was soon torpedoed by a vacillating Izetbegović, backed by the Bosnian Parliament, who apparently believed the United States would ensure the Muslims a better deal than the proposed control over only 30 percent of Bosnia and Herzegovina.[88] In April 1992, as stated previously, the United States and the EC recognized Bosnia and Herzegovina. Subsequently, on 3 September 1992, the London conference on the former Yugoslavia met to carry on the Geneva peace talks.[89]

The best-known attempt to resolve the Bosnian conflict was the so-called Vance-Owen Plan,[90] made public in Geneva in January 1993. U.N. representative Cyrus Vance and EC representative Lord David Owen, cochairs of the EC-U.N. International Conference on the Former Yugoslavia, proposed the creation of a highly decentralized Bosnia and Herzegovina divided in such a way that there would be no national separation of the Muslims, Serbs, and Croats. The plan would have divided Bosnia and Herzegovina into ten units, which would still accede to the Muslim demand for a unitary state. To satisfy Serb and Croat aspirations for ethnic distance, nine of the units would contain a majority from one of the national groups. Sarajevo, the exception, would be designated an open city. The central government would be responsible only for foreign relations and national defense. In effect, as Robert Hayden described it, the Vance-Owen Plan would have made Bosnia and Herzegovina a "protectorate composed of ten mini states."[91]

The Croats quickly accepted the plan, hoping to garner even more territory for their control than they had previously been offered (17 percent during the Carrington phase of negotiations in March 1992). The Serbs rejected the plan, insisting that the lands they had conquered militarily should be part of their portion or the territory they would control and the power they would wield in Bosnia would be insufficient. The Bosnian Muslims favored a viable, secular, centrally governed Bosnian state—which the Vance-Owen plan did not create. Distressed that the plan rewarded Serb aggression and cemented the ethnonational approach to solving the Bosnian problem sought by Serb and Croat nationalists from the beginning, the Bosnian Muslims only reluctantly agreed. However, the Bosnian Serb "parliament" adamantly rejected the plan after Karadžić had signed it, despite pressure to accept by Milošević and the international community. The proposal was then abandoned after much press speculation but little interest by the warring parties in making it work.

U.S. and European diplomats were frustrated in their attempts to resolve the military conflict. Their next proposal, on 4 June 1993, was to create "safe havens" in six major Bosnian cities. The intention was for Sarajevo, Goražde, Tuzla, Srebrenica, Žepa, and Bihać to be placed under U.N. protection.

Vance resigned as U.N. representative and was replaced by Norway's former foreign minister Torvald Stoltenberg. An Owen-Stoltenberg proposal called for a loosely confederated union of nationally determined states, with most decision-making power going to the constituent ethnic republics.[92] The Serbs would control over 50 percent of the territory, the Muslims 30 percent, and the Croats the remainder. The central government would possess almost no autonomous power, not even the ability to control the military, with decisionmaking arrogated to the provinces and independent authorities with trinational representation.

Some leaders in Croatia proper may have dreaded independence for Bosnia and Herzegovina, believing a status quo situation might enable Croatia otherwise to exert influence on the republic, or parts of it, to unite with Croatia if the Bosnian situation remained static for some time. Another, more hard-line group, the nationalist Herzegovinian war lobby, continued to pressure Tudjman to share Bosnia with Serbia. Thus, some of the areas that contained large Croat populations also threatened to secede from Bosnia and Herzegovina if it declared independence. Other Croat leaders, such as Tudjman, welcomed the dissolution of Bosnia and Herzegovina, since it gave Croatia a chance to annex directly a portion of the land. Still other Croat leaders favored cantonization, which would have threatened the unity of Croatia and also of Serbia if cohesive minorities within those units demanded their own cantons. Thus, the concept of cantonization attracted few adherents, although at one point the Serbs and Croats seemed willing to accede to this plan.

The YPA feared that losing Bosnia and Herzegovina to independence would further compromise its mandate to preserve Yugoslavia intact. Thus, the loss of Bosnia was a threat to the military's power, prestige, and prerogatives but also to its stores. For example, Bihać contained a military base and underground airfields, and arms production facilities were spread throughout Bosnia.[93] Thus, the YPA reluctantly left Bosnia and Herzegovina in spring 1992, taking with it what was transportable and destroying what it could not turn over to Bosnian Serbs and did not want the Bosnian government to control.

The Muslims, for their part, feared Serbia and Croatia might agree to partition Bosnia and Herzegovina between them, leaving the Bosnian Muslims either with a nonviable small state or at the mercy of a greater Serbia. They had favored and actively worked for Yugoslav confederation with sovereign republics to parry any Serb-Croat attempts to divide a secularly oriented Bosnia and Herzegovina. The outcome of these political maneuverings was the battle for Bosnia and Herzegovina, which still rages.

Bosnian Muslims as a Bulwark
Between Serbs and Croats

The term *ethnic cleansing* stands for the policy of ridding an area of an undesirable national group to create a homogeneous region.[94] This concept is not historically novel. However, the Serbian version entails not only homogenizing a region but also ensuring that the condition is perpetuated by razing the interdenominational sociocultural network and changing Bosnia and Herzegovina's past. The indigenous Serb population was drawn into the killing so the Croat and Muslim populations would become so terrorized that they would never return.[95] Serbia's initial impetus for its policy of ethnic cleansing of Bosnian Muslims apparently arose from the same idea that had driven the Serbs to the battlefield upon the partition of Yugoslavia: the Serb fear that the newly formed states of Bosnia and Herzegovina and Croatia would create of their Serb populations simply national minorities and eventually destroy the Serb population as a discrete and unique nation in those areas. Thus, Karadžić and others stressed repeatedly that Serb military activity was the only defense against the Muslims and likened themselves to ancient Serbs battling the Turks when they were trying to rule Europe.

In an effort to retain their power in the transition away from communism, Serb elites stressed that to preserve their nation, Serb territory—defined as areas in which Serbs dwelled—should be inhabited and ruled largely by Serbs. In response, Serb populations living in both Croatia and Bosnia and Herzegovina declared autonomy for their regions and proceeded to eliminate non-Serb inhabitants, forming nationalist paramilitary units supported by the YPA. This Serb repugnance for anything but Serb rule was demonstrated forcibly in March 1992 when Bosnian Serbs went to the barricades to protest the outcome of the EC-encouraged referendum that expressed the wish of most Bosnian residents to form an independent state.

The Bosnian Serb fears of dilution of their nation by coexistence in close proximity with other ethnic groups[96] was exacerbated by a yearning for the halcyon days of the Kingdom of the Serbs, Croats, and Slovenes, when the kingdom was essentially organized as a greater Serbia. Furthermore, memories of the atrocities against Serbs during World War II and the large Serbian contribution to Yugoslavia's victories during World Wars I and II were consciously maintained in Serbian communities. Serb opposition member Ljubiša Rajić emphasized the potency of these feelings when he stated that "the Serbs in Croatia and Bosnia feared a recurrence of the massacres of the second world war, and the Muslims feared the same. The Croatian nationalists did not hide that they sought to finish what they had begun during the war."[97] And indeed the conception of Starčević's greater Croatia had again captivated many Croats during the 1980s after Tito's death. Finally, the Serbs complained bitterly that their natural dominant role in Yugoslavia had been watered down by Tito's creation of the autonomous provinces of Kosovo and Vojvodina, which had been granted broad decision-making powers within Tito's version of a federation. Serb leaders saw their moves in the post-Tito era as merely attempts to redress the balance and to take their rightful place of influence in a reconstituted Yugoslavia.

Serbian nationalists can perhaps be forgiven for expecting that exploiting Bosnia and Herzegovina would be so doable. Bosnia and Herzegovina had been carved up by the royal dictatorship in interwar Yugoslavia. In 1929 the Yugoslav kingdom was divided into *banovinas,* but Bosnia and Herzegovina was able to retain its borders; in 1939, however, parts of Bosnia and Herzegovina were given to Croatia under the *Sporazum,* as discussed previously. During World War II, the Nazis awarded all of Bosnia and Herzegovina to the independent state of Croatia.

Even before the twentieth century, Bosnia and Herzegovina spent very little of its history as an independent entity, although it was not sundered as an administrative unit until the twentieth-century Yugoslav Kingdom. The Bosnian Muslims were also not particularly forceful historically in expressing a sense of national self-determination. After a short existence, the independent medieval kingdom of Bosnia was replaced by Ottoman tutelage. Austrian rule at the turn of the twentieth century was not particularly onerous for Bosnia and Herzegovina; neither was Serbian domination in the interwar period, perhaps because the Bosnian Muslims were masters of system manipulation when they were involved in a multinational entity. When Bosnia and Herzegovina became an independent entity, however, Bosnians proved less successful in drawing together successful coalition partners, international defenders, and legitimators of their autonomous status. Apparently, until recently the international community had become more comfortable with Bosnia and Herzegovina serving as the core of a multinational system rather than organizing its own political system.

Furthermore, Bosnia and Herzegovina was the scene of terrible carnage during World War II. Serbs, Croats, and Muslims committed horrible atrocities against each other on this land, which until the recent revival of virulent ethnonationalism may have been forgotten or forgiven. The show trials sponsored by Tito to punish flagrant murderers and other attempts throughout the years to exorcise this demon of ethnic hatred, however, merely ended up eventually inflaming the passions of the survivors and reinforced their martyrology. To this day one can hear—especially in the U.S. émigré community among those who fled Yugoslavia in the wake of Tito's victory—groups of Serbs or Croats declaiming that their particular suffering during World War II was far worse than the suffering of any other group and that the violence their group was accused of has been blown out of proportion.

Nevertheless, even during the contemporary slaughter visited upon Bosnia and Herzegovina by rampaging Serbs and Croats, as well as by Muslims, many Bosnian Muslims have persisted in clinging to the idea of a multinational, secular European country. This anguished statement by a Bosnian Muslim when faced with the evidence of Bosnia's betrayal by its own—Bosnian Serb—inhabitants reflects both that hope and the beginning of its deflation:

> Born 15 years after the war ended, I belong to the second generation of post-war Bosnian Muslims, for whom our Muslim identity was a quaint aspect of family heritage, something to marvel at rather than immerse oneself in. Islam as a religion represented our past rather than our future. I identified myself as a Muslim by nationality, which meant I had ties neither to Serbia nor Croatia, but saw my social and cultural identity as a part of an ethnically-mixed Bosnian tapestry, from which I drew all my cultural and emotional experiences, and in which I belonged together with all other non-Muslim Bosnians. . . . [However] the truth is that the worst and most abhorrent acts of violence are being committed by yesterday's friends and neighbours.[98]

It appears that Muslim-free areas are only one of the targets of Bosnian Serbs. What British journalist Michael Nicholson termed "elitocide"—the destruction of the educated Muslim strata—also seems to be an objective pursued by the Bosnian Serb forces.[99] If elitocide were successful, the Bosnian Muslim community would thus be bereft of leadership when the fighting finally ended.

Economic and Foreign Policy Implications of the Recognition of the Bosnian Muslims

Ethnic hatred is not the sole issue in the Bosnian conflict, although it is the most visible. Two other issues have also fueled the struggle. Economic issues have intermingled with political, geographic, demographic, and other issues, as they did throughout the more than forty-five years of post–World War II Yugoslavia. Foreign policy implications have also driven the conflict.

Bosnia and Herzegovina emerged from World War II an economically devastated land. Many battles were fought on the territory as the Partisans sought to rid their land of both fascist invaders and Serbian monarchists. However, like other regions in Yugoslavia, Bosnia and Herzegovina's economy experienced rapid growth in the post–World War II era. This relative economic prosperity helped to assuage, at least temporarily, the national antagonisms World War II had ignited. Bosnia and Herzegovina—the Yugoslav melting pot—advanced economically because it contained valuable natural resources, such as lead, zinc, manganese, and bauxite. Before the fighting broke out in 1990, Bosnia and Herzegovina provided approximately 85 percent of Yugoslavia's iron ore and 40 percent of its coal and lignite,[100] as well as 40 percent of its industrial production.[101] Furthermore, up to 55 percent of Yugoslavia's defense industries were located in Bosnia and Herzegovina, far from Yugoslavia's vulnerable borders with Warsaw Pact members.[102]

But in Bosnia and Herzegovina, as well as in the rest of the former Yugoslavia, the severe economic downturn in the post-Tito era engendered a fear for and of the future and a concomitant fear and distrust of other Yugoslavs. The failure of Titoism and Tito's social self-management as prescriptions for security—derived by creating conditions for brotherhood and unity—left Yugoslavs searching for some other notion. Post-Tito political leaders such as Milošević were able to harness this economic discontent and other types of disquiet and channel it into ethnonationalism.

The problem of the division of the former Yugoslavia's assets among the successor states is a thorny one. The newly independent states favored a negotiated settlement with all receiving a share. Serbia and Montenegro, however, argued that seceding republics left behind their claims to federal property and assets, which would continue to be administered and exploited by Yugoslavia (made up, of course, of Serbia and Montenegro). No settlement of this issue had been reached before Bosnia and Herzegovina became embroiled in war.[103]

The foreign policy implications of the conflict in Bosnia and Herzegovina are large for the successor states of the former Yugoslavia, as well as for global stability. In light of the Serb offensive against the Bosnian Muslims, the response of the Muslim world has at best been disappointing to the Bosnian Muslims, although as time went on there has been more acknowledgment that Iran and other sources have been providing arms to the Bosnian army.[104] The number of "Muslim volunteers" fighting in Bosnia and Herzegovina remains low, perhaps less than one thousand.[105] Nevertheless, the leadership of Bosnia and Herzegovina has continued to nurture relations with the Islamic world,[106] understanding perhaps that its reticence has stemmed at least in part from a desire to avoid a widespread characterization of the Bosnian-Serb conflict as a showdown between Christianity and radical Islam. Thus, aside from some saber rattling in Muslim-dominated parliaments throughout the world (reflecting the same hollow policies as those followed by the United Nations, NATO, and similar organizations), Islamic states have done relatively little to influence the conflict.[107]

Turkey is in a particularly perilous position. It has acknowledged its geostrategic interest in Bosnia by maintaining close contact and sponsoring some assistance there.[108] However, its religious proclivities must be balanced with its demeanor as a responsible, Europe-oriented country if it wants to be seriously considered for membership in the European Union. Nevertheless, the visit of the prime ministers of Pakistan and Turkey to Sarajevo on 2 February 1994[109] may have sent a message to Europe that the Islamic world considers Europe's nonpolicy on Bosnia to be encouraging (since it is not discouraging) the Serbs and Croats to rid Europe of one of its major Muslim enclaves.[110]

The Muslim world is not alone in its inability to influence the Yugoslav conflict. Germany did its damage by encouraging the Slovenes and Croats to declare independence from Yugoslavia and then recognizing them previous to the settlement of constitutional and human rights issues. But Germany, as with the rest of Europe, was preoccupied with Maastricht and the rigors of its own reunification. Yugoslavia, although a European problem, was not to be permitted to distract European diplomats from the truly important task of integration and was relegated to a secondary position, since its status was deemed easily soluble by a united Europe determined to preempt U.S. involvement in a European problem. Thereafter, Germany withdrew from an active role in policy formation over Yugoslavia to deal with its domestic problems, leaving multilateral European mechanisms to deal with the issue. But the EC, the Conference on Security and Cooperation in Europe (CSCE), the Western European Union (WEU), and similar organizations proved incapable of providing definitive solutions for Yugoslavia's future configuration, thereby abandoning the problem to settlement by combat rather than diplomacy. The role of European diplomatic institutions in providing more than merely diplomatic cover for their state constituents remains to be delineated, as the handling of the Yugoslav breakup amply demonstrated.

With the collapse of the much touted institutions set up by Tito to propel a cohesive Yugoslavia into the post-Tito era, the only chance the South Slavs had of maintaining any unity—short of the notoriously lacking goodwill among the nations—was from a vigilant and willing Western alliance. Through a variety of misjudgments, badly formed policies, and unfortunate goals, the Western alliance failed Yugoslavia even as policymaking was grabbed out of the hands of reasonable, Yugoslav-oriented elites by those who used chauvinistic appeals to maintain themselves in power.

Premature recognition of the independence of Yugoslavia's successor states exacerbated already tense relations between Serbia and Croatia. If that conflict could not be settled peacefully, then it was all but certain that Bosnia and Herzegovina—whose urban areas were the epitome of a cosmopolitan, non-chauvinistic society—would be drawn into a gruesome ethnonationalistic bloodletting. Serb leaders whipped up among their people a fear of the resurgence of Ottoman-type or radical Islamic domination if the Bosnian Muslims, who formed a growing plurality of Bosnia's population, succeeded in gaining any kind of political leadership.[111]

Yet the Serb and Croat leaders' fears about Bosnian Muslim nationalism have been overblown. For example, since the time of his imprisonment, Izetbegović has expressed a more pragmatic and even conciliatory point of view than appeared in the Islamic Declaration. Izetbegović's contemporary writings and pronouncements have expressed the realization that the Bosnian Muslims and their Muslim religion had "to be compatible with [the views] of modern Western society."[112] In fact, since Bosnia's declaration of independence, Izetbegović has emphasized recognition of the equal rights of citizens rather than of nationalities and has retained the loyalty of those Bosnian Serbs and Croats who rejected the radicalism of Croat and Serb chauvinism. Following in the footsteps of preceding leaders of the Bosnian Muslim community, Izetbegović cleaved to a policy of coalition building and multinational decisionmaking, which had stood

Bosnian Muslims in good stead from the experience in Austria-Hungary throughout most of the twentieth century. Although some consider Izetbegović to be an Islamic religious leader, his writings and pronouncements have portrayed him as a religious man who aims to create and lead a secular state that would protect the interests of the Bosnian Muslim community.[113]

Izetbegović's constituents, too, have expressed bewilderment at the turn of events in Bosnia. One young soldier communicated his orientation in this way:

> I never thought of myself as a Muslim. I don't know how to pray, I never went to mosque, I'm European, like you. I do not want the Arab world to help us, I want Europe to help us. But now, I do have to think of myself as a Muslim, not in a religious way, but as a member of a people. Now we are faced with obliteration, I have to understand what it is about me and my people they wish to obliterate.[114]

Conclusion

Thus, the Bosnian Muslims have been caught up in a game that has been larger and tougher than their capacity to cope. Throughout their history up to the present, they were safest when they were part of a multinational coalition, with their position protected by a strong central government. Their vulnerability increased when they were recognized as a nation within Yugoslavia, because their needs had to be met and recognition meant that the Serbs and the Croats could no longer use them as subordinates. Instead, until war struck the area, the Bosnian Muslims had become equal partners in Bosnia and Herzegovina and as such had to be dealt with rather than manipulated. Izetbegović expressed this altered situation through a parable of two brothers who coexisted harmoniously until the younger brother tired of being dominated by the elder and demanded his rights. Thus, the Muslims "are demanding only our rights, and people are afraid as though we want to take something away from someone."[115]

Finally, because of the international turmoil caused by the collapse of the Soviet Union, the West was caught flat-footed, unable or unwilling to expend the necessary effort to protect the Bosnian Muslims. The Bosnian Muslims were caught without shelter in the crossfire between Croatia's desire to be free of Serbian hegemony and Serbia's aspirations to recreate its dominant role in Yugoslavia.

NOTES

1. Cited in Mushtak Parker, *Muslims in Yugoslavia: The Quest for Justice* (Toronto: Croatian Islamic Centre, 1986), p. 1.

2. Cited in S. Nelson Drew, "NATO from Berlin to Bosnia: Trans-Atlantic Security in Transition," McNair Paper 35 (Washington, D.C.: National Defense University, 1995), p. 36.

3. *Balkan WarReport* 14 (September 1992), p. 6.

4. One of the grossest examples of ethnonationalistic insensitivity was Tudjman's attempted rehabilitation of the NDH and the Ustaše within Croatia with the claim that their crimes were no worse than those of the Četniks during World War II. Milan Nikolić, "What Is Showing White in the Sava Near Jasenovac?" *Duga* (30 September–14 October 1989), pp. 69–71, in *FBIS* (25 January 1990), pp. 14–17.

5. In a private conversation, Ellen Comisso pointed out that from the Serb and Croat point of view, mutual fears helped to create a self-fulfilling prophecy—the fear of Tudjman helped to elect Milošević and vice versa. See also *Yugofax* (9 December 1991), p. 3. Zoran Pajić characterized the nationalist choices of the Yugoslav elections in this way: "With the fall of Communism, the old ideologies were destroyed overnight, but new values have not yet been created. Yugoslav society has never known a real democratic experience: so a tremendous gap was created between the fall of the previous regime or previous ideals and the civic society. . . . In nature, such a gap has to be filled and it is being filled by nationalism. People simply went full flight into another type of collective identity, which (in the case of former Yugoslavia) means nationalism. That explains why the majority of voters in Bosnia-Herzegovina, in the first so-called multiparty elections. . . . voted by a large majority for a nationalistic party." "Violation of Fundamental Rights in the Former Yugoslavia: I. The Conflict in Bosnia-Herzegovina," David Davies Memorial Institute of International Studies, Occasional Paper no. 2 (February 1993), p. 4.

6. As early as June 1990, in a speech to Serbia's National Assembly, Milošević had threatened that Slovene and Croat attempts to change the nature of the federation could result in alterations of republic borders. *Report on Eastern Europe*, Weekly Record of Events 1 (6 July 1990), p. 59. Serbia's territorial claims in that case would have included large portions of Bosnia and Herzegovina and Croatia, as well as all of Macedonia, Montenegro, Vojvodina, and Kosovo, according to Vuk Drašković. *Telex* (16 November 1989), and *Start* (16 September 1989), cited in Milan Andrejevich, "Nationalist Movements in Yugoslavia," *Report on Eastern Europe* 1 (23 February 1990), p. 29.

7. For opposing conceptualizations of the bases of Serbian nationalism, see Alex N. Dragnich, *Serbs and Croats* (New York: Harcourt Brace Jovanovich, 1994), which focuses on the positive elements of Serbia's historical role in the Balkans and its victimization by the international community as the basis for its reenergized nationalism, as opposed to the alleged fascist basis of contemporary Serb nationalism propounded by Rabia Ali and Lawrence Lifschultz, "In Plain View," in Rabia Ali and Lawrence Lifschultz, eds., *Why Bosnia? Writings on the Balkan War* (Stony Creek, Conn.: Pamphleteer's Press, 1993), pp. xliv–xlv.

8. See, for example, excerpts from a transcript of the January 1991 meeting of the SFRY presidency in "Kupovanje vremena u projelzanom periodu," *Danas* (15 January 1991), pp. 9–14.

9. *Yugofax* (14 September 1991), p. 4.

10. *Yugofax* (31 October 1991), p. 6.

11. Frits W. Hondius, *The Yugoslav Community of Nations* (The Hague: Mouton, 1968), p. 302.

12. Robert M. Hayden pointed out that by this time the South Slavs had in certain respects created a new political language. Thus, when the Slovenes and Croats spoke of "confederation" as their political aspiration, they in effect meant total independence from any central authority. "The Partition of Bosnia and Herzegovina, 1990–1993," *RFE/RL Research Report* 2 (28 May 1993), pp. 15–17.

13. For a description of the Slovene-Croat proposal, see Milan Andrejevich, "Crisis in Croatia and Slovenia: Proposal for a Confederal Yugoslavia," *Report on Eastern Europe* 1 (2 November 1990), pp. 30–31.

14. For an abridged text of the "Platform on the Future Yugoslav Community," proposed by Izetbegović and Macedonian President Kiro Gligorov, see "Na pet ili deset godina," *Borba* (Zagreb), 4 June 1991, p. 10.

15. The 21 September 1991 issue of *Yugofax* was devoted to the topic "Information in Conflict." See also Mark Thompson's *Forging War: The Media in Serbia, Croatia and Bosnia-Hercegovina* (Great Britain: Article 19, International Centre Against Censorship, 1994), in which the main theme is that the media in the former Yugoslavia was captured by nationalists of all sides and used as an instrument to mobilize people to make war on each other.

16. *Yugofax* (6 September 1991), p. 3.

17. *Ex-Yugofax* (7 May 1992), p. 4.

18. Slaven Letica described Marković's vision of Yugoslavia as a formula: Titoism – dictatorship + pluralism + privatization + enterprises + markets. "Jeza," *Danas* (12 April 1990), p. 15.

19. Lenard J. Cohen, *Broken Bonds: The Disintegration of Yugoslavia* (Boulder: Westview Press, 1993), p. 103.

20. Ibid., p. 160.

21. *Yugofax* (14 September 1991), p. 3.

22. For more on the three conferences attended by Yugoslavia's republic presidents to structure the future Yugoslavia, see Robert J. Donia and John V.A. Fine Jr., *Bosnia and Hercegovina: A Tradition Betrayed* (New York: Columbia University Press, 1994), pp. 212–214.

23. See, for example, Slavenka Drakulić's account of a conversation with a young Croat soldier in *The Balkan Express: Fragments from the Other Side of War* (New York: Norton, 1993), p. 96.

24. For the opinion of the Arbitration Committee of the Conference on Yugoslavia, presided over by Lord Carrington, regarding the legality of secession and whether Yugoslavia legally existed, see *Yugoslav Survey* 32, no. 4 (1991), pp. 17–19. The SFRY presidency's views on this opinion follow in the same issue. The Serbian view of the Yugoslav crisis is further explicated in "Memorandum of the Government of Yugoslavia on the Yugoslav Crisis," *Yugoslav Survey* 33, no. 1 (1992), pp. 97–106.

25. *Večernji List* (27 August 1990), cited by Milan Andrejevich, "Croatia Between Stability and Civil War," *Report on Eastern Europe* 1 (28 September 1990), p. 39. Apparently, the YPA forces assigned to recover Slovenia for the Yugoslav federation were composed of "a conscript army with fragile morale and poor motivation, and a mixed ethnic structure, along with treacherous officers of different peoples and nationalities." Ljubica Jelusić, "Why and When Do Generals Not Admit Defeat?" *Neodvisni Dnevnik* (13 July 1991), p. 14, cited in JPRS-EER-91-119 (8 August 1991), p. 25. See Milan Andrejevich, "Yugoslavia's Lingering Crisis," *Report on Eastern Europe* 1 (5 January 1990), p. 35, for a description of the YPA's position regarding Yugoslavia's deterioration. The YPA in 1990 was apparently proreform, although it opposed a multiparty system and republic self-determination or secession. However, at that point the YPA did not consider force to be an option to meet Slovenia's September 1989 proclamations of self-determination. According to Andrejevich, relations between the YPA and Slovenia were publicly frayed as a result of YPA charges that the

Slovenian opposition party DEMOS presidential candidate Joze Pucnik had insulted the YPA during his electoral bid. "Military Attempts to File Charges Against Slovenian Presidential Candidate," *Report on Eastern Europe* 1 (27 April 1990), pp. 38–41. See also Gojko Marinković, "Čija je armija," *Danas* (6 February 1990), pp. 26–27, and Milan Andrejevich, "The Military's Role in the Current Constitutional Crisis," *Report on Eastern Europe* 1 (9 November 1990), pp. 23–27, for more on the attitudes of the military elite toward Yugoslav public policy.

26. Mihailo Crnobrnja chronicled the Slovenian armed struggle with the YPA in *The Yugoslav Drama* (Montreal: McGill-Queen's University Press, 1994), pp. 161–164. He also charged that the YPA was supposed to lose the war against Slovenia so Serbian nationalism would gain through the discrediting of the Marković (the ostensible commander of the YPA) regime and the Yugoslav-oriented officer corps could then be replaced by Serb nationalists. Crnobrnja, *The Yugoslav Drama*, p. 231.

27. Donia and Fine charted the slow but inexorable transition of the YPA from neutral and moderate preserver of Yugoslav integrity to instrument of greater Serbian chauvinism in *Bosnia and Hercegovina*, pp. 221–223.

28. Misha Glenny, *The Fall of Yugoslavia: The Third Balkan War* (New York: Penguin Books, 1992), pp. 13, 77, 107.

29. *Yugofax* (9 December 1991), p. 3.

30. The *šahovnica* as a Croat symbol is many centuries old, but for many Serbs it is repugnant because it symbolized their persecution under the World War II Ustaše regime in the NDH.

31. On 25 July 1990, thousands of Croatian Serbs attended a rally and demanded autonomy within and secession from Croatia if Croatia left the Yugoslav federation. *Report on Eastern Europe* 1 (3 August 1990), p. 60.

32. The text of Slovenia's declaration of independence *(Deklaracija ob neodvisnosti)* appeared in *Delo* (26 June 1991), p. 1.

33. For a description of the issues addressed and the procedures followed by the Carrington-led Hague Conference, see Crnobrnja, *The Yugoslav Drama*, pp. 194–199.

34. *New York Times,* 22 June 1991, p. 1A.

35. Milan Andrejevich, "Retreating from the Brink of Collapse," *Report on Eastern Europe* 2 (12 April 1991), p. 28; Milan Andrejevich, "Republican Leaders Reach Compromise Accord on Country's Future," *Report on Eastern Europe* 2 (28 June 1991), p. 35.

36. Bogdan Ivanišević and Dragan Čičić, "Totalna politika," *NIN* (14 June 1991), p. 21. A Franciscan from Sarajevo, Fra Marko Oršolić, expressed this sentiment, saying, "Bosnia cannot be maintained without Yugoslavia. Who breaks up Yugoslavia, also breaks up Bosnia." Ivanišević and Čičić, "Totalna politika," p. 21.

37. There were reports in May and June 1991 of Serb and Croat militia incursions into Bosnia and Herzegovina. Andrejevich, "Republican Leaders Reach Compromise Accord on Country's Future," p. 35.

38. Alex N. Dragnich, "Case Study: Bosnia-Herzegovina," paper presented at the American Bar Association Conference on Anarchy in the Third World, 3–4 June 1993, p. 10.

39. Crnobrnja, *The Yugoslav Drama*, p. 139. German Foreign Minister Hans-Dietrich Genscher defended his role in the recognition of Slovenia and Croatia in an interview published in *Dnevnik* (12 June 1992), p. 12, cited in JPRS-EER-92-090 (14 July 1992), pp. 27–28.

Others who were more suspicious of his motives claimed Genscher encouraged the Slovenes and Croats to make rapid declarations of independence to show German leadership in the fashioning of a common European foreign policy, which would recognize the desires of the South Slav peoples for independence. John Newhouse also pointed out that an element of "clientitis" was growing in which the Germans felt protective of the Croats and the French were reluctant to criticize their traditional allies, the Serbs, even when they were clearly aggressors. "The Diplomatic Round: Dodging the Problem," *New Yorker* 51 (24 August 1992), p. 61. Dragnich suggested that Germany's actions reflected its historical policy of *Drang nach Osten* (expansion to the East). *Serbs and Croats*, p. xvii. Milos Vasic, writing for *Yugofax* (3 February 1992), suggested an additional motive for German interest in Yugoslavia: the selling to Yugoslavia of arms from the former East Germany that would have been too expensive for the united Germany to maintain.

40. *New York Times*, 22 June 1991, p. A1.

41. *Tanjug* 1 (June 1991), in *FBIS Daily Report* (Eastern Europe), 3 June 1991, p. 43.

42. Newhouse, "The Diplomatic Round," p. 61.

43. See Francine Friedman, "To Fight or Not to Fight: The Decision to Settle the Croat-Serb Conflict," paper presented at the Annual Meeting of the International Studies Association, Acapulco, Mexico, March 1993, for more on the dynamics of the recognition of Croatia and an analysis of the U.S. dilemma. See also Steven L. Burg, "Why Yugoslavia Fell Apart," *Current History* 92 (November 1993), p. 362.

44. See John B. Allcock, "Yugoslavia: Bosnia and Hercegovina," in Bogdan Szajkowski, ed., *New Political Parties of Eastern Europe and the Soviet Union* (Harlow: Longman, 1991), pp. 311–319, for the results of the election and a directory of Bosnian parties. For the platforms of the leading Bosnian parties, see Milan Andrejevich, "Bosnia-Herzegovina: Yugoslavia's Linchpin," *Report on East Europe* 1 (1990), pp. 22–24.

45. Thompson, *Forging War*, p. 203.

46. Patrick Moore, "The Islamic Community's New Sense of Identity," *Report on Eastern Europe* 2 (1 November 1991), p. 20.

47. For a description of the SDA in its formative period and the personalities who initially formed it, see Senad Avdić, "Pehlivan na tankom kanafu," *Danas* (26 February 1991), pp. 14–15.

48. Tuzla was one of only two cities to elect nonnation-based parties to power. *Washington Post*, 16 November 1994.

49. Ali and Lifschultz, "In Plain View," p. xxxiii. The lack of a delegation speaking for Bosnia and Herzegovina's nonnationalistic voters, claimed Ali and Lifschultz, rendered the later peace talks, which eventually sought ethnic division of Bosnia and Herzegovina, unrepresentative of the will of many of its inhabitants.

50. Z. Jahović, "Neither Serbian nor Croatian, but Bosnian!" *Oslobodjenje* (Sarajevo), 27 March 1991, p. 6, cited in JPRS-EER-91-068 (20 May 1991), p. 26.

51. For the composition of the Bosnian State Presidency as of mid-1993, see Milan Andrejevich, "The Presidency of Bosnia and Herzegovina: A Profile," *RFE/RL Research Report* 2 (13 August 1993), p. 21.

52. Thompson, *Forging War*, p. 202.

53. Hayden, "The Partition of Bosnia and Herzegovina," p. 4. National particularism was also evident in the politically motivated members' responses (according to national identification) to the Vance-Owen Plan. See, for example, evidence of a split in the Muslim-

Croat delegation that was conferring with U.S. Vice President Al Gore in the *New York Times,* 28 February 1993, p. A8.

54. Rajko Zivković, "What Awaits Us," *Oslobodjenje* (Sarajevo), 23 May 1991, p. 1, reported in JPRS-EER-078 (10 June 1991), p. 28. See also Ivanišević and Čičić, "Totalna politika," pp. 18–21; Djoko Kesić, "Meni zaručak," *Borba* (Zagreb), 1 June 1991, p. 2; and Mladen Mirosavljević, "I Was Not in Zagreb," *Vjesnik u Srijedu* suppl. (29 May 1991), p. 3, cited in JPRS-EER-91-078, p. 30.

55. Dragica Pusonjić described the escalation of tensions in "Has It Already Burned Out?" *Borba* (Zagreb), 29 May 1991, p. 9, cited in JPRS-EER-91-078, p. 29. See also Thompson, *Forging War,* pp. 203–204, for accusations of early SDS attempts to undermine the integrity of an undivided Bosnia and Herzegovina. Momcilo Mandić, Bosnia's assistant minister of internal affairs, estimated on the basis of gun permits granted that more than 270,000 Bosnian citizens possessed approximately 323,000 firearms as early as 1991. Cited in Mladen Mirosavljević, "In Bosnia, Everyone Is Arming Everyone Else," *Vjesnik u Srijedu* (12 June 1991), p. 3, cited in JPRS-EER-91-090 (24 June 1991), p. 65. Muslim-Serb tensions were highlighted in a rally of 150,000 to 200,000 Muslims in Foča to honor World War II martyrs, many of whom were Muslims killed by Četniks. *Report on Eastern Europe* 1 (7 September 1990), p. 47.

56. Thompson, *Forging War,* p. 230.

57. According to Zulfikarpašić, Muslims and Serbs lived in 102 mixed *opštinas* in Bosnia and Herzegovina in contrast to three mixed Croat-Serb *opštinas* (Derventa, Kupres, and Modriča). Cited in Luka Miceta, "Ja vjerujem Miloševiću," *NIN* (9 August 1991), p. 21.

58. See *ex-Yugofax* (7 May 1992), p. 6, in which correspondent Lee Bryant described his firsthand experiences at the demonstrations.

59. *Ex-Yugofax* interview with Zlatko Hurtić, secretary-general of the U.N. Association of Bosnia and Herzegovina and a member of the Liberal Party (7 May 1992), p. 6.

60. The *New York Times,* 7 April 1992, p. A3, and much of the media claimed the snipers were Serbs. Serbs, however, denied it and claimed the Serb snipers atop the Holiday Inn were not involved in the incident. See, for example, Zoran Petrović-Piroćanac, Vesna Hadživković, Boro Mišeljić, and Tomislav Kresović, *The Media Happened to Be There* (Milići: Boksit, 1994), pp. 6–7.

61. For Croat and Serb statements on their respective views of internal border changes with regard to Bosnia and Herzegovina, see Goran Moravček, "The Opening of the Croatian Question," *Delo* (9 March 1991), p. 20, cited in *JPRS Report—East Europe*, no. 44 (5 April 1991), pp. 16–17, and interviews with Slobodan Milošević and SFRY Constitutional Commission member Budimir Kosutić in *Ilustrovana Politika* (12 February 1991), pp. 10–13. For the difficulties of pursuing a greater Serbia or a greater Croatia to include Bosnia and Herzegovina, see Radovan Pavić, "Fantastika postaje stvarnost," *Danas* (11 June 1991), pp. 10–11.

62. *Yugofax* reported as early as 9 December 1991 (p. 12) that Milošević was inciting Bosnian Serbs to express discontent with their lot within Bosnia and Herzegovina.

63. *Borba* (Zagreb), 27 June 1991, p. 7, cited in JPRS-EER-91-105 (17 July 1991), pp. 53–54.

64. Further evidence of the continuity of thinking between Tudjman and Milošević appeared at the end of 1994 when both took steps within days of each other to limit critical media coverage by harassing *Vjesnik* and *Borba,* respectively. *New York Times,* 29 December 1994, p. A5.

65. See reports of secret meetings in which this topic was allegedly treated. For example, Tudjman and Milošević met secretly on 25 March 1991 as reported in *Report on Eastern Europe*, Weekly Record of Events 2 (5 April 1991), p. 31. See also Andrejević, "Republican Leaders Reach Compromise Accord on Country's Future," p. 36; Muhammed Tunjo Filipović, "Račun bez krčmara," *Vjesnik* (10 June 1991), p. 6; *War Crimes in Bosnia-Hercegovina: A Helsinki Watch Report*, Vol. 1, (New York: Human Rights Watch, 1992), pp. 42–43; Judy Dempsey, "Bosnian Carve-Up in the Making," *Financial Times* (8 July 1992); Ali and Lifschultz, "In Plain View," p. xxvi. Blaine Harden reported on a Serb-Croat meeting to divide Bosnia and Herzegovina on 6 May in Graz, Austria, in "Serbs, Croats, Agree to Carve-Up Bosnia," *Washington Post*, 8 May 1992, p. A17.

66. Izetbegović reaffirmed this in a June 1990 interview in *Borba*, in which he said, "My party [SDA] is for a solution that would create a sense of equality, a sense that this is a common state in which no one will be outvoted . . . a solution for Bosnia and Herzegovina, nevertheless, needs to be sought in the old formula, which runs that Bosnia is for the Muslims, the Serbs, the Croats, and all the others who live in it." "Kompromisi u dva poluvremena," *Borba* (Zagreb), 9–10 June 1990, p. 5.

67. In this formulation, Izetbegović was joined in 1991 by Bosnian Parliament opposition leader Muhammed Tunjo Filipović. Tomić, "Na dva brvna niz reku," p. 25. Fuad Muhić, Republic Party chair, however, squelched tendencies expressed by some Bosnian Muslims (such as Adil Zulfikarpašić) to create a Bosnian, in contrast to a Bosnian Muslim, nation. See his interview in *NIN*, "Muhićev pogled u budućnost" (28 September 1990), p. 34. For the arguments for and against regionalization and cantonization, see Paul Shoup, "The Bosnian Crisis of 1992," in Sabrina Ramet, ed., *Beyond Yugoslavia* (Boulder: Westview Press, 1995), pp. 177–178.

68. Cited in Mustafa Mujagić, "Mi smo muslimani," *Danas* (6 March 1990), p. 13.

69. Cited in Patrick Moore, "The Islamic Community's New Sense of Identity," *Report on Eastern Europe* 2 (1 November 1991), p. 21.

70. "Nova priča o staroj dilemi," *Borba* (Zagreb), 27 May 1991, p. 8. For the obverse argument, see Mustafa Mujagić, "Da, ja sam fundamentalist," *Danas* (9 January 1990), pp. 14–16, who argued that just because the Bosnian Muslims had finally been recognized as a Yugoslav nation, they did not stop being Bosnians. See also Tomić, "Na dva brvna niz reku," p. 25, in which Muhammed Tunjo Filipović argued that "no type of Islamic republic is possible here [Bosnia and Herzegovina] because religion cannot be the basis of a constitution in modern societies." Filipović insisted that "the accusation of pan-Islamism is simply ridiculous. That idea disappeared from the historical stage all of seventy years ago, and for us it did not have great influence even when it was at its zenith." Cited in Tomić, "Na dva brvna niz reku," p. 14.

71. *Yugofax* (9 December 1991), p. 2.

72. Sabrina P. Ramet reported that even before the outbreak of hostilities against Slovenia and Croatia, the YPA had increased its arms purchases, which were then stockpiled in Serbia or transferred to Serb militias outside of Serbia. "The Yugoslav Crisis and the West: Avoiding 'Vietnam' and Blundering into 'Abyssinia,'" *East European Politics and Societies* 8 (Winter 1994), p. 201.

73. By March 1992, claimed Mark Thompson, the YPA had concentrated ninety-five thousand troops in Bosnia. *Forging War*, p. 205.

74. Pajić, "The Conflict in Bosnia-Herzegovina," p. 2.

75. *War Crimes in Bosnia-Hercegovina*, p. 24. Pajić cited unsubstantiated figures that the

YPA had forty-five thousand soldiers in Bosnia and Herzegovina just before its attack on Slovenia and between sixty thousand and ninety-five thousand troops in Bosnia and Herzegovina by April 1992. Ibid., p. 3.

76. Ali and Lifschultz, "In Plain View," p. xxvii.

77. *Ex-Yugofax* (7 May 1992), p. 2.

78. In a speech to the Bosnian Parliament, Izetbegović reportedly threatened that Bosnia and Herzegovina would not remain in Yugoslavia if Croatia left. *Report on Eastern Europe*, Weekly Record of Events 2 (19 July 1991), p. 51.

79. For example, Pierre Elliott Trudeau, former prime minister of Canada, mourned the fact that "places like Bosnia and Czechoslovakia, which were created after the First World War as multi-ethnic, pluralistic societies, are breaking up into little ethnic territories partly because Western nations blindly played footsie with the independentists in these countries. And now we have lived to witness the obscenity of 'ethnic cleansing.'" *Memoirs* (Toronto: McClelland and Stewart, 1993), pp. 353–354. Early in the crisis Adil Zulfikarpašić, leader of the Muslim Bosnian Organization, categorically stated that Bosnia and Herzegovina's fate lay in the hands of the international community. Cited in Fahrudin Radončić, "Tražimo pomoć Evrope," *Danas* (16 July 1991), p. 29.

80. The referendum asked Bosnia and Herzegovina's inhabitants "Are you in favour of a sovereign and independent Bosnia-Herzegovina, a state of equal citizens and nations of Muslims, Serbs, Croats, and others who live in it?" Zoran Batusić, "E Pluribus Unum?" *East European Reporter* 5 (March–April 1992), p. 22.

81. *War Crimes in Bosnia-Hercegovina*, Vol. 1, p. 27 (note).

82. Donia and Fine, *Bosnia and Hercegovina*, p. 238.

83. Hayden, "The Partition of Bosnia and Herzegovina," p. 7.

84. See, for example, Alex N. Dragnich, "'Sense of Fury' Over Bosnia Is Misplaced," *Daily News-Record* (Harrisonburg, Virginia), 30 December 1992, and *ex-Yugofax* (29 June 1992), p. 6. Nevertheless, Izetbegović threatened to mobilize Islamic countries against the West in light of seeming European and U.S. disinterest in the fortunes of the Bosnian Muslims. Sarajevo Radio BiH 1730 GMT, 11 June 1994, cited in FBIS-EEU-94-113 (13 June 1994), p. 25.

85. See Shoup, "The Bosnian Crisis of 1992," for a detailed description of the negotiations among the parties leading up to the declaration of Bosnia and Herzegovina's independence and an analysis of the part played (and blame shared) by all of the actors in this drama.

86. *War Crimes in Bosnia-Hercegovina*, Vol. 1, p. 30.

87. As of late July 1992, Serbs had seized approximately 60 percent of Bosnian territory, displaced one-third of the population (approximately 1.5 million people), and killed almost one hundred thousand persons. *Ex-Yugofax* (1 August 1992), p. 14.

88. *New York Times*, 30 September 1993, p. A1.

89. For more on the London conference and its challenges, see *Balkan WarReport*, no. 14 (September 1992), p. 1.

90. Hayden presented an analysis of negotiations among the Bosnian Serbs, Croats, and Muslims prior to and during the consideration of the Vance-Owen Plan in "The Partition of Bosnia and Herzegovina," pp. 1–14.

91. For a brief description of the prerogatives arrogated to the weak central government under the Vance-Owen Plan, consult ibid., p. 9.

92. Ibid., p. 11.

93. M.V., "Defense Industry: Withdrawal from Bosnia," *Vreme* (21 October 1991), pp. 24–25, cited in JPRS-EER-92-008 (17 January 1992), pp. 41–42.

94. The origin of the term *ethnic cleansing* is shrouded in controversy. Jose-Maria Mendiluce, representative of the U.N. High Commission for Refugees, claimed to have coined a variety of the term—*ethnic cleaning*. Cited in Christopher Hitchens, "Why Bosnia Matters," in Ali and Lifschultz, *Why Bosnia*, p. 7. George Kenney, the former State Department official who resigned to protest the U.S. Bosnian policy, suggested that his reports introduced that term into popular U.S. parlance. Private conversation with the author.

95. David Rieff described the procedure as follows: Local noncombatant Serbs were forced, on pain of death, to kill a Muslim neighbor, thus implicating him in ethnic cleansing. No more would the noncombatant be an innocent bystander, and, therefore, no more could he welcome back Muslim neighbors after the fighting ended. *Slaughterhouse: Bosnia and the Failure of the West* (New York: Simon and Schuster, 1995), p. 84. Nenad Canak described another scenario that was occurring in Vojvodina: "The first step is to make speeches saying that Serbs are threatened in some area. The second is to stage an incident where Serbs are killed by non-Serbs. The third step is the raising of barricades for protection by unnamed citizens. The fourth is that the unarmed citizens begin to shoot. Then you have war." *Balkan WarReport*, no. 14 (September 1992), p. 7.

96. Apparently, Serb leaders were also concerned that the Serb population was not growing fast enough and were considering punitive tax measures against childless Serbian citizens. See the peroration against this policy by Lj. Živkov, "Podstrek odozdo," *Ekonomska Politika* (23 July 1990), p. 13.

97. Cited in Grete Gaulin, "A Serb on the Roots of War: He Blames His Own—and the West," "Klassekampen," from *World Press Review* (June 1993), p. 10.

98. Indijana Harper, "Unwanted, Unarmed and Under Attack," *East European Reporter* 5 (November–December 1992), pp. 64–65.

99. Cited in Rieff, *Slaughterhouse*, p. 113.

100. Patrick Moore, "Croatia and Bosnia: A Tale of Two Bridges," *RFE/RL Research Report* 3 (7 January 1994), p. 115.

101. *Yugofax* (6 September 1991), p. 4.

102. Milan Jelovac, "Collapse of Military Industry in Yugoslavia," *Vjesnik* suppl. (3 April 1991), p. 7, cited in JPRS-EER-91-064 (13 May 1991), p. 32; Fahrudin Radončić, "In an Iron Embrace," *Danas* (10 September 1991), pp. 34–35, cited in JPRS-EER-91-145 (27 September 1991), p. 48.

103. See Bojana Jager, "Whoever Pulled Out Will Come Up Short," *Borba* (Zagreb), 23 March 1992, p. 11, cited in JPRS-EER-92-042 (6 April 1992), p. 54, for figures on the division of assets and the SFRY presidency's views on the subject.

104. See, for example, *Balkan WarReport*, no. 29 (October–November 1994), p. 6.

105. Patrick Moore, "The Widening Warfare in the Former Yugoslavia," *REF/RL Research Report* 2 (1 January 1993), p. 8; V. Stanković, "U BiH muslimanske 'inter-brigade,'" *Borba* (Zagreb), 8–9 August 1992, p. 6; As'ad Taha, "Arab Mujahidin," *Al-Sharq Al-Ausat* (10 September 1992), pp. 1, 4, cited in JPRS-EER-92-150 (23 October 1992), p. 29; Krešimir Meler, "U pomoč muslimanskim bratom," *Delo* (23 November 1993), p. 7; Renato Cemerika and Vito Bulica, "Muslimani tajno sagradili ratnu mornaricu," *Danas* (15 March 1994), pp. 9–11; TANJUG 1229 GMT, 24 June 1994, cited in FBIS-EEU-94-123 (27 June 1994), pp. 42–43.

106. On 20 January 1991, for example, Yugoslavia's Islamic community called for an end to the Gulf War and to internecine Muslim conflict. *Report on Eastern Europe,* Weekly Record of Events 2 (1 February 1991), p. 47. On 17 July 1991, Izetbegović expressed to Turkish President Turgut Ozal his interest in attending the forthcoming conference of foreign ministers of the Organization of Islamic Countries. *Report on Eastern Europe,* Weekly Record of Events 2 (26 July 1991), p. 56. *Reis-ul-ulema* Jacob Selimoski addressed that conference, warning of the danger for Yugoslav Muslims and claiming that some nationalists were openly calling for murder and expulsion of Yugoslavia's Muslims to Turkey. *Report on Eastern Europe,* Weekly Record of Events 2 (16 August 1991), p. 41.

107. "Dobili dva broda puna oružja," *Politika* (31 August 1992), p. 6, on the other hand, reported that weapons were arriving in Bosnia for the government fighters. Thus, for example, Syria sent two ships to Split loaded with weapons for Muslim soldiers.

108. Sarajevo Radio Bosnia-Herzegovina 1800 GMT, 30 December 1993, cited in FBIS-EEU-94-001 (3 January 1994), p. 46. See *ex-Yugofax* (1 August 1992) for an analysis of the political changes in the countries surrounding the former Yugoslavia and the potential for regional warfare.

109. *New York Times,* 3 February 1994, p. A12.

110. Daniel Pipes and Patrick Clawson, "Ambitious Iran, Troubled Neighbors," *Foreign Affairs* 72 (1992–1993), p. 136.

111. For example, Sabrina Petra Ramet reported a conversation in Belgrade in 1989 with this theme. *Balkan Babel: Politics, Culture, and Religion in Yugoslavia* (Boulder: Westview Press, 1992), p. 165.

112. In *Oslobodjenje* (Sarajevo), 28 September 1990; Vuković, "Kompromisi u dva poluvremena," p. 5; *Vjesnik* (11 November 1990).

113. Milan Andrejevich, "Moslem Leader Elected President of Bosnia and Hercegovina," *Report on Eastern Europe* 2 (18 January 1991), p. 31. See also *War Crimes in Bosnia-Hercegovina,* Vol. 1, pp. 22–23. Izetbegović declared that "I am not in favor of an Islamic republic. Yet, I do want Islam to survive in these lands." TANJUG 1615 GMT, 13 January 1994, cited in FBIS-EEU-94-010 (14 January 1994), p. 30.

114. Ed Vulliamy, *Seasons in Hell: Understanding Bosnia's War* (New York: St. Martin's Press, 1994), p. 65

115. Cited in Vuković, "Kompromisi u dva poluvremena," p. 12.

9

The Case of the Bosnian Muslims: Relevance for the Social Sciences

"If the Bosnian Muslims had been bottle-nosed dolphins, would the world have allowed Croats and Serbs to slaughter them by the tens of thousands?"

—Edward Luttwak[1]

"The Balkans are not worth the healthy bones of a single Pomeranian grenadier."

—Prince Otto von Bismarck
5 December 1876

The preceding chapters have detailed the development of the Bosnian Muslims from their Slavic roots to national self-identification. A major theme of this book is the pivotal importance for the Bosnian Muslims of being recognized as a nation during Titoist Yugoslavia. The protective coloring they had maintained throughout many years and under many regimes of minority-religious status was stripped away and replaced with the legitimacy of political and juridical recognition as an equal nation within Yugoslavia. The result of this politically motivated decision was that the Bosnian Muslims began to act like an equal nation, because de facto and in practice the behavior of all the actors in Yugoslavia was predicated on the belief that the Bosnian Muslims constituted a nation. Regardless of whether it was Tito's aim that this decision should be carried through quite as far as it was, the outcome was that the Bosnian Muslims became vulnerable to those who now considered them rivals for power and resources.

Thus, the significance of the Bosnian Muslims graphically illuminates the importance of ethnicity in the political affairs of the international arena. As such, ethnicity has become an important subject for inquiry in the social sciences. This chapter evaluates whether certain concepts in the social sciences—pluralism, mobilization, social stratification, and consociationalism—have any explanatory power for the Bosnian Muslims' situation. Then I examine the feasibility of certain scenarios for the resolution of the conflicts in this region.

235

Factors Influencing Interethnic Tensions

A variety of elements may influence interethnic tensions. Five factors are relevant for understanding the situation of the Bosnian Muslims: (1) the role of pluralism in ameliorating interethnic tensions in multiethnic entities, (2) the mobilization of ethnic groups, (3) the role of religion in the growth of ethnonationalism, (4) the importance of the degree and type of ethnic stratification within a society, and (5) the function of ethnic-based politics in the development of ethnonationalism. These factors, which are of long-standing significance, became increasingly important in the Bosnian Muslims' twentieth-century attempts to adapt their needs to the political realities within both Yugoslavia and the international environment.

Pluralism

I use the term *pluralism* here in the sense of cultural diversity.[2] A pluralist society generally has relatively few absolute common values and frequently manifests deep cleavages. Even in a profoundly divided community, however, there must be some common set of values and interests—not just violence—to hold the society together.[3]

Within a pluralist society, the degree of equality among the various groups characterizes social relations. Racist or inegalitarian ideologies, such as Nazism, are on opposite ends of the scale from the ideals of egalitarianism with the theoretical absence of racism. Yet egalitarian ideologies have a wide range as well. Included in this category are those ideologies that call for the eventual complete assimilation of inhabitants (which some people, however, might consider cultural genocide), as was pursued by Stalin in his attempts to create *Homo sovieticus* or, in a looser sense, the attempted "Yugoslavism" of the earlier years of Communist Yugoslavia. However, *liberal pluralism* would also be included.

Liberal pluralist societies do not permit legal or governmental recognition or standing of racial, religious, linguistic, or national groups as corporate entities; nor do they allow the use of any but universalistic criteria for evaluating standards of performance. *Corporate pluralism,* as was practiced increasingly in both Titoist and post-Titoist Yugoslavia, on the other hand, recognizes racial and ethnic groups as legally constituted entities. Quota systems based, for example, on numerical strength in the population reward groups politically and economically, and emphasis is on equality of condition rather than of opportunity.[4] This tendency encouraged the Bosnian Muslims to seek the legitimacy corporate recognition would endow. But having done so, they also began to reap the bitter fruits of increased vulnerability when Tito's protection of their status ended with his death.

Finally, *ethnic pluralism,* and thus stability, may be encouraged when the various regions of a country are not so tightly integrated that they are totally dependent on each other. However, if harsh pressures on the society—such as deep political or economic distress or, more severely, political suppression of certain groups as a result of conquest—require regional interdependence and pooling of scarce resources, formerly acceptable public manifestations of ethnic pluralism may threaten stability.[5] In such an event, the nondemocratic domination of a society by a single group becomes possible or, indeed, likely as consensus, institutional integration, or structural balance within the society fails. As Croats and Slovenes in the post-Tito era perceived their economic future and political prerogatives to be increasingly circumscribed by a domineering and nondemocratic Serb nation, the ties that bound the South Slavs together after World War II unraveled.

Mobilization of National Groups

Some observers have noted increased and widespread mobilization of opposition to the globalizing tendencies of modern communications and technology among national groups in many areas of the globe. Harold Isaacs termed this phenomenon "a massive retribalization."[6] Daniel Bell noticed a "tendency toward more inclusive identities"—that is, wider economic and social units— coinciding with the breakdown in "civil theology" (for example, Americanism or, for our purposes, a nascent Yugoslavism) that formerly served as a focus for unity and identification. The absence of this focus permits parochial tendencies such as ethnonationalism to take advantage of the ensuing centrifugal forces of separatism,[7] as exemplified by the breakup of the former Soviet Union and the former Yugoslavia.

Simultaneously, national groups have discovered the vulnerability of state actors. Such mobilized nonstate actors are able to enter the world political arena in an influential manner by intelligent use for their own ends of global economic interdependence and modern communication and transportation systems.[8]

Furthermore, mobilized national groups may alter their previous pursuit of cultural, linguistic, or religious goals and instead emphasize the economic and social interests of their members. This was once the area pursued most successfully by class-based groups. National groups in the current era have been increasingly successful in defining themselves also as interest groups to serve their members more effectively.

The appearance of the welfare state in advanced societies and the socialist state in developing areas encouraged organized national groupings to mobilize differently from the way they had before. In both situations, the state directly influences the economic well-being and political status of groups. Successful interest groups must therefore be able to present their claims on the society's distributive mechanisms effectively to appropriate enough of the state's resources for their members. Class-based groups are loosely aggregated and able to make only very broad claims. Thus, even if these claims were granted, the circumstances of the individual group members would be altered only slightly.

The national group, for its part, is less diffuse and can elicit greater responses to its demands from the state than can a class-based group.[9] National groups, which combine both socioeconomic and political expectations and demands, have an advantage in pursuing their claims on the state over such groups as classes or grand ideological movements, which represent only one or the other type of claim. The very aims and structure of the modern multinational state

> Furnish resources, motivations, and (unintentionally) grievances to regionally con-
> centrated, as well as to geographically dispersed ethnic groups. [The state's] increas-
> ing rate and level of intervention in the economy and the society render it even more
> the focus of social discontent (replacing here private-sector employers) and of orga-
> nized targeting.[10]

Leaders of national groups are increasingly able to extract policy concessions from the state by persuading it to utilize them as the point of reference and the conduit for the implementation of its aims and policies.

The situation, then, is self-reinforcing: Government has become more vulner-able to the political demands of the ethnic group; this is an added inducement for the ethnic group to take on the function of an interest group to gain more influence over government policy. As the ethnic group grows stronger, govern-ment becomes even more sensitive and often more responsive to the group's demands.[11] In Communist countries, where whatever class consciousness had existed had inevitably dissipated, this issue was problematic, and again we can view the situation of the Bosnian Muslims in this light. Despite the ostensibly Marxist basis of Yugoslavia, class was nothing and national status was every-thing for the South Slavs. The Bosnian Muslims had to obtain corporate recogni-tion to influence government decisionmaking and distribution of political, as well as economic and other, resources.

Religion and Ethnonationalism

The initial opportunity to mobilize the ethnic group often occurs when that unit begins to experience the differential effects of industrialization and moderniza-tion. These effects "on the one hand, tend to foster functional macrointegration and to encourage expectations of mobility, and yet in fact often sustain and exacerbate the very inequalities whose traditional legitimacy and seeming inevitability they simultaneously undermine."[12]

Indeed, often the impetus for mobilization comes from the aristocracy of a previously marginal ethnic population that feels threatened by the values emphasized by a more cosmopolitan regime. Similarly, a traditional religious elite might encourage such mobilization,[13] as occurred in contemporary Iran. In fact, religious mobilization may be the earliest phase of the political develop-ment of a national group based on "religiously framed demands, religiously legitimized leaders, and religiously oriented organizations."[14] The consciousness of a relatively small religious group could be raised to the point that it becomes a mobilized national group.[15] Under the Babylonians, Greeks, and Romans, for example, religion was an important distinguishing element of group identity for minority peoples, as the empires destroyed the bonds among ethnicity, belief, and political citizenship (to the extent that such citizenship had existed).[16] For the Bosnian Muslims, too, religion had been their distinguishing characteristic, even though they were widely considered a mostly secular group. But the Bosnian Muslims utilized the religious component of their identity to differentiate themselves to the point at which they could achieve separate corporate recognition.

State authorities, in fact, have occasionally sought to invoke the growing strength of religion to counter the threat of ethnonationalism. Embracing an overarching state religion that would bind all groups and legitimate government programs is a way to harness religion for state purposes. On the other hand, central state officials could attempt to secularize the culture in an effort to render obsolete religious differences that helped to stir up ethnonational conflict. In the case of Yugoslavia, Tito discouraged religious manifestations among the populace, but he was only too willing to trot out "his" Muslims for foreign policy purposes.

Ethnic Stratification

Finally, the level of group cohesion and mobilization may depend on whether the society is stratified vertically or horizontally. In a horizontal system of stratification, there are parallel structures for each national group. The elites within each national group enjoy prestige or wealth and thus have a stake in maintaining the social status quo. This form of society obviously has more stability and less revolutionary potential than a vertical system. However, internal tension is possible if, for example, the elites of a mobilized national group are seen as selling out or working against the common people in their group by benefiting from the new conditions of modernity while not actively pursuing the interests of the other social classes within that group. Since the Bosnian Muslim leadership was widely considered to be following the same type of coalition-building, nonconfrontational politics Bosnian Muslim leaders had successfully followed since the end of the nineteenth century, cohesion among the Bosnian Muslims was remarkably high. Therefore, class antagonisms that might have arisen to rob the group of some of its strength through cohesion were absent.

In a vertically stratified system, one national group is dominant in some way over others, and social stratification is synonymous with ethnicity. Upward mobility denotes a change in national identity, which is unlikely to occur when religion and ethnicity unite. If upward mobility or some kind of economic or social betterment is blocked too long by the dominant group, however, a frustrated national group may mobilize itself. Two possible consequences of this mobilization are increased intracommunal cohesion to boost the competitive edge of that national group or a forced restructuring of the division of labor, resources, and power in the entire society, with a consequent sacrifice of the economic growth and social development of the society as a whole.[17]

The Bosnian Muslims' access as a community to the structures of influence was blocked by the Croat and Serb domination of politics at the republic, as well as the national, level. The mobilization of the Bosnian Muslim community to achieve greater political and economic rewards also coincidentally produced a more cohesive national group. In effect, the Bosnian Muslims became a nation because, having become mobilized for political reasons, they believed themselves to be a nation, just like the Serbs and Croats.

Ethnonationalism and the State

If the state should prove consistently resistant to the demands of a strong, mobilized, and geographically concentrated national group, the issue of secession might arise. But short of secession, what responses can the state make to political demands by national groups? One type of state policy toward ethnic or any other ascription-based groups is to adapt the prescriptions of the eighteenth- and nineteenth-century European theory of popular sovereignty to the modern nation-state. Thus, governments would simply ignore national groups and treat the inhabitants as individuals with the same duties and privileges as other citizens. The rationale for this policy is that

> Since, in theory, the legitimacy of the state rests in the will of the people, and since the people are identified with a national community, the state becomes simply the executive of the solidary national will. Any recognition by the state of ethnic subgroups with a special relationship to the state . . . would be, according to this view, inconsistent with the theory of popular sovereignty.[18]

Furthermore, any state-sanctioned or controlled recognition of ethnicity implies official acceptance of inequality among the various constituent groups. Of course, internal diversity cannot be totally ignored, particularly when a national group is geographically concentrated. In such a case, regional autonomy, "without necessarily granting any official status to corporate ethnic groups as such," may be adequate to deflect conflict.[19]

Some degree of territorial identity within the larger community might even engender loyalty to the polity, since national groups appear increasingly to connect their survival with control over a physical territory. Nevertheless, we must ask, how important in fact is land to ethnic preservation?[20] Austro-Marxist Karl Renner (Rudolf Springer, pseud.) suggested that "nationality is not essentially connected with territory; [instead, nationality is] an autonomous union of persons."[21] In the case of Bosnia and Herzegovina, no one of the three major groups physically dominated the entire territory, and Serbs and Croats each had other "homelands" to attract their loyalty. Yet none of the national groups would freely yield an inch of land to the others or concede a greater territorial need to the Bosnian Muslims who possessed no other territorial homeland.

Another option for state policy is assimilation. Coercive assimilation at its most extreme includes *ethnocide,* the systematic destruction of an ethnic group. Many question whether the atrocities of ethnic cleansing, which are currently being practiced in areas of the former Yugoslavia, may at bottom actually pursue ethnocide rather than merely the homogenization of an area.

Noncoercive assimilation includes the encouragement of voluntary integration through various social and cultural inducements, such as jobs, education, status, and technology. To some extent, this policy worked under Tito. Without the cynical manipulation of aggressive nationalism, first by Serb elites and later by others, Yugoslavia might have weathered the post-Tito transition period more effectively.

Finally, if the government does decide that ethnonationalism within its borders cannot be suppressed or ignored, it might try to accommodate or even harness it for the common good in a variety of ways. The most benign variant would include granting some type of official and legalized identity to the mobilized national group. The Yugoslav elite thus used this policy when it granted political and juridical recognition to the South Slav national groups, eventually including the Bosnian Muslims, to bolster the policy of noncoercive assimilation.

Nevertheless, group-based ethnic politics can include such extreme measures as slavery, which is sometimes imposed on people who are part of an ethnic group that is not native to the region or on a conquered indigenous group. In fact, the main characteristic of slavery is the atomization suffered by those deprived of ethnic and kinship support. The most extreme form of slavery in modern terms is found in the concentration camp, which connotes the possibility of genocide.[22] Genocide is often perpetrated on a group that is economically superfluous to the ruling circle: "either thinly settled nomads or semi-nomads who occupy land coveted by more technologically advanced agriculturists, or 'middleman minorities' that are politically powerless but economically successful and therefore become the target of competitiveness, envy, and greed."[23] The Serbs in particular, although not exclusively, engaged in the most recent variant of concentration camps. Serbs targeted the Bosnian Muslims, a vulnerable national group whose past had been so strongly—often negatively—intertwined with theirs.

Imperialism, "the political domination and economic exploitation by one ethnic group (the *Staatsvolk* . . .) of other ethnic groups,"[24] is another type of group policy of which the Serbs stand accused in the former Yugoslavia, particularly with regard to the Hungarian and Albanian minorities. This policy can take the form of (1) unequal status within the state of members of the *Staatsvolk* (dominant people of the state) and of the conquered nations; (2) unequal privileges and obligations, particularly with regard to land ownership, taxation, and legal rights; (3) some form of local and cultural autonomy for the conquered nations under those traditional elites who will collaborate with the ruling authorities; or (4) "a myth of paternalism and trusteeship" that perpetuates and legitimizes the unequal status between various individuals and ethnic groups.[25]

A third type of policy a state may invoke when dealing with national groups is consociation. Also known as segmented pluralism, this form is defined as "a system of government that institutionalizes proportional ethnic representation and a complex, negotiated system of compromises and balances between supposedly equal ethnic groups."[26] On the surface, consociation seems to be pluralism. Nevertheless, this type of policy—found mainly in multiethnic Western constitutional and parliamentary democracies—is, in fact, more fragile than pluralism is considered to be. This fragility is derived from the fact that it is basically a "conservative cartel of ethnic elites sharing power by giving priority to their *class* over their ethnic interests,"[27] and that it is based on an implicit or explicit understanding by society's elites that achievement of their major goals is mutually advantageous.[28] This could be considered a positive situation if, for instance, mass pressure on the political system had encouraged centrifugal forces that were deleterious to national integrity.

Within the boundaries of the concept of consociation, taken in its broadest sense, exist a variety of forms of polity. The most interesting example of consociation for our purposes is the creation of a federal system of government based on "cultural-linguistic-territorial groups."[29] Arend Lijphart forcefully argued that under certain conditions "federalism can be a consociational device,"[30] since both are nonmajoritarian concepts—although with different emphases.

Federalism itself is rather controversial in regard to its efficacy for solving ethnic conflict.[31] William H. Riker defined federalism as "a political organization in which the activities of government are divided between regional governments and a central government in such a way that each kind of government has some activities on which it makes final decisions."[32] In a federal system, the central government undertakes much of the significant decisionmaking, leaving subnational units to manage regional problems.

According to Najdan Pašić, Yugoslav theorist and former president of the Serbian Constitutional Court, in most cases in the twentieth century federalism has tended toward an ever larger monopoly of power for the central government with a concomitant loss of autonomy for regional and local units.[33] However, governments may fear that failure to grant restive ethnic groups some form of political autonomy would permit and even encourage those disintegrative factors federalism might prevent.[34] Confederalism, which mandates a decentralized decisionmaking system with a weak central government and strong regional units, is an (often unattractive) option in those cases. Many new states, therefore, face the following development dilemma:

> Under-development in the modern era creates a need for centralized authority to offset communal fragmentation; yet centralization effective enough to control disintegrative forces requires resources beyond the reach of underdeveloped systems . . . when intergroup animosity is strong and central authority is weak—countries are mired in apparently endless civil strife.[35]

Federalism may well serve an underdeveloped society that must deal with tenacious ethnic loyalty while simultaneously creating a community large enough to provide that society with sufficient human and other resources. In a particularly interesting passage of her book *Ethnic Conflict and Political Development,* Cynthia Enloe described the attraction of federalism for the leaders of such countries:

> Rarely are federalism's advocates men of romantic enthusiasm; usually they are pragmatic compromisers, and it is hard for men of this temperament to generate nationalistic fervor. Imbued with the spirit of the Enlightenment, they believe in the viability of communities artificially contrived to satisfy man-made laws and rational calculation. Federal politics, consequently, are qualitatively different from ethnic communities, which grow naturally out of implicitly shared values and historical interdependence. The seemingly natural and organic character of ethnic groups makes them appear difficult to overcome. Nation-builders find it easier to skirt such groups, accommodating the national structure to them in the hope that eventually they will be dispersed by nonethnic attachments.[36]

Contrary to the optimism with which Enloe predicted that federalism could help attenuate ethnic conflicts, Walker Connor pointed out that "a survey of multinational states does not indicate that any particular form of government has solved this dichotomy between the need for unity and the fissiparous impact of ethnic consciousness."[37] The fact that ethnic dissonance still exists even in authoritarian societies—which can deal with such concerns through a secret police apparatus, internment without formal charges, and control of communications—is a strong indication that ethnonationalism remains a potent force.[38]

The Case of the Bosnian Muslims in the Former Yugoslavia

Yugoslavia attempted to utilize federalism to attenuate ethnonationalism. After World War II, Tito wanted to ameliorate the national hatreds that had congealed as a result of the war's atrocities. As a good Communist, he probably would have preferred to simply cancel all national self-identification and replace it with class identification. However, he was also a Yugoslav who knew it would not be easy to separate the South Slavs from their memories of past glories and communal dreams of future success. Therefore, he attempted to foster elite consensus through a form of consociationalism—federalism.

Yugoslavia's experience with federalism was fairly successful as long as the Communist Party and the federal government remained centralized. However, the elite consensus in Yugoslavia was as artificial as the country's internal borders. The federal system could not ameliorate this artificiality, since all Yugoslav politics, access to resources, and decisionmaking were based on national identification. Thus, Yugoslavia was a pluralist system but of the less stable corporate pluralist type in which national groups were recognized as legally constituted entities and resources, personnel, and the like were distributed according to quota systems and the national key.

Tito's last attempt at tinkering with the system, the creation of a confederation in the 1970s, merely legitimized Yugoslavia's corporate pluralism and underscored the artificiality of its much-vaunted brotherhood and unity. As Slaven Letica noted, confederalism presupposes friendly states gathered together to win advantage or to protect themselves from external threats. The lands of the former Yugoslavia, however, are currently surrounded by mostly friendly entities but are experiencing internal hostility.[39]

The 1974 constitution's creation of a confederal system thus weakened the center's decisionmaking capabilities. The rules of the game now required republic unanimity, which was virtually impossible to achieve on most important issues. Furthermore, the loss of Tito in 1980 irrevocably shattered one of the few remaining centralizing agents. The field was thus given over to the republics, which instead of continuing to integrate the Yugoslav economy with an eye to closer bonding with Western Europe, chose the road of narrow political preference—ethnonationalism—instead.

It is thus fitting to characterize the former Yugoslavia as a pluralist country that was forced to deal with group inequality in a way that had explosive ramifications for the continued viability of the state. By virtue of its Marxist basis, Yugoslavia should have evolved into a liberal pluralist entity. However, it evolved into a corporate pluralist country because of the intensity of national feeling among its groups. This situation exacerbated interethnic tensions and interregional conflict over development resources, which prevented the gradual development of cohesion liberal pluralism depends upon. Furthermore, post-Tito Yugoslavia began to seem to many as if it were being subjugated by an aggressive and powerful pan-Serbian unit. Disintegration followed when the various ethnic groups repelled the Serbian initiative to dominate a tightly federalized Yugoslavia. In this tug-of-war, the federal decisionmaking process became gridlocked.

The failures of the standard prescriptions for ruling a multinational state—consociationalism, federalism, and confederalism—were exacerbated in Yugoslavia's case by the failure of internationalism. The Soviet Union's attempt at internationalism failed when it was unable to replace the lure of national identification with a nonnational identification within either its empire or its commonwealth. Similarly, despite attempts during the interwar period, as well as in the post–World War II period, Yugoslavia failed to create a "Yugoslav" identification to overpower the intense nationalist aspirations of the Serbs and the Croats.

In regard to mobilization of national groups, Milton J. Esman presciently (for Yugoslavia, at least) concluded that "communal cleavages [ethnic, linguistic, racial, or religious] are likely to be more salient and more intractable than class conflicts, more difficult to manage, and more likely to provoke violence not only in emerging states but in many older polities."[40] In Yugoslavia, vertical stratification was enhanced by the close connection between religion and ethnicity. This connection is made all the more clear when we remember that whereas the Bosnian Muslims were recognized as a national group within the former Yugoslavia in response to perceived domestic and foreign policy imperatives, the major characteristic differentiating them from the Serbs and Croats was their religion. Historically, all three groups are of the same Slavic stock, but it was religion that enraged or frightened the Serbs into rejecting a unified Bosnian state. Many Bosnian Serbs refused to live under a Muslim-dominated regime for fear it would also mean Muslim (religious) domination, as had occurred under the Ottoman Empire.

The history of Bosnia and Herzegovina reflects its pluralistic and tolerant nature, long inhabited as it was by members of many religions and later of various national groups. For many Bosnians, in such a mixed area neither national nor religious identification was important, particularly during the secularizing years of post–World War II Yugoslavia. Until 1969, the Bosnian Muslims were not considered, and largely did not widely recognize themselves, to be a precisely national group in the Yugoslav meaning as were the Serbs or the Croats, although it is clear—at least from the censuses—that they considered themselves a separate group from the Serbs and the Croats. Many Bosnian Muslims considered themselves to be no more than a religious minority or, for secular Muslims, part of the Yugoslav nation. When called upon to declare a national identification for census purposes, Bosnian Muslims had traditionally designated themselves nationally undetermined or Yugoslav, when that option was available. Only a minority declared themselves to be nationally Serbs or Croats. Indeed, Izetbegović underlined the tenuousness of the Bosnian Muslim national identification in a 1991 interview in *Borba* when he said that "thanks to the policies of the last forty some years [Muslims] have not sufficiently affirmed themselves as a nationality, nor have they been sufficiently conscious, and their interests have not been articulated in any manner whatsoever."[41]

When Tito recognized the Bosnian Muslims as a national group, however, they became politically and juridically a Yugoslav nation. Although their historical roots had not changed, their standing in society had. With that adjustment in status rather naturally came an alteration in their self-identification. Political and juridical nationhood contributed a new element to their identity, enhancing their differentiation from the other Yugoslav nations by other than religious criteria. The Bosnian Muslims thus became a nation because they were treated as such after 1969 and because they came to believe it of themselves.

Recognition and elevation to national status within the Yugoslav federation was an important step for the Bosnian Muslims, although it also posed numerous problems for the viability of Yugoslavia. In fact, as early as 1984, scholars considered the Muslim issue in Yugoslavia to be one of the "chief axes of nationalist disequilibrium."[42] At that time, the troublemaking connotation of this term almost certainly referred more to the Albanian Muslims in Kosovo, which abuts a foreign country with potential irredentist demands (Albania), than to the more quiescent Bosnian Muslims. But was there increased yearning for national self-determination among the Bosnian Muslims that, if not as threatening as that of the Kosovar Muslims, was still of sufficient strength to have worried other groups? If Bosnia and Herzegovina were troubled by nationality or any other problem, Yugoslavia as an entity would no doubt feel the tension, particularly since that republic contained rich mineral resources and a large proportion of the Yugoslav arms industry. We have seen in the end-of-century Serb—and Croat—devastation of the Bosnian Muslim nation, in the attempt to divide Bosnia and Herzegovina into homogeneous units that could then be united with neighboring ethnic homelands, that the politicization and mobilization of the Bosnian Muslims were more significant than was credited at the time they were occurring.

As a result of their new status, the Bosnian Muslims automatically gained increased prerogatives and, ostensibly, access to the political and economic resources of the society. But Yugoslavia was becoming increasingly vertically stratified after Tito's death, with the Slovenes and Croats seeking greater economic and political autonomy and the Serbs also reaching for greater prerogatives within the state. The rise in numbers and influence of the Bosnian Muslims in Bosnia and Herzegovina and their frequent alliances with the Croats against perceived Serb interests frustrated the Serbs. When Yugoslavia began to break apart, the Bosnian Muslims became targets of the Bosnian Serbs, who wanted to excise a historically noxious group from lands occupied by Bosnian Serbs or adjacent to Serbia.

The raising of the Bosnian Muslims' status and their consequent communal mobilization, which took them out of the Serbian orbit, thus made the Bosnian Muslims more vulnerable to Serb vengeance and weakened their chances for peaceful survival after the collapse of Yugoslavia. Muhammed Filipović recognized this, at least implicitly, when he perorated that "to assert that the Muslims were invented, that they are a product of the anti-Serb policies of the Communists, that they are Serbs who betrayed their ancestral faith, means to resort to a genocidal attitude toward them, to justify today the need for their reintegration into the religious and political context of the primary ethnos."[43]

Implications of the Conflict

Having discussed the foundations of the Bosnian Muslims' situation, I now turn to the future. What might become of the various actors in the Yugoslav conflicts?

It is doubtful that any of the Serb actors is less nationalistic than the others. The ethnonationalistic "quick fix" for Serbia's ills and failure to secure what is seen by many Serbs to be their rightful role in the Balkans seems to appeal to all of the vocal Serbian leaders, and a liberal Serb opposition is little in evidence at present.[44] In fact, the creation of a greater Serbia seems to be the only commonly held value among the strongest Serbian actors that is backed by numerous voters.[45] In contemporary Serbia, according to Milovan Djilas, exists a mixture of socialism and nationalism—that is, "an authoritarian message suffused with elements of genuine democracy."[46] This mixture has produced what Patrick Moore termed an "aggressive, abusive [political culture that] looks backward to an age of Serbian military glories and of a medieval empire, and this at a time when the Croats and Slovenes are debating the best route to joining democratic Europe and the EC."[47] The Bosnian Serbs, who share—indeed, embody—this attitude, have determined to use ethnic cleansing to facilitate a greater Serbia in this era of transnationalism.[48]

One of the results of the Serb expansion outside of the post-1945 borders could be a civil war within the greater Serbia for which Serbs now struggle.[49] Vuk Drašković, leader of the nationalistic opposition party Serbian Movement for Renewal (DEPOS),[50] pointed out that Serb-Serb violence has not been unknown in the twentieth century[51] as he recalled the murder of more than twelve thousand Serb democrats and monarchists in Belgrade alone after World War II by Tito's Serbian Communists. Drašković predicted that Serbian refugees from non-Serb areas might descend upon a destitute Serbia that would be unable to provide them with jobs or housing. The potential for revolutionary terror would increase.[52] Rifts in the Serb line have also appeared, as Milošević has cut links with Karadžić while retaining a relationship with the Bosnian-Serb state *Republika Srpska Krajina*.[53] Furthermore, a victorious Karadžić would be a credible competitor for Milošević in future elections (and vice versa), with Karadžić acting like a president in his own "country."

The reconstituted YPA, which had been the only hope for a cohesive Yugoslavia, is now controlled by hard-liners who support Milošević's definition of a greater Serbia and are willing to use force to attain it.[54] A powerful chauvinistic army, seeking dominion over all lands with Serb inhabitants and prepared to defend its own prerogatives,[55] would probably not scruple to declare nonlike-minded Serbs to be betrayers of the Serb nation and to deal with them accordingly.[56] Furthermore, Drašković charged that the YPA enthusiastically pursued the conflict against Croatia and likely the conflict against Bosnia and Herzegovina to protect its own financial and other interests. Drašković thus claimed the YPA was attempting to protect its privileges and pensions and the military-industrial complex, from which it garnered large profits.[57] In this way, the YPA conceivably positioned itself to take a leading role in the postwar era.

The Bosnian Muslims are bound in a contradiction. Their first inclination was to support and build a pluralistic, democratic state, or at least a confederation of the former Yugoslav republics, with room for Bosnian Muslims, Serbs, and Croats.[58] A forward-looking, European, multiethnic state was thus their first choice, a state in which those who wished could follow Muslim religious rituals but remain Bosnians with their compatriot Bosnian Serbs and Croats. Now this worldview has rejected them in favor of committing new atrocities to avenge old ones. In this settling of historical scores, they are being killed by their former compatriots. What remains for the survivors is to continue to knock at the European, democratic, multiethnic door that has been barred to them by their neighbors or to realize their own identity and ensure their survival by doing what the Serbs and Croats feared in the first place and have now driven them toward in a counterreaction—to create an Islamic enclave in the middle of Europe.

The Bosnian Muslims' confusion about their relationship with and position in Europe was clearly expressed by a Bosnian Muslim religious leader, Mustafa Cerić:

> The truth is that the Muslims in this country do not understand Islam. . . . They do not practise Islam, they have only their names which are Muslim, and that is a tradition. Some of them do not even know they are Muslim. And yet, as Muslims in this country, we live in a paradox all the time. On the one hand we are European, on the other we don't know what to do about Europe. We cannot at the moment love it, we cannot trust it, we cannot hate it, we cannot deny it, for we are part of it. We are in a similar position in relation to the Serbs and the Croats, with whom we share this country, and who disagree between themselves over everything except one thing: their relationship to the Muslims, and their common need to destroy us. We simply do not know what to do, or where to place our faith.
>
>   We are "Muslims" now, because they did not allow us to be Bosnians. And now that we are Muslims, they all say "that is a religious category, not a nationality, it doesn't count." And so we say then can we please be Bosnians after all, and they, Europe included, say no, because there is no Bosnia any more. I feel like screaming to the Serbs and Croats: Why are you so scared of us? Why are you so *obsessed* by us? Why are you incapable of leaving us alone? Why do you need to exterminate us and our culture? Why does our culture offend you so much that you need to do these things to us?[59]

There is a fear throughout Europe that the conflict in Bosnia is the first salvo in the battle between Christians and Muslims (for world domination? toward Armageddon?). The proponents of this idea claim that adhering to Islam precludes development of a democratic, pluralistic, Western-type government in the lands of Bosnia and Herzegovina. However, the nationalist Serbs and Croats[60] who are attacking and "cleansing"[61] the Bosnian Muslims do so professing a religio-ethnic imperative that excludes the possibility of coexistence between different national and religious communities. The Bosnian Muslims, on the other hand, have long proclaimed publicly their desire to create a multinational, democratic country. Although a Muslim might be the leader of the country, they have stated, Bosnia and Herzegovina would not be made into a Muslim enclave in Europe but instead would celebrate the diversity of the Bosnian mosaic.[62]

Now, however, as the world has watched, Catholic Croats and Orthodox Serbs in Bosnia have justified their killing frenzies with ethnonationalistic rhetoric.

But where are the moderate Orthodox and Catholic religious leaders to preach loving-kindness and tolerance toward other nations and religions?[63]

We are then justified in asking whether religion has banked or stoked the fires of nationalism in the former Yugoslavia. The war seems to be using religion as a cover for an all-out land grab, or how could the South Slavs have avoided religious confrontation until now? We can only suppose that Serb (and Croat?) religious leaders approve of the use of religious imagery to condone murder and violence since little has appeared publicly to gainsay that inference.[64] Would, therefore, the Muslims not be justified in following their own religious leaders and in turning whatever abode is left to them when the fighting is over into a stronghold for Islam?[65]

Other intriguing scenarios have been suggested. The concept of cantonization, the reorganization of Bosnia and Herzegovina along ethnic lines, was forwarded at one time as a possible outcome of the war. However, it has been rejected by some in favor of a regional solution (regionalization) whereby Bosnia and Herzegovina would be more rationally restructured according to economic, historical, and ethnic factors rather than ethnic factors alone. Paul Shoup, for example recommended the following series of mutually reinforcing policies:

> Preservation of the republic's boundaries; breaking up the territorial power base of the ethnic extremists; demilitarization; protecting the rights of nationalities in areas where they are a minority; democratization; and the return to law and order. These steps should culminate with free elections which are not dominated by the extremists. All this could be summed up under the rubric "DDI"—Demilitarization, Democratization, and International Guarantees.[66]

However, one suspects that more goodwill than is currently evident (when viewing the raging war) would be necessary to make this solution work. Yet one does hear of isolated islands of support and nostalgia for the old ideal of Bosnia and Herzegovina, even amid the louder, more clamorous extremist statements of demands that alone are reported by the press. Small signs that the bloodlust and urbanocide of the extremists are revolting to many appear in private conversations with inhabitants from all over the former Yugoslavia.

One can also hear reminders that there are chinks in the armor of the most aggressive nationalists. For example, the ease of creating a postwar Greater Serbia, to include the "cleansed" areas of Bosnia and Herzegovina, is questionable. We are reminded of the fact that the homogeneity of Serbian aspirations may be exaggerated. Historically, the Serbs who lived under Ottoman rule differed socially, culturally, and in other ways from the Serbs living in Austria-Hungary. Thus, the Serbian communities outside of Serbia proper, particularly in Croatia and in Bosnia and Herzegovina, may not easily submit to a Milošević vision of a post–civil war greater Serbia, as the Republic of Yugoslavia would be configured. After all, Tito's strongest World War II allies were the Croat and Bosnian Serbs, who fought against Serbian Četniks, as well as Croat Ustaše and the fascist invaders. The fissure between Bosnian Serbs and Milošević was illustrated recently as Milošević began publicly to demonize and undermine the Bosnian Serb leader Radovan Karadžić in an attempt to push him into a negotiated settlement of the war.[67] If there is difficulty integrating all of these Serbs into a newly reconstituted Yugoslavia, where would they go and what would they do? The question also arises with regard to Montenegro's status in rump Yugoslavia. Some reports of dissension and financial competition between Serbs and Montenegrins have been publicized.[68]

If the Bosnian Serbs and the Croatian Serbs declared independence from their respective states, they would constitute poor states with mostly mountainous terrain and little significant industry. Would they look to Yugoslavia for support? Would a devastated and internationally spurned Yugoslavia be forthcoming with help?

What are the real chances, however, for a postwar restructuring of Bosnia and Herzegovina along regional lines when the war has reduced individuals to one dimension—the ethno-religious one? Can a multidimensional view of Bosnians reemerge to replace the bitterness of the universal betrayals and atrocities? Policies that predated the war and that had been generally unopposed—the Croat government's poor treatment of its Serbian minority and the Serb government's repression of the Kosovar Albanians, for example—made people ready to accept even more intolerant and nationalistically inspired activities. The suggested solutions and actions to end the war depend on the position taken.

Depending on temporal as well as national orientation, the Bosnian conflict can be considered either a war of external aggression or a civil war. Evidence is strong for those who consider this a war of Serbian aggression. Belgrade has been strongly implicated in materially supporting the Bosnian Serbs, as well as providing soldiers to attack the sovereign state of Bosnia and Herzegovina; Croatia has occasionally been similarly implicated on behalf of the Bosnian Croats. The solution to this foreign policy problem is to institute political and economic punishments for violating internationally accepted values. When the erring regime is chastened or altered and the international values (that is, sovereignty and inviolable, internationally recognized frontiers) are reestablished for all, the system would again reach status quo.

On the other hand, aspects of this conflict are akin in many respects to a civil war in that inhabitants of one country are ruthlessly fighting and committing atrocities against each other.[69] Thus, Bosnia and Herzegovina's war has also stressed the reinforcing cleavages of ethnicity and religion. In this view, peacekeeping measures were called for to separate the warring units so negotiation toward a political settlement could begin. Negotiations would be manipulated by international civil servants so no party would be too (dis)satisfied and the parties would resettle into a balanced, if not harmonious, coexistence. The disagreements among the various actors over the character of the problem and the solutions to the tragedy have led to contradictory policies that, by often encouraging the combatants to think their view was finally being recognized, allowed the fighting to continue.

If not forgivable or forgettable, can this chapter be moved beyond in the interest of allowing today's generation to get on with their lives? Will future generations erupt on a flimsy (or real) excuse and avenge the atrocities currently being perpetrated, for example, in the name of the grievances of the 1389 defeat of medieval Serbia at Kosovo? Can Bosnian Muslims forgive their isolation by Serbs and Croats on the basis of their religion and on their willingness to forget that they, too, are Slavs with as long a habitation on the land as the Croats and Serbs? Could Bosnian Serbs ever overcome their repugnance toward having a Muslim president and not consider cohabitation with Muslims to be the renewal of their experience as serfs under the Ottoman Empire or as the first step in the Armageddon struggle of Christians versus Muslims for the soul of Europe?

Perhaps there will be a home for the liberal, tolerant antinationalists, people such as Zlatko Dizdarević, an editor of the Sarajevo newspaper *Oslobodjenje* described: "The father of my wife is Serb. The mother of my wife is Croat. My parents are Muslims. So what about my children? Who are they?"[70] Or perhaps a series of new ministates must exist for a time to allow the groups to work out their bloodlust and aggressions. Once the people have visited the reality of poverty and pariah status, perhaps they can eventually make a better consociation-based deal, rooted in economic need, with their neighbors and erstwhile brothers, as may be happening—although bloodlessly—in the former Czechoslovakia.

In fact, the latter may be occurring to some extent in light of the formula worked out between the governments of Croatia and Bosnia and Herzegovina. According to this plan, the Bosnian Croats and Bosnian Muslims created a federation within Bosnia and Herzegovina, and Bosnia and Herzegovina and Croatia then formed a confederation.

The Croatian and Bosnian populations and politicians have reacted to this formulation very gingerly,[71] and Robert Hayden's disdainful description of the constitutional features is disquieting. He characterized the federation as "an empty shell, with a 'government' that has virtually no authority within the supposed country, a 'legislature' that has no real means of reaching final decisions on contested issues, and courts that have beautifully wide grants of authority in regard to protecting human rights and freedoms, coupled with no means to exercise that authority."[72] Furthermore, only Muslims and Croats are enfranchised, a situation that discriminates against all others. A federation including the territory of Bosnia and Herzegovina that excludes the Serbs as equal partners has little chance of enduring, since such a configuration does not easily permit the flourishing of democracy.

The last hope for Yugoslavia's "Yugoslavs" was Bosnia and Herzegovina; now they are homeless. Long a tolerant, religiously and nationally neutral area, Bosnia and Herzegovina has been forced to acknowledge nationalist differences within its populations.[73] But perhaps those who yearn for the return of the ideal of toleration and multiculturalism that was Bosnia and Herzegovina can serve as the core of a new Bosnia and Herzegovina and create a formula to overcome the hurts and fears the current bloodletting has expressed. Those people seemed to be principally urban inhabitants, not only Muslims but also Croats and perhaps some Serbs, too.[74] This division lends credence to the idea that Bosnia and Herzegovina suffered not only from ethnic divisions but also from rural-urban cleavages. In fact, this cleavage has a long history. It stretches back to the medieval period when herders who took easily to brigandage during the late medieval and Ottoman eras harassed commercial routes and maintained a consistent hostility, which has existed up to the present day, toward urban culture and the modern institutions that culture supports. Furthermore, in these rural areas it was religious self-identification that later supplied the national identity. The ancestors of these rural peoples constitute a significant portion of those who today are attacking Bosnia's cities,[75] particularly nationally diverse Sarajevo, as territory hostile to the ethnic uniformity idea of Karadžić's Bosnian Serbs.

The role of the international community, of course, will be crucial in evaluating the viability of the various possible formulations. What are the minimum standards of statehood the international community, or the indigenous inhabitants, would accept? How much support and protection, how much of a presence would the international community be willing to provide to ensure the viability of the chosen options? These questions do not automatically have positive answers, as is evidenced by the miscalculations, misunderstandings, and miscues ("the inability of the West ... to develop a method to make violence counter-productive," as Shoup put it)[76] that have governed the actions of Western diplomats from the beginning of this situation. The current confederal plan between Bosnia and Croatia apparently came about because of U.S. and German political pressure, as well as economic and political inducements to persuade the Bosnian Muslims and the Croats to bury their animosity.[77] Will the international community, particularly its most powerful members, be able to continue to exert such influence on events? Furthermore, the usefulness of protecting the sovereign nation-states is questioned by the breakup of formerly multiethnic East European countries into their component ethnic parts. Yet the continued stability of the international order may depend on just such protection of sovereignty, even as it is being buffeted by the demands made by ethnonationalists on behalf of the principles of self-determination and the protection of minority rights.

The arguments for homogeneity of living space and for ethnic cleansing or other atrocious remedies for attaining such space are made very strongly today in Yugoslavia and in other places, by word and by deed. But I am not convinced that this is a necessary condition for peace. As Ivo Andrić portrayed in *The Bridge on the Drina*[78] and "The Letter from 1920,"[79] Bosnia is a land of deep hatreds. Croats and Serbs who live in Bosnia are more fearful, living as they do on the outposts of their religion commingled with believers of other faiths, and feel their ethno-religious ties more deeply than their coreligionists living in Croatia and Serbia, respectively. And the Muslims, in many rural minds still not separated from the hated Turks despite their common roots, have been resented by all.

Nevertheless, Andrić also expressed the following sentiment about Bosnia:

It is true that there had always been concealed enmities and jealousies and religious intolerance, coarseness and cruelty, but there had also been courage and fellowship and a feeling for measure and order, which restrained all these instincts within the limits of the supportable and, in the end, calmed them down and submitted them to the general interest of life in common.[80]

Thus, an area does not have to be composed only of similar people for some kind of harmony or at least balance to exist. Each person and each group of per sons makes a contribution to the living space. Perfect harmony, rarely attainable in the best of circumstances, is less to be sought than is a modus vivendi, a minimal set of ground rules, if you will, whereby different types of people can occupy the same space more or less harmoniously. There is little to suggest that Bosnia and Herzegovina is different in this regard. Throughout its history, Bosnia has been dominated by one or another power, which ruled cruelly or benignly—as tyrants, administrators, even liberators. During the various phases of Bosnia's history, usually one of its indigenous peoples has had more favorable circumstances or been less at risk than others. Only once before—during World War II—however, was there such wholesale, massive slaughter as we now witness. This suggests that a different response to stimuli and a different view of the world should not preclude harmonious cohabitation and should definitely not lead to violence.

Exogenous factors, not only endogenous elements, have induced much of the trouble in this region throughout its history. Thus, Milošević's openly nationalist policy, which provided a strong incentive for ethnonational conflict in the former Yugoslavia, was aided by international indecision and selfish protection of narrow national interest. Yugoslavia would not have collapsed so easily without the previous implosion of the Soviet Union and the concomitant depreciation of communism. In a more stable international arena, if the people in Bosnia and Herzegovina had been left to their own designs without the machinations of political leaders who had unhealthy agendas that called for the mobilization of mass hatred and fear, perhaps the tensions endemic particularly in the rural areas would have been leavened by an increasingly interdependent view of European life. Perhaps the Bosnian people would still be living in balance, as they had previously.

Importance of the Ethnonationalistic View of International Affairs

Finally, a few words about the importance of ethnonationalism as a subject of analysis would not be amiss, especially in regard to the Yugoslav problem. A number of telling points are frequently made with regard to the Yugoslav tragedy and its predictability:

1. The former Yugoslavia was made up of primitive, semibarbaric peoples who have never learned to settle their disputes except through violence.
2. Therefore, Yugoslavia—and the Balkans of which it was a part—are not quite "European," insinuating not quite civilized.

Counterarguments follow these lines:

1. On a continent that has witnessed such atrocities as Europe has throughout its history, Yugoslavs are neither more nor less civilized than other Europeans.
2. Yugoslavia has at least four recent decades of nonviolence—and Bosnia and Herzegovina in particular was the epitome of multicultural tolerance, lending the lie to its alleged barbaric underpinnings. Instead, the current conflict in Yugoslavia is the result of the cynical manipulation of historical and religious symbols and of misinformation by politicians attempting to retain power during the transition from communism rather than merely the reassertion of the natural Balkan persona.

The fact that these arguments and counterarguments seem to dominate both academic and lay discussions of the Yugoslav crisis suggests that the ethnonationalistic view of international affairs still has utility. Furthermore, the relevance of ethnonationalism becomes even more obvious when one recalls that public policy, including foreign policy, is fabricated in response to decisionmakers' perceptions of the inhabitants of the area. We are thus reminded by the stubborn continuation of this current Balkan war that ethnonationalism continues to be salient and that ethnonationalistic wars are particularly brutal and resistant to easy solution.

NOTES

1. Edward Luttwak, "If Bosnians Were Dolphins. . . ," *Commentary* 96 (October 1993), p. 27.
2. *Webster's Third New International Dictionary* provided a more detailed definition, noting that pluralism is "a state or condition of society in which members of diverse ethnic, racial, religious, or social groups maintain an autonomous participation in and development of their traditional culture or special interest within the confines of a common civilization" (Springfield, Mass.: Merriam, 1976), p. 1745. For a discussion of three propositions "on the relationship between social structure and political behavior in a democracy" identified by pluralist theory, see Arend Lijphart, *The Politics of Accommodation: Pluralism and Democracy in the Netherlands* (Berkeley: University of California Press, 1968), p. 1.
3. Jan Prins, "The World's Plural Societies: An Introduction," *Plural Societies* 1 (1970), p. 3.
4. Milton M. Gordon, "Toward a General Theory of Racial and Ethnic Group Relations," in Nathan Glazer and Daniel P. Moynihan, eds., *Ethnicity: Theory and Experience* (Cambridge: Harvard University Press, 1975), pp. 105–106. See Pierre L. van den Berghe, "Protection of Ethnic Minorities: A Critical Appraisal," in Robert G. Wirsing, ed., *Protection of Ethnic Minorities: Comparative Perspectives* (New York: Pergamon Press, 1981), pp. 343–351, for a description of six circumstances that singly or in combination might force

departure from the egalitarian ideal and induce some degree of group inequality in a plural society.

5. Cynthia H. Enloe, *Ethnic Conflict and Political Development* (Boston: Little, Brown, 1973), p. 22. Dijana Pleština's recent study of economic regionalism in Communist Yugoslavia treated the relationship between conflicts over economic resources and those over politicized ethnicity. *Regional Development in Communist Yugoslavia: Success, Failure, and Consequences* (Boulder: Westview Press, 1992).

6. Harold R. Isaacs, "Basic Group Identity: The Idols of the Tribe," in Glazer and Moynihan, eds., *Ethnicity*, p. 30.

7. Daniel Bell, "Ethnicity and Social Change," in Glazer and Moynihan, eds., *Ethnicity*, pp. 143–144.

8. John F. Stack Jr., "Ethnicity and Transnational Relations: An Introduction," in John F. Stack Jr., ed., *Ethnic Identities in a Transnational World* (Westport, Conn.: Greenwood Press, 1981), p. 5.

9. Glazer and Moynihan added that "the strategic efficacy of ethnicity as a basis for asserting claims against government has its counterpart in the seeming ease whereby government employs ethnic categories as a basis for distributing its rewards." "Introduction," in Glazer and Moynihan, eds., *Ethnicity*, p. 10.

10. Joseph Rothschild, *Ethnopolitics: A Conceptual Framework* (New York: Columbia University Press, 1981), p. 235.

11. Ibid., p. 61.

12. Ibid., p. 2.

13. Ibid., p. 29.

14. Cynthia H. Enloe, "Religion and Ethnicity," in Peter F. Sugar, ed., *Ethnic Diversity and Conflict in Eastern Europe* (Santa Barbara: ABC-Clio, 1980), p. 361. However, Enloe added the caveat that "when assessing what religion adds to ethnic identification and interethnic relations, it is essential to note that there are critical differences among religions which bear directly on how ethnicity is expressed and maintained collectively. It is not simply a matter of 'religion' being a part of the boundary setting package but *which* religion. To add another complexity the boundaries may often be affected by a *sect* of a major religion." "Religion and Ethnicity," p. 353 (emphasis in original).

15. Paul R. Brass, "Ethnic Groups and Nationalities," in Peter F. Sugar, ed., *Ethnic Diversity and Conflict in Eastern Europe*, p. 12.

16. Andrew Bell-Fialkoff, "A Brief History of Ethnic Cleansing," *Foreign Affairs* 72 (Summer 1993), p. 112.

17. Enloe, *Ethnic Conflict and Political Development*, pp. 28–29.

18. Van den Berghe, "Protection of Ethnic Minorities," p. 347.

19. Ibid.

20. Gidon Gottlieb claimed the Wilsonian solution to self-determination based on territory is outmoded. He suggested that nations without territory should be granted nonterritorial status that would give them standing within the international community, which nonterritorial peoples currently do not possess. "Nations Without States," *Foreign Affairs* 73 (May–June 1994), pp. 100–112.

21. Karl Renner, *Das nationale Problem* (Leipzig: 1902), p. 35, as quoted in Joseph Stalin, *Marxism and the National Question: Selected Writings and Speeches* (New York: International, 1942), p. 33.

22. The policy of slavery ranges from "covert state support for 'spontaneous' and spo-

radic pogroms . . . to widespread genocidal massacres aided and abetted by the state, such as through massive deportations and forced marches . . . to systematic methodical extermination of an entire ethnic group as a matter of official state policy." Van den Berghe, "Protection of Ethnic Minorities," p. 351.

23. Ibid.

24. Ibid., p. 349.

25. Ibid., pp. 349–350.

26. Ibid., p. 349.

27. Ibid (emphasis in original).

28. I am grateful to Jill Irvine for sharing with me her views on the strengths and weaknesses of consociation as a policy choice.

29. Brass, "Ethnic Groups and Nationalities," p. 47.

30. Arend Lijphart, "Consociation and Federation: Conceptual and Empirical Links," *Canadian Journal of Political Science* 12 (September 1979), p. 500. See also Lijphart's "Non-Majoritarian Democracy: A Comparison of Federal and Consociational Theories," *Publius* 15 (Spring 1985), pp. 3–15. Others, however, insist on the divergence of consociation from federalism when they define federalism largely in territorial or geographic terms. See the discussion by Daniel J. Elazar, "Federalism," in David L. Sills, ed., *International Encyclopedia of the Social Sciences*, Vol. 5 (New York: Macmillan, 1968), p. 357. Elazar also differentiated the two when he characterized federalism as relating to the form of a polity, whereas consociation treats the character of a regime. "Federalism and Consociational Regimes," *Publius* 15 (Spring 1985), p. 29.

31. For an exhaustive treatment of the subject of federalism, see Ivo D. Duchacek, *Comparative Federalism: The Territorial Dimension of Politics* (New York: Holt, Rinehart and Winston, 1970). On the efficacy of federalism for the autonomous areas in Yugoslavia during the Communist period, see Francine Friedman, "Kosovo and Vojvodina: One Yugoslav Solution to Autonomy in a Multiethnic State," in Daniel J. Elazar, ed., *Governing Peoples and Territories* (Philadelphia: Institute for the Study of Human Issues, 1982), pp. 59–88.

32. William H. Riker, "Federalism," in Fred I. Greenstein and Nelson Polsby, eds., *Handbook of Political Science*, Vol. 5: *Governmental Institutions and Processes* (Reading, Mass.: Addison-Wesley, 1975), p. 101.

33. Najdan Pašić, "Federalism in Yugoslavia's Contemporary Development Period: Between or Beyond Federalism and Confederalism," *Florida State University Proceedings and Reports* 18–19 (1984–1985), p. 3.

34. Brass, "Ethnic Groups and Nationalities," p. 48.

35. Enloe, *Ethnic Conflict and Political Development*, p. 92.

36. Ibid., p. 93.

37. Walker Connor, "Self-Determination: The New Phase," *World Politics* 20 (October 1967), pp. 44–45.

38. Ibid.

39. Slaven L. Letica, "Jeza," *Danas* (4 December 1990), p. 15.

40. Milton J. Esman, "The Management of Communal Conflict," *Public Policy* 21 (Winter 1973), p. 49.

41. Cited in Željko Vuković, "Kompromisi u dva poluvremena," *Borba* (9 June 1990), p. 5.

42. See, for example, Pedro Ramet, *Nationalism and Federalism in Yugoslavia, 1963–1983* (Bloomington: Indiana University Press, 1984), p. 144.

43. Cited in M. Mujagić, "Da, ja sam fundamentalist," *Danas* (9 Jan. 1990), p. 15.

44. Christopher Hitchens uncovered a few influential Serbs (and Croats) who rejected the Milošević and Tudjman visions of Yugoslav division, such as Mirjana Miocinović, widow of Serbian novelist Danilo Kiš, and Croat academician Rudi Supek, among others. "Why Bosnia Matters," in Rabia Ali and Lawrence Lifschultz, eds., *Why Bosnia? Writings on the Balkan War* (Stony Creek, Conn.: Pamphleteer's Press, 1993), pp. 10–11. *Yugofax* reported on 14 September 1991 that a peace movement had formed in Serbia composed of Citizens for Peace Actions, the Centre for Anti-War Activities, the Helsinki Citizens Assembly for Yugoslavia, Physicians for Prevention of War, soldiers' mothers, Greens, the Women's Lobby, the Feminist Party, and others. Little evidence of their movement has been seen since then.

45. Nicholas J. Miller, "Serbia Chooses Aggression," *Orbis* 38 (Winter 1994), p. 63.

46. Milovan Djilas and G. R. Urban, "The End of the Bolshevik Utopia," *World Today* 47 (October 1991), p. 177. See Robert M. Hayden, "Constitutional Nationalism in the Former Yugoslav Republics," *Slavic Review* 51 (Winter 1992), pp. 654–673, for a definition of the collective and exclusive democracy pursued by Serbs.

47. Patrick Moore, "Where Is Yugoslavia Headed?" *Report on Eastern Europe* 2 (6 September 1991), p. 33.

48. Muhammed Filipović characterized the Serb position as follows: "Victors in warfare and losers in peacetime, the Serbs, as an object of the general hatred of the others, seek the causes of their problems in the existence of permanent public and hidden enemies of Serbism (the Comintern, the Vatican, the Croats, the Slovenes, the Muslims, the Albanians, Islam, etc.)." Cited in Mujagić, "Da, ja sam fundamentalist," p. 15.

49. In a press interview, Crown Prince Alexander Karadjordjević speculated that a constitutional monarchy would avoid a Serb civil war and perhaps begin the admittedly long and tortuous healing process necessary to enable the South Slavs to live peacefully in proximity to each other. See his interview in *Die Presse* (Vienna), 1 March 1990. Alexander expressed his willingness to serve in a radio interview on 25 September 1990. See *Report on Eastern Europe*, Weekly Record of Events 1 (5 October 1990), p. 52.

50. In an interesting note about Drašković, Milovan Djilas stated in 1991 that Drašković was, in his opinion, worse than Milošević, because "Drašković would generate even more intolerance than Milošević is doing. . . . Drašković stands for the Četnik tradition, which is discredited." Djilas and Urban, "The End of the Bolshevik Utopia," p. 175.

51. Violent Serb versus Serb clashes were also reported in March 1991 when Serb demonstrators in Belgrade protested Milošević's policies. See *Report on Eastern Europe*, Weekly Record of Events 2 (22 March 1991), p. 46. More recently, Sarajevo Radio Bosnia-Herzegovina claimed there was "inter-Chetnik fighting near Brško on 27 January 1994." Cited in FBIS-EEU-018 (27 January 1994), p. 38.

52. "To Save Serbia, Stop the War: Interview with Vuk Drašković," *East European Reporter* (January–February 1992), p. 15.

53. For an analysis of why Milošević would profit by distancing himself from Karadžić, see *Balkan WarReport*, no. 28 (September 1994), pp. 21–22. See also the same issue, p. 3.

54. Robert Guskind, "Ethnic Time Bombs," *National Journal* 24 (18 January 1992), p. 158.

55. The YPA has felt its prerogatives increasingly threatened since at least 1990. See, for example, Aleksandar Ćirić, "Hleb—Sudbina vojske," *NIN* (27 July 1990), pp. 24–25.

56. Vojvodina resident Nenad Canak charged this in *Balkan WarReport*, no. 14 (September 1992), p. 7.

57. "To Save Serbia, Stop the War," p. 14.

58. "Muhićev pogled u budučnost," *NIN* (28 September 1990), p. 34.

59. Cited in Ed Vulliamy, *Seasons in Hell: Understanding Bosnia's War* (New York: St. Martin's Press, 1994), pp. 68–69 (emphasis in original).

60. Patrick Moore suggested that Tudjman may have instigated the Croat-Muslim conflict to increase his political stock with the so-called Herzegovinian lobby, rather than pursuing the traditional Muslim-Croat alliance against Serbia to the benefit of Croats in Croatia and central Bosnia. "Changes in the Croatian Political Landscape," *RFE/RL Research Report* 3 (3 June 1994), p. 11.

61. Documented reports of ethnic cleansing are numerous. See, for example, Amnesty International, *Genocide: Ethnic Cleansing in Northwestern Bosnia* (Zagreb: Croatian Information Center, 1993).

62. In an interview with the Belgrade daily *Borba*, 4–5 April 1992, *Reis-ul-ulema* Jakub Selimoski noted that "Europe has 20 million adherents of the Islamic religion, i.e., indigenous Muslims." Almost one-fifth, or approximately 4.5 million Muslims, live in the lands of the former Yugoslavia. Cited in Darko Tanašković, "Muslims and muslims in Former Yugoslavia, Part 1," *East European Reporter* 5 (May–June 1992), p. 13. They live mostly in Bosnia and Herzegovina, Macedonia, and Kosovo. Yet the existence of these Muslims does not automatically suggest a united front of Muslims against Christians, as witness the fissure between the Izetbegović government forces and the breakaway units of Velika Kladuša near Bihać who were loyal to Fikret Abdić. Abdić had previously been imprisoned for his participation in the 1987 Agrokomerc scandal, which involved collusion between Bosnian republic officials and Agrokomerc officials in the issuance of unbacked promissory notes. However, he emerged from the scandal a local hero, which during the current upheavals in Bosnia and Herzegovina allowed him to create his own autonomous area dedicated to pursuing commercial relations with surrounding areas and to ignore Izetbegović's political sovereignty. See Milan Andrejevich, "Bosnia-Herzegovina: Yugoslavia's Linchpin," *Report on East Europe* 1 (1990), p. 21.

63. *Dnevnik* reported that the Serbian Orthodox Church, in fact, supported Serbia's ultranationalist forces in their bid to achieve a greater Serbia. Maroje Mihovilović, "Serbia: The Church Has Turned Its Back," *Dnevnik*, 24 January 1992, p. 11, cited in JPRS-EER-92-017 (12 February 1992), p. 29; I. Mlivončić, "Blessing of Violence," *Slobodna Dalmacija*, 6 May 1992, p. 9, cited in JPRS-EER-92-060 (15 May 1992), p. 46. See also *Reis-ul-ulema* Selimoski's plea to Serb Orthodox patriarch Pavle for intervention in "Why Is There Not an Outcry Against Genocide?" *Flaka e Vellazerimit*, 3 July 1992, p. 6, cited in JPRS-EER-92-117 (27 August 1992), p. 42.

64. Ali and Lifschultz, "In Plain View," in Ali and Lifschultz, eds., *Why Bosnia*, p. xliv.

65. David Rieff noted that Islamists began to make headway in undercutting multiculturalism in Bosnia and Herzegovina and in the SDA only in late 1994, "when most Bosnians had completely lost hope in any just outcome." *Slaughterhouse: Bosnia and the Failure of the West* (New York: Simon and Schuster, 1995), p. 142. Furthermore, predicted Zdravko Grebo, a University of Sarajevo law professor, Serb and Croat nationalism aided by European appeasement policies could conceivably become the midwives of the very Muslim radicalism in Europe they purported to be trying to prevent. *Balkan WarReport*, no. 24 (February 1994), p. 20.

66. Paul Shoup, "The Bosnian Crisis of 1992," in Sabrina Petra Ramet and Ljubiša S. Adamović, eds., *Beyond Yugoslavia: Politics, Economics, and Culture in a Shattered Community* (Boulder: Westview Press, 1995), pp. 177–178.

67. *New York Times,* 11 July 1994, A1. A fissure between the Bosnian Serb military leadership and Radovan Karadžić was later reported, with General Ratko Mladić the apparent winner. *U.S. News and World Report,* 17 April 1995, p. 23.

68. See, for example, *ex-Yugofax* (29 June 1992), p. 7.

69. The Western press has been accused of selective, anti-Serb reporting of the Bosnian conflict—of underplaying Bosnian atrocities against Serbs and falling for Muslim-created photo opportunities, which have increased pressure for Western military and diplomatic intervention on the side of the Bosnian government. See, for example, Peter Brock, "Dateline Yugoslavia: The Partisan Press," *Foreign Policy* 93 (Winter 1993–1994), pp. 152–171, and J. P. Maher's letter to the editor, *Boston Globe,* 6 December 1994.

70. Susan Miller, "Bleak Letters from Sarajevo," *Newsweek* (13 December 1993), p. 73. One source estimated that 12 percent of Yugoslavia's youth, nearly 1 million children, were products of nationally mixed marriages. *Yugofax* (28 September 1991), p. 4.

71. Moore, "Changes in the Croatian Political Landscape," p. 11.

72. Robert M. Hayden, "The Constitution of the Federation of Bosnia and Herzegovina: An Imaginary Constitution for an Illusory 'Federation,'" *Balkan Forum* 2 (1994), pp. 77–78. Hayden proceeded to illustrate the weaknesses and inconsistencies of this new structure and to characterize its result as the partition of the Croat and Muslim portions of Bosnia and Herzegovina.

73. For example, Miroslav Toholj, a leader of the Bosnian SDS, expressed dismay at the declaration of independence of the multinational Bosnian state, observing that "the Serb name has finally been taken away from the Serbs; they have been turned into citizens, which Serbs won't accept." *Vreme,* 9 March 1992, cited in Mark Thompson, *Forging War: The Media in Serbia, Croatia and Bosnia-Hercegovina* (Great Britain: Article 19, International Centre Against Censorship, 1994), p. 52 (note).

74. Robert M. Hayden, "The Partition of Bosnia and Herzegovina, 1990–1993," *RFE/RL Research Report* 2 (1993), p. 3 (note).

75. Donia and Fine, *Bosnia and Hercegovina,* p. 28. Tihomir Loza described the Bosnian Serb orientation as "rural Nazism." *Yugofax* (7 May 1992), p. 3.

76. Shoup, "The Bosnian Crisis of 1992," p. 180. Colin Heywood was somewhat more blunt when he wrote that "it is rare, at least in the history of the last half century, for a people and a culture based on a continent ostensibly at peace to be destroyed in the full view of the world and with the apparent complicity of the unelected functionaries who purport to represent the people of the world in its tragically misnamed global forum." "Bosnia Under Ottoman Rule, 1463–1800," in Mark Pinson, ed., *The Muslims of Bosnia-Herzegovina: Their Historic Development from the Middle Ages to the Dissolution of Yugoslavia* (Cambridge: Harvard University Press, 1994), p. 22.

77. Heywood, "Bosnia Under Ottoman Rule," p. 22. For more on the variable Croat-Muslim relationship, see Patrick Moore, "Endgame in Bosnia and Herzegovina?" *RFE/RL Research Report* 2 (13 August 1993), pp. 17–23.

78. Ivo Andrić, *The Bridge on the Drina* (New York: Macmillan, 1959).

79. Extracts printed in *Yugofax* (9 December 1991), p. 8.

80. Andrić, *The Bridge on the Drina,* p. 283.

Selected Bibliography

Aldiss, Brian W. 1966. *Cities and Stones: A Traveller's Jugoslavia.* London: Faber and Faber.

Alexander, Stella. 1979. *Church and State in Yugoslavia Since 1945.* Cambridge: Cambridge University Press.

Ali, Rabia, and Lawrence Lifschultz. 1993. "In Plain View," in Rabia Ali and Lawrence Lifschultz, eds., *Why Bosnia? Writings on the Balkan War.* Stony Creek, Conn.: Pamphleteer's Press.

Allcock, John B. 1991. "Yugoslavia: Bosnia and Hercegovina," in Bogdan Szajkowski, ed., *New Political Parties of Eastern Europe and the Soviet Union.* Harlow: Longman.

Allworth, Edward. 1971. "Restating the Soviet Nationality Question," in Edward Allworth, ed., *Soviet Nationality Problems.* New York: Columbia University Press.

Amnesty International. 1993. *Genocide: Ethnic Cleansing in Northwestern Bosnia.* Zagreb: Croatian Information Center.

Andrejevich, Milan. 1990. "Bosnia-Herzegovina: Yugoslavia's Linchpin." *Report on East Europe* 1:20–26.

———. 1990. "Crisis in Croatia and Slovenia: Proposal for a Confederal Yugoslavia." *Report on Eastern Europe* 1:28–33.

———. 1990. "Croatia Between Stability and Civil War." *Report on Eastern Europe* 1:12–15.

———. 1991. "The Future of Bosnia and Herzegovina: A Sovereign Republic or Cantonization?" *Report on Eastern Europe* 2:28–34.

———. 1990. "Military Attempts to File Charges Against Slovenian Presidential Candidate." *Report on Eastern Europe* 1:38–41.

———. 1990. "The Military's Role in the Current Constitutional Crisis." *Report on Eastern Europe* 1:23–27.

———. 1991. "Moslem Leader Elected President of Bosnia and Hercegovina." *Report on Eastern Europe* 2:30–32.

———. 1990. "Nationalist Movements in Yugoslavia." *Report on Eastern Europe* 1:27–31.

———. 1993. "The Presidency of Bosnia and Herzegovina: A Profile." *RFE/RL Research Report* 2:21–24.

———. 1991. "Republican Leaders Reach Compromise Accord on Country's Future." *Report on Eastern Europe* 2:33–37.

———. 1991. "Retreating from the Brink of Collapse." *Report on Eastern Europe* 2:25–31.

———. 1990. "Yugoslavia's Lingering Crisis." *Report on Eastern Europe* 1:33–36.

Andrić, Ivo. 1959. *The Bridge on the Drina.* New York: Macmillan.

"Anti-Moslem Feelings Denied." 1984. *Yugoslavia: Situation Report, Radio Free Europe Research* (Yugoslavia) 1:5–7.

Arnakis, George G. 1969. *The Near East in Modern Times.* Vol. 1: *The Ottoman Empire and the Balkan States to 1900.* Austin: Pemberton Press.

———. 1963. "The Role of Religion in the Development of Balkan Nationalism," in Charles Jelavich and Barbara Jelavich, eds., *The Balkans in Transition: Essays on the*

Development of Balkan Life and Politics Since the Eighteenth Century. Berkeley: University of California Press.

Avakumović, Ivan. 1964. *History of the Communist Party of Yugoslavia.* Aberdeen: Aberdeen University Press.

Banac, Ivo. 1983. "The Communist Party of Yugoslavia During the Period of Legality, 1919–1921," in Ivo Banac, ed., *The Effects of World War I: The Class War After the Great War: The Rise of Communist Parties in East Central Europe, 1918–1921.* Boulder: Social Sciences Monographs.

———. 1984. *The National Question in Yugoslavia: Origins, History, Politics.* Ithaca: Cornell University Press.

"Baron de Kállay's Achievement." 1895. *Spectator* 75:428–429.

Bartlett, C.N.O. 1980. *The Turkish Minority in Yugoslavia.* Bradford, West Yorkshire: Postgraduate School of Yugoslav Studies, University of Bradford.

Bartolović, Dragan. 1976. "Political Tendencies in the Church," in Erich Weingartner, ed., *Church Within Socialism: Church and State in East European Socialist Republics.* Rome: IDOC International.

Batusić, Zoran. 1992. "E Pluribus Unum?" *East European Reporter* 5:22–24.

Beals, Ralph C. 1977. "The Rise and Decline of National Identity." *Canadian Review of Studies in Nationalism* 4:147–166.

Begić, Dana. 1965. "Akcije muslimanskih gradžanskih političara poslije skupštinskih izbora 1935. godine." *Godišnjak Društva istoričara Bosne i Hercegovine* 16:173–189.

Belin, Ivo. 1923. "Malo izborne statistike." *Nova Evropa* 7:329–336.

Bell, Daniel. 1975. "Ethnicity and Social Change," in Nathan Glazer and Daniel P. Moynihan, eds., *Ethnicity: Theory and Experience.* Cambridge: Harvard University Press.

Bell, Wendell, and Walter E. Freeman, eds. 1974. *Ethnicity and Nation-Building: Comparative, International, and Historical Perspectives.* Beverly Hills: Sage Publications.

Bell-Fialkoff, Andrew. 1993. "A Brief History of Ethnic Cleansing." *Foreign Affairs* 72:110–121.

Beloff, Nora. 1985. *Tito's Flawed Legacy: Yugoslavia and the West Since 1939.* Boulder: Westview Press.

Bennigsen, Alexandre. 1980. "Soviet Muslims and the World of Islam." *Problems of Communism* 29:38–51.

Birnbaum, Henrik. 1987. "The Ethno-Linguistic Mosaic of Bosnia and Hercegovina." *Die Welt der Slaven* 32:1–24.

Borowiec, Andrew. 1977. *Yugoslavia After Tito.* New York: Praeger.

Brass, Paul R. 1980. "Ethnic Groups and Nationalities," in Peter F. Sugar, ed., *Ethnic Diversity and Conflict in Eastern Europe.* Santa Barbara: ABC-Clio.

———. 1991. *Ethnicity and Nationalism: Theory and Comparison.* London: Sage.

Brock, Peter. 1993–1994. "Dateline Yugoslavia: The Partisan Press." *Foreign Policy* 93:152–171.

Brown, J. F. 1991. "The Resurgence of Nationalism." *Report on Eastern Europe* 2:35–37.

Bukowski, James. 1975. "Yugoslavism and the Croatian National Party in 1867." *Canadian Review of Studies in Nationalism* 3:70–88.

Burg, Steven L. 1983. "The Political Integration of Yugoslavia's Muslims: Determinants of Success and Failure." Pittsburgh: Carl Beck Papers in Russian and East European Studies, University of Pittsburgh.

———. 1993. "Why Yugoslavia Fell Apart." *Current History* 92:357–363.

Byrnes, Robert F., ed. 1976. *Communal Families in the Balkans: The Zadruga.* Notre Dame: University of Notre Dame Press.

Carter, April. 1984. "The Republics and the Party." *Government and Opposition* 19:385–390.

Ceranić, Ivan. 1971. "Religious Communities in Yugoslavia," in Zlatko Frid, ed., *Religions in Yugoslavia: Historical Survey, Legal Status, Church in Socialism, Ecumenism, Dialogue Between Marxists and Christians, etc.* Zagreb: Binoza.

Ćerić, Salim. 1968. *Muslimani srpskohrvatskog jezika.* Sarajevo: Svjetlost.

The Četniks: A Survey of Četnik Activity in Yugoslavia, April 1941–July 1944. 1944. G-2 (PB), Λ.F.H.Q.

Charanis, Peter. 1976. "The Slavs, Byzantium, and the Historical Significance of the First Bulgarian Kingdom." *Balkan Studies* 17:8–12.

Cicak, Fedor Ivan. 1965. "The Communist Party of Yugoslavia Between 1919–1934: An Analysis of Its Formative Process." Ph.D. dissertation, Indiana University.

Ćimić, Esad. 1970. *Socijalističko društvo i religija.* Sarajevo: Svjetlost.

Ćirković, Sima. 1964. *Istorija srednjovekovne bosanske džava.* Belgrade: Srpska književna zadruga.

Clissold, Stephen, ed. 1975. *Yugoslavia and the Soviet Union 1939–1973: A Documentary Survey.* London: Oxford University Press.

Cohen, Lenard J. 1993. *Broken Bonds: The Disintegration of Yugoslavia.* Boulder: Westview Press.

———. 1983. "Regional Elites in Socialist Yugoslavia: Changing Patterns of Recruitment and Composition," in T. H. Rigby and Bohdan Harasymiw, eds., *Leadership Selection and Patron-Client Relations in the USSR and Yugoslavia.* London: Allen and Unwin.

Connor, Walker. 1972. "Nation-Building or Nation-Destroying?" *World Politics* 24: 319–355.

———. 1973. "The Politics of Ethnonationalism." *Journal of International Affairs* 27:1–21.

———. 1967. "Self-Determination: The New Phase." *World Politics* 20:30–53.

Crnobrnja, Mihailo. 1994. *The Yugoslav Drama.* Montreal: McGill-Queen's University Press.

Cviic, K. F. 1980. "Yugoslavia's Moslem Problem." *World Today* 36:108–112.

De Asboth, Janos. 1890. *An Official Tour Through Bosnia and Herzegovina with an Account of the History, Antiquities, Agrarian Conditions, Religion, Ethnology, Folk Lore, and Social Life of the People.* London: Swan Sonnenschein.

Dedijer, Vladimir. 1966. *The Road to Sarajevo.* New York: Simon and Schuster.

Dedijer, Vladimir, and Antun Miletić, eds. 1990. *Genocid nad muslimanima, 1941–1945: Zbornik dokumenata i svjedočenja.* Sarajevo: Svjetlost.

Denitch, Bogdan. 1976. *The Legitimation of a Revolution: The Yugoslav Case.* New Haven: Yale University Press.

———. 1975. "Religion and Social Change in Yugoslavia," in Bohdan R. Bociurkiw and John W. Strong, eds., *Religion and Atheism in the U.S.S.R. and Eastern Europe.* Toronto: University of Toronto Press.

Deroc, M. 1985. "The Former Yugoslav Army." *East European Quarterly* 19:363–374.

Djilas, Aleksa. 1984. "Communists and Yugoslavia." *Survey* 28:25–38.

———. 1991. *The Contested Country: Yugoslav Unity and Communist Revolution, 1919–1953.* Cambridge: Harvard University Press.

Djilas, Milovan, and G. R. Urban. 1991. "The End of the Bolshevik Utopia." *World Today* 47:173–180.

Djordjević, Dimitrije. 1986. "Three Yugoslavias—A Case of Survival." *East European Quarterly* 19:385–393.

Djordjević, Jovan. 1966. "La République Socialiste," in *Le Fédéralisme Yougoslave*. Paris: Librairie Dalloz.

Doder, Dusko. 1993. "Yugoslavia: New War, Old Hatreds." *Foreign Policy* 91:3–23.

Donia, Robert J. 1978. "The Battle for Bosnia: Habsburg Military Strategy in 1878." Paper presented at the conference Otpor austrougarskoj okupaciji 1878. godine u Bosni i Hercegovini, Sarajevo, October.

———. 1979. "Imperial Occupation and Its Consequences: The Army and Politics in Bosnia and Hercegovina, 1878–1914." Unpublished paper, Ohio State University, Lima.

———. 1981. *Islam Under the Double Eagle: The Muslims of Bosnia and Hercegovina, 1878–1914*. Boulder: East European Monographs.

———. "The Urban Sources of Political Success: The Case of the Bosnian Moslem Nobility, 1890–1910." Ann Arbor: University of Michigan.

Donia, Robert J., and John V.A. Fine Jr. 1994. *Bosnia and Hercegovina: A Tradition Betrayed*. New York: Columbia University Press.

"Dr. Izetbegović's Address at the 1983 Sarajevo Trial." 1985. *South Slav Journal* 8:94–97.

Dragnich, Alex N. 1993. "Case Study: Bosnia-Herzegovina." Paper presented at the American Bar Association conference Anarchy in the Third World, 3–4 June.

———. 1980. "The Serbian Government, the Army, and the Unification of Yugoslavs," in Dimitrije Djordjević, ed., *The Creation of Yugoslavia 1914–1918*. Santa Barbara: Clio Books.

———. 1992. *Serbs and Croats*. New York: Harcourt Brace Jovanovich.

Dragosavac, Dušan. 1983. "Present-Day National Problems." *Socialist Thought and Practice* 23:16–34.

Drakulić, Slavenka. 1993. *The Balkan Express: Fragments from the Other Side of War*. New York: Norton.

Drew, S. Nelson. 1995. "NATO from Berlin to Bosnia: Trans-Atlantic Security in Transition." McNair Paper 35. Washington, D.C.: National Defense University.

Duchacek, Ivo D. 1970. *Comparative Federalism: The Territorial Dimension of Politics*. New York: Holt, Rinehart and Winston.

Duke, Kenneth. 1981. "German Foreign Policy in S. and S.E. Europe, 1942–1945." *South Slav Journal* 4:4–18.

Dvornik, Francis. 1964. *The Slavs Between East and West*. Milwaukee: Marquette University, Slavic Institute.

Eden, Anthony. 1965. *The Memoirs of Anthony Eden, Earl of Avon: The Reckoning*. Boston: Houghton Mifflin.

Edwards, Lovett F. 1967. *Introducing Yugoslavia*. London: Methuen.

Ekmečić, Milorad. 1980. "Serbian War Aims," in Dimitrije Djordjević, ed., *The Creation of Yugoslavia 1914–1918*. Santa Barbara: Clio Books.

Elazar, Daniel J. 1985. "Federalism and Consociational Regimes." *Publius* 15:17–34.

Enloe, Cynthia H. 1973. *Ethnic Conflict and Political Development*. Boston: Little, Brown.

———. 1980. "Religion and Ethnicity," in Peter F. Sugar, ed., *Ethnic Diversity and Conflict in Eastern Europe*. Santa Barbara: ABC-Clio.

Esman, Milton J. 1973. "The Management of Communal Conflict." *Public Policy* 21:49–78.

Evans, Arthur J. 1878. "The Austrians in Bosnia." *Macmillan's Magazine* 38:495–504.

———. 1877. *Through Bosnia and the Herzegovina on Foot During the Insurrection, August and September 1875, with an Historical Review of Bosnia*. London: Longmans, Green.

Fawcett, Millicent Garrett. 1877. *The Martyrs of Misrule,* in Eastern Question Association, *Papers on the Eastern Question,* no. 11. London: Cassell Petter and Galpin.

Filipović, Milenko S. 1962. "Forms and Functions of Ritual Kinship Among South Slavs." *International Congress of Anthropological and Ethnological Sciences* (6th). Paris: Musee de l'homme.

Filipović, Nedim. 1985. "Forming of Moslem Ethnicon in Bosnia and Herzegovina," in Ranko Petković, ed., *Moslems in Yugoslavia.* Belgrade: Review of International Affairs.

Fine, John V.A., Jr. 1975. *The Bosnian Church, A New Interpretation: A Study of the Bosnian Church and Its Place in State and Society from the 13th to the 15th Centuries.* Boulder: East European Quarterly.

———. 1983. *The Early Medieval Balkans: A Critical Survey from the Sixth to the Late Twelfth Century.* Ann Arbor: University of Michigan Press.

———. 1987. *The Late Medieval Balkans: A Critical Survey from the Late Twelfth Century to the Ottoman Conquest.* Ann Arbor: University of Michigan Press.

———. 1994. "The Medieval and Ottoman Roots of Modern Bosnian Society," in Mark Pinson, ed., *The Muslims of Bosnia-Herzegovina: Their Historic Development from the Middle Ages to the Destruction of Yugoslavia.* Cambridge: Harvard University Press.

———. 1966. "Review of Sima Ćirković, *Istorija srednjovekovne bosanske države,* Belgrade, 1964." *Speculum* 41:527–528.

———. 1969. "Was the Bosnian Banate Subjected to Hungary in the Second Half of the Thirteenth Century?" *East European Quarterly* 3:167–177.

Flere, Sergej. 1991. "Denominational Affiliation in Yugoslavia 1931–1987." *East European Quarterly* 25:145–165.

Foot, M.R.D. 1976. *Resistance: An Analysis of European Resistance to Nazism 1940–1945.* London: Eyre Methuen.

Forbes, N., A. J. Toynbee, D. Mitrany, and D. G. Hogarth. 1915. *The Balkans: A History of Bulgaria, Serbia, Greece, Rumania, Turkey.* Oxford: Clarendon Press.

Franzius, Enno. 1967. *History of the Byzantine Empire: Mother of Nations.* New York: Funk and Wagnalls.

Friedman, Francine. 1996. "The Bosnian Muslims: The Making of a New Nation in the Former Yugoslavia," in Jill Irvine, Carol Tilly, and Melissa Bokovoy, eds., *From Partisans to Politics.* New York: St. Martin's Press.

———. 1994. "Ethnic Conflict in Yugoslavia: The Rise of Tribalism." Paper presented at the annual meeting of the Midwest Political Science Association, Chicago, Illinois, 16 April.

———. 1982. "Kosovo and Vojvodina: One Yugoslav Solution to Autonomy in a Multiethnic State," in Daniel J. Elazar, ed., *Governing Peoples and Territories.* Philadelphia: Institute for the Study of Human Issues.

———. 1993. "To Fight or Not to Fight: The Decision to Settle the Croat-Serb Conflict." Paper presented at the annual meeting of the International Studies Association, Acapulco, Mexico, March.

Furlan, Boris. 1943. "The Nationality Problem in the Balkans." Lecture delivered at the Hoover Institution, Stanford, California, 20 February.

Gavrilović, Michael. 1922. "The Early Diplomatic Relations of Great Britain and Serbia." *Slavonic Review* 1:86–109.

Georgiev, Vladimir I. 1972. "The Earliest Ethnological Situation of the Balkan Peninsula as

Evidenced by Linguistic and Onomastic Data," in Henrik Birnbaum and Speros Vryonis Jr., eds., *Aspects of the Balkans: Continuity and Change.* The Hague: Mouton.

Gilfond, Henry. 1975. *The Black Hand at Sarajevo.* Indianapolis: Bobbs-Merrill.

Gimbutas, Marija. 1972. "The Neolithic Cultures of the Balkan Peninsula," in Henrik Birnbaum and Speros Vryonis Jr., eds., *Aspects of the Balkans: Continuity and Change.* The Hague: Mouton.

Glazer, Nathan, and Daniel P. Moynihan. 1975. "Introduction," in Nathan Glazer and Daniel P. Moynihan, eds., *Ethnicity: Theory and Experience.* Cambridge: Harvard University Press.

———. 1974. "Why Ethnicity?" *Commentary* 58:33–39.

Glen, Alexander 1975. *Footholds Against a Whirlwind.* London: Hutchinson.

Glenny, Misha. 1992. *The Fall of Yugoslavia: The Third Balkan War.* New York: Penguin Books.

Gordon, Milton M. 1975. "Toward a General Theory of Racial and Ethnic Group Relations," in Nathan Glazer and Daniel P. Moynihan, eds., *Ethnicity: Theory and Experience.* Cambridge: Harvard University Press.

Gottlieb, Gidon. 1994. "Nations Without States." *Foreign Affairs* 73:100–112.

Gow, James. 1988. "Legitimacy and the Military: Yugoslav Civil-Military Relations and Some Implications for Defence," in Marko Milivojević, John B. Allcock, and Pierre Maurer, eds., *Yugoslavia's Security Dilemmas: Armed Forces, National Defence and Foreign Policy.* Oxford: Berg.

Guldescu, Stanko. 1972. "Bosnia and Herzegovina in Medieval and Modern Times." *Balkania* 3:24–27.

Guskind, Robert. 1992. "Ethnic Time Bombs." *National Journal* 24:156–159.

Hadžijahić, Muhamed. 1974. *Od tradicije do identita: Geneza nacionalnog pitanja bosanskih muslimana.* Sarajevo: Svjetlost.

Hadžijahić, Muhamed, Mahmud Traljić, and Nijaz Šukrić. 1977. *Islam i muslimani u Bosni i Hercegovini.* Sarajevo: Svjetlost.

Hamilton-Hill, Donald. 1973. *SOE Assignment.* London: Kimber.

Harper, Indijana. 1992. "Unwanted, Unarmed and Under Attack." *East European Reporter* 5:21–23.

Hauptmann, Ferdo, ed. 1967. *Borba muslimana bosne and hercegovine za vjersku vakufsko-mearifsku autonomiju.* Sarajevo: Arhiv SRBiH.

Hayden, Robert M. 1994. "The Constitution of the Federation of Bosnia and Herzegovina: An Imaginary Constitution for an Illusory 'Federation.'" *Balkan Forum* 2:28–35.

———. 1992. "Constitutional Nationalism in the Former Yugoslav Republics." *Slavic Review* 51:654–673.

———. 1993. "The Partition of Bosnia and Herzegovina, 1990–1993." *RFE/RL Research Report* 2:1–14.

Headlam-Morley, Agnes. 1929. *The New Democratic Constitutions of Europe: A Comparative Study of Post-War European Constitutions with Special Reference to Germany, Czechoslovakia, Poland, Finland, the Kingdom of the Serbs, Croats and Slovenes and the Baltic States.* London: Oxford University Press.

Hehn, Paul. 1984. "Capitalism and the Revolutionary Factor in the Balkans and Crimean War Diplomacy." *East European Quarterly* 18:155–184.

Hershberg, Theodore. 1973. "Toward the Historical Study of Ethnicity." *Journal of Ethnic Studies* 1:1–21.

Heywood, Colin. 1994. "Bosnia Under Ottoman Rule, 1463–1800," in Mark Pinson, ed., *The Muslims of Bosnia-Herzegovina: Their Historic Development from the Middle Ages to the Dissolution of Yugoslavia*. Cambridge: Harvard University Press.

Hitchens, Christopher. 1993. "Why Bosnia Matters," in Rabia Ali and Lawrence Lifschultz, eds., *Why Bosnia? Writings on the Balkan War.* Stony Creek, Conn.: Pamphleteer's Press.

Hodgkinson, Harry. 1955. *The Adriatic Sea*. London: Cape.

Hoettl, Wilhelm. 1953. *The Secret Front: The Story of Nazi Political Espionage*. London: Weidenfeld and Nicolson.

Hoffman, George W., and Fred Warner Neal. 1962. *Yugoslavia and the New Communism*. New York: Twentieth Century Fund.

Hondius, Frits W. 1968. *The Yugoslav Community of Nations.* The Hague: Mouton.

Höpken, Wolfgang. 1985. "Party Monopoly and Political Change: The League of Communists Since Tito's Death," in Pedro Ramet, ed., *Yugoslavia in the 1980s*. Boulder: Westview Press.

Hoptner, Jacob B. 1962. *Yugoslavia in Crisis 1934–1941*. New York: Columbia University Press.

Ilić, Andrew. 1971. "The Truth About the Croatian Catholics and Croatian Moslems." *Balkania* 5:20–23.

Inalcik, Halil. 1972. "The Ottoman Decline and Its Effects Upon the *Reaya*," in Henrik Birnbaum and Speros Vryonis Jr., eds., *Aspects of the Balkans: Continuity and Change*. The Hague: Mouton.

Irwin, Zachary T. 1984. "The Islamic Revival and the Muslims of Bosnia-Hercegóvina." *East European Quarterly* 17:437–458.

Isaacs, Harold R. 1975. "Basic Group Identity: The Idols of the Tribe," in Nathan Glazer and Daniel P. Moynihan, eds., *Ethnicity: Theory and Experience*. Cambridge: Harvard University Press.

———. 1975. *Idols of the Tribe: Group Identity and Political Change*. New York: Harper and Row.

———. 1979. "Power and Identity: Tribalism and World Politics." *Headline Series* (Foreign Policy Association), no. 136.

"Islam in Yugoslavia." 1938. *Moslem World* 28:309–310.

Jancar, Barbara. 1981. "Women in the Yugoslav National Liberation Movement: An Overview." *Studies in Comparative Communism* 14:143–164.

Janković, Branimir M. 1988. *The Balkans in International Relations*. New York: St. Martin's Press.

Jelavich, Charles. 1953. "Revolt in Bosnia-Hercegovina." *Slavonic Review* 31:41–49.

Jelavich, Charles, and Barbara Jelavich. 1977. *The Establishment of the Balkan National States, 1804–1920*. Seattle: University of Washington Press.

Jelić-Butić, Fikreta. 1971. "Bosna i Hercegovina u koncepciji stvaranja Nezavisne Države Hrvatske." *Pregled* 12:663–670.

Job, Cvijeto. 1993. "Yugoslavia's Ethnic Furies." *Foreign Policy* 92:52–74.

Johnson, A. Ross. 1978. *The Role of the Military in Communist Yugoslavia*. Santa Monica, Calif.: Rand Corporation, no. 6070.

Jugoslavia: Basic Handbook. Part 1: *Pre-Invasion*. 1943. London.

Jugoslavia: Basic Handbook. Part 2: *Post-Invasion*. 1943. London.

Jukić, Ilija. 1970. "Tito's Legacy." *Survey* 77:93–108.

Kann, Robert A. 1950. *The Multinational Empire: Nationalism and National Reform in the Habsburg Monarchy 1848–1918*. Vol. 2: *Empire Reform*. New York: Columbia University Press.

Kaplan, Robert D. 1993. *Balkan Ghosts: A Journey Through History*. New York: St. Martin's Press.

Kardelj, Edvard. 1977. *Political and Military Strategy: Creative Role of Josip Broz Tito in the National Liberation Uprising and Socialist Revolution in Yugoslavia*. Belgrade: Socialist Thought and Practice.

Karlović, N. L. 1982. "Internal Colonialism in a Marxist Society: The Case of Croatia." *Ethnic and Racial Studies* 5:276–299.

Karpat, Kemal. 1973. *An Inquiry into the Social Foundations of Nationalism in the Ottoman State: From Social Estates to Classes, From Millets to Nations*. Princeton: Princeton University, Center of International Studies, Research Monograph no. 39.

Kemura, Ibrahim. 1969. "Bosna i muslimani u očima jednog posmatrača iz sredine XIX stoljeća." *Glasnik Vrhovnog islamskog starješinstva u socijalističkoj federativnoj republici jugoslaviji* 32:418–424.

Kerr, Donal A. 1992. "Religion, State and Ethnic Identity," in Donal A. Kerr, ed., *Religion, State and Ethnic Groups*. New York: New York University Press.

Kimball, Stanley. 1973. "The Austro-Slav Revival: A Study of Nineteenth-Century Literary Foundations." *Transactions of the American Philosophical Society*, no. 63.

King, Robert R. 1981. "Eastern Europe," in Robert G. Wirsing, ed., *Protection of Ethnic Minorities: Comparative Perspectives*. New York: Pergamon Press.

Klaić, Nada. 1989. *Srednjovjekovna Bosna: Politički položaj bosanskih vladara do tvrtkove krunidbe (1377 g.)*. Zagreb: Grafički zavod hrvatske.

Knežević, Anthony. 1989. *A Short History of the Croatian Nation*. Philadelphia: Croatian Catholic Union.

Knežević, Oton. 1942. "Bosna i Hercegovina od seobe naroda do XII. st.," in *Poviest hrvatskih zemalja Bosne i Hercegovine od najstarijeh vremena do godine 1463*. Sarajevo: Napredak.

Knežević, Radoje L., ed. 1956. *Knjiga o Draži*. Vol. 1. Windsor, Canada: Srpska narodna odbrana.

Kočović, Bogoljub. 1985. *Žrtve drugog svetskog rata u Jugoslaviji*. London: Biblioteka *Naše delo*.

Konjević, Mile. 1971. "O nekim pitanjima politike ustaša prema bosanskohercegovačkim muslimana 1941. godine." *Pregled* 12:671–682.

Konjhodzich, Alija. 1981. "Serbians of the Moslem Faith in Chetnik Ranks," in *Draža Mihailović Memorial Book*. Chicago: Organization of Serbian Chetniks "Ravna Gora."

Kortepeter, Carl Max. 1972. *Ottoman Imperialism During the Reformation: Europe and the Caucasus*. New York: New York University Press.

Kovacs, Frederic W.L. 1942. *The Untamed Balkans*. London: Hale.

Kowalewski, David. 1982. "The Religious-National Interlock: Faith and Ethnicity in the Soviet Union." *Canadian Review of Studies in Nationalism* 9:97–111.

Krimper, Ronald L. 1973. "The Diplomatic Prelude to the Destruction of Yugoslavia, January to April 1941." *East European Quarterly* 7:125–147.

Krizman, Bogdan. 1989. *Hrvatska u prvom svjetskom ratu: Hrvatsko-srpski politički odnosi*. Zagreb: Globus.

Kulišić, Spiro. 1953. "Razmatranja o porijeklu muslimana u bosni i hercegovini." *Glasnik Zemaljskog muzeja u sarajevu* 8:121–131.

Kuzmany, N. 1925. "Notes on the Moslems of Bosnia." *Moslem World* 15:177–181.

Lampe, John R., and Marvin R. Jackson. 1982. *Balkan Economic History, 1550–1950: From Imperial Borderlands to Developing Nations.* Bloomington: Indiana University Press.

Laveleye, Baron Emile de. 1887. *The Balkan Peninsula.* London: Unwin.

Lavrin, Janko. 1929. "The Bogomils and Bogomilism." *Slavonic Review* 8:269–283.

Lazić, Ivan. 1971. "The Legal and Actual Status of Religious Communities in Yugoslavia," in Zlatko Frid, ed., *Religions in Yugoslavia: Historical Survey, Legal Status, Church in Socialism, Ecumenism, Dialogue Between Marxists and Christians, etc.* Zagreb: Binoza.

Lea, Henry Charles. 1887. *A History of the Inquisition of the Middle Ages.* Vol. 2. New York: Harper.

Lendvai, Paul. 1971. *Anti-Semitism Without Jews: Communist Eastern Europe.* Garden City, N.Y.: Doubleday.

———. 1972. *National Tensions in Yugoslavia.* London: Institute for the Study of Conflict.

Lewis, Bernard. 1976. "The Return of Islam." *Commentary* 61:39–49.

Lijphart, Arend. 1979. "Consociation and Federation: Conceptual and Empirical Links." *Canadian Journal of Political Science* 12:3–15.

———. 1985. "Non-Majoritarian Democracy: A Comparison of Federal and Consociational Theories." *Publius* 15:3–15.

Lockwood, William G. 1978. "Bosnian," in Richard V. Weekes, ed., *Muslim Peoples: A World Ethnographic Survey.* Westport, Conn.: Greenwood Press.

———. 1975. *European Moslems: Economy and Ethnicity in Western Bosnia.* New York: Academic Press.

———. 1978. "Living Legacy of the Ottoman Empire: The Serbo-Croatian Speaking Moslems of Bosnia-Hercegovina," in Abraham Ascher, Tibor Halasi-Kun, and Béla K. Király, eds., *The Mutual Effects of the Islamic and Judeo-Christian Worlds: The East European Pattern.* Brooklyn: Brooklyn College Press.

Lopašić, Alexander. 1979. "Islamisation of the Balkans: Some General Considerations," in Jennifer M. Scarce, ed., *Islam in the Balkans: Persian Art and Culture of the 18th and 19th Centuries.* Edinburgh: Royal Scottish Museum.

Lukac, Dušan. 1969. "Doprinos revolucionarnog radničkog pokreta urazrešavanju ključnih problema nacionalnog pitanju u Jugoslavijii." *Jugoslovenski istorijske časopis* 4:163–170.

Luttwak, Edward. 1993. "If Bosnians Were Dolphins …" *Commentary* 96:27–32.

MacKenzie, David. 1985. *Ilija Garašanin, Balkan Bismarck.* Boulder: East European Monographs.

———. 1982. "Serbian Nationalist and Military Organizations and the Piedmont Idea, 1844–1914." *East European Quarterly* 16:323–344.

Madej, W. Victor, ed. 1979. *German Operations in the Balkans (Spring 1941–1944).* New Martinsville, W. Va.: Game Marketing.

Madol, H. R. 1942. *The League of London: A Book of Interviews with Allied Sovereigns and Statesmen.* London: Hutchinson.

Magaš, Branka. 1993. *The Destruction of Yugoslavia: Tracking the Break-up of 1980–92.* London: Verso.

Marković, Sima. 1923. *Nacionalno pitanje u svetlosti Marksizma.* Belgrade: Narodna Misao.

Massacre of Croatians in Bosnia-Hercegovina and Sandzak. 1978. Toronto: Croatian Islamic Centre.

Mates, Leo. 1972. *Nonalignment: Theory and Current Policy.* Dobbs Ferry, N.Y.: Oceana.

May, Arthur J. 1951. *The Hapsburg Monarchy, 1867–1914.* Cambridge: Harvard University Press.

Meier, Viktor. 1983. "Yugoslavia's National Question." *Problems of Communism* 32:47–74.

Mellor, Roy E.H. 1975. *Eastern Europe: A Geography of the Comecon Countries.* New York: Columbia University Press.

Memorandum Addressed by the Jugoslav Socialists to the International Socialist Peace Conference in Stockholm. 1917. London: Jugoslav Workmen's Association.

Menges, Karl H. 1953. *An Outline of the Early History and Migrations of the Slavs.* New York: Department of Slavic Languages, Columbia University.

Meriage, Lawrence P. 1977. "The First Serbian Uprising (1804–1813): National Revival or a Search for Regional Security." *Canadian Review of Studies in Nationalism* 4:187–205.

Mestrović, Matthew M. 1960. "The Elections of 1923 in the Kingdom of the Serbs, Croats, and Slovenes." *Journal of Croatian Studies* 1:3–24.

Milazzo, Matteo J. 1975. *The Chetnik Movement and the Yugoslav Resistance.* Baltimore: Johns Hopkins University Press.

Miletić, Antun. 1972. "O saradnji komandanta četničkih odreda istočne Bosne Jezdimira Dangića sa nemcima (avgust 1941–april 1942)." *Vojnoistorijski glasnik* 23:135–147.

Miller, Nicholas J. 1994. "Serbia Chooses Aggression." *Orbis* 38:59–66.

Miller, William. 1898. "Bosnia Under the Austrians." *Gentleman's Magazine* 61:340–352.

———. 1898. "Bosnia Under the Ottomans." *Gentleman's Magazine* 61:241–245.

———. 1898. *Travels and Politics in the Near East.* London: Fisher Unwin.

Mladenović, Milos. 1976. "Family Names of Osmanli Origin in Bosnia and Herzegovina," in Donald P. Little, ed., *Essays on Islamic Civilization Presented to Niyazi Berkes.* Leiden: Brill.

———. 1958–1959. "The Osmanli Conquest and the Islamization of Bosnia." *Slavic and East European Studies* 3:219–225.

Mlivončić, Ivica. 1967. "Crkve i religija u vrijeme narodno-oslobodilačke borbe." *Naše teme* 11:24–26.

Moore, Patrick. 1994. "Changes in the Croatian Political Landscape." *RFE/RL Research Report* 3:24–27.

———. 1994. "Croatia and Bosnia: A Tale of Two Bridges." *RFE/RL Research Report* 3:15–18.

———. 1993. "Endgame in Bosnia and Herzegovina?" *RFE/RL Research Report* 2:17–23.

———. 1991. "The Islamic Community's New Sense of Identity." *Report on Eastern Europe* 2:19–23.

———. 1991. "Where Is Yugoslavia Headed?" *Report on Eastern Europe* 2:30–35.

———. 1993. "The Widening Warfare in the Former Yugoslavia." *RFE/RL Research Report* 2:12–15.

Moynihan, Daniel Patrick. 1993. *Pandaemonium: Ethnicity in International Politics.* New York: Oxford University Press.

Muftić, Mahmud Kemal. 1970. "Hundred Years of Mistakes in Croatian National Politics." *Balkania* 5:1–6.

Murvar, Vatro. 1989. *Nation and Religion in Central Europe and the Western Balkans—The Muslims in Bosna, Hercegovina and Sandžak: A Sociological Analysis.* Brookfield: FSSSN Colloquia and Symposia, University of Wisconsin.

"Muslims in Yugoslavia: Adaptation and Accommodation." 1977. *Impact International* 7:14.

Neal, Fred Warner. 1954. "From Particularism to Unity: The Kaleidoscope of Nationalism(s) in Yugoslavia." *American Universities Field Staff* (Southeast Europe Series) 2:12–13.

———. 1982. "Yugoslav Approaches to the Nationalities Problem—The Politics of

Circumvention." Paper presented at the annual meeting of the American Association for the Advancement of Slavic Studies, Washington, D.C., 16 October.

Neville-Bagot, G. H. 1960. "The Muslims of Bosnia and the Other Autonomous States of Yugoslavia." *Islamic Review* 48:31–34.

Newhouse, John. 1992. "The Diplomatic Round: Dodging the Problem." *New Yorker* 51:60–71.

"The October 12, 1941, Resolution of the Sarajevo Moslems." 1983. *South Slav Journal* 6:37–39.

Okey, Robin. 1982. *Eastern Europe 1740–1980: Feudalism to Communism.* Minneapolis: University of Minnesota Press.

———. 1992. "State, Church and Nation in the Serbo-Croat Speaking Lands of the Habsburg Monarchy, 1850–1914," in Donal A. Kerr, ed., *Religion, State and Ethnic Groups.* New York: New York University Press.

Olson, Robert W. 1976–1977. "The Ottoman Empire in the Middle of the Eighteenth Century and the Fragmentation of Tradition: Relations of the Nationalities (Millets), Guilds (Esnaf) and the Sultan, 1740–1768." *Die Welt des Islams* 17:72–77.

Pajić, Zoran. 1993. "Violation of Fundamental Rights in the Former Yugoslavia: 1. The Conflict in Bosnia-Herzegovina." David Davies Memorial Institute of International Studies, Occasional Paper no. 2.

Pamuk, Sevket. 1984. "The Ottoman Empire in the 'Great Depression' of 1873–1896." *Journal of Economic History* 44:107–118.

Parker, Mushtak. 1986. *Muslims in Yugoslavia: The Quest for Justice.* Toronto: Croatian Islamic Centre.

Parsons, Talcott. 1975. "Some Theoretical Considerations on the Nature and Trends of Change of Ethnicity," in Nathan Glazer and Daniel P. Moynihan, eds., *Ethnicity: Theory and Experience.* Cambridge: Harvard University Press.

Pašić, Najdan. 1984–1985. "Federalism in Yugoslavia's Contemporary Development Period: Between or Beyond Federalism and Confederalism." *Florida State University Proceedings and Reports* 18–19:3–14.

Pavlovich, Kosta St. 1972. *Razgovori sa Slobodanom Jovanovićem, 1946–1958.* Windsor, Canada: Avala.

Pavlowitch, Stevan K. 1978. "Yugoslav-British Relations 1939–1941 as Seen from British Sources." *East European Quarterly* 12:309–339.

Pearson, Raymond. 1983. *National Minorities in Eastern Europe 1848–1945.* New York: St. Martin's Press.

Petričević, Jure. 1983. *Nacionalnost stanovništva jugoslavije: Nazadovanje Hrvata manjine napredovanje Muslimana i Albanaca.* Brugg: Adria.

Petrović-Piroćanac, Zoran, Vesna Hadživković, Boro Mišeljić, and Tomislav Kresović. 1994. *The Media Happened to Be There.* Milići: Boksit.

Pinson, Mark. 1994. "The Muslims of Bosnia-Herzegovina Under Austro-Hungarian Rule, 1878–1918," in Mark Pinson, ed., *The Muslims of Bosnia-Herzegovina: Their Historic Development from the Middle Ages to the Dissolution of Yugoslavia.* Cambridge: Harvard University Press.

Pipes, Daniel, and Patrick Clawson. 1992–1993. "Ambitious Iran, Troubled Neighbors." *Foreign Affairs* 72:124–141.

Pleština, Dijana. 1992. *Regional Development in Communist Yugoslavia: Success, Failure, and Consequences.* Boulder: Westview Press.

Pozderac, Hamdija. 1983. "The National Question and the Formation of the Yugoslav Federation." *Socialist Thought and Practice* 23:31–47.

Prins, Jan. 1970. "The World's Plural Societies: An Introduction." *Plural Societies* 1:1–23.

Prpić, George. 1969. "Communism and Nationalism in Yugoslavia." *Balkan Studies* 10:23–50.

Purivatra, Atif. 1974. *Jugoslavenska muslimanska organizacija u političkom životu Kraljevine Srba, Hrvata i Slovenaca.* Sarajevo: Svjetlost.

———. 1970. *Nacionalni i politički razvitak muslimana.* Sarajevo: Svjetlost.

Raičević, Jovan. 1979. "Savez komunista Jugoslavije i nacionalno pitanje," in *KPJ-SKJ: Razvoj teorije i prakse socijalizma, 1919–1979.* Belgrade: Savremena administracija.

Ramet, Pedro. 1984. "Religion and Nationalism in Yugoslavia," in Pedro Ramet, ed., *Religion and Nationalism in Soviet and East European Politics.* Durham: Duke University Press.

Ramet, Sabrina P. 1992. *Balkan Babel: Politics, Culture, and Religion in Yugoslavia.* Boulder: Westview Press.

———. 1992. *Nationalism and Federalism in Yugoslavia, 1963–1983.* Bloomington: Indiana University Press.

———. 1992. "War in the Balkans." *Foreign Affairs* 71:79–98.

———. 1994. "The Yugoslav Crisis and the West: Avoiding 'Vietnam' and Blundering into 'Abyssinia.'" *East European Politics and Societies* 8:189–219.

Redžić, Enver. 1987. *Muslimansko autonomaštvo i 13. SS divizija: Autonomija Bosne i Hercegovine i Hitlerov Treći Rajh.* Sarajevo: Svjetlost.

———. 1980. "Nacionalne manjine u jugoistočnoj evropi." *Pregled* 70:138–165.

———. 1970. "O posebnosti bosanskih muslimana." *Pregled* 60:25–41.

———. 1963. *Prilozi o nacionalnom pitanju.* Sarajevo: Svjetlost.

Remington, Robin Alison. 1993. "Bosnia: The Tangled Web." *Current History* 92:364–369.

———. 1993. "Ethnonationalism and the Integrity of the Sovereign State: The Disintegration of Yugoslavia." Paper presented at the Conference on Race, Ethnicity and Nationalism at the End of the Twentieth Century, University of Wisconsin–Milwaukee, 30 September–2 October 1993.

———. 1984. "The Politics of Scarcity in Yugoslavia." *Current History* 83:370–374.

Rieff, David. 1995. *Slaughterhouse: Bosnia and the Failure of the West.* New York: Simon and Schuster.

Riker, William H. 1975. "Federalism," in Fred I. Greenstein and Nelson Polsby, eds., *Handbook of Political Science.* Vol. 5: *Governmental Institutions and Processes.* Reading, Mass.: Addison-Wesley.

Ristić, Dragiša N. 1966. *Yugoslavia's Revolution of 1941.* University Park: Pennsylvania State University Press.

Roskin, Michael G. 1994. *The Rebirth of East Europe.* Englewood Cliffs, N.J.: Prentice-Hall.

Rothschild, Joseph. 1974. *East Central Europe Between the Two World Wars.* Seattle: University of Washington Press.

———. 1981. *Ethnopolitics: A Conceptual Framework.* New York: Columbia University Press.

Runciman, Steven. 1947. *The Medieval Manichee: A Study of the Christian Dualist Heresy.* Cambridge: Cambridge University Press.

Rusinow, Dennison I. 1985. "Nationalities Policy and the 'National Question,'" in Pedro Ramet, ed., *Yugoslavia in the 1980s.* Boulder: Westview Press.

———. 1977. *The Yugoslav Experiment 1948–1974.* London: Hurst.

————. 1982. "Yugoslavia's Muslim Nation." *Universities Field Staff International Reports* (Europe).

S. C. 1946. "Political Forces in Yugoslavia Today." *World Today* 2:535–545.

Said, Abdul A., and Luiz R. Simmons. 1976. "The Ethnic Factor in World Politics," in Abdul A. Said and Luiz R. Simmons, eds., *Ethnicity in an International Context.* New Brunswick, N.J.: Transaction Books.

Šarac, Zajim, et al. 1947. *Yugoslav Muslims' Message to India.* Bombay: People's Publishing House.

Schöpflin, George. 1973. "The Ideology of Croatian Nationalism." *Survey* 19:123–148.

————. 1980. "Nationality in the Fabric of Yugoslav Politics." *Survey* 25:1–19.

"The September 22, 1941, Resolution of the Mostar Moslems." 1982. *South Slav Journal* 5:31–33.

Seton-Watson, Hugh. 1977. *Nations and States: An Enquiry into the Origins of Nations and the Politics of Nationalism.* Boulder: Westview Press.

Seton-Watson, R. W. 1930. "Russian Commitments in the Bosnian Question and an Early Project of Annexation." *Slavonic Review* 8:578–588.

Shoup, Paul. 1995. "The Bosnian Crisis in 1992," in Sabrina Petra Ramet and Ljubiša S. Adamović, eds., *Beyond Yugoslavia: Politics, Economics, and Culture in a Shattered Community.* Boulder: Westview Press.

————. 1968. *Communism and the Yugoslav National Question.* New York: Columbia University Press.

Sijerčić, Irfan. 1985. "The Activities of the 'Young Moslems' at the End of the War 1944–1945." *South Slav Journal* 8:23–28.

Sivrić, Ivo. 1982. *The Peasant Culture of Bosnia and Herzegovina.* Chicago: Franciscan Herald Press.

Sloane, William M. 1914. *The Balkans: A Laboratory of History.* New York: Abingdon Press.

Smajlović, Ahmed. 1978. "Muslimani u Jugoslaviji." *Glasnik Vrhovnog islamskog starješinstva u socijalističkoj federativnoj republici jugoslaviji* 41:548–582.

Smith, Anthony D., ed. 1992. *Ethnicity and Nationalism.* Leiden: Brill.

————. 1972. "Ethnocentrism, Nationalism, and Social Change." *International Journal of Comparative Sociology* 13:1–20.

————. 1992. "Introduction: Ethnicity and Nationalism," in Anthony D. Smith, ed., *Ethnicity and Nationalism.* Leiden: Brill.

Solovjev, Aleksandar. 1952. "Engleski izveštaj XVII vijeka o bosanskim Poturima." *Glasnik Zemalskog muzeja u Bosni i Hercegovini* 7:101–109.

Sosnosky, Theodor von. 1913. *Die Balkanpolitik Osterreich-Ungarns seit 1866.* Vol. 1. Stuttgart: Deutsche Verlags-Anstalt.

Stack, John F., Jr. 1981. "Ethnicity and Transnational Relations: An Introduction," in John F. Stack Jr., ed., *Ethnic Identities in a Transnational World.* Westport, Conn.: Greenwood Press.

Stalin, Joseph. 1934. *Marxism and the National and Colonial Question.* New York: International Publishers.

————. 1942. *Marxism and the National Question: Selected Writings and Speeches.* New York: International Publishers.

Stanković, Slobodan. 1982. "Arab Countries Finance Construction of a Mosque in Zagreb." *Radio Free Europe Research,* RAD Background Report/176 (Yugoslavia).

————. 1983. "Campaign Against 'Khomeini-Inspired' Moslems in Yugoslavia." *Radio Free Europe Research*, RAD Background Report/119 (Yugoslavia).

————. 1981. *The End of the Tito Era: Yugoslavia's Dilemmas.* Stanford: Hoover Institution Press.

————. 1983. "Further Attacks Against Yugoslavia's 'Young Moslems.'" *Radio Free Europe Research*, RAD Background Report/102 (Yugoslavia).

————. 1984. "On the Eve of the 12th Yugoslav Party Congress." *Radio Free Europe Research.*

————. 1983. "Tito's Successors Fear 'Moslem Nationalism.'" *Radio Free Europe Research*, RAD Background Report/82 (Yugoslavia).

Stoianovich, Traian. 1962. "Factors in the Decline of Ottoman Society in the Balkans." *Slavic Review* 21:623–632.

————. 1963. "The Social Foundations of Balkan Politics, 1750–1941," in Charles Jelavich and Barbara Jelavich, eds., *The Balkans in Transition: Essays on the Development of Balkan Life and Politics Since the Eighteenth Century.* Berkeley: University of California Press.

Stokes, Gale. 1980. "The Role of the Yugoslav Committee in the Formation of Yugoslavia," in Dimitrije Djordjević, ed., *The Creation of Yugoslavia 1914–1918.* Santa Barbara: Clio Books.

Sućeska, Avdo. 1969. "Istorijske osnove nacionalne posebnosti bosansko-hercegovačkih Muslimana." *Jugoslovenski istorijski časopis* 4:47–54.

Sugar, Peter F. 1963. *Industrialization of Bosnia-Hercegovina 1878–1918.* Seattle: University of Washington Press.

————. 1977. *Southeastern Europe Under Ottoman Rule, 1354–1804.* Seattle: University of Washington Press.

Sulzberger, C. L. 1973. *Unconquered Souls: The Resistentialists.* Woodstock, N.Y.: Overlook Press.

Symmons-Symonolewicz, Konstantin. 1979. "Ethnicity and Nationalism: Recent Literature and Its Theoretical Implications." *Canadian Review of Studies in Nationalism* 6:98–102.

Tanašković, Darko. 1992. "Muslims and muslims in Former Yugoslavia, Part 1." *East European Reporter* 5:13–15.

Thompson, Mark. 1994. *Forging War: The Media in Serbia, Croatia and Bosnia-Hercegovina.* Great Britain: Article 19, International Centre Against Censorship.

Tochitch, Desimir. 1984. "Titoism Without Tito." *Survey* 28:1–23.

Tomasevich, Jozo. 1975. *War and Revolution in Yugoslavia, 1941–1945: The Chetniks.* Stanford: Stanford University Press.

————. 1969. "Yugoslavia During the Second World War," in Wayne S. Vucinich, ed., *Contemporary Yugoslavia: Twenty Years of Socialist Experiment.* Berkeley: University of California Press.

Tomašić, Dinko. 1942. "Croatia in European Politics." *Journal of Central European Affairs* 2:64–86.

Trhulj, Sead. 1992. *Mladi Muslimani.* Zagreb: Globus.

"The Trial of Moslem Intellectuals in Sarajevo." 1983. *South Slav Journal* 6:55–89.

van den Berghe, Pierre L. 1981. "Protection of Ethnic Minorities: A Critical Appraisal," in Robert G. Wirsing, ed., *Protection of Ethnic Minorities: Comparative Perspectives.* New York: Pergamon Press.

Vryonis, Speros, Jr. 1972. "Religious Changes and Patterns in the Balkans, 14th–16th Centuries," in Henrik Birnbaum and Speros Vryonis Jr., eds., *Aspects of the Balkans: Continuity and Change*. The Hague: Mouton.

Vucinich, Wayne S. 1969. "Interwar Yugoslavia," in Wayne S. Vucinich, ed., *Contemporary Yugoslavia: Twenty Years of Socialist Experiment*. Berkeley: University of California Press.

———. 1977. "Mlada Bosna and the First World War," in Robert A. Kann, Béla K. Király, and Paula S. Fichtner, eds., *The Habsburg Empire in World War I: Essays on the Intellectual Military, Political and Economic Aspects of the Habsburg War Effort*. Boulder: East European Quarterly.

———. 1962. "The Nature of Balkan Society Under Ottoman Rule." *Slavic Review* 21:597–616.

———. 1949. "Yugoslavs of the Moslem Faith," in Robert J. Kerner, ed., *Yugoslavia*. Berkeley: University of California Press.

Vulliamy, Ed. 1994. *Seasons in Hell: Understanding Bosnia's War*. New York: St. Martin's Press.

Vušković, Boris. 1986. "Nacije u SKJ: Nacionalna struktura članstva Saveza komunista u većim gradovima republika i pokrajina." *Naše Teme* 30:375–404.

War Crimes in Bosnia-Hercegovina: A Helsinki Watch Report. Vol. 1. 1992. New York: Human Rights Watch.

Wendel, Hermann. 1923. "Marxism and the Southern Slav Question." *Slavonic Review* 2:289–307.

Wiles, J. W. 1928. "Moslem Women in Yugoslavia." *Moslem World* 18:61–65.

Woodhouse, Edward James, and Chase Going Woodhouse. 1920. *Italy and the Jugoslavs*. Boston: Badger.

Ye'Or, Bat. 1978. *Dhimmi Peoples: Oppressed Nations*. Switzerland: Editions de l'Avenir.

Zimmerman, William. 1987. *Open Borders, Nonalignment, and the Political Evolution of Yugoslavia*. Princeton: Princeton University Press.

Zukin, Sharon. 1985. "Self-Management and Socialization," in Pedro Ramet, ed., *Yugoslavia in the 1980s*. Boulder: Westview Press.

Zwemer, S. M. 1927. "Islam in South Eastern Europe." *Moslem World* 17:35–38.

About the Book and Author

Although their plight now dominates television news worldwide, until recently the Bosnian Muslims were virtually unknown outside of Yugoslavia. Who are these people? Why are they the focus of their former neighbors' rage? What role did they play in Yugoslavia before they became the victims of ethnic cleansing? Why has Bosnia and Herzegovina, once a model of ethnic tolerance and multicultural harmony, suddenly exploded into ethnic violence?

Focusing on these questions, Friedman provides a comprehensive study of this national group whose plight has riveted governments, the press, and the public alike. With a name reflecting both their religious and their national identity, the Bosnian Muslims are unique in Europe as indigenous Slavic Muslims. Descendants of schismatic Christians from the Middle Ages, they converted to Islam after the Ottoman conquest of Bosnia.

The book follows them as they went from victims of crusades during the Middle Ages to members of the ruling elite within the Ottoman Empire; from rulers back to subjects under Austria-Hungary; and later to subjects again, this time under the Serbs in the interwar Yugoslav Kingdom and under the Communists after World War II. The Bosnian Muslims have survived through it all and have even thrived during certain periods, most notably when they were recognized as a nation by Tito.

Meticulously tracing their turbulent history and assessing the issues surrounding Bosnian Muslim nationhood in Yugoslavia, Friedman shows us how the mixed secular and religious identity of the Bosnian Muslims has shaped the conflict in which they are now so tragically embroiled.

Francine Friedman is assistant professor of political science and director of the Office of European Studies at Ball State University.

Index